The BIG 6

TEACHING ELEMENTARY

INFORMATION LITERACY

SKILLS WITH THE BIG6™

Joyce Needham

...worth Publishing

Columbus, Ohio

The "Big6™" is copyright © (1987) Michael B. Eisenberg and Robert E. Berkowitz. For more information, visit: www.big6.com. The Big6 steps are reprinted with permission.

Trademarks: Rather than put a trademark symbol with every occurrence of a trademarked name, we note that we are using the names simply in an editorial fashion and to the benefit of the trademark owner, with no intention of infringement of the trademark.

Library of Congress Cataloging-in-Publication Data

Needham, Joyce.
  Teaching elementary information literacy skills with the Big6? / Joyce Needham.
      p. cm.
  Includes bibliographical references and index.
  ISBN-13: 978-1-58683-326-8 (pbk.)
  ISBN-10: 1-58683-326-X (pbk.)
  1. Information literacy--Study and teaching--United States. 2. Electronic information resource literacy--Study and teaching--United States. 3. Information retrieval--Study and teaching--United States. 4. Information technology--Study and teaching--United States. I. Title.
  ZA3075.N433 2009
  028.7071'0973--dc22

                          2008032126

Cynthia Anderson: Editor
Judi Repman: Consulting Editor

Published by Linworth Publishing, Inc.
3650 Olentangy River Road
Suite 250
Columbus, Ohio 43214

Copyright © 2009 by Linworth Publishing, Inc.

ISBN 13: 978-1-58683-326-8
ISBN 10: 1-58683-326-X

5 4 3 2 1

TABLE OF CONTENTS

Table of Figures viii
Table of Lesson Plans x
About the Author xi
Acknowledgments xii
Introduction xiii
   The Purpose xiii
   The Organization and Content xiii
   The Big6 Problem Solving Process xv
   Application of the Big6 xv
   Works Cited xvi

PART 1: Getting Started—Focusing on the Student 1
Chapter 1: What? Helping Students Understand the Task 3
   What Is Information Literacy? 3
   What Are Problems? 4
   How Can the Big6 Problem Solving Process Help? 4
   Tips and Strategies to Introduce and Teach Students the Big6 Problem Solving Process 5
   Works Cited 7

Chapter 2: Why? Motivating Students to Become Better Problem Solvers 9
   Why Do Students Need to Develop Problem Solving Skills and Become Lifelong Learners? 9
      Our Rapidly Changing World 9
         Examples of Impact on Occupations 10
         Examples of Devices and Activities 11
      The Desire to Become Independent 11
   Why Focus on Mastering a Problem Solving Process Such as the Big6? 13
      Why Consciously Use the Process? 13
         Problems and Practice 13
         Learning Both Content and Process 13
      Can the Process Be Used to Improve Our Problem Solving Skills? 13
      Can the Process Help Solve Difficult Problems? 14
   Works Cited 14

PART 2: Making It Work—Focusing on Fundamentals of Learning 15
Chapter 3: Empowering Students Through Knowledge of the Learning Process 17
   How Do We Learn? 17
   How Does the Big6 Connect to the Learning Process? 19
      Step 1: Task Definition. What is my problem or task? What information do I need? . . .19
      Step 2: Information Seeking Strategies. What sources can I use to gather information? . . .19
      Step 3: Location and Access. Finding the source and the information within the source . . .21
      Step 4: Use of Information. Engaging and extracting, and Step 5:
         Synthesis. Organizing and presenting information. 21
      Step 6: Evaluation. Assessing product and process. 21
   Tips and Strategies to Help Students Become Better Learners .21
      The Big6 Problem Solving Process 21
      Task Definition 22
      Location and Access & Use of Information 23
      Evaluation 26
   Works Cited 26

Chapter 4: It's All About Process—About Teaching Process .27
   What Is Process? 27
   Do We Have Time to Teach Process? 28

TABLE OF CONTENTS | continued

Are We Using the Process or Teaching the Process? 29
How Do We Teach Process? 29
    Name the Process 29
    Teach the Steps in the Process, Including the Vocabulary 29
    Use Vocabulary as a Strategy 29
Scaffold Instruction 31
    Move from Simple to Complex 32
    Provide Many Opportunities for Practice 32
    Include Student Evaluation or Feedback 34
Works Cited 36

Chapter 5: Connecting Processes: Big6 Problem Solving, Reading, Listening,
Speaking, Writing, and Technology 37
What Do Reading, Listening, Speaking, Writing, and Problem Solving Have in Common? 37
Where Does Technology Fit? 40
Where Does Reading Fit Within the Big6 Problem Solving Process? 40
Where Does Writing (Including 6 + 1) Fit Within the Big6 Problem Solving Process? 41
Sample of an Integrated Lesson 43
Works Cited 43

Chapter 6: Making Problems Work for Us 47
Why Use Problems? 47
How Do I Create *Good* Student Problems? 48
    Suggestions for Creating Engaging Problems 48
    Getting Started Creating *Good* Student Problems 48
What Is the Desired Level of Learning? 50
Letting Students Be the Problem Solvers 51
Works Cited 52

PART 3: Focusing on Mastering the Six Steps 53
Chapter 7: Task Definition (What Is My Task?) 55
What Is Task Definition? 55
Why Is Task Definition Important? 56
Tips and Strategies to Help Students Identify Their Task 58
Works Cited 62

Chapter 8: Information Seeking Strategies (What Source Can I Use?) 67
What Are Information Seeking Strategies? 67
Possible Sources of Information 67
    Prior Knowledge or Schema 68
    The Internet 68
Why Are Information Seeking Strategies Important? 68
What Factors Determine the Best Source? 69
Tips and Strategies to Help Students Determine Sources 70
    Strategies for Identifying and Selecting Sources 70
    Sample Lessons to Improve Source Selection Skills 85
    Teaching Internet Skills 85
        Awareness of the Need for Internet Skills 85
        Knowledge of the Variety of Sources on the Internet .86
        Internet Reliability: Awareness of and Development of Skills 87
Works Cited 88

Chapter 9: Location and Access (Where Is the Source and the Information?) 89
What Is Location and Access? 89

TABLE OF CONTENTS | continued

Why Is Location and Access Important? 89
What Does Accessing Information from a Source Look Like? 91
    Components of Accessing Information from Text 91
        Scanning and Skimming 91
        Scanning 92
        Skimming 93
        Keywords 93
        Text Aids, Features, or Conventions 93
    Location and Access on the Internet 94
        Locating the Source or Navigating on the Internet 94
    Accessing Information from the Internet 96
        Scanning and Skimming 96
        Keywords 96
        Text Aids, Features, or Conventions 96
Tips and Strategies to Help Students Find Information More Quickly 96
Location and Access Strategies 97
    Strategies to Assist in Location of Source 97
    Strategies to Assist in Location of Information Within the Source 98
        Strategies for Teaching Scanning 98
        Strategies to Increase Scanning Speed 99
        Strategy for Teaching Skimming 105
        Strategies for Teaching Keywords 105
        Strategies for Teaching Text Aids, Conventions, or Features 106
        Strategies for Teaching Internet Skills 106
    Culminating Lesson 112
Works Cited 112

Chapter 10: Use of Information 113
What Is Use of Information? 113
Why Is Use of Information Important? 114
Tips and Strategies to Help Students Develop Use of Information Skills 116
    Tips and Strategies to Develop Engaging and Extracting Skills 116
    Tips and Strategies to Improve Engaging Skills 117
    Tips and Strategies to Improve Extracting Skills 117
    Citation Tips and Strategies 117
        Preventing Plagiarism 117
        Why Do Sources Need to be Cited? 120
Works Cited 122

Chapter 11: Synthesis 123
What Is Synthesis? 123
Why Is Synthesis Important? 124
Tips and Strategies to Help Students Synthesize More Effectively 124
    Strategies to Improve Synthesis 124
    Strategies for Organizing 126
    Strategies for Communicating 127
    Determining the Form of Synthesis 128
Works Cited 129

Chapter 12: Evaluation 131
What Is Evaluation? 131
Why Is Evaluation Important? 133
    Example One 133

Example Two 133

Why Self-Evaluation? 134

Tips and Strategies to Help Students Become More Effective and Efficient Evaluators 135

Evaluating Product and Process 135

Evaluating Product 137

Evaluating Process 138

Works Cited 142

PART 4: Plugging in the Big6 Problem Solving Process 143

Chapter 13: Applying the Big6 to Research Problems 145

How Do I Introduce the Big6 as a Research Strategy? 145

What Might Big6 Research Look Like with Primary Students? 149

Research Topics 149

Use of Mnemonics 149

Sample Research Project 149

What Might Big6 Research Look Like with Intermediate Students? 157

Modeling and Guiding 157

Incorporating Choice 157

Sample Research Project 158

Tips and Strategies to Strengthen Students' Research Skills 158

Works Cited 162

Chapter 14: Note Taking 163

What Is Note Taking? 163

Why Is Note Taking Instruction Important? 164

Tips and Strategies for Teaching Successful Note Taking 165

Accessing Information from Print and Oral Sources 165

Identifying and Extracting Important Information 165

Recording the Important Information 168

Write Phrases 169

Notes Which Can Be Read .169

Organize Notes 169

Scaffold for Teaching Note Taking 169

Modeling 170

Guiding 170

Independent Practice 171

Works Cited 172

Chapter 15: Answering Questions from the Text and Test Taking 173

Should Students Answer Questions from Text? 173

Can the Big6 Be Applied to Answer Questions? 174

What About the Big6 and Test Scores? 177

How Can Students Be Taught to Utilize Big6 in Test Taking? 180

Task Definition 180

Reading Selection Questions .180

Maximum Use of Limited Knowledge 183

Works Cited 183

Chapter 16: Classroom Management and the Big6 185

How Can Classroom Management Be Used as an Opportunity to Teach the Big6? 185

What Does Classroom Management Look Like Using the Big6? 186

How Important Are Consequences and Consistency? 186

How Do I Implement the Big6 into Classroom Management? 190

TABLE OF CONTENTS | continued

Establish Concrete Behavior Expectations 190
Make the Process Visible 191
Scaffold Instruction 191
    Scaffolding Classroom Routines and Procedures 191
    Modeling Classroom Routines and Procedures 191
    Guiding Classroom Routines and Procedures 191
    Independent Practice of Routines and Procedures 192
Scaffolding Behavior 192
    Modeling Behavior 192
    Guiding Behavior 192
    Independent Practice of Behavior 193
Pose Problems 193
Provide Opportunities for Student Evaluation 193
How to Begin Integration of Big6 into Classroom Management 200
Works Cited 200

Chapter 17: Math and the Big6 201
What Does the Big6 Look Like Applied to Math Word Problems? 201
What Basic Math Concepts Can Develop Through the Use of Big6? 206
How Can I Guide My Students to Use Big6 to Solve Math Problems? 207
Strategies That May Be Used to Address Specific Weaknesses 210
    When Students Have Difficulty Breaking the Process into Small Steps 210
    When Students Have Difficulty Identifying the Task or Information Needed 211
    When Math Strategies Are the Weakness 213
    When Students Need to Strengthen Their Evaluation Skills 214
    When Students Are Ready to Move to the Next Level 217
Works Cited 218

Chapter 18: Science and the Big6 221
Where Does the Big6 Fit into the Science Curriculum? 221
Sample Lessons Integrating the Big6 Problem Solving Process and Science Content 223
Works Cited 261

Chapter 19: Social Studies and the Big6 263
Where Do Problems and the Big6 Fit within Social Studies? 263
Creating Integrated Social Studies Lessons 265
Integrating Problem Solving into Existing Lessons 267
Sample Lessons Integrating Big6 and Social Studies 268
    Motivators 268
    Skills 268
    Time Requirements 269
Works Cited 269

Chapter 20: Parting Thoughts 297
Why Teach Problem Solving? 297
Why the Big6 and Not Another Problem Solving Process? 298
Teaching the Big6: Are You Ready to Tackle the Problem? 299
Helping Our Students Succeed 299
Works Cited 302

Appendix A: Picture Books and Information Literacy Skills 303
Appendix B: Historical Fiction Picture Books, American History 304
Appendix C: Science Content and Picture Books 305
Index 306

TABLE OF FIGURES

Figure 1.1:   Big6 Problem Solving Process with the Little 12 4
Figure 1.2:   Using the Big6 to Solve an Authentic Problem 6
Figure 2.1:   Problem Solving Continuum 12
Figure 3.1:   A Functional Model of Information Processing 18
Figure 3.2:   A Functional Model of Information Processing through the Big6 Lens 20
Figure 3.3:   Comparing the Dictionary and Encyclopedia 24
Figure 4.1:   The Big6 Organizer 33
Figure 4.2:   Planning Form 35
Figure 5.1:   Connections between the Big6 Process and Communication Arts (CA) 39
Figure 5.2:   Technology Integrated into Big6 40
Figure 5.3:   Integrating Big6 Process with the Writing Process and 6 + 1
              Traits of Writing 42
Figure 6.1:   Examples of *Good* Student Problems 50
Figure 7.1:   Web of Questions 60
Figure 7.2:   List of Questions 61
Figure 7.3:   List of Sorted Questions 61
Figure 7.4:   Strategies to Help Know or Identify Task (Bloom's Knowledge Level) 64
Figure 7.5:   Strategies to Help Students Understand the Task and Identify
              Information Needed (Bloom's Level Two) 65
Figure 8.1:   Comparison of Book Publication and Internet Publication 86
Figure 9.1:   Internet Index or Menu 94
Figure 9.2:   Word Search 99
Figure 9.3:   Guide Word Champ 100
Figure 9.4:   Differentiating Between Scanning and Skimming 104
Figure 9.5:   Keyword Organizer 105
Figure 10.1: Teaching Extracting Skills 118
Figure 10.2: How Do We Cite Sources? 121
Figure 11.1: Synthesis Forms 128
Figure 12.1: Accurate Evaluation 132
Figure 12.2: Suggested Evaluation Questions 139
Figure 13.1: Compare Student Research Process with Big6 Process 146
Figure 13.2: Comparison of Faulty Research Process with Big6 Process 147
Figure 13.3: Opportunities for Choice 157
Figure 14.1: Nonlinguistic Representation of Note Taking 164
Figure 14.2: Wilson's Creek Battle 166
Figure 15.1: Answering Questions from Text 175
Figure 15.2: Social Studies Test Item 177
Figure 15.3: Connecting Electronic Testing to Paper and Pencil Testing 179
Figure 15.4: Comparison of Answering Questions from Text to Answering
              Questions on Tests 181
Figure 15.5: Sample Reading Selection Questions 182
Figure 15.6: Sample Test Item 182
Figure 16.1: Comparison of Directing to Questioning 187
Figure 16.2: Telling vs. Questioning 194
Figure 16.3: Establishing a Classroom Management System Utilizing Big6 197
Figure 16.4: Addressing Faulty Behavior 198
Figure 17.1: Big6 Organizer for Math Problems 202
Figure 17.2: Big6 Math Organizer—How Many More Dogs Than Snakes 203
Figure 17.3: Big6 Math Organizer—Marbles 204
Figure 17.4: Math Concepts 206
Figure 17.5: Big6 Math Organizer 209

TABLE OF FIGURES | continued

Figure 17.6:   Mnemonics 210

Figure 17.7:   Rotation 211

Figure 17.8:   Following One Problem through the Process 212

Figure 17.9:   Using Drawing and Visualization 213

Figure 17.10: Math Strategy Bank 215

Figure 17.11: Creating a Math Strategy Bank 214

Figure 17.12: Student Evaluations 217

Figure 17.13: Sample Diagnostic Practice 219

Figure 18.1:   Problem Solving and Science 222

Figure 18.2:   Scientific Inquiry and the Big6 Planner 223

Figure 18.3:   Science Content Standards 224

Figure 19.1:   Social Studies Skills and the Big6 Skills 264

Figure 19.2:   American Revolution Journal Entry 266

Figure 20.1:   Task: Teaching Big6 300

TABLE OF LESSON PLANS

Number	Title	Content	Grade Level	Page #
5.1	Writing a Fiction Animal Story	**Reading** Writing Science: Life Science	4-5	44-45
8.1	Introduction to Sources	Any Content	K-2	72-75
8.2	Test Preparation Sources: What source do I use to study for tests?	Any Content	3-5	76-78
8.3	Introduction to Reference Sources	Any Content	3-5	79-82
8.4	Student Selection of Sources for Research	Any Content	2-5	83-84
9.1	Unit Plan for Guide Word Champ: Building Scanning Ability and Speed	Any Content	2-5	101-103
9.2	Text Aids, Features, or Conventions: The What and Why	Reading Nonfiction Writing Nonfiction	3-5	107-108
9.3	Identifying the Best Source and Locating Information	Any Content Example: Social Studies	3-5	109-111
13.1	Answering a Simple Research Question	Any Content	K-2	150-151
13.2	Author Study	Reading Literature	K-2	152-153
13.3	Classification of Animals	Science: Life Science Writing	1-3	154-156
13.4	Civil War Study	History: Civil War	4-5	159-161
18.1	Properties of Objects: Comparing, Sorting, and Describing	Science: Physical Science	K-2	225-226
18.2	Life Cycles	Science: Life Science	K-1	227-228
18.3	Dinosaur Report	Science: Life Science Could be adapted to any content	K-2	229-231
18.4	Class Animal Book	Science: Life Science	K-2	232-234
18.5	An Australian Rainforest Living Museum	Science: Life Science	2-4	235-237
18.6	Objects in the Sky	Science: Earth and Space Science	1-3	238-239
18.7	Creating Our Safety Rules	Science: Science in Personal and Social Perspective	K-4	240-241
18.8	Simple Machines and Westward Expansion	Science: Physical Science Social Studies: History, Westward Expansion	5	242-243
18.9	Animal Classification Riddle Step Book	Science: Life Science	3-5	244-246
18.10	Internet Scavenger Hunt: Earthquakes and Volcanoes	Science: Earth and Space Science	3-5	247-249
18.11	Planets Brochure	Science: Earth and Space Science	3-5	250-252
18.12	Necessity is the Mother of Invention	Science: Personal and Social Perspectives; History and Nature of Science; Science and Technology	1-5	253-254
18.13	Inventions and Our Life	Science: Personal and Social Perspectives; History and Nature of Science Communication Arts: Fact and Opinion	3-5	255-257
18.14	Invention Timeline	Science: History and Nature of Science	3-5	258-260
19.1	Using Picture Books to Teach Social Studies	Social Studies: History	1-5	270-271
19.2	Landforms Book and Game	Social Studies: Geography	1-3	272-275
19.3	Class Luau	Social Studies: Geography and Multicultural Awareness	3-5	276-277
19.4	Learning About Our State	Social Studies: Geography Writing: Letters	3-5	278-279
19.5	Creating a State Scrapbook	Social Studies: Geography	3-5	280-281
19.6	Exploring Our City	Social Studies: Government and Geography	3-5	282-283
19.7	History Timeline	Social Studies: History	3-5	284-286
19.8	Paul Revere via Primary and Secondary Sources	Social Studies: History, Revolutionary War	4-5	287-288
19.9	Comparing Famous Americans	Social Studies: History, Biography	1-2	289-291
19.10	Famous African Americans	Social Studies: History, Biography Can adapt to study of any people	3-5	292-294
19.11	Timeline of American Presidents	Social Studies: History, Biography and Geography	2-5	295-296

ABOUT THE AUTHOR

Joyce Needham

Joyce currently serves as a consultant to Springfield (Missouri) Public Schools providing Big6 training for K-12 staff and assisting with a variety of district library projects. She is also a certificated Big6 trainer and has provided training across the state of Missouri. She has published articles in *TeacherLibrarian*, *Library Media Connection*, and the *Big6 e-newsletter*. Joyce served 32 years as a Missouri educator before retiring in 2006. She spent 17 years as a secondary business education teacher and 15 as an elementary library media specialist where she implemented an integrated, flexible library program. Prior to her service at Springfield, Joyce taught in Oak Ridge and Jackson, Missouri. She holds a B.S. and M.A. from Southeast Missouri State University in Cape Girardeau. Joyce is a farm girl having grown up on the family farm in southeast Missouri. She was one of 40 graduates of the Delta High School Class of 1970.

ACKNOWLEDGMENTS

Some books are born from the imagination; other books are born from books themselves. This book was born from the *experiences* shared with students and staff at Springfield Public Schools. It is with humility I say thank you to:

- The teachers at Sequiota and Weller who collaborated with me to integrate problem solving and discover the power of the Big6,

- Teacher and daughter, Julie, who both served as a sounding board and shared her own Big6 classroom experiences,

- Springfield administrators (Bonnie Tabor, Nancy Colbaugh, Gary Prouty, and Anita Kissinger) who shared my vision and helped make it a reality,

- The Springfield family of librarians, especially partner Janet McBride, who provided support in the form of knowledge and friendship, and

- Mary Kay Carson, district library coordinator, who was responsible for the birth of the vision.

For making the book a reality, special thanks are extended to:

- Kevin, *favorite son-in-law and talented editor*, who "faithfully" searched for frags, "not only/but also" statements and reminded of the need to cite,

- Mike Eisenberg and Robert Berkowitz for the creation of the Big6, and

- Linworth Publishing and their editing staff, Cyndee Anderson, Kate Vande Brake, and Christine Weiser, for assistance provided during the publishing process.

Finally, for providing the nurturing support needed to write this book and for the joy they bring to each of my days, love and gratitude are extended to all my family, especially:

- My husband of 34 years, Jordan; daughter Julie; son Jordan III; son-in-law Kevin; granddaughter Ayla; and parents Clyde and Dorothy.

INTRODUCTION

The Purpose

Reading, writing, math, and information literacy or problem solving are four basics which have been identified as necessary if students are to become lifelong learners, critical thinkers, and productive members of our society.

Information Literacy/Problem Solving is the topic of this book. Unfortunately, just because a teacher or library media specialist has problem solving skills and uses them does not guarantee students will develop these skills. Providing direct instruction and guidance/coaching greatly enhance the possibility of producing information-literate students. **This book provides tips, strategies, and lessons which may be used to provide direct instruction and coaching.**

Teachers and library media specialists share the responsibility of creating information-literate students. The tips, strategies, and lessons in this book utilize the Big6 to teach information literacy. They may be used effectively by either the teacher or the library media specialist. Used by teachers and library media specialists who collaborate and team teach, they become more effective. Such collaboration has the potential to positively impact student achievement and provide a support system for teachers and library media specialists.

The Organization and Content

Learning has been identified as having three parts: what we learn, why we learn it, and how we learn it (Brennan). Ruby Payne validates this with her Payne Lesson Design which includes: What, Why, How, and Proof (Payne 6). Closer examination reveals why each of these parts are important to make learning more effective and efficient.

What: Being able to name or label the content or process being taught. Knowing what is to be learned allows for more effective and efficient storage and retrieval, e.g. 4th grade students were asked to create a graphic organizer in the form of a t-chart to solve a math problem. Students were at a loss. The teacher commented, "You know how to do t-charts, we did them in communication arts! Remember when we did . . . in communication arts. That was a t-chart." Students immediately began to solve their problem. They needed to know WHAT they had learned in order to retrieve the information and skills.

Why: To motivate and engage learners. Why gives purpose to activities, and as research tells us, the brain is always trying to make sense (Wolfe 103). For example, a library media specialist began instruction of the library catalog by simply telling students it was one of the skills they needed to master. Instruction took approximately two hours and many did not master the skill. When the library media specialist gave students a reason for learning by asking, "Do you have favorite books? Do you sometimes have trouble finding those favorites? Would you like to learn a tool that will help you locate your favorite books in the library?" Instructional time decreased to approximately one-half hour and students were seen using the catalog after the instruction.

How: The activities or actions necessary for learning to take place. The how of learning has long been a focus in the field of education. As a result, many hours have been invested in research and field study and now provide information enabling teachers to design and implement effective instruction. Individual teachers are developing effective instructional strategies and lessons. However, because of the isolated nature of teaching, others remain unaware of these effective strategies and spend many hours and much work re-creating effective activities, strategies, and lessons (i.e. reinventing the wheel).

This book is organized into four parts. Part One focuses on the **what** and **why** of the Big6 and problem solving. Parts Two through Four focus on the **how**.

- Part One provides information and strategies that will help teachers and library media specialists ensure students know **what** they are learning—the Big6 problem solving process—and **why** they need to learn it to be problem solvers and information literate.

- Part Two makes connections between Big6 problem solving and information available from research. The intent is to provide information enabling teachers and library media specialists to design and implement more effective lessons and strategies to teach Big6, e.g. problem solving/information literacy skills.

- Part Three offers tips and strategies for each Big6 step enabling teachers and library media specialists to introduce the steps and build prescriptive practice for students. Prescriptive practice is designed to allow students to build upon their strengths and strengthen their weaknesses.

- Part Four provides activities and lessons which integrate the Big6 problem solving process into existing classroom activities and content. These activities and content may be used by teachers as is or as a springboard to creating more effective and efficient lessons for students. They are offered in recognition of the power of integrating content into process (making connections), and the importance of practice or repetition in learning. With the integration of Big6 problem solving into existing classroom activities, students improve their problem solving/information literacy skills, and do so by utilizing the limited amount of instructional time more fully.

The Big6 Problem Solving Process

The Big6 problem solving process, the brainchild of Mike Eisenberg and Robert Berkowitz, "is a process model of how people of all ages solve information problems" (4). It is the process upon which the lessons and strategies in this book are based. The six steps identified are:

1. Task Definition
2. Information Seeking Strategies
3. Location and Access
4. Use of Information
5. Synthesis
6. Evaluation

Application of the Big6

Before you begin your journey through this book, take a moment to think about what you hope to obtain from the information in this book, or what problem you need to address. By applying the six steps you will discover the adaptability of the process, and see how the process guided me in writing this book.

#1 Task Definition: Your task is to provide the direct instruction and coaching which will enable students to become efficient, effective problem solvers and information literate individuals.

#2 Information Seeking Strategies: You could use the Internet (www.big6.com), other books published by Big6 Associates, speak with or train with Mike Eisenberg or Bob Berkowitz (developers of the Big6 process), or use this book. Since this book is already in your hand and I am partial to it, let's make it our source. Do not forget, you will also need to use prior knowledge, schema, or (as the kids would say) "the stuff you know."

#3 Location and Access: As the book is in your hand, you have already located the source. The information within the source may be accessed in a couple of ways. You may read cover-to-cover or use text aids, e.g. table of contents and index, and scan for keywords. If you have difficulty retrieving prior knowledge, you may try making connections (suggestions in Chapter 3).

#4 Use of Information: Since this information is in text format there is only one way to get the information into your brain so it may be used. You must read. But do not try to clutter your brain with all of the information in the book, just extract information you need at the moment or, as Barbara Jansen (109) would say, "the treasure." You might want to take notes to make it easier to find the extracted information in the future. My favorite way to note the treasure is to highlight text (phrases only) and then paper clip the top of the page.

#5 Synthesis: This is where you solve your problem, or in this case the student's problem. Remember you can only synthesize if you use your new information in the classroom to ensure your students are conscious of the Big6 process, engage in learning the process, and apply the process to solving the problems they face.

#6 Evaluation: Evaluation of the product: Did you provide direct instruction and coaching? Have your students become more effective and efficient problem solvers? Can they identify the Big6 steps? **Evaluation of the process:** What worked for you? (You'll want to do that again!) What would you do differently next time? Did you remain focused on your task of helping students become problem solvers as you used the lessons, strategies, and tips suggested in the book? Did the lessons, strategies and tips suggested in the book work?

Works Cited

Brennan, Marilynn. "The Learning Journey: Software for the Brain." Regional Consortium for Educational Technology (RCET) Conference. University Plaza Hotel, Springfield, MO. May, 2002.

Eisenberg, Michael and Robert Berkowitz. *Teaching Information & Technology Skills: The Big6 in Elementary Schools.* Worthington, OH: Linworth Publishing Company, 1999.

Jansen, Barbara A. *The Big6 in Middle School: Teaching Information and Communications Technology Skills.* Worthington, OH: Linworth Publishing Company, 2007.

Payne, Ruby K. *Learning Structures, Modules 10-16 Workbook.* Highlands, TX: Aha Process, Inc., 1998.

Wolfe, Patricia. *Brain Matters: Translating Research into Classroom Practice.* Alexandria, VA: Association for Supervision and Curriculum Development, 2001.

PART 1

The BIG 6

GETTING STARTED—
FOCUSING ON THE STUDENT

Ensuring students know **what** they are learning
(problem solving) and **why** they need to learn it is a first step
in the journey of teaching Big6 problem solving. Information and
strategies in this section are designed to help you ensure your
students understand what problem solving and information
literacy skills are and why they are needed.

CHAPTER 1

WHAT? HELPING STUDENTS UNDERSTAND THE TASK

What is the task of students in school? If you asked this question two generations ago you would probably have been told reading, writing, and arithmetic. Asked a generation ago, after the Russians launched Sputnik, advanced mathematics and science would have been added. Today, as information and technology explode around us, many still recognize reading, writing, and arithmetic or mathematics as basics; but also add a fourth basic, information literacy.

What Is Information Literacy?

The American Association of School Librarians (AASL) and Association of Educational Communications and Technology (AECT) define information literacy as the ability to **access** information efficiently and effectively, **evaluate** information critically and competently, and **use** information accurately and creatively (AASL and AECT 8). Information literacy skills allow us to continue learning once our formal education is complete. These are the skills we utilized to learn how to use a debit card or to make an online purchase. Information literacy enables us to utilize new information and call upon prior knowledge in order to solve new problems. It is the ability which ensures lifelong learning. Information literate students possess the skills needed to solve information problems, to access, evaluate, and use information for the purpose of solving problems, minor or major, personal or school related.

What Are Problems?

This chapter began with a problem: What is the task of students in school? Problems require action to be taken or choices made. Students face a range of problems each day at school and home. Some are as simple as "What book do I want to read?" or "Where am I supposed to meet Mom?" Other problems are as complex as learning to read, completing a research project on the Civil War, or answering questions on state-mandated tests. These problems may be solved successfully and without stress when students are information literate.

How Can the Big6 Problem Solving Process Help?

As an educator you solve problems daily, hundreds of problems. You solve many of them automatically, without conscious thought, because you have mastered the problem solving process. Direct instruction of a problem solving process can enable your students to master the process and become efficient and effective problem solvers.

Big6, developed by Mike Eisenberg and Bob Berkowitz (11), consists of six steps which identify the process used to solve problems. Each of the six steps is further defined by two small steps known at the Little 12 (See Figure 1.1). The vocabulary used to identify the steps is authentic and learner friendly.

1. Task Definition
1.1 Define the problem
1.2 Identify the information needed
2. Information Seeking Strategies
2.1 Determine all possible sources
2.2 Select the best sources
3. Location and Access
3.1 Locate sources
3.2 Find information within sources
4. Use of Information
4.1 Engage
4.2 Extract
5. Synthesis
5.1 Organize information from multiple sources.
5.2 Present the result
6. Evaluation
6.1 Evaluate the product (effectiveness)
6.2 Evaluate the process (efficiency)

Figure 1.1
Big6 Problem Solving
Process with the Little 12

Efficient and effective problem solving is more likely to occur when students consciously apply each of the steps when attempting to solve problems. This ability to use the Big6 process is facilitated when problem solvers know and understand the vocabulary and receive direct instruction and guidance when applying the steps to problem solving.

Effective problem solvers use all of the steps in the process when solving problems. Those steps are, however, not always applied in a sequential manner, progressing from step one through step six. Authentic problem solving is not always linear. For instance, it may be necessary to evaluate (Big6 #6) immediately after identifying the task (Big6 #1). Or when completing research a student may be using information (Big6 #4) and find it necessary, because all the needed information has not been found, to revisit information seeking strategies (Big6 #2).

Knowledge of the steps involved in problem solving allows students to focus upon each specific step and the skills required to master each step. It allows for individual steps in the problem solver's process to be analyzed and weaknesses identified and addressed. These strengthened steps may then be placed back within the framework of the process.

The Big6 makes a powerful tool for improving problem solving skills because it:

- provides specific steps which logically guide problem solving

- provides vocabulary allowing verbalization of the process and making the process visible

- can be used to solve authentic problems from a variety of areas, e.g. science, research or personal

- can be used repetitively when solving problems leading to mastery of the process

- allows the problem solver to identify and address problem solving weaknesses

- actively engages students in their learning

- encourages students to take responsibility for their learning

Tips and Strategies to Introduce and Teach Students the Big6 Problem Solving Process

So where do you start in teaching students to be problem solvers using the Big6? Some strategies which might be utilized include:

Let students know Big6 is a series of steps. Following these steps, like a recipe, can help solve problems at school and home.

Develop a sense of problems. Make sure students understand what problems are. Help them identify the problems they must solve.

Ensure students know why they should spend time learning Big6. Help them recognize the occurrence of problems in their everyday life, the importance of developing problem solving skills, and how Big6 can aid in developing those skills. (See Chapter 2).

Introduce the steps. Possible ideas might include:

- **Pose an authentic problem.** Present authentic problems students face such as going to the movies, purchasing a bicycle, or signing up for the summer community baseball program. Apply the steps of Big6 to solve the problem. See Figure 1.2 for a sample problem and application of the six steps.

1. Task Definition (What is my task?)
I want to play baseball this summer on the community team.

2. Information Seeking Strategies (What sources can I use?)
I can call the City Park program, ask my teacher, ask a friend.
I decide to ask my friend Tommy, because he told me his Mom just signed him up to participate in the program.

3. Location and Access (What is my task?)
Tommy and I walk home together and so on the way home I ask him who his Mom called. He tells me to stop by his house because his Mom has the phone number to call and register.

4. Use of Information (Where can I find the sources and the information?)
I stop by Tommy's and write down the number, which I give to my Mom at dinner. She calls the number and registers me to play baseball.

5. Synthesis
I play ball this summer.

6. Evaluation
Product: Did I get to play ball this summer? Do I want to play next summer?
Process: What did I do that worked well this time? Asking Tommy? Getting number from his mother? What would I do differently next time? Write numbers so it is easier for Mom to read them.

Figure 1.2
Using the Big6 to Solve an Authentic Problem

- **Solve a problem and then apply the Big6 process**. Divide students into teams. Have each team create a symbol of a concept or of content recently taught using aluminum foil. Give some criteria, e.g. must be 3-dimensional or minimum size. After students have completed the symbols, talk them through the Big6 steps to illustrate how they are already using the process to solve problems. They use the process unconsciously. Stress the goal in class will be to verbalize and consciously use the process to solve difficult problems.

- **Write the steps of problem solving**. Pose a problem and have students write down the steps they would use to solve the problem. Then model solving the problem using the Big6 steps. Have students compare the steps they used and the steps in Big6. There should be several similarities.

- **Arrange the steps in proper sequence**. Give each team a set of six strips with the steps of Big6 written in random order. Ask students to arrange the strips in the order they would use to solve a problem. Think aloud as you solve a problem using the Big6 steps.

- **Introduce vocabulary before the process**. Before introducing Big6, teach and use Big6 vocabulary with students, e.g. task, evaluate, sources. After students have mastered the vocabulary, introduce the Big6 and the six steps as a problem solving process.

Post the steps in the classroom. Display the Big6 steps so they may be referred to throughout the day by students. Having students create the posters may be a powerful way of increasing awareness of the six steps.

Help students visualize the process. Verbalize and model for students as you solve problems during the school day, e.g. our problem is . . . our task is . . . the source I am using is . . . .

Where are we? Ask students to identify where you are in the problem solving process at various times throughout the school day.

Review the process. After initial introduction to the steps, review:

- **Create a nonlinguistic set of Big6 posters**. Write each of the steps of Big6 at the top of a poster or chart paper. Divide the class into six teams. Assign each team to one poster. Have teams draw a picture or pictures to illustrate that step. Allow a couple of minutes to complete the task. Rotate the team to next step or poster and ask them to add illustrations. Continue until each team has the opportunity to add to each of the six posters. Keep posters displayed as a visual reminder of the steps.

- **Pop-Up Relay**. Hand out 18 strips, each containing one of the Big6 steps or the Little 12 steps. Have students stand, or pop-up, to identify the Big6 and the Little 12 in order, e.g. the person with step 1 stands and reads, "Task definition." The person who has 1.1 will stand and read, "Define the problem." Continue until all the Big6 and Little 12 have been presented. You may wish to post strips on the board for all to see following the activity.

- **Pop-Up Application**. Hand out the 18 strips, the Big6 and Little 12, again. This time pose a problem and use the Big6 steps to solve the problem. The individual with step 1 would stand and say, "Task definition." The person with 1.1 would then stand and identify what the task is and the person with 1.2 would stand and identify what information is needed. Proceed until the problem has been solved using all of the Big6 and Little 12 steps.

Works Cited

American Association of School Librarians (AASL) [and] Association for Educational Communications and Technology (AECT). *Information Power, Building Partnerships for Learning.* Chicago, IL: American Library Association, 1998.

Eisenberg, Michael and Robert Berkowitz. *Teaching Information & Technology Skills: The Big6 in Elementary Schools.* Worthington, OH: Linworth Publishing, Incorporated, 1999.

CHAPTER 2

WHY? MOTIVATING STUDENTS TO BECOME BETTER PROBLEM SOLVERS

Teachers often lament about the students who do not pay attention in class and thus do not learn. For some students, knowing the teacher considers the content or process being presented important ensures they will engage in the lesson and learn. Many others are not motivated to learn just because the teacher believes the lesson to be important. How can we motivate these students to learn? Research reports that much of the information entering the brain is filtered out because it is not considered relevant or important (Wolfe 79). If students are provided an authentic purpose, prior to receiving information, the new information has a better chance of being identified as relevant and thus passing into the brain. Consequently it becomes important to take the time and ensure our students know *why* they *need* or *want* to learn a specific process or content.

Why Do Students Need to Develop Problem Solving Skills and Become Lifelong Learners?

Our Rapidly Changing World

The world is experiencing an information and technology explosion. As a result some of today's students will work in jobs that do not yet exist. Many, unlike their parents and grandparents, will change careers. The knowledge and skills required to be a successful, contributing citizen continue to change. To keep pace with the evolving knowledge and skills requires continued learning, making it impossible to reach a point where everything is known and thus learning can stop. Developing the skills to continue learning after our formal education is complete is a necessity. Information literacy skills, or problem solving skills, enable students to become lifelong learners.

Understanding the need for problem solving skills can motivate students. By looking at specific examples of how our world has changed, students may begin to understand the importance of lifelong learning and problem solving skills.

Examples of Impact on Occupations

Examples of careers and how they have been impacted by the information technology explosion is one strategy which may help students comprehend the need for information literacy skills.

If you were among the college graduates of the seventies, you probably felt you possessed all of the skills and knowledge needed to succeed in your life's work, or career, upon graduation. If you were a business education teacher you graduated prepared to teach:

- typing using manual typewriters
- bookkeeping, perhaps with the use of an adding machine
- banking with three types of accounts possible: checking account, passbook savings, certificate of deposit
- shorthand

If you are a business education teacher in today's world, because of the advent of technology, you are actually teaching:

- keyboarding using computers
- accounting utilizing automated record keeping systems
- banking with dozens of account options
- use of audio recording and videotaping devices instead of shorthand, which has become obsolete

If the business education teacher of the seventies was not a lifelong learner, she followed the path of the dinosaurs and became extinct. Many occupations have been impacted by the information and technology explosion. Examples of some of these other occupations and changes within the last 30 years include:

- auto mechanics: electronic systems instead of just mechanical systems
- retailers: e-mail and Internet
- broadcasters and television commentators: cable and satellite capabilities
- farmers: global positioning satellites and electronic systems in equipment
- doctors and nurses: utilization of new devices for diagnosis and treatment, and increased knowledge about the human body

After beginning this discussion on the effects of the information and technology explosion upon careers, challenge students to visit with friends and relatives. Ask students to discover changes in their respective fields and the requisite learning necessary for continued success. The need for lifelong learning and its impact upon future careers may motivate students to hone their problem solving skills.

Examples of Devices and Activities

Our personal lives have been impacted as a result of the information and technology revolution. New devices are in abundance. The way we complete a variety of activities has changed. Raise students' awareness of the impact of information and technology on our devices and activities and thus our lives:

1. Brainstorm with students. Create a list of devices and activities which have only existed for the past 20 or 30 years. The listing of devices may mention microwaves, laptop computers, remote controls, and CDs. Activities may include sending and receiving e-mail, scanning credit and debit cards, making online purchases, and finding information on the Internet.

2. Use this brainstormed list and the adults in the students' lives to emphasize the speed with which our world is changing. Have students take the brainstormed list and ask parents or other adults to answer these questions:

   - Do you remember life before this device or activity?

   - Did you learn to use this device, or complete this activity, while in school?

   - Do you use this device or complete this activity?

   - If yes, how did you learn to use this device or complete this activity? For example, did you read, have someone show you how, take a class, etc.

3. An awareness of how rapidly our world is changing should result when students analyze the information gathered from adults. Students may also comprehend the need for continued learning if they are to enjoy the benefits of new devices and changing activities.
   After students have gathered information discuss the following ideas:

   - Do you think the changes your parents and others have experienced will continue in your lifetime?

   - If so is there a need for you to continue learning after you finish your formal education?

   - Is it smart to invest time and effort in improving your problem solving skills?

Many students will not remember life before these devices and activities. By visiting with adults, who do remember, students may better appreciate how rapidly our world changes. In addition, discussion of the information gathered may help students recognize the power of being a lifelong learner. Many of the adults questioned will have had no opportunity to learn about the devices and activities during formal education because they did not exist when the adults were students. Students should grasp that only by recognizing a need and then using problem solving skills were these adults able to function effectively and efficiently in the changing world. This awareness may motivate students to improve their problem solving skills.

The Desire to Become Independent

No one likes to be told what to do. The need to be independent tends to grow as students progress through school. As a high school teacher I frequently heard students exclaim they could not wait to graduate. The students went on to voice their opinion that after graduation no one would tell them what to do. Those students were unaware that perhaps even more people would be telling them what to do. Bosses, spouses, children, government, church, and associates all have expectations to be met and tasks to be completed. It is not possible to stop these demands. Individuals can, and do, control whether the problems are solved independently or whether they wait and rely on others to tell them what to do.

The level of independence with which problems are solved may be placed upon a continuum (see Figure 2.1). Both problem solving ability and personality play a part in where an individual falls on the continuum.

Levels of independence		
←		→
Independent problem solvers	Semi-dependent problem solvers	Dependent problem solvers

Figure 2.1 Problem Solving Continuum

1. **Independent problem solvers**. These individuals recognize the problem and immediately take steps to solve it. They do not wait to be told they must solve the problem. Independent problem solvers often operate at the unconscious level, or on autopilot, when solving problems.

2. **Semi-dependent problem solvers**. These individuals are, sometimes, independent problem solvers. At other times they must be prompted, or reminded, of the problem and what steps should be taken to solve the problem.

3. **Dependent problem solvers**. These individuals rarely identify and solve problems on their own. Instead they wait until someone tells them there is a problem and what they should do to solve the problem.

Those who operate at the independent level rely upon themselves. This self-reliance seems to result in positive feelings and feelings of empowerment by the problem solver. Associates of the independent problem solver may enjoy less stress. As the problem solver assumes responsibility for problem solving, that responsibility is lifted from their associates' shoulders. To be an independent problem solver requires mastery of the problem solving process.

Operating as a dependent problem solver appears to require less brain power and effort. There are, however, disadvantages to this approach to problem solving. One disadvantage is the frustration which often results from always being told what to do. Another disadvantage involves those who must do the telling. Many people find it frustrating to have to constantly direct, or tell, an individual. As the frustration builds there is a tendency to begin telling in a rude manner. If this situation arises both the problem solver and the person directing the problem solver have a negative experience. Dependent problem solvers often do not possess problem solving skills.

The semi-dependent problem solver, the middle of the continuum, usually represents individuals who are developing their problem solving skills. At times they may solve problems independently. At other times they still need the modeling and guidance that a teacher may provide.

Students who desire independence may be motivated to improve problem solving skills as they become aware of the effect of the levels of problem solving. Assuming students understand the need to be lifelong learners and the role of problem solving skills in attaining that goal, the next objective is to help them understand why a process such as Big6 is important.

Why Focus on Mastering a Problem Solving Process Such as the Big6?

Using a problem solving process provides consistency. The same steps can be taken to solve the problem, even though the problems to be solved constantly change. The power of the process may be explained to students using an analogy: a recipe is to a cook what the Big6 process is to a problem solver. Just as a cook uses a recipe to produce a meal more efficiently and effectively, a problem solver can use a process such as Big6 to more efficiently and effectively solve problems (see analogy in Chapter 3). Problems can be solved without awareness of the process being used. The resulting trial and error type of problem solving, however, is not as productive as consciously identifying and using the steps involved in problem solving.

The Big6, as discussed in Chapter 1, breaks the process of solving problems into six small steps. Focusing on each step enables students to master the problem solving process. Once the process has been mastered, many problems can be solved on autopilot, or without conscious thought.

Why Consciously Use the Process?

Problems and Practice

Teachers and students face hundreds of problems each day. Research indicates that practice is effective for learning procedures or processes (Wolfe 101). Thus a tremendous opportunity exists to help learners improve their problem solving skills—by practicing each of the steps as the problems are solved. The Big6 steps can be practiced if the problems are school problems such as preparing for a social studies test or writing a book report. The Big6 steps can be practiced if the problems are personal in nature such as deciding what to do on Saturday night or deciding how to spend the $25 you received for your birthday. Because of this diversity the opportunities to master the problem solving process are even greater.

Learning Both Content and Process

Every problem solved involves both content and process. Because of the focus on content in schools, many opportunities to teach the problem solving process are missed. Problems are often solved via instruction which is limited to the content, e.g. the civil war, photosynthesis, or the setting of the story. These missed opportunities for teaching the problem solving process are even more disturbing when it is realized that the content may not be used again, but the process will be used every time a problem is solved.

Can the Process Be Used to Improve Our Problem Solving Skills?

It is possible to diagnose the weak links in a student's problem solving skills by focusing on individual steps. When students identify specific weaknesses in their problem solving skills it becomes possible to identify the specific step that is weak. Once the step has been identified the student and teacher may focus on strategies to improve the weakness. Some samples of common weaknesses and the Big6 step that needs strengthening are listed below:

- Have you ever had a teacher assume you had knowledge from earlier instruction, but you had no memory of having learned that information? (Weakness: #3 Location and Access, inability to access prior knowledge).

- Have you ever accidentally left an answer blank when taking a test? (Weakness: #6 Evaluation, failure to evaluate).

- Have you ever done poorly on a test because you forgot to take home your book or your notes the night before the test? (Weakness: #2 Information Seeking Strategies, not realizing needed sources or #3 Location and Access, failure to locate materials).

- Have you ever had trouble finding papers and materials? (Weakness: #3 Location and Access, failure to locate materials).

- Have you ever been clueless as to what you are supposed to do on an assignment, even after the teacher has spent a great deal of time explaining? (Weakness: #1 Task Definition).

Those students who identify some of the weaknesses listed may benefit from knowing they are not the only students to experience these weaknesses. The bulleted list includes weaknesses frequently identified in the problem solving process. It is important for students to understand that these weaknesses are not indicators of intelligence. Rather they are symptoms of poor problem solving skills. This is actually good news. Intelligence is the knowledge we are born with and extremely difficult, if not impossible, to change. Problem solving skills, however, are much easier to change. Prescriptive practice can positively impact problem solving skills once these weaknesses are diagnosed.

Can the Process Help Solve Difficult Problems?

Many of the problems staff and students face each day might be called no-brainers. They are simple problems that can be solved without conscious thought to the process. Some of the problems, however, are difficult problems or brain busters. There is a greater chance of success if the problem solver knows each of the steps in the problem solving process and can consciously apply it.

Armed with an understanding of what problem solving is, why it is desirable to become a problem solver, and why using a problem solving process can help them become more effective and efficient problem solvers, students are ready to begin learning and using the Big6 process. They are ready to begin working smarter, not harder. This is one of the very best motivators.

Works Cited

Wolfe, Patricia. *Brain Matters: Translating Research into Classroom Practice*. Alexandria, VA: Association for Supervision and Curriculum Development, 2001.

PART 2

The BIG 6

MAKING IT WORK— FOCUSING ON FUNDAMENTALS OF LEARNING

This section makes connections between the Big6 problem solving process and information available from research and field study. The intent is to provide information enabling you to design and implement more effective lessons and strategies to teach Big6 or problem solving and information literacy skills.

CHAPTER 3
EMPOWERING STUDENTS THROUGH KNOWLEDGE OF THE LEARNING PROCESS

How do we learn? The process of learning is unclear for many students and teachers. If you ask your students where learning takes place, you will probably see fingers pointed at the top of heads. Additionally you may hear students respond, "in my brain." However, if you ask students how they learn you are likely to hear an array of answers. Responses such as studying, working hard, not talking during class, going to school, staying awake, and doing math and stuff like that. These responses reveal how abstract the process of learning is to many students.

It is not surprising that the learning process is not fully understood by all educators and learners today. Only recently have technological advances enabled scientists to observe the brain at work learning. These observations offer insights into the process of learning. These insights may be utilized by teachers to develop effective learning strategies like the Big6. They also may be utilized to empower students to actively engage in and take control of their own learning.

How Do We Learn?

The functional model of the brain processing information (Wolfe 77), as illustrated in Figure 3.1, reveals learning occurs when new information enters our **sensory memory** through one of our **five senses**. New information is then passed from sensory memory into our **working or short-term memory**. Learning takes place when the new information is mixed with prior information which is retrieved from **long-term memory**. This new learning is then stored in long-term memory.

A Functional Model of Information Processing

Based upon the work of Patricia Wolfe (p. 77)

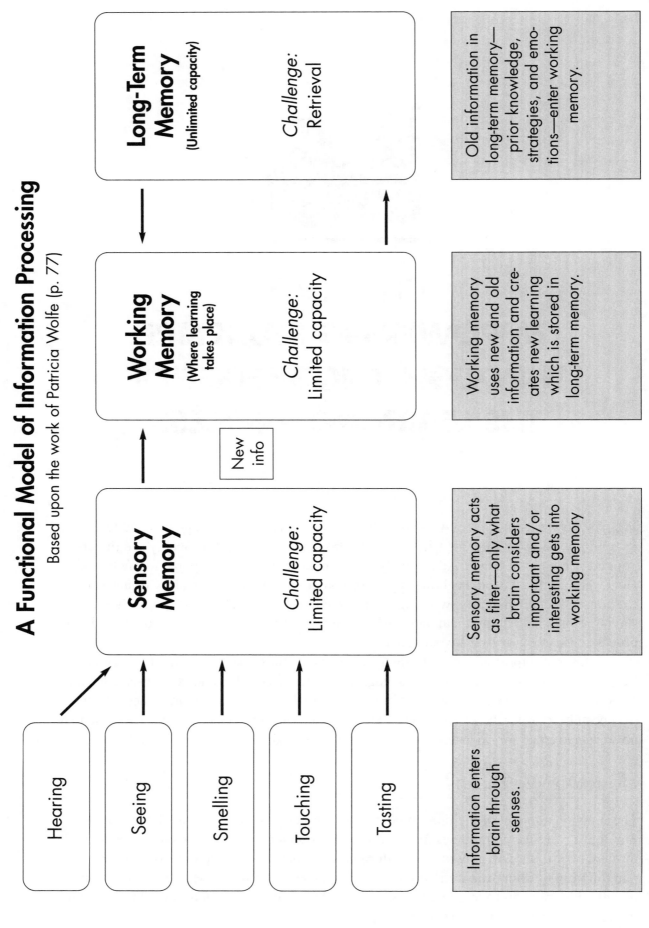

Hearing

Seeing

Smelling

Touching

Tasting

Sensory Memory

Challenge: Limited capacity

New info

Working Memory

(Where learning takes place)

Challenge: Limited capacity

Long-Term Memory

(Unlimited capacity)

Challenge: Retrieval

Information enters brain through senses.

Sensory memory acts as filter—only what brain considers important and/or interesting gets into working memory

Working memory uses new and old information and creates new learning which is stored in long-term memory.

Old information in long-term memory—prior knowledge, strategies, and emotions—enter working memory.

From *Teaching Elementary Information Literacy Skills with the Big6™* by Joyce Needham. Columbus, OH: Linworth Publishing, Inc. Copyright © 2009.

Figure 3.1 A Functional Model of Information Processing

The learning process presented in this simplified functional approach appears uncomplicated and efficient. However, there are some inherent weaknesses:

- **Needed information may fail to be accessed.** Not all information makes it through our senses and into the sensory memory. Additionally not all information entering sensory memory makes it to the working memory. This is an obvious problem. If information fails to enter the brain it cannot become part of our learning. Why does some information get lost? The cause is a combination of the quantity of information continuously bombarding our senses and the limited capacity of sensory and working memories.

- **Retrieval is another weakness in our learning process.** Have you ever struggled to recall the name of a former student or colleague? Or a week after taking a test had difficulty recalling the facts you retrieved in order to pass that test? If so you experienced the downside of long-term memory's unlimited capacity, which is the difficulty of retrieving or recalling stored information.

With knowledge of the weaknesses in the learning process teachers and library media specialists may develop effective learning strategies which:

- Guide students to use their senses to access new information and to use prior knowledge to access old information.

- Encourage students to consciously set filters to allow entry of important information.

- Assist students in retrieving prior knowledge by making connections between new learning and prior knowledge.

How Does the Big6 Connect to the Learning Process?

The Big6 process is a process for solving problems. Solving problems encourages making sense of information which is a natural tendency of the brain (Wolfe 104). Looking at the functional model of information processing using a Big6 lens (see Figure 3.2) reveals how effectively Big6 may assist in the learning process.

Step 1: Task Definition. What is my problem or task? What information do I need?

Information must be filtered through the senses, sensory memory, and working memory to become part of our learning. Research indicates the brain filters information considered important and emotional or important and factual (Schiller 11). When students know the task, and the information needed, they are better able to identify the important information. This increases their learning possibilities.

Step 2: Information Seeking Strategies. What sources can I use to gather information?

Students must be engaged to identify sources which may be used to solve the problem. They must focus on what information is needed. This focus increases the probability of filtering needed information into the brain. Recognizing when the needed source is prior knowledge allows the brain to actively engage long-term memory and retrieve the needed information.

A Functional Model of Information Processing through the Big6 Lens

Based upon the work of Patricia Wolfe (p. 77)

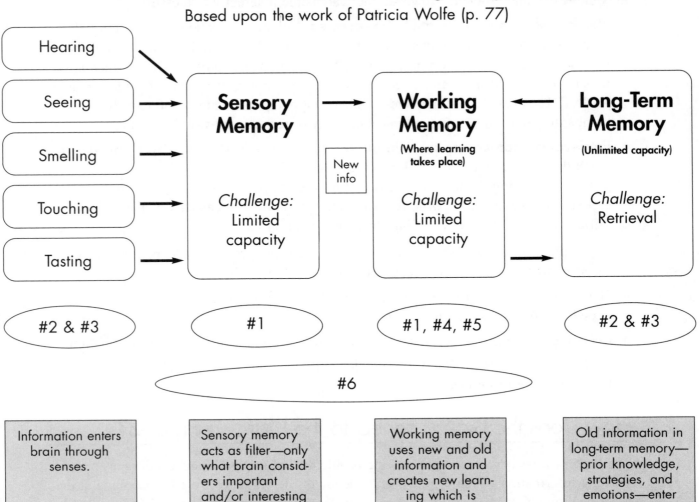

#1 Task Definition:
Sensory memory only passes to working memory the information that is considered interesting or important. If the brain identifies the task and recognizes the information as necessary to complete the task it will be deemed important. In working memory, recognition of our task or problem aids in creating desired learning.

#2 Information Seeking Strategies and #3 Location and Access:
Knowing what source to use and locating that source enables us to gather the new and old information necessary for learning to take place.

#4 Use of Information and #5 Synthesis:
These steps describe what happens in the working memory as new learning is created.

#6 Evaluation:
This step is ongoing, occurs at all stages of learning, and helps to ensure that we learn as effectively and efficiently as possible.

Figure 3.2 A Functional Model of Information Processing through the Big6 Lens

Step 3: Location and Access. Finding the source and the information within the source.

Information must first be located before it can be filtered into the brain. The ability to quickly locate and access the needed information from sources facilitates the learning process.

Step 4: Use of Information. Engaging and extracting, and Step 5: Synthesis. Organizing and presenting information.

The actual learning or synthesis occurs in the working memory. Learning within the working memory is a multi-step process. First information is used or actively filtered into the working memory. Next the important information must be extracted. Finally synthesis takes place as information is organized and communicated to the intended audience and to long-term memory. Utilizing Steps 4 and 5 of the Big6 process may more efficiently and effectively guide students through this portion of the learning process.

Step 6: Evaluation. Assessing product and process.

The brain constantly monitors or evaluates (Wolfe 103). Much of the evaluation of the learning process occurs at an unconscious level. We ask ourselves questions such as: Do I need this information? Does this make sense? What is my task? This ongoing evaluation by the brain leads to successful learning and the development of skills needed for future learning. Teaching students to *consciously* evaluate both product and process (Step 6) assists students in improving these important evaluation skills.

Tips and Strategies to Help Students Become Better Learners

With understanding of the learning process and its inherent weaknesses, it is possible to design specific teaching strategies based upon the Big6 problem solving process. Integrating strategies within the framework of Big6, rather than presenting them as a list of things to do, results in a connectedness which may facilitate learning. The following strategies may be used within the context of the Big6 problem solving process or one of its steps.

Big6 Problem Solving Process

Teach students the functional model of learning. Connect that knowledge to using the Big6 steps. This knowledge may motivate students and help them become actively engaged in learning.

Help students become aware of what learning looks like and feels like. Catch students engaged in learning. Catch students reading, listening, writing, thinking, or locating information. Then raise their awareness that those are the activities involved in learning. Try this strategy to help students focus on what learning looks like and feels like:

- *Observe the class.* When you notice students actively involved in learning activities ask students to "freeze." (As a librarian, instead of commanding students to freeze, challenge students to "be a book." The results will be the same because books do not move and books do not talk.)

- *Then identify and connect for students*: "What you were doing was learning, e.g. letting information into the sensory memory, using information, and so on. That is what it looks and feels like."

Task Definition

Ensure that students are conscious of their basic task at school. The basic task or job of students at school is learning. Student consciousness of their task has the potential to facilitate learning. Along with awareness of task, developing an understanding and consciousness of the learning process and its realities may be powerful.

■ *Learning takes place in the brain.* Learning is something the individual has to do for himself. While teachers or parents may guide and assist, *the learning must be accomplished by the student.*

■ *Learning is hard work.* Teachers and library media specialists are learners and as such know the reality of this statement. Do not assume all students comprehend that learning is hard work. For instance, a teacher was introducing her 5th graders to the Big6 as a successful strategy for solving math problems. To further convince students of the power of the Big6 process, she shared that the 4th graders, when using the Big6 process to solve math problems, went home exhausted. Instead of being impressed, students expressed concern about the usefulness of the Big6 process. The students perceived anything which made them tired as being negative. To help students understand that learning can be hard work and tiring, the teacher used this analogy comparing a sports practice session with a learning session:

  • Think of a sport you play. Now think of one of your practice sessions. Sometimes after practice do you feel that you only have enough energy to drag yourself out of the door and into the car? Do you feel that there is no way you could run out and hop in the car?

  • Think about those times you have been really tired. Did you work hard? Would you say you had a good practice session? Would you say that as a result of the practice your game will improve?

  • Think about those days you leave school feeling refreshed. Think about those days you go home exhausted. When have you learned the most?

  • Just as physical exercise may result in immediate physical fatigue, learning may also result in fatigue. Sometimes it may even seem recovering from mental fatigue requires more time than recovering from physical fatigue.

■ *The more we learn the easier learning becomes.* The process of learning becomes easier with repetition and practice. Using an analogy of strengthening muscles and strengthening learning skills may help students understand.

  • Walk over to a somewhat heavy object in the classroom and attempt, unsuccessfully, to lift or pick up the object.

  • Ask students, "Is there anything I can do to make it easier to lift this object?"

  • Suggest: "What if I practiced lifting this object 10 times a day for 10 days? Would it get easier? What if I started lifting weights? With repetition or practice would my muscles get stronger? Would it be easier to lift the object? Just as our muscles get stronger with use, our brain becomes stronger with use. So the more you consciously practice the skills needed for effective learning (listening, retrieving information, making connections, and so on.) the easier learning will become for you."

- *Intelligence need not limit the ability to become a better learner.* Many skills needed for successful learning are those which learners may excel in regardless of intelligence. For instance while the following actions may not require above average intelligence, any one of the following actions could lead to improved student achievement:
  - taking the book home the night before a test. This is part of *location and access* (Big6 #3) and may lead to a higher test score.
  - taking organized notes. This is part of *use of information* (Big6 #4) and can be taught, having a positive effect on student performance.
  - evaluating the test before turning it in to make sure there are no blanks and that writing is legible. This is part of *evaluation* (Big6 #6) and may be powerful as a strategy enabling students to improve learning achievement by correcting silly mistakes.

As a teacher identify task (what you want students to learn and why) before giving any assignment. A beginning business law teacher, expecting students to learn everything in a chapter, assigned students to read the chapter and answer the questions at the end. It is clear, based on current knowledge of the limited capacity of sensory and working memory, why students were unable to meet the teacher's expectations. The teacher failed to identify the task for her students, to identify what information was needed and why. Had the teacher identified the task as students read the chapter, they could have filtered the information needed into the brain.

An example of the effectiveness of identifying the students' task prior to making assignments was demonstrated when 4th graders were learning about volcanoes. The teacher identified that students needed to be able to name and identify characteristics of the four types of volcanoes, i.e. cinder cones, composite, shield, and lava domes. The teacher located an article containing the desired information. Questions for students to answer were included at the end of the article. These questions asked students to explain how composite volcanoes were formed and to identify an example of each of the four types of volcanoes. Would answering the questions have met the students' goal of naming and identifying the four types of volcanoes? The teacher decided it wouldn't. Instead of answering the questions on the worksheet, students were assigned to create a chart including the four types of volcanoes and characteristics of each. Having identified the students' task, the teacher was able to direct students to more effective and efficient learning.

Location and Access & Use of Information

Guide students in making connections between new learning and prior knowledge. Without making these connections students may fail to store information or may have trouble retrieving prior knowledge. The importance of making connections is illustrated in the following two experiences:

In the first situation 3rd grade students were to be tested on their knowledge of the dictionary. Prior to the test students were given a dictionary and entry words. Students used the guide words to locate the entry word and then used the entry word to find the definition in the dictionary. On the test the students' ability to use guide words was assessed with a chart rather than a dictionary page. To assess the ability to use the dictionary students were given a sample dictionary page. However, instead of being given an entry word and finding the definition, they were given a definition and asked to find the entry word. Though the majority of students mastered dictionary use during instruction, test performance was low. Most students failed to make connections between what they were taught and the test because of the different format (chart vs. actual dictionary) and focus (definition leads to entry word rather than entry word leads to definition) used for instruction and testing. When the teacher asked students if she ever tested them over content they were not taught, a majority of the students responded yes. This response validated the belief that poor test grades were the result of difficulty making connections between instruction and testing rather than lack of student learning.

The second experience illustrates how making connections can impact student achievement. In a school-wide assembly held before state testing, the principal asked, "What can you do to help you do your best on the test?" The principal reluctantly called upon Don, a 4th grader who was known for speaking first and thinking later, who was frantically waving his hand in the air. When Don shouted "Big6", the principal asked, "How can Big6 help with the test?" To the principal's amazement Don rattled off each of the six steps. Don had been using the Big6 process to solve math word problems in his classroom and obviously made the connection that state mandated tests, like math problems, were problems. He identified Big6 as a problem solving strategy he knew and could use.

Comparing the Dictionary and Encyclopedia

Step 1: Randomly call on students to tell you what they know about a familiar source, in this case the dictionary. Write that information on the left side of a table or t-chart:

Dictionary	
• gives definitions • helps us spell • is arranged in alphabetical order • it gives a little information, about a paragraph	

Step 2: Introduce and write the name of the new resource, in this case the encyclopedia, on the right side of the table or t-chart.

Dictionary	Encyclopedia
• gives definitions • helps us spell • is arranged in alphabetical order • it gives a little information, about a paragraph • has lots of words or entries	

Step 3: Using the student created list, compare the dictionary to the encyclopedia noting similarities and differences, and writing similarities on the right side of the chart.

Dictionary	Encyclopedia
• gives definitions • helps us spell • is arranged in alphabetical order • it gives a little information, about a paragraph • has lots of words or entries	• is arranged in alphabetical order • has a lot of information, sometimes pages • has lots of words or entries

Figure 3.3 Comparing the Dictionary and Encyclopedia

Posing problems and integrating process within content are two powerful Big6 strategies which also help students make connections. In addition, the following four strategies within the problem solving process may aid students in making connections:

- **Questioning**. Ask questions of students to help them verbalize connections. For instance, to help students make connections between the many problems faced within the classroom, you might ask, "Is this a problem? Can you name another problem we have had today?" Or to make the connection that the same process is used to solve all problems you might ask, "What process do we use to solve problems? Can you name the steps of the process? Can you apply those steps to this problem?"

- **Comparisons**. Compare prior knowledge to new knowledge. Graphic organizers, such as Venn diagrams and t-charts, may be very helpful. For instance, when you are ready to introduce the encyclopedia, draw a t-chart or table (see Figure 3.3). Write dictionary on the left. Ask students to tell you what they know about the dictionary. Put this information under dictionary on the chart. Then introduce the encyclopedia and note similarities and differences as you complete the right side of the chart.

- **Prompting**. Help students retrieve prior knowledge by prompting. You might say, "Remember when we…" or "This is the same as…" or "What does this remind you of?" Frequently students who successfully make the connection are able to provide prompts to classmates and so you might say, "Sally, you remember, can you give a hint or clue that might help your classmates remember?"

- **Analogies**. Start with a familiar item or idea and use an analogy to compare the new to the known. For instance, you might use the following analogy between a cook and a recipe and a problem solver and the Big6 process to help students understand the Big6 process:

I love chocolate. (To engage students, ask if any of them love chocolate!) If I were to put you in the kitchen with the ingredients and utensils needed, could you bake a chocolate cake? Without a recipe, you might have to try several times, but you could eventually bake the cake. If I put you in the kitchen with the needed ingredients, utensils, and a RECIPE (listing of the steps), do you think you could make that chocolate cake faster and easier?

Analogy to Big6: Given enough time you can probably solve your information problem. But if you have the recipe (Big6), you will solve your problem more quickly and easily.

Let's take the analogy a step further. The "chef" has mastered the process of cooking. He can probably bake that chocolate cake quickly and easily because the recipe is stored in his brain, or if he has the recipe he can tweak it (add a bit of this and little of that) to create an even better chocolate cake.

Analogy to Big6: When you have mastered the Big6 steps you will be like the chef. You will not need to consciously use the recipe or the Big6 steps (you will have it stored in your brain and will use them on autopilot). If needed you will be able to take the Big6 steps and tweak them to solve your problem even more quickly and easily.

Evaluation

Guide students in monitoring their actions and evaluating if they are actively engaged in learning. After students have an awareness of what learning looks and feels like, again ask students to "freeze." Next ask students to evaluate: "Were you learning? What could you have done to be a better learner?" For instance, ask: "If you were talking about content of lesson were you learning? If you were talking about recess were you learning? If you were listening to the teacher share information were you learning? If you were playing with a pencil while the teacher was talking were you learning? What if you were talking to a friend?" Next ask students, "What could you do differently next time to make you a better learner?"

Understanding how we learn helps us as teachers to guide and to direct our students to more effective and efficient learning. Helping students develop an understanding allows them to engage and take responsibility for their own learning. With knowledge of the learning process, teachers and students can utilize the natural fit of the Big6 process to improve learning.

Works Cited

Schiller, Pam. *Start Smart! Building Brain Power in the Early Years.* Beltsville, Maryland: Gryphon House, Inc., 1999.

Wolfe, Patricia. *Brain Matters: Translating Research into Classroom Practice.* Alexandria, VA: Association for Supervision and Curriculum Development, 2001.

CHAPTER 4
IT'S ALL ABOUT PROCESS—
ABOUT TEACHING PROCESS

What Is Process?

Process may be described as a series of steps. Baking a cake, tying a shoe, reading, writing, and problem solving are all examples of processes. For each process there is a series of steps which leads to completion of the task. If the process is baking a cake, the recipe lists the steps or procedures to produce a delicious cake. If the process is solving problems, the steps of the Big6 identify the steps.

It is possible to bake a cake without a recipe. If our cook chooses not to rely upon a recipe, the process for baking the cake is recalled from prior knowledge. If the cook has mastered the process, relying on use of prior knowledge to create a delicious cake is a successful strategy. However, if the cook has not mastered the process, baking the cake without a written recipe will probably take longer and may not yield the same quality product.

Big6, like the recipe for our cake, identifies the steps involved in our process. Without Big6 the steps in problem solving may not be visible. This is not a problem once the process has been mastered, e.g. the chef who recalls the process from prior knowledge rather than the recipe. However, if the process has not been mastered and is not visible, the problem solver is likely to try trial and error to solve the problem. Trial and error as a problem solving strategy usually takes more time and does not yield the same quality. Teaching the process, or making it visible to our students, empowers students to become more effective and efficient problem solvers.

Do We Have Time to Teach Process?

The school day is packed with curriculum which must be taught. Teachers and library media specialists wonder how to find time to teach one more lesson. However, it is the very nature of process which demands it be taught. The brain can use processes on auto-pilot, with no conscious thought, once the process or procedure has been learned. In a sense the process becomes invisible (Wolfe 114).

You may have experienced completing a process on autopilot or unconsciously. For instance, have you arrived at your destination via car and suddenly realized you do not remember turning onto a particular street or stopping at a particular intersection? You know you must have completed certain actions to arrive safely at your destination but you do not recall them. This is because you have mastered the process of driving and can function on autopilot or unconsciously. This is frightening unless you also know about the brain's monitoring system. If something unusual happens, e.g. a deer runs in front of your car or the brake lights of the car in front of you come on, then your monitoring system can alert you and you switch back to a conscious-level of operation.

Completing procedures, such as problem solving, on autopilot requires less effort and time. Think back to when you were first learning a process you have now mastered. Perhaps you remember when you were first learning to type or to cook. Can you remember the amount of time and effort involved in completing the process then? Can you complete the process faster and with less effort now? One goal when learning a process is that the process will be learned so thoroughly that it can be performed on autopilot.

While it is desirable to function at the autopilot level, procedures can be learned more efficiently and effectively in manual mode. In manual mode, conscious thought is given to the process and each step as it is being used. Operating in manual mode is a powerful learning strategy. It is also an effective strategy when the problem to be solved is difficult, e.g. the first time you type on a word-processor or prepare a gourmet recipe.

Examining reading and writing instruction provides evidence that educators recognize the importance of consciously teaching process. When teaching children to read, teachers identify and verbalize the steps in the process for students. If the task is to decode the words the teacher encourages students to get your mouth ready, look for parts you know, and think about what would make sense. If the task is comprehension then the teacher models questioning, making connections, and inferring. Instead of giving students a topic and expecting a finished product with the first writing, teachers today guide students through gathering their ideas, writing a rough draft, revising, editing, and finally publishing their writing. While teaching process requires time, the learning which results justifies the use of that time.

There is a bonus for taking the time to teach process: less time is required to solve a problem operating at the autopilot level than operating at the manual level. Initially taking more time to teach the process can lead to less instructional time required as students develop the ability to independently solve problems. The time required to teach students process can be recovered when students have mastered the process, e.g. by spending 30 minutes teaching process today, 30 minutes of instructional time will be saved tomorrow when students use the process independently.

Are We Using the Process or Teaching the Process?

A concern was raised at a faculty meeting after students were observed struggling with the Big6 vocabulary: "Are students actually being taught the problem solving process?" One of the teachers responded, "Teachers are using the problem solving process. Students just do not recognize the name Big6 or the six steps. Is that really important?" Think for a moment. The goal of teaching problem solving is that students will be able to independently apply the steps in the process to successfully solve a problem. Will students be able to recall and apply the steps if they cannot verbalize the steps?

There is a difference between using the process and teaching the process. Using the process, or modeling, is an important strategy in teaching the process. However, teaching the process means the student will be able to recognize when he has a problem, to recall the six steps in the problem solving process, and to apply each step and actively solve the problem.

How Do We Teach Process?

Think of the strategies that work to teach other processes such as reading, writing, or math. Those same strategies are effective when teaching problem solving strategy.

Name the Process

Make students conscious of both the content and the process to be learned. It is possible for students to use a process and not learn the process. Learning the process is facilitated when the steps of the process are verbalized or communicated to students as the process is completed. When students are made aware of not just the content objectives, e.g. social studies and science objectives, but also of the process being used, e.g. the writing process, the reading process, and the Big6 problem solving process. Integrating content into the process provides for authentic problem solving. Coupled with conscious and direct instruction in the process, students have the opportunity to really learn the process.

Teach the Steps in the Process, Including the Vocabulary

Break the process into small steps and then teach the steps. Verbalize the steps in the process using the Big6 vocabulary to make the process visible for students. Using the vocabulary will assist students in both storing the process and recalling it when needed to solve a problem. (See Chapter 1 for additional strategies to teach the Big6 steps.)

Use Vocabulary as a Strategy

Each content area has its own vocabulary. For example if our content is music the vocabulary will include notes, rhythm, flats, sharps, etc. If the content is cooking it will include ingredients, stir, bake, etc. It is possible to be proficient at a process such as problem solving and be unaware of the vocabulary. However, knowledge and use of the vocabulary lead to improved communication and can result in more effective and efficient teaching and learning of the process.

The teacher, or library media specialist, can better communicate the process to the student by knowing and using the vocabulary. Would it be easier to teach someone to play the piano using words such as keys, notes, and pedal or to teach without using those words? Would it be easier to teach someone to bake a cake using words such as stir, batter, or bake or to teach without being able to use those words?

A common, shared vocabulary allows students to communicate their knowledge of the process. More importantly, it provides students the tools needed to ask effective questions leading to increased learning. Without knowledge of Big6 vocabulary a student might say, "I don't understand." Equipped with the Big6 vocabulary that student might say, "I don't understand the task or I don't understand the source that I should use." Knowledge and use of the vocabulary makes the communication between teacher and learner more specific and clear. This aids in learning the process.

Knowledge of vocabulary also helps the student make connections to and access to prior knowledge. Connecting new knowledge to prior knowledge helps the learner make sense of the new information. It also increases future recall of the information. (See suggestions for making connections in Chapter 3.)

- Students are introduced to a Venn diagram. Yet when asked to compare, instead of using the Venn diagram they organize information in paragraphs.
- Students are taught to recognize text features such as indexes and guide words. Yet when asked to find information in text they begin turning from page to page to locate the information.
- Students create a t-chart in reading. Yet when asked to create a t-chart in a math problem they are unable to do so.

These examples illustrate the importance of student awareness of what is being learned to increase learning, and the importance of making the process or knowledge visible so students may connect what is being learned to its purpose in order to recall and use it. In these examples students did not connect:

- The Venn diagram to a method of organizing information when making comparisons.
- Text features a tool to locate information quickly.
- The chart they made in reading to a t-chart.

Using and verbalizing the vocabulary associated with the process and the knowledge is one method of helping students make these necessary connections. What would it look like if teachers or library media specialists had verbalized the vocabulary in each of the examples?

- When introducing the Venn diagram: "The Venn diagram is one method of *organizing information*." When students are asked to compare, ask, "How will you *organize your information?*"

- When introducing text features such as the index or guide words: "The purpose of text features is to help us *locate information* quickly." When students need information from a book, ask, "What might help you *locate the information*?"

- When creating the t-chart in reading: "This is called a *t-chart*. Do you think that is a good name for it?" Ask students to "Create a *t-chart* to solve this math problem." Assist those students who are unable to create the t-chart by prompting, "You have used a *t-chart* before. Remember in reading when . . .?"

Scaffold Instruction

Provide plentiful support to students as they begin to learn the process. Gradually withdraw the support and allow students to be the problem solvers.

Begin by modeling the process. Throughout the day verbalize for students the steps of the process as problems are solved. For example, if you are going on a field trip, arranging for bus transportation is one problem you might need to solve. Utilize this as an opportunity to model the problem solving process by thinking aloud as you identify each step to solve the problem. Arranging bus transportation might look and sound like this as the teacher thinks aloud:

1. "The first step is *task definition*. What is my task? I need to get a bus for our field trip. I will need to know where we are going, when we are going, how long we will be there, and how many students will be going."

2. "Next I need to identify *information seeking strategies*. What sources of information can I use? I can use the place we are visiting on our field trip, my prior knowledge, and you."

3. "My third step is *location and access*. Where is the source and where is the information? You are right here, I am here, and I have the phone number of our field trip location."

4. "Now I am ready to *use the information*. This means using the information found in steps 2 and 3 to solve the problem identified in step 1. Using my knowledge of our schedule I determine possible dates we might be able to take the field trip. Calling the site of our field trip I find out which date they can give us our tour and how long the tour will last. Finally, I ask you, the student, how many will be able to go on the field trip."

5. "The problem is now ready to be solved or *synthesized*. As the school secretary arranges all buses I visit her office. I tell her we need a bus at 8:30 a.m. on Friday, September 24 to take us to *Wonders of Wildlife* at Campbell and Sunshine. We will need to leave the *Wonders of Wildlife* at 2:30 p.m."

6. (This will occur after the field trip.) "There is one final step to be completed. That is *evaluation*. Because I *may* need to solve this problem again it is important to evaluate my product. Did we complete our task? Did we get the bus? Did we get there and back on time? Because I *know* there will be problems to solve in the future, I also want to evaluate my use of the Big6 problem solving process. What steps worked really well? For instance, it really helped to think about our schedule before calling *Wonders of Wildlife*. What should I do differently next time? It would probably be easier for the secretary if the next time I give her a written copy of the details."

Provide opportunities for guided practice. An easy way to provide students guided practice is to question students and let them verbalize the steps in the process. For instance, at the beginning of an assignment you might ask, "What is our task? What information do we need?" (Big6 #1), "What sources could we possibly use? Which is the best source for us to use this time?"(Big6 #2), and "Where is the source? How can we find the information within the source?" (Big6 #3). As students begin to use the information and then complete the assignment, you might ask, "What step is next?" (Big6 #4 & #5). Finally, as the assignment is completed, students may be asked to evaluate. To evaluate *product*, "Did you complete your task? Are you pleased with your results?" To evaluate *process,* "What worked for you? What would you do differently next time?" (Big6 #6). In this example all six steps of the process are focused upon. As students are guided through the problem solving process, it may be desirable to focus on all six steps or only on one or two steps. This will depend upon the particular assignment involved and the students' knowledge of the process.

Provide opportunities for independent practice. Pose a problem to students. Have the student identify each of the steps taken to solve the problem. Consider letting students work in groups or pairs when independent practice first begins. It is also helpful to provide students an organizer (see Figure 4.1). Completing an organizer the first few times problems are solved may help the student learn the steps. When the student is comfortable completing the organizer, take it away and ask the student to use a mnemonic (www.use, see Chapter 1) to list the six steps and then identify the actions taken. If an organizer is not used writing the mnemonic at the top of the assignment may remind students to list the six steps and then identify the actions taken. While learning the Big6 process, it is important for students to consciously use all six steps. Completing an organizer or using a mnemonic requires conscious use of all the steps. It is also important to remember our goal is for students to automatically use the six steps as they solve their problems. When student have reached this goal it is not necessary to consciously apply each step and so it is not necessary to use the organizer or the mnemonic. It is important for students to understand that the use of an organizer and a mnemonic are learning tools and will only be used until the steps have been mastered.

Move from Simple to Complex

When you introduce the process, apply it to solving problems that are easy for students. This allows the student to focus on the process. Attention must be divided between the process and the content when the problem to be solved is difficult. Once the Big6 process becomes familiar and students use it to solve difficult problems, they will be able to appreciate the power of the process and be motivated to master it.

Provide Many Opportunities for Practice

According to research, we have only a 10 percent chance of remembering something done once in 30 days, and a 90 percent chance of remembering something done six times in 30 days (Schiller 95). You may be thinking: How do I find the time to teach the steps even once in 30 days? Should I set aside 30 minutes a day, or a week, for problem solving instruction? My schedule is already so full! While setting aside instructional time to teach the steps in isolation would be better than not teaching the steps, there is a better option: integrate.

Big6© (www.use) **Problem Solving Worksheet**

#1 What is my task?
(Task Definition)
 	
  ■ Define the problem or task.
 	
  ■ What information is needed?	

#2 What source can I use?
(Information Seeking Strategies)
 	
  ■ Brainstorm possible sources.
    Don't forget prior knowledge.
 	
  ■ Select the best source (easiest
    and fastest).	

#3 Where are the sources?
(Location and Access)
 	
  ■ Locate the source.
 	
  ■ Locate the information within
    the source (scan and skim for
    keywords using text aids).	

#4 Use of Information
 	
  ■ Engage (read, listen, view).
 	
  ■ Extract (Trash & Treasure).	

#5 Synthesize
 	
  ■ Organize your information.
 	
  ■ Complete your task (#1).	

#6 Evaluate
 	
  ■ Effectiveness: Go back to #1
    and make sure task is
    completed.
 	
  ■ Efficiency: Did I do it the
    easiest, fastest way? What
    would I want to do differently
    if I did this task again?	

From *Teaching Elementary Information Literacy Skills with the Big6™* by **Joyce Needham**. Columbus, OH: Linworth Publishing, Inc. Copyright © 2009.

Figure 4.1 Big6 Organizer

Students solve hundreds of problems every day. These existing math, communication arts, social studies, art, etc. problems may be utilized to integrate and teach the problem solving process. For instance, when it is time for science, pose a problem and have students use Big6 to solve the problem. Integrating the problem solving process is not only a time-saving method of teaching the process, it is a powerful practice.

Several professionals or teachers are involved in helping the student learn in a typical elementary school. If all of these professionals, e.g. the classroom teacher, the library media specialist, the art teacher, the music teacher, the counselor, are aware of students' learning goals then integration can become a reality. Communicating students' learning goals among the teachers can be a challenge with the time constraints each face. One possible method of communication is to use a planning form (see Figure 4.2). This form, which communicates the learners' goal in the classroom, may be completed by the classroom teacher and distributed to the related arts teachers. In one building the teachers took this tool to a higher level of communication. Each related arts teacher provided feedback on integration efforts on the form and returned it to the classroom teacher. By integrating the Big6 into content areas, the student has the opportunity for repetitive practice using the same process while solving a variety of real problems.

Include Student Evaluation or Feedback

In *Classroom Strategies that Work*, Marzano, Pickering, and Pollock identify feedback as one of the nine research-based strategies that work. A powerful effect on student learning has been found when students are provided feedback identifying where they stand relative to a specific learning goal. It is important to recognize that students can effectively monitor or evaluate their own learning (Marzano 96-99). Requiring students to evaluate, Step 6 of Big6, provides students the opportunity to determine weaknesses and strengths. Knowledge of these strengths and weaknesses helps students identify specific skills on which to focus continued practice. It is difficult to ensure that continued practice will focus on the skills most needed by the learner without the knowledge gained from evaluation.

Observation of athletic coaches during practice sessions may provide an opportunity to observe this strategy in action. Guided by the coach, the athlete evaluates and diagnoses his strengths and weaknesses. The evaluation is followed up with prescriptive practice designed to address the specific strengths and weaknesses of the athlete. This same strategy can be used to help students become more effective and efficient problem solvers. For example, if a student's weakness is using information, or specifically note taking, spending time practicing taking notes may be more beneficial than spending time locating information or writing a final report. This practice becomes even more powerful as the student recognizes his need to improve this specific skill. The knowledge learned by the teacher and student through evaluation may be used to make more effective use of our limited time and may also result in greater gains.

Process leads us to successful completion of a task. Big6 is a process which leads us to successful problem solving. Process may be taught. To teach process requires time. Once the process has been learned, however, time can be saved as students independently and efficiently solve problems. Teaching process requires more than just using the process. Teachers and library media specialists collaborating to integrate problem solving within content may effectively utilize limited time by guiding students as they use the Big6 process.

Planning Guide

(Art, Computers, LMS, Music, Physical Education, Speech, Counselor, LD)

For the month of _____   Please return to the LMC by: _____

Teacher/Team: _____   Meet in LMC: _____

Subject	Name of Unit, Concepts, Date of next test, etc.	Vocabulary
Communication Arts		
Math		
Social Studies		
Science		
OPTIONAL: Technology/Computer Skills	Complete the following section if it applies.	
Information Literacy Skills		
LMC Materials Need		

Figure 4.2 Planning Form

Works Cited

Marzano, Robert J., Debra J. Pickering, and Jane E. Pollock. *Classroom Instruction That Works, Research-Based Strategies for Increasing Student Achievement.* Alexandria, VA: Association for Supervision and Curriculum Development, 2001.

Schiller, Pam. *Start Smart! Building Brain Power in the Early Years.* Beltsville, Maryland: Gryphon House, 1999.

Wolfe, Patricia. *Brain Matters: Translating Research into Classroom Practice.* Alexandria, VA: Association for Supervision and Curriculum Development, 2001.

CHAPTER 5
CONNECTING PROCESSES:
BIG6 PROBLEM SOLVING, READING, LISTENING, SPEAKING, WRITING, AND TECHNOLOGY

If teachers and library media specialists were asked what they need more of in a day, a likely answer would be *time*. Increased curriculum demands have turned time into one of an educator's most precious commodities. Knowing what students need to learn is not the challenge. Finding time to teach all the skills and knowledge students need to be successful in today's world is the challenge. One method of using time more effectively is to teach skills simultaneously rather than separately. This becomes a viable option when we understand the natural connections between reading, listening, speaking, writing, technology, and problem solving.

What Do Reading, Listening, Speaking, Writing, and Problem Solving Have in Common?

The processes of reading, writing, listening, speaking, and problem solving/information literacy are identified as the communication arts. How are these processes connected?

One might say reading, writing, listening, and speaking are to information literacy what the fingers are to the hand. While fingers are important in their own right, they become even more important when they function as part of the hand. The hand is most capable with all five fingers functioning well. Reading, writing, listening, and speaking are each important in their own right. However, when they function within the process of problem solving, or information literacy, they become even more important. Accessing, evaluating, and using information, or information literacy, is severely limited without the skills of reading, listening, writing, and speaking. For how is information accessed if not by reading or listening, or used and communicated without speaking or writing?

When students need to read, listen, write, and speak in order to complete assignments and solve problems, they are confronted with an authentic reason to learn these skills. Understanding this reason may provide student motivation. Instruction which integrates the communication arts skills helps establish the need for each skill and provides opportunities to practice the skills, thus leading to student mastery of each process. Specific skills identified as part of communication arts instruction and the connections to problem solving and Big6 are shown in Figure 5.1.

By consciously connecting these skills to the problem solving process through use of Big6, instead of teaching the skills as isolated lessons, a real need to learn the skill is established and an authentic learning opportunity results. Students are taught the skill and when and how the skill should be used. For example, when the teacher verbalizes note taking is necessary when using information (Big6 #4), students:

- recognize the need for learning to take notes thus encouraging mastery

- identify when note taking skills are needed

- improve their problem solving skills

The connections between the communication arts processes—reading, writing, listening, speaking, and problem solving—make it possible to teach the processes while students focus on learning other content such as science and social studies. Designing lessons that focus on more than one skill allows for a natural integration of skills. It also allows students to focus on two or more skills at the same time utilizing limited time wisely. For instance, when students complete a research project about animal life, one of the science goals, opportunities for learning include:

- reading from the information found

- writing as the students prepare the final project

- problem solving as the six steps of Big6 are followed to complete the project

- science content

In essence we are *killing two birds with one stone*. Instead of students spending one hour learning about animal life and another hour practicing reading for a total of two hours, students can spend one hour reading about animal life. Students meet two additional learning goals, writing and problem solving, at the same time. Lessons of this type also encourage students to make valid connections to prior learning and result in purposeful learning (see Chapter 3).

Connections between Big6 Process and Communication Arts (CA)

Big6	Connections to CA Skills
Task Definition: What is my task? What information do I need?	■ KWL Charts (what do you Know, Want to know, what did you Learn) ■ Graphic organizers and/or outline ■ Concept mapping ■ Questioning—QAR (question answer relationship), developing essential questions ■ Keywords ■ Vocabulary ■ CUC—Check is evaluation (Circle, underline, count, check) ■ Major instructional goals as sources of problems ■ Developing thesis: timeline, compare/contrast, classify, etc.
Information Seeking Strategies: What sources, which is best?	■ Prior knowledge (schema) ■ Teacher ■ Text (fiction and nonfiction) ■ Technology: Internet, CDs, databases ■ Other sources specific to the task including: encyclopedia, dictionary, atlas, almanac, thesaurus ■ Keywords
Location and Access: Find the information	■ Scanning/skimming ■ Text features (aids or conventions) ■ Keywords
Use of Information: Engage and Extract	■ Reading ■ Use of senses ■ Note taking strategies ■ Trash and treasure ■ Note taking formats ■ Citing sources
Synthesize or Solve: Organize and Communicate	■ Writing ■ Appropriate products, e.g. reports, displays ■ Technology: word processing, PowerPoint
Evaluate: Product/Effectiveness Process/Efficiency	■ Rubrics ■ 6 + 1 writing traits ■ Metacognition—thinking about your thinking

From *Teaching Elementary Information Literacy Skills with the Big6™* by **Joyce Needham**. Columbus, OH: Linworth Publishing, Inc. Copyright © 2009.

Figure 5.1 Connections between the Big6 Process and Communication Arts (CA)

Where Does Technology Fit?

Technology provides tools to assist in solving problems. Eisenberg and Berkowitz (26) identify a variety of technology tools (see Figure 5.2) which may be utilized when problems are solved using the Big6 process.

Big6 Steps	Technology Integrated
Task Definition	Brainstorming software
Information Seeking Strategies	Full-text electronic resources
Location and Access	Online library catalog Electronic magazine index
Use of Information	Word processing Electronic magazine index Full-text electronic resources Copy-paste (in various programs)
Synthesis	Word processing Desktop publishing Presentation/multimedia software Electronic spreadsheets
Evaluation	Spell/grammar checking
Used with permission of Eisenberg and Berkowitz (p. 26)	

Figure 5.2 Technology Integrated into Big6

Specific technology skills, when fit within the existing Big6 framework, may be easier to recall. Teaching technology skills in this manner utilizes an integrated approach rather than an isolated approach to instruction. Compare the two approaches to teaching technology skills: Using an isolated approach, students may receive an unconnected list of 10 or 15 technology tools and be given the task of learning how to use the tools. Using an integrated approach, students receive information about specific technology tools at the time those tools may be used to solve the students' problem. For instance, a student identifying what source to use to locate information (Big6 #2) may be introduced to the Internet. A student ready to synthesize (Big6 #5) may be introduced to word processing or electronic slide shows. Students then use these technology tools to solve the problem.

Student learning can also be facilitated when the teacher or library media specialist makes connections between familiar technology and new technology: If you needed to extract important information (Big6 #4.2) in a print article, you might highlight it. If you accessed that same article on the computer, instead of highlighting, what technology skill might you use? *You could cut and paste.*

Where Does Reading Fit Within the Big6 Problem Solving Process?

Reading is often required when students reach Step 4, Use of Information. Use of information involves engaging and extracting. Engaging means students transfer information from the world around them, and from prior knowledge, into the brain. When that information is presented in printed form, then the act of engaging requires students to read. Students must either read to themselves or have someone else read to them if the information is to be transferred to their brain. Information cannot be used to help solve the problem until it enters the brain.

Reading is also essential when the problem is presented in printed form. Without the ability to read, or listen as the words are read, it is impossible to identify the task (Big6 #1). Poor reading skills have a direct effect on how successful students are in problem solving.

Students often find it easy to engage in a good story or literature. Using literature or picture books is an effective way to help students engage and improve reading and problem solving skills while also increasing content knowledge. Appendices A-C offer bibliographies which may help you begin incorporating picture books into Big6 problem solving instruction.

Where Does Writing (Including 6 + 1) Fit Within the Big6 Problem Solving Process?

Writing is often required when students reach Step 4, Use of Information, and Step 5, Synthesis. The purpose of writing differs when using information (Big6 #4) and when synthesizing information (Big6 #5). When using and extracting information, it is often necessary to take notes in order to remember the important information or treasure. The information written only needs to make sense to the problem solver as they are the one to use it. Teaching students the purpose of the writing may help them focus on more effective use of time. For instance, it is not necessary to take time to write in complete sentences. However, taking the time to ensure spelling is correct and notes make sense to the problem solver is wise.

Synthesizing, organizing, and presenting the solution may require writing depending upon the form it takes. Often the solution is presented in written form whether in a report, PowerPoint® presentation, poster, brochure, or simply the answer to a question. It is again important for the problem solver to understand the purpose of the writing. For instance, it is important to write in complete sentences and to follow conventions of writing as the purpose is to communicate to others.

Writing may also be necessary, depending upon the assignment, as students complete Step 1, Identify the Task, and Step 6, Evaluate. Poor writing skills negatively affect the problem solving process.

The steps of Big6 may also be used to guide students through the process of writing if that is the problem to be solved (see Figure 5.3). Connections are also made to 6 + 1 Traits of Writing (Culham 11) which may be integrated within the problem solving process.

A student's knowledge of how the Big6 steps are embedded within the writing process may strengthen both mastery of the problem solving process and the writing process. One of the simplest ways to make students aware of the connections between problem solving and writing is to verbalize both the writing step and the Big6 step which is being completed: You are revising in the writing process but you are also synthesizing and evaluating in the problem solving process. Students may use both Big6 and the writing process to solve their problem when they recognize *writing* as a problem. Using both processes simultaneously allows students to develop a deeper understanding of problem solving and to experience the varying emphasis upon each step depending upon the nature

Integrating Big6 Process with the Writing Process and 6 + 1 Traits of Writing

Process	Steps of the Process					
Writing Process	Prewriting/ Collecting	Drafting	Revising	Editing	Publishing	Celebrating
6 + 1 Traits of Writing	Ideas	All Traits	Organization Voice Word Choice Sentence Fluency	Conventions	Presentation	
Big6 Process	Task Definition Info. Seeking Strategies Location and Access Use of Information	Synthesis	Synthesis and Evaluation	Synthesis and Evaluation	Synthesis	Evaluation

6 + 1 Traits of Writing

1 — Ideas: Ideas make up the content of the piece of writing—the heart of the message.

2 — Organization: Organization is the internal structure of the piece, the thread of meaning, logical pattern of the ideas.

3 — Voice: Voice is the soul of the piece. It's what makes the writer's style singular, as his or her feelings and convictions come out through the words.

4 — Word Choice: Word choice is at its best when it includes the use of rich, colorful, precise language that moves and enlightens the reader.

5 — Sentence Fluency: Sentence fluency is the flow of the language, the sound of word patterns—the way the writing plays to the ear, not just to the eye.

6 — Conventions: Conventions represent the piece's level of correctness – the extent to which the writer uses grammar and mechanics with precision.

+1 — Presentation: Presentation zeros in on the form and layout—how pleasing the piece is to the eye.

Culham, Ruth. 6 + 1 *Traits of Writing: the complete guide grades 3 and up.* Portland, OR: Northwest Regional Educational Laboratory, 2003. (Revised by Bob Berkowitz, 4/1/2005)

From *Teaching Elementary Information Literacy Skills with the Big6™* by Joyce Needham. Columbus, OH: Linworth Publishing, Inc. Copyright © 2009.

Figure 5.3 Integrating Big6 Process with the Writing Process and 6 + 1 Traits of Writing

of the problem being solved. For instance, while writing requires less emphasis upon information seeking strategies (Big6 #2) than research, evaluation (Big6 #6) is extremely important to successful revision and editing. Students are better prepared to face a world in which they must continue to learn in order to be successful when they develop this deep understanding of the problem solving process.

Sample of an Integrated Lesson

The number and type of lessons which may be designed to integrate instruction of these processes are limited only by the imagination of the teacher and library media specialist. Lesson Plan 5.1 Writing a Fiction Animal Story provides just one sample.

Natural connections exist between Big6 and the processes of reading, listening, speaking, writing, and technology. Utilizing these connections, teachers and library media specialists may design lessons integrating these process skills with content such as science, social studies, or literature using Big6. The resulting lessons fully utilize limited instructional time and create a brain-friendly learning environment. An environment which engages students through problem solving, makes connections between new and prior knowledge, and provides students opportunities for authentic use of the processes.

Works Cited

Culham, Ruth. *6 + 1 Traits of Writing, The Complete Guide for Grades 3 and Up*.
    Portland, Oregon: Northwest Regional Educational Laboratory, 2003.
Eisenberg, Michael and Robert Berkowitz. *Teaching Information & Technology Skills: The Big6 in Elementary Schools*. Worthington, OH: Linworth Publishing, Incorporated, 1999.

LESSON PLAN 5.1

LESSON TITLE: WRITING A FICTION ANIMAL STORY

Grade Level: 4th or 5th

Time Frame:
4 or more 30-minute sessions:
- One session: intro
- One or two sessions: gather information
- Sessions to write (homework?)
- One session: to share and evaluate

Content Objective:
Reading:
- Select a fiction story and identify facts within the story

Writing:
- Create a fiction story about an animal. Include facts about the animal within the story.

Science: Life Science
- Identify characteristics of animals

Information Literacy Objective:
- Practice the steps of the problem solving process
- Information Seeking Strategies & Location and Access: locate and use encyclopedias to gather facts
- Location and Access: locate fiction and nonfiction books

Materials and Sources:

- Fiction books about animals, such as:
  - *KBUG Radio, up close and personal: an interview with Harry the Tarantula* by Leigh Ann Tyson
  - *Diary of a Worm* by Doreen Cronin
  - *Caterpillar and the Pollywog* by Jack Kent
  - *Clara Caterpillar* by Pamela Duncan Edwards
  - *What Newt Could Do for Frog* by Jonathan London
  - *Bubba and Trixie* by Lisa Campbell Ernst

PLAN

Problem:

- Read one or two fiction stories about animals from the above list.
- After each read aloud discuss with students: Is this fiction or nonfiction? Are there any facts in the story?
- Use a story and create a chart of facts the author had to know about the animal to write the story. Ask: Did you ever think the author of a fiction book might need to know facts about the animal to write a story?
- Do you think it was more fun to learn the facts through the story or would it have been more fun to memorize the facts from our list? More fun to learn through the story.
- Pose problem: I agree. One of our science goals is to study animals. What if you each chose an animal, studied about the animal, and wrote a fiction story about the animal? Would you learn about animals? Could you read the books of your classmates and learn about a lot of different animals?
- What do you think? Do you like the idea of studying about animals by writing fiction books?

Note: *Completion of a Big6 Organizer (Figure 4.1) will help students solve this problem. Depending upon the level of student skills in the process, the teacher may choose to guide students through completion of the organizer or have students complete it independently.*

Task Definition:

- What is our task? To learn about animals by writing and reading fiction stories about animals.
- What information will we need? An animal and facts about the animal. Let's see if we can select our animals and determine what specific facts are needed:
  - Select animal: Students may brainstorm a list of animals or, if science objectives dictate specific animals to be studied, teacher may compile list. Let students select one animal from list. If two students wish to use the same animal, have the students draw to determine who may use the animal.
  - Develop a list of information needed. This will help streamline the process for students. Ask students: I would like to write a story about a giraffe. What do I need to know about the giraffe to write my story? Use story elements to develop a list of information needed, e.g.:
    - Character: physical characterisitics and personality traits
    - Setting: habitat, other animals which might be friends or enemies

Information Seeking Strategies:

- What source can we use? Internet, encyclopedia, nonfiction books.

Location and Access:

- Locate the source and the information within the source.

Use of Information:

- Have students create a note taking organizer identifying the information that is needed.
- Students read and extract facts about their animal. Facts are recorded on the note taking organizer.

Synthesis:

- Using facts about their animal and the writing process, student write the fiction story about their animal.
- Students read classmate's stories. After reading they create a list of facts about the animal in the story.

Evaluation:

- Product:
  - Together with students, create a rubric to evaluate the story. Students should complete the rubric before submitting the story.
  - Knowledge gained about the animals may be assessed by having students list facts they know about the animals included in the stories.
- Process: Evaluate the process or the Big6 organizer and the writing process by providing students a written reflection form with questions such as: What step of the process was hardest for you? Why? What step of the process was easiest for you? Why? What would you do the same next time? What would you do differently next time?

Technology Suggestion: Technology skills may be integrated by using electronic sources to gather information and/or using a word processing program when the writing story.

From *Teaching Elementary Information Literacy Skills with the Big6™* by **Joyce Needham**. Columbus, OH: Linworth Publishing, Inc. Copyright © 2009.

CHAPTER 6

MAKING PROBLEMS WORK FOR US

Why Use Problems?

Problems may be defined as questions or situations which are puzzling, unresolved, or difficult. Problems compel us to take action or make choices. Problems engage us. These characteristics make the use of problems a valuable learning strategy.

There may be concern about presenting learning as a series of problems if the word problem has a negative connotation for you. Consider, however, that riddles and puzzles are problems. Two plus two is a problem. Is it possible that the negativity attached to problems is not a result of the problem itself but of the degree of difficulty involved in solving the problem? If the answer is yes, then posing learning as a series of problems becomes even more powerful as a teaching strategy. By posing problems, the number of opportunities students have to hone their problem solving skills is increased. Students are provided lots of practice while guidance is provided by the teacher. Utah library media specialist JaDene Denniston (Denniston) uses the power of problems to motivate her students. As students begin their information literacy instruction in the library, she challenges students to become better problem solvers. Each lesson presented is posed as a problem. Students are guided through the Big6 process as they solve the problems. JaDene has seen the power of problems to engage students as her students begin to enter the library and ask, "What problem are we going to solve today?"

Using problems to engage students is a powerful teaching strategy. Turning learning objectives into problems also provides the opportunity to guide students through the Big6 problem solving process, thereby actively teaching students to become effective and efficient problem solvers.

How Do I Create *Good* Student Problems?

Not all problems are equal. Students find some problems more motivating or engaging than others. As a teacher or library media specialist it is important to create engaging problems.

Suggestions for Creating Engaging Problems

The following suggestions, along with the accompanying saga detailing the creation of a *good* problem, may offer some ideas as you seek to develop engaging problems:

Create problems that belong to the students. As a library media specialist, I initially began instruction on the library catalog by saying, "I need to teach you how to use the library catalog." This was presenting learning as a problem. The problem, however, was not the students' problem. It belonged to the library media specialist. While I was motivated to solve the problem, the students were not. I eventually recognized the need to present the learning as the students' problem. As a result instruction was initiated by saying, "According to our district instructional goals, you need to learn to use the library catalog. So your task today is to learn to use the catalog." This transferred ownership of the problem to the student. Many students, however, were not motivated to learn a skill simply because the school district had identified it as a needed skill.

Create authentic problems. Authentic in this instance may be defined as instilling in students a real need or desire to solve the problem. With continued efforts to create a *good* problem, I finally thought from the student's point of view: As a student why do I want or need to use the library catalog? The problem emerged. Initial instruction began as students were asked, "Do you have favorite books? Do you ever have trouble finding them in the library? What if I told you about a computer program which would help you find your favorites? Is anyone interested in learning about this program?" At this point heads began to nod. Students were then introduced to the program called the library catalog and instruction on the process of using the catalog began.

The library catalog problem evolved. It went through several versions before finally qualifying as a *good* student problem. A problem which presented learning as the students' problem, a problem which students had a need to solve. The majority of students thought finding their favorite book was a problem and one they wanted to solve. Posing the objective—learning to use the library catalog—as the students' problem resulted in student engagement, which led to successful completion of the objective.

Further evidence of the power of *good* problems may be observed if we look at our saga of learning to use the library catalog one more time. The students presented with the *good* problem not only achieved their objective but did so in less time. Instruction which originally required two hours was completed in less than one hour. In addition more of these students were observed using the catalog to find their favorite books after instruction. This was an indication that a higher level of learning had been attained than previously.

Getting Started Creating Good Student Problems
The first step in creating problems is to identify the learning goal or objective. With so much to teach it is extremely important that the limited time available for instruction focuses on goals and objectives identified as essential for students.

Once the learning goal is identified try to state it as a problem for the students.
Focus on students' needs and wants rather than the needs of the teacher or library media specialist. A casual discussion with an individual student may be helpful in providing student perspective. Remember the person who has ownership of the problem will be the person motivated to solve it. The secret to creating problems to engage students is to think like your students.

The final step before presenting the problem is to identify why your students will need, or want, to solve this problem. Understanding the importance of creating an authentic problem may be facilitated by reflecting upon staff development sessions you previously have attended. Think back to sitting in training sessions and being taught new teaching strategies. Did you learn the strategies? If the strategy was one that your supervisors had identified as important but that you were not convinced was important, it was probably difficult for you to engage. As a result you may not have mastered the strategy. If you felt you needed to know the strategy, or if you wanted to learn the strategy, you probably engaged. As a result you were able to learn more effectively and efficiently. The same is true of our students.

Looking at exercise in our world today may also help us understand the power of identifying need or purpose. In today's world there are many people who exercise or have the intent to exercise. There appears to be an increase in the availability of exercise equipment, the number of spas and gyms, and even the number of runners and walkers on our streets. Why? Are we exercising for the purpose of exercise? Are we exercising because the exercise itself is fun or enjoyable? My husband comments he does not see many runners with smiling faces! A better explanation for the increase in exercise is probably our awareness of how exercise improves our health. Exercise is needed to solve an authentic problem.

Consider the skills of reading and writing. As an educator you have probably done some reading and writing lately. In all likelihood when you read it was because you needed information or wanted to enjoy the written word. When you wrote it was probably for the purpose of communicating. While these purposes are why we need to learn to read and write, do you think your students can identify these authentic purposes? By posing authentic problems which require reading and writing, students may develop an understanding of the need to improve reading and writing skills, leading to student motivation and engagement. Consider which of the following assignments you find more motivating:

- *It is time to read. Read from this book until 20 minutes is up.* Purpose: Read so you will have read for 20 minutes.

- *I just love to read Dr. Seuss. His words have a rhythm and rhyme that I really like. Do you like his way with words? Take the next 20 minutes and read some of Dr. Seuss's words. Listen to the rhythm and rhyme as you read and be prepared to share if you like that style or not.* Purpose: Read to decide if you like the rhythm and rhyme of Dr. Seuss's words.

Completion of either assignment will meet the objective of practicing reading skills. The second assignment, however, provides the reader an engaging reason to practice reading.

Information literacy skills may be integrated into all areas of the curriculum as a result of consciously presenting learning goals in the form of problems. The creation of *good* student problems will become an effective habit with practice. To help establish that habit, Figure 6.1 includes additional examples of learning goals presented as problems designed to engage students.

- **Goal:** Learn about award programs such as Caldecott, the Newbery Award, The Coretta Scott King Award, and state award programs such as the Mark Twain Award

- **Problem:** Do you ever have trouble finding a good book to read? Did you know there are awards that recognize books that are considered good? Could it help you find a good book to read if you knew about these awards and some books that have won the awards?

- **Note:** Focusing on book selection as the purpose for learning about book awards will encourage students to not only learn about the award programs but to use this knowledge as a strategy when searching for a book to read.

- **Goal:** Test Taking Strategies.

- **Problem:** Does taking tests make you nervous? Are you pleased with your performance on tests? Would you like to do better with less worry and maybe less work? Tests have been around for a long time and lots of different people have spent time trying to determine just what test takers do that help them perform well on the tests. Would it be helpful to you if we spent some time looking at the skills and strategies that have been identified?

- **Note:** Begin instruction presenting various strategies for taking tests such as note taking, listening in class, quizzing, etc.

- **Goal:** Learn the causes of the American Civil War.

- **Problem:** Did you know there was a time when the men in our country fought each other? Men from New York fought men from Virginia. Men from Virginia fought other men from Virginia. Men in one family even fought other men in their own family. This happened during what we call the Civil War. What would cause men with so many connections and so much in common to fight each other? Would you like to understand why men fought each other? To understand what caused the Civil War and what it was like during that period of our history?

- **Goal:** Note taking.

- **Problem:** Are there times you need to remember what you read or what your teacher tells you? Is it ever a problem to remember what you read? What about remembering what your teacher tells you? Do you take notes when your teacher is sharing information? Do you have difficulty identifying what is important and getting it written? Have you ever taken notes and then had trouble reading the notes after you have written them? Would you like to learn some strategies to make it easier for you to take notes from what you read and hear?

Figure 6.1 Examples of *Good* Student Problems

What Is the Desired Level of Learning?

Learning occurs at various levels. One of the most widely used classification systems describing these various levels of learning is Bloom's Taxonomy (Bloom 201-207). It is important to comprehend that the problems or questions posed for students to solve will affect the level of learning which results. For instance the task, *write about Abraham Lincoln's life,* will probably result in a lower level of learning than the task, *how did Abraham Lincoln's life impact the kind of leader he became?* Asking students to *describe the purpose of the library catalog* will result in a lower level skill than asking students to *use the library catalog to find a book.* It is important, therefore, to determine what level of learning is desirable before posing problems.

It may not be necessary for students to reach the highest level of understanding on every learning goal. For instance, reaching the highest level of learning for reading—evaluation—may be desirable, while reaching the evaluation level of the periodic chart in chemistry would probably not be necessary. Posing higher level problems for students to solve may have the positive side effect of creating assignments which are plagiarism-proof. For example, if the task is to write about Abraham Lincoln's life, it is possible, and very easy, to go to an encyclopedia and copy what is written about his life. However, if the task is to identify what impact his life had on his leadership style, it will be very difficult to find a source from which to copy. The nature of the question will force the learner to combine and edit the information found to adequately answer the question.

Use of the verbs at the various levels of Bloom's Taxonomy may help to create problems which lead to the desired level of learning. For instance, to reach a lower level of learning, students might be asked to tell, name, or list. By using the verbs adapt, design, or combine in the problem, students will be challenged to a higher level of learning.

Letting Students Be the Problem Solvers

Teachers are caretakers. As such, it is tempting to solve our students' problems. Many times it is initially easier, or faster, to solve the problem for our students. Students must practice solving problems using Big6, not only watch adults, if they are to learn to solve problems. Consider a toddler faced with the problem of picking up toys. There are two options possible. One is having the toddler pick up the toys himself, which will probably require an adult to spend time guiding the child. The other option is for the adult to pick up the toys for the child. Given the fact the toddler's physical skills and attention span are just beginning to develop, it will be faster if the adult picks up the toys. Reflect for a moment on who needs to learn to solve the problem: the toddler or the adult. Remember we learn problem solving, or processes, by practice. Initially it may appear easier for the parent to pick up the toys. However, if the goal is for the toddler to become the problem solver, letting the toddler pick up the toys allows the child to practice the process. The adult acting as guide and director is more effective in teaching problem solving than the adult picking up the toys. This same temptation to solve our students' problems exists within the classroom. Teachers and library media specialists know students must solve their own problems. Yet within daily school life the temptation to become the problem solver is great. Consider the following scenario:

Low mid-quarter grades. When Josie, a 4th grade teacher, computed mid-quarter science grades, she was dismayed to find students grades were low, Cs and Ds rather than As and Bs. She knew parents would be concerned. Immediately she started stressing over what actions she could take to improve student grades. All of the actions she considered added to her already heavy work load. None of the actions required extra effort on the part of the students who had earned the low grades.

The teacher assumed ownership of the problem and attempted to solve it. Students suffered no consequences from their poor problem solving and were quite content. They obviously recognized letting the teacher solve the problem required less effort on their part. Even if the teacher is able to solve the problem, the concern is students are not improving their Big6 problem solving skills. Opportunities are being missed for valuable Big6 problem solving practice—opportunities to practice Big6 skills while the teacher is available to provide any needed assistance and guidance. What would our scenario look like if students became the problem solvers and teacher the guide?

Josie first needs to ensure students understand that while she is willing to offer guidance, the poor grades are a student problem. Students need to recognize grades are earned by students and not given by teachers. Guiding students through problem solving using Big6 Josie may help students identify the problem (Big6 #1) by acknowledging mid-quarter grades are much lower than she believes they should be based on ability. She may ask students if they are happy with their grades. With her guidance students should identify their problem as low mid-quarter grades and find a way to improve those grades. Students may utilize both prior knowledge and Josie as a source (Big6 #2 and #3). The information available may be used (Big6 #4) as students are guided in a discussion identifying the learning strategies they have been using, whether the strategies have been successful, and changes which may make learning more effective. Josie may guide students as desired strategies are used (Big 6 #5 Synthesis) by reminding students of suggested strategies and changes. She may also guide students as they evaluate (Big 6 #6) whether grades are improving and which strategies are helping. The students engage and solve the problem of low grades and the teacher becomes a valuable guide.

Presenting learning goals in the form of problems to be solved by students is a powerful strategy. It provides the opportunity for students to practice Big6 problem solving skills in a guided setting. It integrates content and process in an authentic matter and encourages students to become actively engaged in their learning.

Good student problems are truly student problems. Students recognize that it is important these problems be solved. Careful thought should be given to identifying essential learning goals and developing problems which address the goals and the level of learning desired.

Finally, while teachers and teacher librarians may feel a responsibility and desire to help students, we must recognize students are best helped when allowed to solve their own problems. The best help the teacher may offer takes the form of guiding and supporting students through the process. Letting students become the problem solvers helps the students gain valuable skills in problem solving. It may even reduce teacher stress. More importantly the problems are more effectively solved.

Works Cited

Bloom, Benjamin S. *Taxonomy of Educational Objectives, Handbook One.* New York: Allyn & Bacon, 1984.

Denniston, JaDene, Certified Big6 Trainer. Conversation with Author. August, 2001.

PART 3

The BIG 6

FOCUSING ON MASTERING
THE SIX STEPS

This section focuses on helping students learn each of the six steps of the Big6 problem solving process. On understanding **what** the step is, **why** he or she needs to learn the step, and finally **how** he or she can master each step. Tips and strategies presented may be utilized in initial instruction or as prescriptive practice helping students build upon their strengths and strengthen their weaknesses.

The BIG 6

CHAPTER 7
TASK DEFINITION
(WHAT IS MY TASK?)

What Is Task Definition?

Task definition is the first step in solving a problem. It requires the problem solver, or the student, to identify the task to be solved or the action to be taken. Once identified, the problem can be verbalized or written. The problem thus becomes concrete and specific.

You engage in task definition frequently. For instance, every time you get into your automobile to travel. Before you start the engine, back out of your drive, and take off you have identified your task, "Where am I going?" Without task identification, you would not know whether to turn left or right or if you had enough gas in the tank. The process of task definition allows the problem to be solved with less time and effort.

Task definition in the classroom begins when the teacher states the problem or assignment for students. Stating the problem may be the only action needed to enable successful identification of the task when the task is simple. At other times, because of the difficulty of the problem or a breakdown in the student's problem solving process, the task may not be successfully identified. Evaluation may enable the problem solver to determine if task identification is successful.

Successful task definition depends upon first filtering the relevant information, or task, into the brain. The brain must then access prior knowledge from long-term memory in order to make sense of the task (see Chapter 3). It is important to remember the brain can only access information through one of the five senses—seeing, hearing, smelling, tasting, or touching (Wolfe 79). Seeing and hearing, the senses needed to read and listen, may be the two senses most often used in the typical classroom.

Successful task definition requires an understanding of the task. Understanding the task makes it possible to determine information needed. To develop questions which, when answered, will solve the problem. To develop questions which broaden or narrow the topic as needed. To develop questions which reflect the required level of understanding, e.g. knowledge only, application, or perhaps synthesis (Bloom 201-207). Finally, understanding the problem allows the problem solver to identify the keywords which can be utilized to locate the information (Big6 #3).

Successful task definition makes it possible to comprehend the nature of the needed information. Do you need:

- a lot of information or only one or two facts?

- current information as facts may have changed recently?

- facts or opinions?

- primary or secondary sources?

- text, graphic, audio, or video?

Why Is Task Definition Important?

The ability to identify the task may be one of the most important steps in solving problems. How can a problem be successfully solved if the problem solver does not know what the task or problem is? Incomplete or inaccurate understanding of the task often results in the inability to solve the problem.

Problem solvers are constantly being bombarded with information—more information than it is possible to access (Chapter 3). Identifying the important, or relevant, information is facilitated when the task has been identified.

Engaged students tend to be more successful learners (Wolfe 142). Identification of the task allows learners to engage and focus energies on the important information and the steps of the problem solving process. The following visualization illustrates the impact of task definition and student engagement on learning, or problem solving:

- **8:00 a.m., any weekday morning**. You are on your way to work. You parked your car at school and are walking into the building, down the hall, and towards your classroom or library. As you walk you think of each of the many tasks you need to complete including lessons to prepare, assignments to grade, papers to copy, phone calls to be made, etc. You are defining your task.

- **3:30 p.m., same day. Evaluate**. How successful was your day? Did you complete some or all of the tasks you identified this morning? Did identifying the tasks help you focus on and complete more tasks or solve more problems?

- **4:00 p.m., same day**. While you have finished teaching, your day is not yet over. You are walking down the same hall you walked down this morning. Only this time you are on your way to the auditorium for an hour of inservice training. While you walk you wonder what the topic of training is. You decide it does not matter because at 5:00 p.m. you can go home. You leave task definition in the hands of the trainer.

- **5:00 p.m., same day**. Training is over. Evaluate. Did you complete your task of spending an hour in training? Did you also complete the task the trainer identified? Are you leaving with new information? Will you use this new information in your classroom or library? If you answered yes to the above questions, at some point during the training you probably engaged and identified, for yourself, the task presented by the trainer.

Our goal for students is increased achievement. Increased achievement is more likely when students identify their own tasks rather than rely on the teacher to do so. In other words, you want your students to be the 8 a.m. teacher who arrives at school identifying all the tasks he or she needs to complete rather than the 4 p.m. teacher content to let the trainer identify the problem. When teachers or students identify their tasks they are engaged. Task definition may be considered one of the first steps towards student engagement.

The effect of task definition upon learning efficiency is illustrated by the following example of 2nd graders challenged to go on a call number scavenger hunt.

Students were given envelopes on which the book's address (title and call number) were written. The task was to use the call numbers on the envelopes to locate books in the library. The library media specialist stressed it was not necessary to find the *specific title* written on the envelope, only to find a book which *matched the first two letters or numbers* in the call number. In each of five classes the majority of students matched every letter or number in the call number and found the specific title written on the envelope. You may be thinking, "So why are you concerned? The students did find the books. In fact they did even more than asked to do." While students did find books, they did not find as many books as they would have by completing the task as directed. Matching every letter required more time and effort which was not necessary to solve the problem. The number of books found did not measure how quickly students could match the first two letters of a call number. Students worked harder and less efficiently because they did not accurately identify the task. Faulty task definition may have an even more profound effect upon the next problem they attempt to solve.

The following examples illustrate how problem solving may be impacted by student failure to correctly identify the task:

- The directions instructed students to <u>underline</u> the correct answer, yet 56 out of 57 5th grade students circled their answers.

- The question asked in what year and <u>where</u> Elvis Presley was born. The student answered 1935 and 1977.

- The question noted that Noah Webster was famous for writing a dictionary and asked students to use a dictionary, look up the word famous, and write the guide words. One student's answer to the problem was, "very well-known individual."

- Directions on a state-mandated test were, "What is *the best word* to fill in the blank in the following sentences?" The student asked the teacher if he could use two words.

Improving task definition skills should lead to increased student achievement. Requiring students to evaluate (Big6 #6) not only reveals whether the task has been successfully identified but also provides an opportunity to determine why task definition might not have been successful. The teacher or library media specialist may guide students in understanding why the task was not correctly identified and provide assistance as the students consciously focus on developing their task identification skills.

There are several possible reasons why students may have difficulty identifying the task.

Not listening. Being *told* by the teacher does not guarantee that the problem solver *heard and understood.*

- The student may have a physical problem interfering with the ability to hear.

- The student may fail to focus on and gather the important information as a result of the large amount of information he or she is bombarded with, not just words but other stimuli in the environment.

- The noise or movement of classmates may interfere with hearing.

- Nerves or tension may impact the ability to listen.

A possible solution to this problem is to make students aware of listening as a skill. Help students diagnose what interferes with their listening, and help them utilize strategies to overcome the weaknesses.

Assuming the task is already known. Working memory pulls old, or prior information, from long-term memory and new information from sensory memory to identify and solve problems. When the new problem is similar to tasks previously completed, the problem solver may assume it is the same problem and use prior information instead of the needed new information. For example, if a new assignment appears similar to previous assignments on which answers were circled, students will likely rely on previous knowledge and circle the answers even though new information indicates answers should be underlined. Another example is the student who, although asked to identify guide words, writes the definition because that is what he typically does when the dictionary is used. A possible solution to this problem is to encourage students to compare new information, obtained from senses, with prior information, obtained from long-term memory. When students think they know the task, encourage them to read and compare. "Yes, that is what I thought" or "Oops this is different."

The complexity of the task. Another reason students might fail to define the task correctly has to do with the task itself. If it is a complicated task, it might take conscious thought to determine all the parts or components involved in understanding the task. The problem solvers experience may impact how difficult the task is considered. For example, I asked kindergartners to…"go home, talk with your parents, and find a safe place to keep your library book." When asked at the end of the lesson, "What is your task?" The majority responded the task was to *keep their book safe*. The kindergartners were able to focus on the more general task of *keeping their book safe*, but did not comprehend the more specific task of *finding a safe place* to keep the book. When this same task was posed to 1st graders, most all were able to identify the task as finding a safe place to keep their book.

Tips and Strategies to Help Students Identify Their Task

As a teacher or library media specialist, you play a key role in helping students evaluate and develop task definition skills. Following are some strategies which may be utilized to design effective instruction promoting task definition.

Evaluate the tasks assigned to students. A good place to begin is to examine the assignments given to students. (See Chapter 6 for suggestions on creating problems or tasks.) Does the task focus on an essential skill or concept? Will the task provide the learner an opportunity to master the identified skill or concept? Is the goal obvious? Is the assignment stated clearly? Once satisfied with the assignment, or problem, consider the assessment. Will the assessment you have designed evaluate the goal? Does it evaluate both process and product? For instance, answering questions at the end of the chapter may be a beneficial assignment if the questions assigned address the essential skills and concepts students need to master. The skills and concepts you wish students to master will determine whether you have students:

- write their answers as phrases: students need to learn the content

- write answers in complete sentences: students need to learn the content and improve their ability to construct sentences

- include the page number and paragraph number where the answer was found: students need to improve their location and access skills (Big6 #3)

Foster students' belief in task definition. Help students understand the significance of task definition in the problem solving success. Nurture an environment which encourages students to spend time thinking about the assignment rather than immediately jumping in and beginning. This environment may be encouraged by providing students time for the sole purpose of identifying the task, randomly asking students to identify their task, and providing students credit in the form of grades when they correctly identify the task.

Provide a scaffold for students. First identify the task *for* students. Then work *with* students to identify the task. Finally, expect task definition to be completed *by* the students. Assignments can be communicated to students by simply telling, writing it on a whiteboard, or providing a handout with the problem identified. For instance, begin by giving an assignment and then stating, "Your task is to . . ." and restate the problem. Next, give the assignment and randomly call on students to restate the task. If a student has difficulty restating the problem, guide them by asking questions until they have identified the complete task. Finally, present assignments and expect students to identify or restate the task independently.

Develop vocabulary. Teach the concept of task definition and the vocabulary which may be used to communicate about the concept such as task definition, objective, goal, and problem.

Guide, but do not solve. Insist students take ownership of problems. Limit your role to that of coach and guide. When students come to you to solve their problems: "How many library books do I have checked out? I can't find my pencil. Do you want this paper?" Instead of providing the answer, ask, "What is your task? How can you solve that problem?" Provide the guidance that empowers students to solve their own problems. Remember the first step to solving problems begins by identifying the task.

Student success in identifying the task may also be enhanced when students improve their abilities to identify tasks in written instructions, ask questions, and identify keywords. The following paragraphs offer some suggestions for improving these skills.

Identifying the task in written instructions. Both student and adult learners are often presented problems in the form of written instructions. An understanding of characteristics of written instructions is valuable in identifying the task. For instance:

- the task is usually associated with a verb such as identify, list, write, or compare
- the verb which identifies the task is usually followed by a keyword which further identifies the task
- the task or problem usually appear at the end of the instructions

Knowledge of these characteristics may encourage the learner to develop effective habits such as skimming the instructions for verbs.

Questioning. After the task has been identified, it is necessary to determine the questions which must be answered to complete the task. These questions identify the important information as you begin to locate (Big6 #3) and use information (Big6 #4). Having students brainstorm questions is an effective strategy to help develop questioning skills. Depending upon the learners' needs, these questions may be recorded on a web (see Figure 7.1) or in a list (see Figure 7.2).

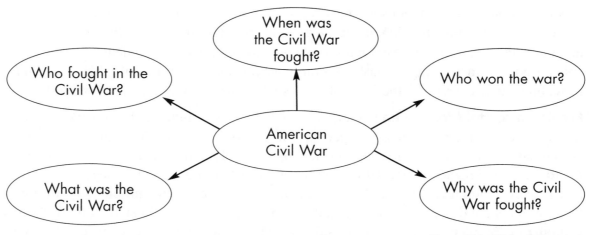

Figure 7.1 Web of Questions

After all questions have been written, it is helpful to group or sort questions into groups by topic (see Figure 7.3).

Each group of questions should be labeled and arranged in a logical order. This list of questions serves as a guide as sources are identified and located and the information is used and synthesized. When roman numerals and letters are added to this list of questions, e.g. I, II, a. b., the learner has the outline required for longer papers.

Identifying keywords. Keywords are also known as treasure words, important words, the topic, the subject, or the theme. Keywords are like a *key to a door* but instead of unlocking the door, the keyword unlocks the answer to our questions or the information needed. When searching for information in a book or on the Internet, keywords help locate the information. In a book you scan the guidewords, index, or contents for the keyword. On the Internet you enter the keyword and ask the computer to search or match it. Without the keyword it is difficult, if not impossible, to locate information. Identifying keywords is difficult because there is often more than one keyword that might be used to obtain the desired information. For instance, if information is needed on the topic of dogs, dogs

Civil War
■ What was the Civil War?
■ Who fought the Civil War?
■ When was it fought?
■ Why was the war fought?
■ Who won the war?
■ Who were some of the commanding generals for the South?
■ Who were some of the commanding generals for the North?
■ Who were the commanding generals representing the North and South at the surrender at Appomattox?
■ Who was the president of the United States?
■ Who was the president of the Confederacy?
■ How long did the war last?
■ Who fired the first shot of the war?
■ Where was the shot fired?
■ What was the pivotal battle in 1863 which swung the civil war to the North?

Figure 7.2 List of Questions

Civil War
■ What was the Civil War?
■ When was it fought? ■ How long did the war last?
■ Why was the war fought?
■ Who won the war? ■ What was the pivotal battle in 1863 which swung the Civil War to the North?
■ How did the war begin? ■ Who fired the first shot of the war? ■ Where was the first shot fired?
■ Who fought the Civil War? ■ Who were some of the commanding generals for the South? ■ Who were some of the commanding generals for the North? ■ Who were the commanding generals representing the North and South at the surrender at Appomattox? ■ Who was the president of the United States? ■ Who was the president of the Confederacy?

Figure 7.3 List of Sorted Questions

might be the keyword needed. But it is also possible that the authors creating the desired information used canine, mutt, collie, poodle, or even puppy. To locate the desired information, the problem solver must be able to identify the possible keywords or risk not finding all the needed information. Students may start to identify keywords by highlighting or underlining them in the questions they develop. As teachers or library media specialists, the next step is to raise student awareness that others might not use the same words. You might guide students by asking, "Are these the words you would use to write or communicate about the information? Do you think that everyone who wrote about this topic would use the same words? What are some other words that authors might have used?" Students may then brainstorm and create a list of other possible keywords or synonyms. Introducing and using the thesaurus to assist in identifying possible keywords is also a powerful strategy. Having a list of keywords in hand as students begin to locate information (Big6 #3) provides a focus and can make locating the information quicker.

The concepts and strategies discussed thus far may be used to help create a classroom atmosphere where task definition is an integral and conscious part of daily problem solving. As teachers or library media specialists, a need may also exist for a quick strategy designed to strengthen students' task definition skills. A number of such strategies are presented in Figure 7.4. Rather than use all the strategies you will probably wish to choose only one or two strategies which best meet the needs of your problem solvers. The strategies listed in Figure 7.4 are designed to help students reach the knowledge, or first level of Bloom's Taxonomy (Bloom 201-207).

At the knowledge level students should be able to identify the task. The next step is for students to understand the problem and identify the information needed to solve the problem. Figure 7.5 provides specific strategies which may be used to provide students the guidance and practice necessary to move their task definition skills to the next level.

Task definition is vital to become a successful problem solver. As teachers or library media specialists, our first task is to help our students comprehend what task definition is and why it is important. The next task is to create a classroom or library environment which supports students' ability to identify and understand the task and identify the information needed to solve the problem. Within this supportive environment students should be provided opportunities to evaluate their task definition strengths and weaknesses and to practice their task definition skills with the guidance of the teacher and/or library media specialist.

Works Cited

Bloom, Benjamin S. *Taxonomy of Educational Objectives, Handbook One.* New York: Allyn & Bacon, 1984.

Eisenberg, Michael and Robert Berkowitz. *Teaching Information & Technology Skills: The Big6 in Elementary Schools.* Worthington, OH: Linworth Publishing, Incorporated, 1999.

Wolfe, Patricia. *Brain Matters: Translating Research into Classroom Practice.* Alexandria, VA: Association for Supervision and Curriculum Development, 2001.

Strategies to Help Know or Identify Task (Bloom's Knowledge Level)

1	**Simon Says.** Play a game of Simon Says. Then provide students a printed copy of the commands. Have students treasure or highlight the task in each command. Share or reflect what it looks like, sounds like, and feels like when focusing on your task e.g. students might say "I listen for the verbs." Play another game of Simon Says with students focusing on task definition.
2	**Model or *Think Aloud.*** Throughout the day model for students, e.g. My task is to . . . . Use Big6 vocabulary to raise students' awareness of the problem solving process.
3	**Create a *need* for students to know. Do not repeat task.** ■ Expect each student to identify his or her task the first time. ■ If he or she cannot, make it his or her responsibility to identify the task by finding an alternate source, such as a classmate or the whiteboard. ■ If a student has difficulty recalling his task, be caring and concerned as you guide. Avoid being sarcastic or judgmental. ■ Ask students to evaluate why they are having difficulty with task definition. Use evaluation to help students understand the impact of task definition on quickly and easily solving problems.
4	**Create the expectation students will be able to verbalize task at any time. Verbalizing the task helps ensure the task is internalized.** ■ Initially require every student to repeat the task. This reinforces your expectation that each student is responsible for knowing his or her task. Task may be repeated to classmate or teacher. ■ Next randomly call on students to repeat task. ■ If a student cannot tell you the task, call upon another student, and then go back to original student and ask them to identify the task. Do NOT let him or her off the hook! ■ Periodically have students turn to partner and share task. Follow up by randomly calling upon students and having them repeat what their partner said.
5	**Occasionally ask students to identify their task in writing.** This will provide feedback and allow students and teachers to assess strengths and weaknesses and design further instruction. Sharing the results with class may be helpful. If you share students' work, do be conscious of students' feelings, e.g. let students' responses remain anonymous. Sharing can help students realize: ■ Task identification can be difficult. ■ Others find task definition difficult also, e.g. "You are not the only one." ■ It is helpful to consciously think: What is my problem? ■ Task identification is not a matter of intelligence. With conscious practice all can successfully identify task.
6	**Have students create a graphic organizer or a nonlinguistic representation of their problem.** Creating a graphic organizer or nonlinguistic representation requires an in-depth understanding of the problem.
7	**Guide students when solving written problems (questions in book, test question, reading selection, math problem, etc.).** Before they start to read the problem guide students: ■ What is your purpose in reading? ■ Answer: To identify the problem. ■ Begin reading and when you have found the problem underline or highlight it.
8	**Practice, Practice, Practice.** Using problems students face at home and school, practice identifying task.

	- Gather typical problems students face both at home and at school. The teacher or students may write the problems. Some problems should be simple and others more difficult. Problems might include: Where do I go after school today? How do I get signed up for the city parks' program? What do I need to study for the science test?
	- Use a game format and have students practice identifying the task. This will provide guided practice. Possible game formats:
	Team relay
	   - Divide class into teams.
	   - Give each team a task or problem.
	   - Working as a group, identify the task.
	   - Send one team member to assess or check if problem is correctly identified.
	   - If incorrect, member returns to team and again tries to correctly define problem.
	   - If correct, member picks up a new problem and returns to team.
	   - Continue for a set period of time.
	   - Winning team is the team which accurately identifies the most tasks.
	- **Showdown**
	   - Divide class into halves.
	   - Have one student from each half come stand in front of you.
	   - Read a problem.
	   - Student who first correctly identifies the task stays.
	   - Other student returns to seat and another challenger from the team comes up to compete.
	   - Teacher acts as judge. In case of tie, give another task.

9	**Practice Task Definition When Preparing for Tests.** Write possible test questions on sentence strips. Questions may be actual questions from prepared tests, questions from the text, or questions the teacher has posed to students. Model highlighting the words which describe the task. Break class into groups; give each group one sentence strip and a highlighter. After each group is done, they stand and share the original question and the highlighted task. The rest of the class should evaluate if task has been correctly identified. Stress the importance of getting the task into working memory so you can evaluate to make sure you are solving the task.

10	**Have students evaluate their ability to identify their task.**
	- Provide students with a tally sheet.
	- During a specified time period, e.g. Monday morning from 8 a.m. to 12 p.m., periodically ask students: What is your task? Do you know what you are supposed to be doing? Ask support staff, such as art teacher and lunchroom aides, to also prompt students during this time period.
	- If a student knows the task when prompted, a plus (+) is made on the tally sheet. If the task is not known, a minus (-) is made on the tally sheet.
	- At the end of the time period, the student should evaluate use of Step 1 Task Definition: Did you always know what your task was? If not, why did you not know?
	- A discussion of why task definition is important may be needed.
	- If task definition is a weakness, have student identify behaviors preventing him or her from knowing the task. For instance, maybe the student is having difficulty listening or paying attention. After a student identifies a possible cause for the weakness in identifying the problem, guide him or her in thinking of and using a concrete strategy to help identify task, e.g. if the problem is listening the student might choose one of the following strategies:
	   - Sit with hands together on table or desk.
	   - Do not sit beside best friend.
	   - Do not hold anything in hands.
	   - Mentally repeat or reword what speaker is saying.
	   - Take notes to help stay focused.
	   - Compare what is being said with what is already known.
	   - Try to predict what the speaker is going to say.

Figure 7.4 Strategies to Help Know or Identify Task (Bloom's Knowledge Level)

Strategies to Help Students Understand the Task and Identify Information Needed (Bloom's Level Two)

1	**Establish mindset that for every test and assignment student needs to identify information needed.** "Never go into a test or assignment without knowing exactly what is going to be covered. Know what it is going to look like and how it is going to be graded." e.g. Will test be comprehensive or only over latest material? Will test be multiple choice or essay? Will it be 10 points or 100 points? "You have to do 'brain surgery' (without knives) on your teachers. (They are the source!). Try to get into their heads and figure out what they want. Why waste time and effort studying the wrong materials or expecting the wrong style of test. Take control! Make sure you define the task!" Berkowitz and Eisenberg
2	**Have students "discuss" what a successful assignment or exam answer will look like BEFORE starting to complete assignment or take exam.** Focus: If the teacher is evaluating the assignment, she/he is the best source of knowing what an "A" will look like. Teach students to consider what teacher is looking for in this assignment not just what student thinks an assignment should look like. Berkowitz and Eisenberg
3	**Have students evaluate samples of a completed assignment before beginning work on the assignment.** Give students an assignment. Offer two or three samples of completed work for the assignment including at least one sample that is definitely poor. Have students assess the samples in terms of the assignment: "Does it do what was required? Is it complete? How could it be improved?" (This works well as cooperative learning activity.) Berkowitz and Eisenberg
4	**Have students evaluate assignments before they are turned in. Extend the above activity by gathering a few samples of student work.** Examples can be gathered while the assignment is in progress and then before assignment is turned in. Have students evaluate whether the task has been completed. To provide a more positive learning experience, allow time for students to make corrections or revisions to work after evaluation and before turning it in for a grade. Also be careful that samples remain anonymous so student whose work is evaluated will not feel threatened.
5	**Purposely give assignments that are vague.** Do not give "details" or "spell out" some of your assignments. Make it a game. After making initial assignment say, "I am not going to TELL you anything else about the assignment but I will ANSWER your questions." Be willing to answer any and all relevant questions about the assignment, but answer a question only once. This places the burden of finding out exactly what is expected on students. Berkowitz and Eisenberg.
6	**Provide opportunities for students to practice identifying keywords.** Task definition requires students to recognize and understand key terms in assignments and on tests. Give students an assignment and have them highlight or underline keywords. Evaluate to determine if students identified the correct words *and* if they have a concrete understanding of the meaning of those words. Having students do a nonlinguistic representation is an effective way to check for understanding.
7	**Use riddles to practice task definition and zero in on keywords.** Read or display riddles to class, have students identify the keywords and then try to answer riddles. Fit the level of the riddle to your students' ability. ■ When does a ghost have breakfast? Focus or keywords: ghost; breakfast time (answer: In the moaning) ■ What kind of pants does a ghost wear? Focus or keywords: ghost; pants (answer: Boo-jeans) ■ As I was going to St. Ives . . . Focus or keywords (going to St. Ives)
8	**Prompt students to focus on keywords (by any name).** The needed information becomes the *keyword or treasure or important word or subject or theme or main idea.* To solve the problem, keywords must be a constant focus. Prompt students as they work through the problem solving process to help focusing become a habit. "What is your treasure? What info are you looking for? Is that information important?"

9	**Provide guided practice in identifying the task and the information needed.** Gather several assignments or problems or tasks students typically complete in your class. Group students and give each group one assignment and a large piece of paper. Have the group identify the task and what information is needed to complete the task on large paper. Then pass the paper to another group for evaluation of the task and information needed. Any needed corrections and/or agreement with original work should be written on the paper. Continue passing paper from group to group for evaluation until each group receives their original and feedback. Discuss those strategies that helped successfully identify the task and those that lead to errors in determining task.
10	**Require students to identify information needed prior to solving the problem.** Give an assignment. Have students write: "The information I need is . . . " The resulting list will guide students as they search for information by providing the keywords for skimming and scanning (location and access) and suggesting an organization for the product (synthesis). If writing a research paper, the information identified on the "list" actually becomes the body of the paper. By adding the introduction and conclusion the paper will be complete. Encourage students to do this preplanning by giving credit/grade for completion of the list or require students to complete list before they move to the next step in research, i.e. "You cannot start using sources (Internet, encyclopedia, etc.) until I have seen your list."
11	**Guide students to determine questions/information needed and method of organization.** Give students a research topic. Have each student write at least three questions they think should be answered. Write one question per sticky note. Randomly call on an individual student to read his or her question and have class identify a category that question would fit within (e.g. if doing Famous Americans I might have category of personal life, accomplishments, etc.) Post large sheets of paper around the room. As categories are suggested write on large paper and then have all students place questions that fit within that category on the paper. Continue randomly calling on students until all sticky notes have been placed on large sheets. Evaluate: Is there any other information that we would want to include? Do we have categories that are logical? Also discuss what type of information is needed to answer the questions and what sources we can use to find answers (don't forget prior knowledge which will be important on higher level questions). Teacher can guide and direct to ensure that all required content is included in the questions.

From *Teaching Elementary Information Literacy Skills with the Big6™* by **Joyce Needham**. Columbus, OH: Linworth Publishing, Inc. Copyright © 2009.

Figure 7.5 Strategies to Help Students Understand the Task and Identify Information Needed (Bloom's Level Two).

CHAPTER 8
INFORMATION SEEKING STRATEGIES (WHAT SOURCE CAN I USE?)

What Are Information Seeking Strategies?

Task definition (Big6 #1) identifies needed information. The next logical step is to locate the needed information. Information seeking strategies describes the process of identifying the source you will use to solve your problem. The first step in information seeking is to brainstorm possible sources of the needed information. An awareness of a variety of sources is invaluable in compiling this list. Once a list of possible sources has been created, each needs to be assessed to determine which is best. There are many factors which determine what makes the best source. Problem solvers need to be familiar with these factors.

Possible Sources of Information

Possible sources of information include the traditional reference sources such as the dictionary, thesaurus, encyclopedia, almanac, and atlas. Nonfiction books, on a variety of topics or subjects, are possible sources. The Internet must also be included. Our list is not complete, however, without including the most common sources used in our school and daily life. These would include textbooks, teachers, classmates, parents, and our prior knowledge. Our prior knowledge, schema, or the stuff we know is one of the most useful sources for our students.

Students benefit when they consider all of the above as possible sources. Comprehending that asking the teacher or a classmate a question is using a source of information raises awareness of the importance of sources in problem solving and also increases student familiarity with and understanding of sources. Learning is facilitated when students can make connections between the known, sources they use daily in the classroom and at home, and the unknown, traditional reference sources.

Prior Knowledge or Schema

Prior knowledge is perhaps the source students are required to use most often in school. When students take a test, their prior knowledge and the test itself are the only sources available to them. When students solve a math problem, it is required that they access information not just from the problem but also from their prior knowledge. Even defining our task requires use of prior knowledge.

If you observe students taking tests you may see some students read, reread, and then read a test question again. The student is obviously searching for the needed information using the test as the source. Unfortunately, the student will find it difficult to solve the problem unless he recognizes that prior knowledge is the needed source. The probability that students will access prior knowledge to solve problems increases when students consciously identify it as a source. This awareness that prior knowledge is often needed as a source when solving problems may also motivate students to increase their prior knowledge.

The Internet

A preferred source of information for many of our students is the Internet. A seasoned problem solver may believe the Internet is not always the best source. Based upon this belief, use of the Internet may be limited or students may be required to also use print sources. It is important, however, to recognize that the Internet is a part of our lives today.

The Internet can be a powerful source of information. Its importance as a source is enhanced because students appear so motivated to use it. Efficient and effective use of the Internet relies upon a set of skills. Some of the skills are the same as those required to use print sources such as identifying keywords, scanning, and skimming. Other skills, such as efficiently navigating the abundance of information and judging the reliability of the information found, are specific to the Internet. If our students are to effectively and efficiently use the Internet, definitely a lifelong skill, it is important they have the opportunity to develop these skills. Specific skills for locating information on the Internet will be discussed in Chapter 9, Location and Access.

Why Are Information Seeking Strategies Important?

Unfortunately information does not magically jump into your hands when you enter the library. Nor is it possible to have the needed information just appear on the computer screen when you sit down. Locating the needed information begins by first identifying what sources can provide that needed information.

There is a constant need, as a problem solver, to determine what source to use, e.g. to use our information seeking strategies. Even embarking upon a fun outing such as an overnight trip to Kansas City, Missouri, to attend a Royal's baseball game requires the problem solver to select and use a variety of sources as the following partial list illustrates:

- Royal's ticket office via the telephone and the Internet to obtain tickets

- Internet to access hotel and make room reservations

- <u>Travel companions and a map</u> to find directions to Kansas City and the hotel
- <u>Hotel staff</u> to locate the room and access key
- <u>Hotel concierge</u> to determine whether to walk or ride the hotel shuttle to the game
- <u>Tickets</u> to locate seats at the ball park
- <u>Menu board</u> at the ball park to determine food wanted and cost of food
- <u>Menu</u> at restaurant to determine what to eat for breakfast
- <u>Companions</u> to locate the person with car keys so car can be unlocked and belongings loaded for the trip home

Information seeking strategies impact the success of our problem solving. Selecting an appropriate source ensures the needed information can be located. It also ensures the information will be found using the least amount of time possible. Selecting an inappropriate source may result in either not solving the problem or, at the very least, not reaching the best solution. A greater investment of time may also be required.

The following scenarios from real life illustrate the impact of information seeking strategies upon our lives:

- A kindergartner tried to explain that the source of ink marks in his book was his parents. Library media specialist might have believed the student if the source had been identified as a classmate or younger brother or sister.

- A high school student incorrectly identified the source of an overdue book as the public library. The student returned the book to the public library rather than the school library. This resulted in the student's grades being held. It also required the investment of time of the school librarian, public librarian, and school's central library office staff in getting the book back to its rightful owner.

- After standing in line to vote for 15 minutes, a voter was told he could not vote because he was at the wrong poll. When the voter asked where he could vote, the voting official consulted with a colleague and even placed a phone call to the voting registrar. After these sources were unsuccessful the voter looked at his voter registration card, which had been in his hand the entire time, and found his proper precinct listed on the face of the card. If the voter had initially used the voter registration card as his source he would have saved himself, the election officials, and even the other voters time.

What Factors Determine the Best Source?

There are many factors which affect our choice of source. The following are some of those which make the source a good choice:

- contains the needed information
- easily accessible
- easy to use
- accurate and reliable
- timely

- appropriate format of the information, i.e. pictures, text, graphs
- amount of information

One important consideration when selecting a source relates to accuracy and reliability. More specifically, is the source impartial? Some content, such as religion and politics, is more likely to be biased. Because of the biased nature of some sources, it is a good idea to identify our source. Consider political announcements which routinely identify the source of the information, e.g. brought to you by the Democratic Party or approved by the candidate. Knowing the source of the information allows the problem solver to consider the source.

Tips and Strategies to Help Students Determine Sources

Strategies for Identifying and Selecting Sources

- **Provide Modeling and Guidance**. Sharing with students as you select and use sources throughout the school day is a quick strategy to raise students' awareness of sources and increase their skill in selecting the best source. Think aloud or model for students, e.g. "We need to know what is for lunch today so let's use the school menu as a source." Provide opportunities for guided practice. For instance, as students prepare to go home at the end of the day ask, "What task do you have tonight? What homework do you need to complete? What sources will you need?" Before starting a lesson in the classroom, e.g. science, art, or reading, ask students, "What is our task? What sources will we need?"

- **Acknowledge the Levels of Information Required**. Bloom (201-207) identified levels of learning (see Chapter 6). The level of learning addressed by the problem affects the type of information needed and the preferred source. To answer knowledge level questions such as when was the first microwave manufactured or who won the World Series in 2000, a text source such as an encyclopedia, almanac, or Internet may be needed. To answer synthesis or evaluation level questions (such as what was the impact of the microwave) both a text source and prior knowledge may be required. Successful completion of the task at this level normally requires that facts taken from the text source be manipulated using prior knowledge to arrive at an answer. Students taught to recognize the various levels of learning addressed by problems may be better able to select the needed sources.

- **Make Connections Between New and Familiar Sources**. Introduce new sources by first connecting with familiar sources. The teacher or library media specialist should first label as sources those most familiar to students, such as friends, teachers, parents, television, radio, and prior knowledge. Next, make connections between the above sources and the text sources students find in their environment such as billboards, cereal boxes, newspapers, magazines, and telephone directories. Finally, introduce traditional sources which teachers and library media specialists tend to focus on such as nonfiction books, textbooks, encyclopedias, dictionaries, almanacs, atlases, and thesauruses. Making the connections between all these sources will confirm for students that a source is where you find information. That the differences between the various sources are the information provided by the source and the way that information is accessed.

- **Begin Identification of Source Early**. Eisenberg suggests that even in kindergarten and the primary grades students can begin identifying the sources of information being used (Eisenberg, Workshop). He suggests at this age students stamp assignments to identify the source used. The teacher or library media specialist may provide a choice of three or four stamps. Depending upon the source used, students may use a smiley face for prior knowledge, stick figure for teacher, parents, or another individual, book for information found in a book, or computer for information found on the Internet or a CD-ROM. This process may raise awareness of the variety of sources used to solve problems and also lay the groundwork for citing sources at upper levels.

- **Avoid the "I know" Pitfall**. Prior knowledge is the quickest and easiest source to use if the information needed to solve the problem is already known. Using prior knowledge as the source, however, is a problem when students *think* they know, but in reality do not. You may already be identifying those students who frequently *think* they know. Some students truly believe they know the answer. Others may simply be a bit lazy and not want to take the time required to use another source. Requiring students to verify information may be a solution regardless of the reason for the problem. Students may be told, "Even if you know the answer, you must verify it in a text source. By finding the answer in print you are proving you knew the correct answer and also getting important practice in identifying and using sources."

- **Identify the Essential Question**. The essential question students need ask when trying to determine if a specific source is a good source of the needed information is "Does this source have the information I need?" In addition to asking the essential question, students need to be taught to answer the question by utilizing the table of contents and index to identify what information is included in the book.

- **Identify Type of Information Found in Specific Sources**. Knowledge of the type of information found in reference books such as dictionaries, encyclopedias, atlases, almanacs, and thesauruses is valuable when selecting the best source. A quick activity to assess this knowledge is to copy one page from several different reference sources. Display each page using a projection device such as an overhead. Ask students to determine what type of reference book the page came from and why, e.g. it came from a dictionary because it has definitions or it came from an atlas because it is a map.

- **Develop a List of Criteria**. Instead of presenting students a list identifying criteria to use when selecting the best source, *let students tell you the criteria* by creating a class list. In training sessions Eisenberg frequently poses a research problem to participants, has them brainstorm a list of possible sources, and select the best source. Participants are then asked to explain why they chose that particular source. What results is a list of the criteria or factors to be considered in selecting the best source (Eisenberg, Workshop). Such a list, created by your class and posted in the classroom or library, could be used to guide students as they develop the skills needed to select sources. Eisenberg also suggests the teacher or library media specialist allow students a chance to edit this list as learning progresses (Eisenberg, Workshop).

LESSON PLAN 8.1

LESSON TITLE: INTRODUCTION TO SOURCES

Grade Level: K-2nd
Depending upon questions used in game

Time Frame:
- One 30-minute session

Content Objective:
- May be connected to any content area through the problems posed

Information Literacy Objective:
- Practice using the steps of the problem solving process
- Information Seeking Strategies: awareness of what sources are and specific sources used

Materials and Sources:
- Directions and rules for playing Showdown (Found at the end of the Lesson Plan)
- Showdown Questions (Sample at the end of the lesson plan, following directions for Showdown)

PLAN

Problem:
- Often when you have problems to solve, the information needed to solve the problem is right inside your head. This is called prior knowledge or schema. For instance, if I ask you what your name is or what you ate for breakfast, you can probably tell me using yourself. You do not have to ask anyone else for the answer. You are the source.
- Sometimes, especially at school, you are asked to solve problems when you do not have the prior knowledge needed or you cannot be the source. In those cases, is it important to know who or what you can use as a source or to find the information you need.
- Do you think it might be a helpful to practice identifying sources? Would you like it if we could turn our practice into a competition or game?

Task Definition:
- What is our task? *To identify sources which can help us find the information we need to solve our problems.*

Information Seeking Strategies:
- What source can we use to solve this problem? I know a game we can use to practice our sources. I can be source of that information. I also happen to have a list of some problems you might need to solve and I have identified the sources needed. Could we use that? (See sample questions at the end of the lesson plan following Showdown.).

Location and Access:
- I am here, and here (hold up list of questions) are the problems.

Use of Information:
- Explain to students how Showdown is played. See directions at the end of the lesson plan.

Synthesis:

- Using the game format, Showdown, ask students to identify the best source to locate information needed to solve the problems.

- Make sure students understand they are not solving the problem. They are to identify the source which will have the information needed to solve the problem.

- Begin game by having students choose from among three possible sources (a multiple choice format). As the game progresses, let students rely on their prior knowledge to identify the best source.

Evaluation:

- Product:
    - Following the game have students discuss with a neighbor the following: Explain what a source is. Name two or three sources you use often. After students discuss, randomly call on a couple of students to share what their neighbor said.
    - Ask students to evaluate by thumbs up/thumbs down: Are sources important in helping you solve problems? Is it important to know what source to use?"

- Process:
    - Was the game fun?
    - Do we know more about sources after having played the game?
    - Would you like to play the game to help you learn other information?

DIRECTIONS & RULES FOR SHOWDOWN

Getting started:

- Separate into two teams and sit opposite each other.
- Have one student from each team face the emcee (teacher or library media specialist).
- Read the question.
- The student who raises his or her hand first tries to answer the question.
- If he gets it wrong, or does not know, the other person gets a chance to answer.
- The student with the right answer stays until unseated or until another student raises his or her hand faster and gives the correct answer. The student, who does not get the answer first, takes his seat and is replaced by a teammate.
- If a student raises his or her hand before the question has been completely read: Stop reading immediately and expect student to answer. If answer is incorrect, the question may be reread in its entirety for the other student.

Playing the game fairly:

- Why are we playing this game? *To have fun and to learn.*
- I will be the judge or referee. Just like the referee or umpire in a ballgame, my decision stands.
- I will try not to make any mistakes. But I cannot guarantee I will not make mistakes. Remember I am the referee so, just like at a ballgame, my word is final.
- We will not argue. If I make a mistake, someone gets lucky. I like to judge, because when you judge, you sometimes end up getting upset with each other and that takes the fun out of the game. I would rather you get upset with me.

■ If I am unsure as to who raised their hand first or feel there is a tie, then I will pick a number between 1 and 10 and have the two students guess to see who is closest to the number and who will get to go first.

Keeping the game moving:

■ To ensure all students are listening, refuse to read any questions until all are quiet.

■ Encourage students, waiting for their turns, to practice by mentally answering the questions. Unseating a classmate is less difficult if students have been paying attention and are actively engaged.

QUESTIONS FOR SHOWDOWN
Italics: substitute personal information for your situation.

Round One:

Choose the best source

1. Tanya wants to know if there are monarch butterflies in *our state*. Who is the best person to ask?
   a. lawyer
   b. clerk in store
   c. conservation agent

Hint: you may not know what a conservation agent does, but should know the other two sources will not work. Teach process of elimination as a test taking strategy.

2. *I* need to know how to spell economics. What is the best source to use?
   a. textbook
   b. dictionary
   c. telephone directory

3. Who would be the best person to ask to find out how much sales taxes are in *our county*?
   a. state governor
   b. county tax collector
   c. Easter bunny

4. Who can *I* ask to find out what is for lunch tomorrow?
   a. Ms./Mr. _____, *art teacher*
   b. Ms./Mr._____, *secretary*
   c. Ms./Mr._____, *librarian*

5. To find the address to the *local movie theater* the best source would be:
   a. telephone directory
   b. textbook
   c. dictionary

6. Who would be my best source to find out the author of *Harold and the Purple Crayon*?
   a. Ms./Mr. _____, *music teacher*
   b. Ms./Mr. _____, *library aide*
   c. Ms./Mr. _____, *principal*

Round Two:

Name the best source to find the information needed to solve the following problems. Information in parenthesis represents the best answers.

7. Do elephants live in China? (encyclopedia, book, Internet)

8. What animal has lived at the *city zoo* the longest? (someone who works at the zoo)

9. How much hay does a cow eat in a day? (farmer, encyclopedia)

10. What is the next science topic or subject we will study in *our grade*? (teacher)

11. What programs are on television tonight? (*TV Guide*, TV)

12. Do dogs get cancer? (encyclopedia, veterinarian)

13. Which teacher has taught at *our school* the longest? (principal, secretary)

14. Will electric rates in *our city* go up this year? (city utilities)

15. How much does it cost for one semester at *our local college*? (worker at that college)

16. When was Eric Carle born? (encyclopedia or biography)

17. What are the symptoms of diabetes? (doctor, nurse, encyclopedia, Internet)

18. Who will teach 3rd grade next year at *our school*? (principal, secretary)

19. Will the local book store give away books in their summer reading program this year? (worker at the local book store)

20. Will the local library have story telling sessions this summer? (worker at the local library, especially someone who works in the children's department)

LESSON TITLE: TEST PREPARATION SOURCES: WHAT SOURCE DO I USE TO STUDY FOR TESTS?

Grade Level: 3rd-5th
Depending upon questions used in game

Time Frame:
- Two or three 30-minute sessions
- Sessions will not be back to back

Content Objective:
- Test Preparation, any content area

Information Literacy Objective/Big6 Objective:
- Practice using the steps of the problem solving process
- Information Seeking Strategies

Materials and Sources:
- Returned test in some content area
- Second unit of content to be tested
- Chart paper

PLAN

- This lesson may be more meaningful if students have previously taken a test. Especially if they are not pleased with their test scores.
- Prior to lesson: Provide students a study guide, test the content of the study guide, grade and return test to students.

Problem:
- Discuss the test which has been returned. Ask: Are you pleased with your score? Do you wish your score was higher? Would you like to get the same score with less work?
- Does test preparation affect your score? Have you thought about what sources are available or what sources you should use to prepare for tests? Would it be helpful to spend some time learning how to prepare for tests?

Task Definition:
- What is our task? *To figure out how we can best prepare for tests. To determine what sources we can and should use.*

Information Seeking Strategies & Location and Access:
- Ask students to write how they studied or prepared for the previous test. *Responses received from a 3rd grade class included: Mom/Dad quizzed me, used the study guide, read important pages in the chapter, studied a lot, studied every night, reread the chapter, questioned myself, watched a video, reread chapters in text, focused, studied hard, concentrated, practiced, paid attention in class.*
- Create a list of all the sources and strategies students used and the number of students who used each source.

Use of Information:
- Share the list with the class and discuss the various methods used:
    - How do you study hard? How do you concentrate? You probably need to study and concentrate, but those are kind of vague.

- Let's look at some other specific responses. How about using the study guide? Why would the study guide be a good source? *Teacher created the study guide and teacher created the test. Several of you indicated you reread the chapters.* Would there be any benefit to reading the study guide instead of the chapter itself? The study guide is about four pages, chapters are over 50 pages. That's right, you have less information. Is that O.K. to have less information? Who created the test? Teacher. Who created the study guide? Teacher. So should you have all the important information on the study guide?

- How about having Mom or Dad quiz you? Is that a concrete strategy you can use? What source would be the best to have parents use to quiz you? *Study guide.*

- Someone mentioned they paid attention in class. Is that a good source of information? Does your teacher ever test you over information discussed in class? *Yes.* What about information you have not discussed in class? *Usually not.* So if you discuss information in class is that a clue that it is important? *Yes.* If you listen in class, does that help you learn the information? So can you really begin to study for your test by listening in class?

Synthesis:

- Develop a class list of sources to use for test preparation. Following is a list developed by a 4th grade class.

Sources to use for test prep:

1. Class: Pay attention and listen during class.
2. Identify all other sources to use:

    Text (identify which chapters), notes, and study guides
3. Before the test study the important information only.

    Find this information in: study guides, text and graphic aids in textbook.
4. Quiz yourself: Ask questions and say or write the answer.
5. Have someone quiz you.

- Post this list and refer to it as instruction begins on the next unit to be tested. Throughout the rest of the year refer students to these sources.

Evaluation:

- Prior to the next test ask: Have you been using the sources on our chart? How do you feel about the sources?

Problem:

- What source do you not yet have for the next test? *The study guide.*

- Would you like to help me construct the study guide? Do you think every teacher you have for the rest of your school life will provide you with a study guide? *Probably not.*

- If you can create your own would that be helpful?

Task Definition:

- What is your task? *To create a study guide for the next test.*

Information Seeking Strategies:

- What sources could we use to construct our study guide? *Text, notes, prior knowledge or memory from class, teacher.*

Location and Access:

- Have students gather text and notes.
- Ask them to jot down from memory information remembered from the unit.

Use of Information:

- Have students, working in groups of four, create a list of questions they believe could or should be included on the upcoming test.
- Post chart paper. Do a round table share to transfer questions from groups to chart. One person from each group stands. Go around the room and have each person who is standing read one question and write it on the posted chart paper. Everyone who has that question on their list marks it off. Ask the second member of the group to stand and repeat procedure. Continue until all the questions students created in groups are written on the chart paper.
- At this point review the questions and indicate those which definitely could be on the test. If there is information which will not be included, let students know this and also explain why, e.g. This is just a detail. I do not expect you to know every detail.

Synthesis:

- Type a study guide using the questions left on chart paper and give each student a copy.
- Students take test.

Evaluation:

- Product: Return the test to students and ask: Are you pleased with your score? Is your score higher than on the last test?
- Process:
    - Think about the sources you used for the test. Refer to chart created in first lesson. Did you pay attention in class? Did you use the text? Notes? Study Guide? Did you study or read only the important information in the sources? Did you quiz yourself? Did you have someone else quiz you? What worked well for you? What did you do differently in preparing for this test that made a positive difference?
    - How did the study guide work for you? On the next unit, do you think it will be easier to identify the information? Will this be helpful to you?

From *Teaching Elementary Information Literacy Skills with the Big6™* by **Joyce Needham**. Columbus, OH: Linworth Publishing, Inc. Copyright © 2009.

LESSON PLAN 8.3

LESSON TITLE: INTRODUCTION TO REFERENCE SOURCES

Grade Level: 3rd-5th	**Time Frame:** ■ Two 30- to 40-minute class sessions ■ Do not have to be consecutive
Content Objective: ■ Any content area in which reference sources may be used to answer questions	**Information Literacy Objective/Big6 Objective:** ■ Practice use of the steps of the problem solving process ■ Information Seeking Strategies

Materials and Sources:

■ Note taking organizer

■ Copy of a variety of reference sources: dictionary, encyclopedia, thesaurus, atlas, almanac, magazine, newspaper

■ Directions for Battle of the Reference Sources (see end of lesson plan)

■ Questions for Battle of the Reference Sources (sample found at the end of the lesson plan, following Directions for Battle of the Reference Sources)

PLAN

Problem:

■ Who can tell me what a source is? Turn to your neighbor and name two or three sources you use daily here at school or at home when solving problems.

■ Randomly call on a couple of students to share what their neighbors said.

■ There is another set of sources which are useful when we are doing research or need to learn about a specific concept, idea, or event. These are usually called reference sources. Maybe because we *refer* to them.

■ You usually go to these sources, locate or find a specific piece of information (Big6 #3) and read or use (Big6 #4) just that section. In other words, you normally would not read them from cover to cover as you might other books or sources. You can find all of these in print form or online in electronic form.

■ Do you think it might be important for you to know about these sources? Do you think you will need to be doing research and finding information in books very much this year? . . . next? . . . in high school? . . . in college?

■ What if we could combine learning about these sources with a game? Would that spark your interest to learn about these reference books?

Task Definition:

■ What is our task? *To learn about reference sources and to try to win a game using those sources.*

■ What information do we need to learn about reference sources? *Need to know the name of the source and when to use it.* The answers to three questions can help you decide if a particular source will solve your problem. The three questions are:

■ What type of information or content is found in the source?

- ■ What is the format of the information, e.g. maps, paragraphs, charts?
- ■ How current is the information?
- ■ Do you want to work smarter or harder? *Smarter.* I agree. How can we all get this information with the least amount of work? *Divide into groups and each group find information on one source or book. Each group can share information found with others.*
- ■ Randomly call on a student to identify the task and the three pieces of information needed about each book.

Information Seeking Strategies & Location and Access:

- ■ Give each group a book and a note taking organizer on which to record information.
- ■ Ask: Do you want to turn page-by-page and read the entire book to answer the questions? What text aids (see Chapter 9) will help us find the information needed to answer the questions? *Title page, table of contents, foreword or introduction if available.*

Use of Information:

- ■ Using books, each group completes the note taking organizer.
- ■ Information gathered by each group is used to create a class chart. See sample below.

Name of book	Type of info or content	Format of info	How current?

Synthesis:

- ■ Next class session students compete in Battle of the Reference Sources.
- ■ Directions and rules for Battle of the Reference Sources follow at the end of the lesson plan.

Note: Other game formats such as Jeopardy (search Internet for electronic version) or Showdown (see Lesson Plan 8.1) may also be used.

Evaluation:

- ■ Product:
  - ■ Ask students to write the name of each reference source studied, the type of information contained, the format of the information, and if the information is current.
  - ■ Ask students to evaluate: Were you able to identify the best source in our game? Which sources are the easiest to remember? Which sources do you need to become more familiar with?
- ■ Process: How did it work for you to break into groups and gather information? Did the class chart we created provide the information you needed? Did you enjoy the game? Are you better able to identify the best source now than before we played the game? What would you suggest we do the same when this lesson is taught to the next class? What would you suggest we do differently?

Follow-up activity: Strengthening familiarity and use of electronic sources

- ■ Visit the Internet with students and find each type of reference source online.
- ■ Share that sometimes access is free and sometimes subscriptions must be paid. Be sure to share any sources provided through the school.
- ■ Discuss reliability of electronic sources.
- ■ Create a list of pros and cons for using print and/or electronic sources.

DIRECTIONS AND RULES FOR BATTLE OF THE REFERENCE BOOKS

Note: The format of this game may be used for many different skills.

- Divide the class into Teams A, B, C, D, etc. Four members to a team work well. Teams may be named if desired. Within each team, students decide who will answer first, second, etc.

- A question is asked of Team A. The first person on the team may answer by himself for two points or the team may confer and earn one point. Only one answer is allowed. If the team does not give the correct answer, another team can steal the question. To steal, as soon as a wrong answer is given, the next person on the team to answer raises his or her hand. The first team with a raised hand has the opportunity to answer for one point. If that team is incorrect, the second team to raise hand is called upon. This continues until all teams who wish are given an opportunity to answer the question. Each team has only one opportunity to answer the question.

- The second question goes to the second team. Game continues with teams and members taking turns answering the question.

- Play can be divided into three rounds with points increasing for each succeeding round. Conferring and stealing always provide half the points available to the first person asked the question who answers on his or her own. One possible scoring chart is shown below:

Round	Points if first person answers alone	Points if confer or steal
Round 1	2	1
Round 2	4	2
Round 3	6	3

- An emcee is needed to read questions and conduct the game.

- One person to watch for raised hands is very helpful. If it is not clear who raised their hand first or if there is a tie, have each team involved guess a number between 1 and 10. Whoever guesses closest gets the first opportunity to steal the question.

- Having a designated scorekeeper is helpful. The scorekeeper can tally the score per round and then transfer totals to the chart.

- Establish amount of time allowed for each round. It usually works well to allow each team to have the same number of opportunities to answer questions.

- To keep the game moving, establish a time limit within which answers must be given. One quick and easy way is for the emcee to simple count to three. At the end of that time, he or she says: I need an answer.

Notes about Battle Game format:

- While topic of questions may vary, connecting the topic with the currently studied social studies or science content is desirable.

- Consider letting students write the questions to be used in the competition. This can encourage good question writing as students experience firsthand the frustration of trying to answer unclear questions or having opposing teams get points for answering questions which are too obvious.

- This game format works well with any content. For instance, one school used it as Battle of the Books. Each class selected a team to represent the class. These teams battled to determine who could identify the most award-winning books. Questions were about books on the state's book award program. The answer was the title of the specific book.

SAMPLE QUESTIONS FOR BATTLE OF THE REFERENCE BOOKS

Answer should reflect the BEST source

Q: What was the magnitude of the San Francisco earthquake of 1906?

A: *Almanac*

Q. In 2004 the volcano, Santa Maria, erupted in Guatemala. On what continent is Guatemala located?

A. *Atlas*

Q. What other word could I use for earthquake?

A. *Thesaurus*

Q. Can scientists predict exact times when volcanoes will erupt?

A. *Encyclopedia*

Q. The news reported that a volcano erupted in South America. What does erupt mean?

A. *Dictionary*

From *Teaching Elementary Information Literacy Skills with the Big6™* by **Joyce Needham**. Columbus, OH: Linworth Publishing, Inc. Copyright © 2009.

LESSON PLAN 8.4

LESSON TITLE: STUDENT SELECTION OF SOURCES FOR RESEARCH

Grade Level: 2nd-5th	**Time Frame:** ■ One 30-minute session
Content Objective: ■ Any content area in which reference sources may be used to answer questions	**Information Literacy Objective/Big6 Objective:** ■ Practice using the steps of the problem solving process ■ Information Seeking Strategies

Materials and Sources:
- A question students need to answer using a reference source
- Chart paper and marker
- Prior knowledge of student and teacher

PLAN

- This lesson may be used anytime a reference source is needed by students to solve a problem.
- Students need to be able to identify the problem.
- Selecting the best source may take as little as 10 to 15 minutes.

Problem:
- In order to solve our problem we are going to need to use a reference source.
- Will using a source help us learn about that source so we may better use it in the future?
- How can we determine which is the best source to use to solve this specific problem?

Task Definition:
- What is our task? *Find the best source to solve our problem and to learn about other sources as we do so.*

Information Seeking Strategies:
- Ask the class to brainstorm a list of possible sources. Record these possible sources on a chart.
- Select the best source:
  - Refer to the first item on the chart. Ask students to identify the pros and cons of using this source. For instance, if the source is the dictionary, a pro might be it gives definitions; a con might be it provides only a small amount of information.
  - Continue listing pros and cons of each source on the class chart.
  - Based upon pros and cons determine which source will be best. Scaffold selection:
    - First level: The teacher or library media specialist selects the best source from the class chart. Identify for students why that particular source was chosen.
    - Second level: Allow students to choose the source from two or three appropriate sources identified on the class chart. Teachers may establish criteria for the choices such as one text source and one electronic source must be used. This assures students get practice using a variety of sources.
    - Third level: Students select the best source from those sources listed on the class chart.

Synthesis:

- Pose a problem to be solved, e.g. what is a characteristic of a mammal?
- It is recommended students immediately report to the teacher or library media specialist the source they select to use.
    - This encourages students to commit to a source rather than wandering from source to source wasting precious time.
    - It also enables the teacher to offer guidance if the best source has not been selected.
- Source is cited when the problem is solved.

Evaluation:

- Process: Have students evaluate in writing or orally. If evaluation is written, providing credit for completion of the evaluation is recommended. After the source has been used to solve the problem, have students evaluate:
    - What about using this source did you like?
    - What about using this source did you not like?
    - If you were solving this problem again would you use this source? Why or Why not?
    - What have you learned about using the source that will be valuable in the future?

Sample Lessons to Improve Source Selection Skills

Elementary students, even at the primary level, are capable of understanding the concept of sources. These students rely on many sources, e.g. teachers, parents, siblings, friends, bus drivers, and so on, to solve their problems. Raising student awareness of what sources are and identifying sources they use is the first step to preparing them to use reference sources in later years. It also helps students become more independent, logical problem solvers. An example of how the concept of sources may be introduced to K-2 students is presented in Lesson Plan 8.1.

Students typically begin to take content tests, such as science and social studies, in 3rd grade. One of the major factors affecting the success of test taking is the information seeking strategy (Big6 #2) or identifying the sources needed to prepare for the test. However, students are often left to solve this problem independently. Student achievement may be positively impacted when students recognize the sources available to help with test preparation and identify those which may be used most easily and effectively. Lesson Plan 8.2 provides a lesson which may be used to offer students guidance with test preparation sources. It is suggested that students experience at least one content test before the lesson is taught. The prior knowledge acquired from preparing for a test will make the lesson more meaningful. There is also the possibility, if students did not perform as well as they hoped on the test, students will be motivated to improve their test preparation skills.

As students begin 2nd or 3rd grade they are normally given opportunities to solve problems using traditional reference sources, e.g. dictionary and encyclopedia. After students begin to experience the need to use these reference sources, a lesson designed to distinguish differences between the types of sources may be helpful. The lesson in Lesson Plan 8.3 is designed for that purpose.

Choice is an important motivator for students. Modeling, followed by guided practice and independent practice, or scaffolding, is an effective strategy to help students master process. The lesson presented in Lesson Plan 8.4 relies upon choice and scaffolding and provides one option for helping students develop information seeking strategies when using a reference source to solve problems.

Teaching Internet Skills
Awareness of the Need for Internet Skills

Students have a tendency to believe they know all there is to know about using the Internet because of the amount of exposure they have to the Internet. The reality is that many of our students do not possess the skills to effectively and efficiently use the Internet. Teaching students skills they perceive they already have is usually not very effective. It is important, therefore, to help students recognize a need for Internet instruction. The following strategy may be successful in convincing students of the need for instruction:

Allow a class which needs to access information to use either a print source or a source found on the Internet. Watch for the first students to locate the needed information (Big6 #3) and begin to use information (Big6 #4). In most classes, this will be the students who use the text source. When the first students reach step 4, stop the entire class. Ask students to evaluate, "Raise your hand if you have completed step 3.1, if you have located your source. Raise your hand if you have completed step 3.2, if you have located your information within the source. Raise your hand if you are beginning step 4, reading and extracting the information." The results of this evaluation will likely reveal those students using text sources, such as the encyclopedia or books, are further along in the problem solving process. If this is true it is important for students to be aware of the fact and to realize it indicates Internet use has not been mastered. Ask students to evaluate by responding with thumbs up/thumbs down: Is using the Internet always faster? Is using the Internet always easier? Would you be interested in learning strategies to make use of the Internet faster and easier for you?" At this point students may be open to any strategies you may share which improve Internet usage. If your experience is the majority of students using the Internet are further along in the process, the need may be for more skills instruction in using text rather than using the Internet.

Knowledge of the Variety of Sources on the Internet

The Internet contains a variety of sources. Electronic versions of reference books such as dictionaries, encyclopedias, and thesauruses may be found. A variety of subscription services such as World Book, EBSCO, SIRS are often available to students. The Internet also has a number of search engines, Web browsers, or indexes available. Students benefit from understanding what is available on the Internet. They also benefit when teachers and library media specialists model using these various sources and provide opportunities to use the sources in an environment where assistance is available. Experiencing the use of these sources may help students comprehend why they may be preferable to searching the Internet.

As teacher or library media specialist, have the following discussion with your students:
■ You know me. You know I am a library media specialist or teacher. Would you be interested in buying my book telling you how to perform brain surgery? Or would you be interested in my book with directions on building your own airplane? No, definitely not!
■ Why? You know I do not have the skills necessary to do either brain surgery or to build an airplane.
■ Proceed to inform students: I will probably never have a book published about either of these two topics. This is because no publisher would publish my books on those topics.
■ Publishers are in business. This business is how the owners earn a living. To stay in business they must make a profit. They make their profit by selling books.
■ If you bought a book with incorrect or bad information, would you buy from that publisher again? Probably not. So the publisher has an intense interest in publishing accurate information. To ensure this happens, publishers have editors and nothing can be printed without the editor's approval.
■ Move the comparison to publishing on the Internet: Is there anyone to stop me from publishing my directions for conducting brain surgery or how to build an airplane on the Internet? No.
■ If I have access to the technology needed and I pay a fee to have the Web page displayed, I can publish just about anything I want. If it is illegal I might be stopped. But think of all the information on the Internet. There are hundreds, thousands, even millions of Web pages. Do you think it possible to monitor everything that is published on the Internet?
■ When you pick up a book, you are probably safe assuming the information is accurate because it has been checked. When you go to the Internet, you cannot make that same assumption.
■ This does not mean you should not use the information. The Internet can be a wonderful source of information.
■ What it does mean is that when using the Internet, it is your responsibility to look at the information and determine if it is accurate.

Figure 8.1 Comparison of Book Publication and Internet Publication

Internet Reliability: Awareness of and Development of Skills

A group of 5th grade students were dismayed to learn the Web site they used to gather information for their animal reports was actually created by a 3rd grade class. This can easily happen when students lack Internet search skills. It is important for students to be aware not all information available on the Internet is reliable or accurate. In some cases the information might even be dangerous information.

Students need to be taught how to evaluate information found on the Internet. This instruction needs to be designed to help students evaluate Web sites for accuracy, objectivity, authority, currency, and coverage. Students may be more receptive to such instruction if they are first made conscious of the need to evaluate.

The discussion of differences between publishing a book and publishing on the Internet (see Figure 8.1) may raise student awareness of the need to evaluate Web sites. Following this discussion by sharing a variety of Web sites which are not reliable may further convince students of the necessity to evaluate Web sites. An easy way to find a variety of unreliable Web sites is to use a search engine and conduct a search for *bogus Web sites.* Such a search should lead you to many sites. One site, McWhortle Enterprises, Inc. is actually sponsored by a government agency, the Federal Trade Commission (FTC). The seriousness of Web reliability is attested to by the fact that the FTC has created such a page.

An effective way to use these sites is to access the site and ask students to, "Read over the site. Be on the look-out for anything that bothers you or surprises you or causes you to question as you read." Give students a few minutes to complete the task and then ask for their feedback. If you choose a site with a topic students have some prior knowledge of they should be able to identify the faulty information. For instance, if you choose the Mankato City site students will probably question the picture of the windmill and the statement that a tourist enjoyed whale watching on the river.

Another way to help students evaluate Web sites is to select a topic or person who might be controversial, such as a public figure or conflict with another country. For instance, a search of the Internet for information about a candidate for the United States presidency would yield sites reflecting a variety of views. Depending upon the source the candidate may be portrayed as the person who will save our nation, the person who will lead to the downfall of our nation, or the person who will help our health care system but hurt our economic system. Experiencing varying perceptions about one person or one topic may help students understand the need to evaluate information gathered on the Internet. It may also help students to understand the need for consulting more than one source when conducting research.

After viewing several sites it is time to create a class list of criteria for evaluating Web sites. Students' prior knowledge obtained from viewing unreliable Web sites and the Internet are valuable sources. Conducting an Internet search for a specific individual's work, such as Kathy Schrock, or using the keywords, *evaluating Web pages,* may provide more specific information on Web page evaluation.

The list of criteria for evaluating Web sites may include checking the source of the Web site, e.g. the source for:

- .gov is government agencies
- .edu is educational institutions
- .org is nonprofit organizations

- .mil is military
- .com is commercial business

Knowledge of the source may be important in helping students evaluate Web sites, e.g. educational sites are usually reliable; however, be careful because they often publish their students' work.

The created list of criteria may then be used by students as they practice evaluating Web sites. Having students practice evaluation skills using Web sites which are actually needed by students or staff is one strategy which makes the practice more meaningful for students and assists the teacher and library media specialist in identifying helpful sites.

It is strongly suggested that students be directed to specific Web sites until teachers and library media specialists feel confident students have mastered Web site evaluation skills. These acceptable Web sites may be communicated to students by placing a shortcut on the desktop, creating links on the library or classroom Web page, or marking the sites as favorites.

If there is a specific Web site a teacher or library media specialist prefers students not use, it is a good idea to share with students reasons for prohibiting the use of that specific site. For instance, instead of just saying, "You may not use Wikipedia," say, "Because of reliability issues you are not to use Wikipedia for this project." Another consideration, when prohibiting sites, is whether students are likely to use the site when accessing information for their own purposes. Instruction in effectively using the source may be desired if this is the case. For example, some teachers or library media specialists may prefer their students not use the Google search engine. However, if students are going to use Google for their own personal searches, any instruction provided which makes student use of Google more efficient is important for the students.

Information seeking strategies are often used automatically or without conscious thought. Many problem solvers may not recognize the sources most often used to gather information such as prior knowledge, peers, or teachers as sources. Awareness of these information seeking strategies and recognition of commonly used sources is important. It enables the problem solver to consciously choose the best source to solve the problem. It also leads to a quicker and deeper understanding of new sources as they are presented. It is possible to provide direct instruction in information seeking strategies. In today's world the direct instruction needs to include the Internet as a source.

Works Cited

Bloom, Benjamin S. *Taxonomy of Educational Objectives, Handbook One.* New York: Allyn & Bacon, 1984.
Eisenberg, Michael. Pre-AASL National Conference Big6 Workshop. Kansas City, Missouri: 2003.

CHAPTER 9
LOCATION AND ACCESS (WHERE IS THE SOURCE AND THE INFORMATION?)

What Is Location and Access?

At this point in the problem solving process the task is identified (Big6 #1) and the source of information is identified (Big6 #2). The next step is to locate the source and access the information within the source (Big6 #3). Students need to be aware of each step as distinct and tangible, requiring its own set of skills. The teacher or library media specialist may facilitate this awareness by verbalizing the individual steps of the problem solving process.

Locating the source and accessing the information are two distinct tasks. Locating the source involves physically accessing the source, e.g. going to the teacher, finding the book, or logging on to the Internet. Accessing the information within the source requires that the information be found in preparation for use (Big6 #4). If the teacher is used as the source, accessing the information will involve asking questions and preparing to listen to the answer or the needed information. If a book, or the Internet, is the source, accessing the information will involve scanning and skimming text aids to locate the keywords. Before information can be used it must be located and accessed (Big6 #3).

Why Is Location and Access Important?

Location and Access (Big6 #3) and Information Seeking Strategies (Big6 #2) are essential steps in the problem solving process. Yet these two steps are often missing in other problem solving strategies or processes. This may be explained by the past reality of our world.

In the traditional classroom the teacher assumed the responsibility of identifying sources and then locating information. For example, it was the teacher's responsibility to provide students the textbooks and identify the page on which information was located, hand out any handouts, and write information on the board. The student's responsibility was to identify the task (Big6 #1), use the information (Big6 #4), and solve the problem (Big6 #5). The actual process of identifying sources and locating information was typically not part of the student's problem solving process. Perhaps this was because access to information was quite limited, making it difficult for the student to successfully locate information.

The arrival of computers and the Internet have changed our world. Information is more readily available to our generation than any other. The Internet and television have not only made it possible, but desirable, for students to locate information independently. Access to sources such as books, television, and the Internet does not automatically lead to possession of the skills needed to effectively and efficiently utilize these sources. As a teacher or library media specialist, you may have witnessed students who:

- race into the library with the expectation that the information needed will fly off the shelves and into their hands

- check out a nonfiction book and carry it with them but never open it

- move from one book to another when trying to find needed information

- sit down at a computer and expect the needed information to appear on the screen

- spend hours browsing the Internet without locating the needed information

If so, you may recognize that location and access are skills. Students need to master these skills in order to become lifelong learners and problem solvers. An appreciation for the impact of location and access may encourage mastery of the skills. One possible way to increase student awareness is by sharing the following dialogue with students:

1. Do you ever need to use a book or the Internet to find information? Do you think you will be expected to find information more often or less often as you get older . . . become a high school student . . . college student . . . worker? Would you like to be able to find information more quickly?

2. If you cannot locate the source, or the information within the source, can you use the needed information? Can you successfully solve your problem if you do not use the information?

3. If I give you a book, and the information needed is in the book, can you eventually find the information? Is it possible to thumb through the book, page by page, skimming until you locate the information? Would it take a long time to find the information in this way? Would you mind searching through one book in this manner to find information? What about five books? Ten books? A hundred? This kind of searching reminds me of the adage, *it is like searching for a needle in a haystack*. Would you benefit by learning to quickly locate information in a written source? *(It may be helpful to hold up a typical reference book with its hundreds of pages and tiny print to help students appreciate the time required to locate information in this manner.)*

4. Extend the above example of searching page by page to searching for information on the Internet. Do you agree if given enough time you can eventually find the information you need if it is in a book? Think about the Internet for a

moment. Would you agree information on the Internet is unlimited? So you should be able to find any needed information on the Internet. Think about how you access information on the Internet. You type in an address, use an index, or do a search. But what if you do not know how to find the address? Or you do not know which index to use? Or you do not identify the keywords when searching? Will you be able to access the information? Is it important then for you to learn strategies to locate information on the Internet?

5. Would you rather spend your time solving problems or would you rather spend your time on your favorite pastime such as sports, hobbies, or even napping? Location and access of information is just one step in the problem solving process. However, can you successfully solve the problem without the needed information? You might get lucky sometimes, but what about the majority of the time? Do you need to locate the information? Think about this: Let's say Johnny can find the needed information in 10 minutes and Jason takes 60 minutes to find the information. Johnny has an extra 50 minutes. Can he choose how he will spend that time? Jason, on the other hand, has no extra time or no choice. Becoming proficient at finding information is one of the easiest ways to reduce the time we spend solving problems.

What Does Accessing Information from a Source Look Like?

The type of source used determines how information will be accessed. The sources students most often rely on are probably prior knowledge, oral sources, visual sources, or sources with text or print. Each of these sources relies on use of one or more senses for access. For instance, accessing information from:

- prior knowledge relies heavily upon making connections (Chapter 3)

- oral sources, such as the teacher or a friend, require listening

- visual sources, such as pictures and movies, require seeing

- text sources, such as books and articles, require seeing in a unique way via reading

- multimedia sources, such as television and Internet, require both seeing and listening

Much of the information accessed by students comes from text sources. Consider the number of textbooks, handouts, writing on the board, books, Internet sites, and magazines to which students are exposed. Students benefit from having a clear understanding of the process of accessing text sources because of the prevalence and complexity of text. The process may be described as: *Scanning or skimming to find keywords using text aids, features, or conventions.*

Components of Accessing Information from Text

To better understand the process, it may be helpful to examine each of the components or parts of the process.

Scanning and Skimming

While often used synonymously, scanning and skimming are two distinct tasks whose purpose should not to be confused with that of using information (Big6 #4) or reading.

Scanning and skimming are location skills (Big6 #3). Reading is typically used to acquire information and is actually a use (Big6 #4) strategy. There is a tendency for students to begin reading when attempting to locate information. This tends to slow down the location process as reading generally is a more time-consuming activity than either scanning or skimming. An even more dangerous tendency is trying to scan and skim during the use portion of problem solving. While scanning and skimming are important in helping locate information quickly, if information is to enter our brain it must be read. Encourage students to first locate the information, scan or skim, and then use the information, or read. By differentiating between the skills of scanning, skimming, and reading, each of the skills become more concrete and easier for students to master.

Scanning and skimming may be considered a type of reading utilized to locate information. Scanning is the process used to find details, such as dates and locations, and skimming is the process used to find big ideas. The purpose of scanning and skimming, however, has more to do with matching than reading. The purpose of scanning and skimming is to compare and match two pieces of information: the information you are trying to find and the information actually found. When scanning and skimming are used to match they become powerful location skills. Teaching scanning and skimming as matching skills render them concrete strategies students may utilize.

Scanning

Explaining scanning to students as the process used when locating a car in the parking lot is an effective strategy. When trying to locate a car in the parking lot, you look at each car and compare it to the picture of your car in your mind. That picture might include the color of the car, the shape of the car, or the make and model of the car. As you scan the parking lot, you do not take in any information about the cars you are looking at except to compare and say, *no that is not it* or *yes that is it*.

To scan text, one letter at a time is matched. Like the cars in the parking lot, no meaning is attached to the letters scanned. The letter scanned is just compared to the letter being searched for and is identified as matching or not matching. For instance, when scanning for the word *number,* the student would first scan for the letter *n* or look at the beginning letter of each word in the text and compare it to the *n*. If the letter is not an *n* the student moves to the first letter of the next word. The process continues until an *n* is found. When the *n* is matched, the student scans for the next letter or the *u*. The scanning continues until each letter in the word is matched and the word *number* is located in the source. Scanning one letter at a time is a process that may be mastered by any student who recognizes the letters of the alphabet. Reading is not required for success. Scanning is the process used when:

- a call number is used to locate a book in the library
- a page number is used to find a specific page
- a guide word is used to find a word in the dictionary
- an index is used to locate a word
- a telephone directory is used to locate a telephone number
- a search engine on the Internet conducts a simple search

Skimming

An entire word or concept is matched when skimming. Skimming requires that each word be read, not to input the word or meaning into the brain, but for the sole purpose of comparing or matching the word to the keyword. If the word does not match the keyword, it is ignored and the problem solver moves on to the next word. When a match is found, the problem solver is ready to begin use of the information (Big6 #4), which involves reading the information found. For instance, when skimming for the word *number,* the student might read *the* or *letters.* As neither of these words matches *numbers,* the student would dismiss these words from his memory and move to the next word in the text, comparing it to *number.* If *number* or *count* or *numeral* or another word that matches *number* is found, the problem solver is ready for Step 4, Use of Information.

Skimming requires the problem solver to match ideas. Skimming requires higher level skills as the problem solver must read the words and recognize the meaning of the words being compared. Skimming becomes necessary when there is more than one word which may be used to convey the word or idea being matched. Scanning is sufficient to find the needed information if all of the information about farming is located under *farming.* It is possible, however, that information about farming is also located under agriculture, cultivation, crops, or livestock, making it necessary to skim if this information is to be located. Information about doctors may be located under the term doctors, physician, medical doctor, M.D., or even surgeon. Therefore it is necessary to skim, rather than scan, to find all the information needed. Skimming is often required when trying to find information in a textbook, on a Web page, or in an encyclopedia article. Some search engines, such as Google, may provide a synonym search as an advanced search option. Such a search will skim, matching the idea, rather than scan, matching specific letters.

Keywords

Keywords, as discussed in conjunction with task definition in Chapter 7, identify the information needed to solve a problem. The keyword is the word, or words, the problem solver scans or skims to locate. To scan, the keyword is usually found within the problem itself. If skimming is required, other words which may be used to describe the keyword must also be identified. For example, if the problem is: What is a GPS? GPS is identified as the keyword and the problem solver scans for G . . . P . . . S. To skim, the problem solver identifies other words which may be used in place of GPS, such as global positioning satellite, location, directions, etc. The problem solver skims for any of these matching words or ideas.

Text Aids, Features, or Conventions

Nonfiction or informational books include devices to assist the problem solver in locating information in the text. These devices are designed so that information can be located without reading the text from cover to cover. Depending upon who is labeling these devices, they might be known as aids, features, or conventions. These aids include both text aids such as indexes, tables of content, labels, headings, and captions, and graphic aids such as pictures, diagrams, charts, tables, bold or highlighted print. These aids can be scanned or skimmed to quickly locate needed information.

Location and Access on the Internet

Locating the Source or Navigating on the Internet

To locate information in a book, you pick up the book and physically open it. Locating information looks different when using the Internet. With the Internet, you begin by sitting down at the computer. But there are no pages to physically open. There are three ways to locate the information available electronically. They include:

1. Type in the URL or address
2. Use an index, directory, or menu
3. Use a search engine

Effectively using these methods to locate information requires specific knowledge and skills. Mastery of these skills is facilitated when teachers and library media specialists provide students the knowledge and opportunities to practice using the knowledge to locate information. Some of the information students need includes:

Using the URL or Address. Accessing information by typing in the URL or address is one of the quickest access methods. The biggest obstacle to accessing information using the address is that the problem solver must type the *exact* address. The spelling, spacing, punctuation, etc. must be exactly as it appears in the address.

Using an Index. The index might also be known as a directory or menu when using the Internet. Indexes, directories, or menus are found on many search engines, such as Yahoo, and on many Web pages. See Figure 9.1 for a sample of a typical index.

The index consists of a list of choices. The problem solver scans or skims these choices for the entry which matches the keyword. Scanning or skimming an index, directory, or menu might look like this:

LINKS—LMS SELECTED SITES		
Table of Contents Click on the desired topic (keyword) to find links in that category!		
Authors & Illustrators	Links for Teachers	Search the Library
Big6 & Research	Literature and Reading	Search the Net: Google
Fun Time	News & Weather Media	Social Studies
Homework Help	Reference & Libraries	Springfield Public Schools
Links for Parents	Science & Math	Technology Support

Figure 9.1 Internet Index or Menu

The problem solver needs information about Jan Brett. Using Figure 9.1, the problem solver skims the menu and matches *Brett* with *Author*. *Author* is then selected. On the next index to appear the problem solver scans for Brett and selects or clicks on *Brett, Jan*. At this point the information sought is accessible on the computer. Other examples using Figure 9.1 might include:

- scan for *weather* select *News and Weather Media*
- scan for *Big6* select *Big6 & Research*

The effective use of indexes, menus, or directories is often hindered by the inability to make connections or match the choices to the keyword being sought. The teacher or library media specialist may help students overcome this obstacle by helping students:

- develop a list or web of possible keywords (see Chapter 7) during task definition (Big6 #1)

- master the skills of scanning and skimming

- experience locating information using an index as the teacher or library media specialist thinks aloud while using indexes to locate information

Using a search engine. Search engines may be the most frequently used method of locating information on the Internet. Yet they are probably the most difficult to effectively use.

Because of the growth of the Internet, it is not unusual to get over a million *hits* when using a search engine. As an effective problem solver you may recognize this as a problem. Many students, however, may not be concerned with the number of hits. The following discussion may help students recognize the importance of the effective use of a search engine:

Conduct a search on the Internet which results in millions of hits. Ask students to look at all the hits, "Is this good?" Some students may respond, "yes." They may assume the more information available, the easier it will be to solve the problem. Guide students to realize this is not always a true assumption. Ask students, "Can we read all of these sources? If we visited 100 of the sites and spent three minutes at each, how much time would be spent locating information? Over three hours! Do you think each site will have the information we need? Even if all 100 sites have the information, do we need all that information? Can we include that much information in our five-page paper?"

After this discussion, students may have a better understanding of the importance of identifying the task (Big6 #1) and be motivated to learn how to effectively use search engines. More effective use of search engines is facilitated with an understanding of how search engines function. Search engines do the actual location of information for the problem solver. The problem solver must enter the keyword used to locate the information.

The inability of the problem solver to correctly identify the keyword impacts effective use of search engines. Observation reveals many search engines scan rather than skim. This means the only information located will be that which matches the keyword letter by letter. For instance, when *doctor* is entered as the keyword, the search engine scans and locates all articles containing the word *doctor.* It will not access articles or information if the author used *physician* or *surgeon* instead of *doctor*. The choice of keywords is, therefore, important in conducting an effective search. Knowledge and use of advanced search options and Boolean operators, such as *and* or *not*, may also lead to more effective use of search engines.

Accessing Information from the Internet

The process of accessing information from the Internet is the same as accessing information from text. It involves *scanning or skimming to find keywords using text aids, features, or conventions.* While the same components are involved, because of the electronic format, the components look and sometimes operate differently.

Scanning and Skimming

With text it is necessary for the problem solver to scan and skim. When using the Internet the computer scans for the problem solver and locates the desired Web page. It is important to remember that the computer does not usually skim unless we use advanced search options. Once the Web page has been accessed, it once again becomes the responsibility of the problem solver to scan and skim for keywords to locate the needed information.

Keywords

Keywords are even more important when using electronic sources than when using text sources. While not efficient, given enough time, it is possible to turn every page in a text source to locate the information needed. Using an electronic source, if the keyword is not entered, the information remains hidden and unavailable to the problem solver.

Because of the way the human brain functions (Chapter 3), when humans scan it is more efficient to scan for one keyword at a time. A student using a text source to locate the population of Missouri would find it easier and faster to first scan for Missouri and then population. Because computers are extremely efficient at scanning it is possible, and even desirable, to scan for several keywords at one time. A student using an electronic source to locate the population of Missouri would want to enter both Missouri and population as keywords. By entering two or more keywords the number of hits is reduced. It is also more likely one of the resulting hits will contain all of the needed information.

Text Aids, Features, or Conventions

Electronic sources, such as the Internet, contain the same text and graphic aids found in print sources. These aids, just as in print sources, assist in locating information when scanned or skimmed for keywords. Students' learning curve may be reduced when connections are made between the familiar text aids found in print sources and the text aids found on electronic sources. For instance, prior to introducing students to electronic indexes such as the library catalog or EBSCO, share or review a traditional print index found at the end of a book. This encourages students to connect known information with new information and results in a quicker and more thorough understanding of the new indexes. Challenging students to find electronic versions of familiar print aids, e.g. labels, pictures, bold text on Internet sites, also allows students to apply what is previously known to the electronic aids and reduces instructional time.

Tips and Strategies to Help Students Find Information More Quickly

The following tips or strategies are intended to assist you as you help students develop effective and efficient location and access skills.

Location and Access Strategies

Acknowledge success and build upon it. Recognize students who quickly locate the source or the information within a source, e.g. the first student to find his or her science book or the first student to open his or her journal to the correct page. Recognizing those students will provide them encouragement in the future and may also motivate classmates. Give students the opportunity to think about the process used by asking them to share their strategies, e.g. "Jim, would you share how you were able to find your book so quickly? Jean, you found that page so quickly, could you share what you did?" Verbalizing actions taken may make the process more concrete for the student responding and the entire class.

Think aloud. Any time you need to locate information, think aloud as you model your process for students. For example, you need to find Humpty Dumpty to share with the kindergarten class. Instead of quickly and silently finding the nursery rhyme, think aloud.

> "I need to find Humpty Dumpty. I know Humpty Dumpty is a nursery rhyme. I think I may find it in this book because this is a book of nursery rhymes. Rather than looking at every page, I think I will use what we call an index. It is usually found at the back of the book. It is a listing of everything in the book. I am going to scan for H because that is the first letter in Humpty. Here it is. Now I need to find a u, etc. . . . "

Distinguish between the skills. Have students first locate the source of information. Then have students locate the information within the source. Separate the skills.

Teach two guiding questions. Once students have an understanding of information seeking strategies (Big6 #2) and location and access (Big6 #3), teach them the two questions which may be utilized to guide students through both steps:

- *Does this source have the information I need?* With a possible source in hand, answering this question will help students determine if they have actually identified the source. The title, index, and table of contents can be used to answer this question.
- *How is the book arranged?* This question helps determine how to locate information in the source. Guide words are the preferred aid if the book is arranged in alphabetical order. The index is the preferred aid if the book is arranged by subject or some other format such as chronological order.

Strategies to Assist in Location of Source

Explain the importance of organization. Instead of demanding, e.g. straighten your desk or clean out your backpack, take a few moments to explain why this is important. For instance, "If you have a place for everything and everything is in its place, it will take less time to locate your sources. Please check your backpack and your desk and make sure they are organized."

Explain the importance of timing. Ask students, "When do you need to locate sources for homework? After you sit down to study or before you leave school for the day?" Help students develop the habit of locating sources prior to the need by prompting and asking.

Catch students succeeding. The next time students need a source after they have cleaned out their desks, ask them to evaluate (Big6 #6): "Is it faster to find the source this time? Why? Will staying organized help you locate sources?" This will increase students' awareness of the role organization plays in locating sources. It allows them to experience the benefits rather than being told of the benefits.

Provide individual support. Identify those students who have difficulty staying organized. They will be the students who constantly lose materials and have trouble finding things. Help students identify their problem: location and access (Big6 #3), not intelligence. Provide students guidance as they develop their own system to organize their materials. For instance, one student may need one separate folder for homework, while another may need one folder for each content area with the homework for each area kept in the individual folders. Parents and guidance counselors may also be able to assist students in developing a workable system. Follow up with students and evaluate how their system is working. Help students tweak the system to make it better and practice it until it becomes a habit.

Strategies to Assist in Location of Information within the Source

Have students locate information in a source before you give any instruction. Give students a book. Do not give instruction on how to find information within a source. Ask students to locate information independently. Time how long it takes students to locate the information. Next, time yourself as you model or think aloud and find the information. As students observe you, ask them to compare what they did with what you are doing. After you find the information, compare the time required. Have students discuss how the strategies were similar or different. What worked and what did not work? Challenge students to locate information a second time. Compare the time required and discuss what they learned about using sources to locate information.

Strategies for Teaching Scanning

Teach students that scanning is matching. To scan students need to compare one letter to another to see if there is a match. Focus on only one letter at a time to speed up the comparison process. Warn students of the tendency to look at the entire word. Explain when this happens it is easy to get distracted and start pronouncing that word and thinking of the meaning of that word. Both of these actions require time and slow down the scanning process. A fun and effective strategy to help students develop the habit of scanning or matching one letter at a time is to use word searches. Guiding students through the process of scanning using a word search (see Figure 9.2) might look like this:

Try to find the following words:

SCAN
SKIM
INFO
AID

C	S	B	A	L
M	S	C	A	N
O	F	N	I	D
E	I	C	D	E
M	I	K	S	A

Figure 9.2 Word Search

Scan to find the word *SCAN*.
1. The first letter to match is *S*.
2. Start at the box in the top left corner of the table in Figure 9.2. The letter is *C*, this is not a match.
3. Since it does not match, move right, to the next box. That box has a letter *S*. This is a match.
4. Since there is a match, look at the second letter in *SCAN* or *C*.
5. Search the boxes surrounding the *S* to see if there is a *C*.
6. The search reveals a *B*, which does not match. Look at another box surrounding the *S*. It has a *C*, which is a match.
7. Since we have a match, look at the third letter in *SCAN* or the *A*.
8. Find the *S* and *C* and continue diagonally. The next letter is *I*, which does not match.
9. Go back to the first *S* found. Scan the next block surrounding it, which is an *S*.
10. This does not match, so move to the next box. This is an *M*, which is not a match.
11. Continue this process until all four letters in the word *SCAN* are matched.

Make connections for students. Label the process of using call numbers to locate books as scanning when it is introduced to students. First review or model scanning for call numbers before introducing students to using guide words to locate words in the dictionary. Make the connection, "When you use guide words you are scanning. It is the same process of matching or comparing one letter at a time. Instead of scanning the call numbers you will scan the words at top of page, or the guide words, to find or locate information on that page."

Strategies to Increase Scanning Speed

Motivate students to scan quickly. The speed with which a problem solver scans will have a direct effect upon the total time required to solve the problem. Strategies that may encourage faster scanning include:

Timed scanning practice with recognition to those who scan quickly may motivate students. Scanning can easily be practiced locating names in the telephone directory. The possibility of learning to locate information in the telephone directory faster than parents or siblings may motivate students.

Select a Guide Word Champ. Prepare a list of guide words and words that may or may not be found on that page (see Figure 9.3).

The words in bold below represent the guide words for one page in a reference book. For each word in the two columns below, your job is to scan and put a check (√) before the word if the word would be found on that page. Example, there is a check in front of ashe because it would be found on the page.	
ash	**Austria**
☑ ashe	☐ Australia
☐ arrow	☐ autograph
☐ Aspen	☐ award
☐ atlas	☐ aviation
framework	**frequent**
☐ freckle	☐ franc
☐ free	☐ freedom
☐ fox	☐ freak
☐ fragrant	☐ freeze

Figure 9.3 Guide Word Champ

In order to determine who uses guide words most quickly be sure to include more words than any student can find. Time students as they identify whether specific words will or will not be on a given page. The student with the most correct answers is named the Guide Word Champ. While there are many possibilities for recognizing this student, one simple and effective method is to display a sign with Guide Word Champ and the name of the winner in the classroom or library. The sign also serves as a visible reminder of the importance of being able to scan quickly.

The Guide Word Champ activity works well as a culminating activity. Lesson Plan 9.1 provides a unit that begins with introducing students to scanning. It takes them through guided practice and ends with the Guide Word Champ activity.

LESSON PLAN 9.1

LESSON TITLE: UNIT PLAN FOR GUIDE WORD CHAMP: BUILDING SCANNING ABILITY AND SPEED

Grade Level: 2nd-5th

Time Frame:
- Three to six sessions depending upon amount of practice provided students

Content Objective:
- Skill at scanning may be utilized in any content area as students use dictionaries, thesauruses, encyclopedias, etc.

Information Literacy Objective/Big6 Objective:
- Practice use of the steps of the problem solving process
- Location and Access: specifically scanning

Materials and Sources:
- Two or three different handouts with guide words and words to scan for (see Figure 9.3)
- Dictionaries
- Timer

PLAN

Problem:
- How do you locate information in a book that is arranged in alphabetic order? *Guide words.*
- Do you like using guide words to find information in books like the dictionary? Would you rather use guide words and look up information or go outside and play? . . . read a good book? . . . talk to a friend? *At this point students will probably acknowledge there are activities they would rather do than use guide words.*
- Think. Be a problem solver. Is there anything you can do to decrease the amount of time you spend looking up information? Can you simply choose not to look up the information? What if you were really, really fast at scanning and finding the information? If you could find a word or the information in less than a minute rather than in three minutes. If you had to look up 20 words, it would take less than 20 minutes rather than 60 minutes. That means you would have 40 minutes of *extra or free* time!
- Who should really want to be fast at scanning? *The student who least likes to do it!*
- What if I told you I could help you become a very fast scanner? Raise your hand if you are interested.
- Would you be interested in a little competition or race? The student who is the fastest at scanning will be honored as our *Guide Word Champ.* Our champ will have his or her name posted in the library/classroom until next year when the new champ is determined.
- Are you ready to start?

Task Definition:
- What is our task? *To learn to scan as fast as we can and to determine the fastest scanner!*

Information Seeking Strategies:
- What sources are we going to need? *Guide students as sources are identified: prior knowledge, teacher, your voice, dictionary, and some words to locate.*

Location and Access:

■ I have gathered all of our sources except your prior knowledge and voice. You will be responsible for those! Remember, the whole reason we want to be fast scanners is to Locate and Access (Big6 #3) Information!

Use of Information:

■ Let's think about what we already know:

  ■ To use guide words do you read or scan? *Scan*

  ■ When you scan do you read or match? *Match*

  ■ Do you match a letter or a word? *Letter*

  ■ Scanning requires focus. Do you have time to think about what's for lunch or what you are going to do when you get home tonight if you are scanning? *No, you only have brain power to think of the letter you are looking for and compare it to the letter found.*

■ Let's do a couple of samples together:

■ I am going to write two guide words on the board.

  Cat   Dog

■ Tell me what you know about these guide words. *Cat is the first word on the page and dog is the last word on the page.*

■ Let's begin scanning. The first word we want to find is **bunny**. Let's talk our way through this. The secret to being fast at scanning is to get this conversation memorized so you can do it very quickly.

■ The first letter in bunny is **b**. Compare **b** from bunny with the **c** from **cat**. Does it come before or after? Saying the alphabet will help answer that question. a . . . b . . . c. **b** comes before. Since it comes before the first word on the page it will not be on the page.

■ Let's try a second word: **duck.** Remember: Secret to being fast is to memorize this conversation.

■ The first letter in **duck** is **d**. Compare **d** from **duck** (what we are looking for) with the **c** in **cat** (what we have found.) Question: Does d come before or after **c?** a . . . b . . . c . . . d. After. Since it comes after it MIGHT be on this page. Will need to look at the second guide word.

■ Scan or match the **d** from **duck** with the **d** in dog. It matches. If it matches what do we do? That's right, go to the next letter. So let's compare the **u** from duck (what we are searching for) with the **o** in **dog** (what we found.). Say your alphabet o . . . p . . . q . . . r . . . s . . . t . . . u. **u** comes after **o**. Since it comes after the last word on the page it will not be on this page.

■ Let's try another. This time you tell me. Will **cow** be on our page?

■ Scan: Does **c** in **cow** match **c** in **cat?** *Yes.* What do we do if it matches? *Go to the next letter.*

■ What next? Scan the **o** in **cow** with the **a** in **cat**. **o** *comes after* **a** *so it might be on the page.* How will we find out? *Scan the next guide word.*

■ **c** in **cow** and the **d** in **dog**. a . . . b . . . c . . . d. **c** *comes before*. So our word comes after the first word on the page and before the last word on the page. Will it be on the page? *yes*

■ Continue guided practice. Make sure students are thinking aloud with you. The questions students should ask and answers include:

  ■ Does it match? If yes, then go to next letter.

  ■ Does it match? If no, then does it come before or after?

- If it comes before the first guide word, it is not on the page.
- If it comes after the first guide word, it might be on the page.
- If it comes before last guide word, it is on the page.
- If it comes after last guide word, it is not on the page.

- Provide independent practice. Remind students their task is not just to scan but to scan quickly.

Evaluation:

- Students complete a trial test, use same format competition will use. Allow a limited amount of time to complete, only 5 or 10 minutes. See Figure 9.3 for format.
- Collect and evaluate papers. Identify the lowest scores, students who obviously have not mastered the process.

Use of Information:

- Working with groups of four or less, again model scanning and provide guided practice for these students. Help students evaluate why they may be having difficulty scanning quickly.

Synthesis:

- Provide authentic practice by having students scan guide words to quickly locate words in the dictionary. It is desirable to model or guide locating the first couple of words. This will help students realize the process is the same. The differences are: the guide words are found on a page in the book rather than on our paper, and instead of simply saying the word is on the page, they need to scan the entry words and actually locate the word on the page.
- Let students experience scanning guide words to locate words in other sources such as telephone directory, thesaurus, biographical dictionary, encyclopedia, etc.
- Students complete a timed event, same format as Figure 9.3 to determine the champ.
  - To determine who is fastest: limit time and provide more words than even the fastest scanner can locate in the allowed time.
  - Students receive one point for each word correctly identified as being on the page or not being on the page.
  - Before students begin competition remind them to:
    - Focus: Can you be thinking about how fast you are going? What's for lunch? Reading the words you are searching for? Focus on each letter, scan or compare the letter you are searching for with the letter in the guide word. Remember your conversation. Does it come before . . . if yes . . . if no . . .
    - Work Fast: Normally how fast we do something may not be important. However, because information has to be found before it can be used, being able to find information quickly is really important to efficient problem solving.
- Announce and post the *Guide Word Champ*. He or she will be the reigning champ until next year when a new champ will be determined from the class which succeeds them.

Evaluation:

- Product: Ask students to evaluate via thumbs up/thumbs down: Are you faster at scanning and finding words now than before we began this unit? Why do you think you are faster? Turn to your neighbor and share the conversation you have with yourself when finding words using guide words.
- Process: Did it help to break the process into steps? Did it help to evaluate?

Differentiating between Scanning and Skimming

Missouri Cities	
Bolivar	Poplar Bluff
Branson	Sarcoxie
Cabool	Seymour
Cape Girardeau	Skyline
Delta	Spokane
Fair Play	Springfield
Galena	St. Louis
Half Way	Urbana
Jackson	West Plains
Jefferson City	Winona
Joplin	

Completing this exercise may help students see scanning and skimming as two distinct skills. It is then possible to become more proficient at each skill by focusing and practicing one skill at a time.

1.   Remind students:
Scanning = matching one letter at a time.
Skimming = matching the entire word or concept.

2.   Ask students to locate, as quickly as they can, the following Missouri cities on the above table:
- Delta
- Poplar Bluff
- Capitol of Missouri
- Skyline
- City along the Mississippi River
- Home of Bass Pro Shops and third largest city of Missouri
- Springfield

3.   After each city is located, students should identify if they scanned or skimmed to locate the city on the chart.
Answers:
- Delta: scan
- Poplar Bluff: scan
- Capitol of Missouri (Jefferson City): skim
- Skyline: scan
- City along the Mississippi River (St. Louis or Cape Girardeau): skim
- Home of Bass Pro Shops and third largest city of Missouri (Springfield): skim
- Springfield: scan

4.   Evaluate: Ask students:
- Which process is the most difficult and why? skimming, you have to use prior knowledge and make connections
- Do you read when scanning? no, match letters
- Do you read when skimming? yes, but only to see if the word matches your word or concept

From *Teaching Elementary Information Literacy Skills with the Big6™* by **Joyce Needham**. Columbus, OH: Linworth Publishing, Inc. Copyright © 2009.

Figure 9.4 Differentiating between Scanning and Skimming

Strategy for Teaching Skimming

Teach the difference between scanning and skimming. Provide students an opportunity to experience the difference between scanning and skimming (see Figure 9.4). Consciously experiencing the differences between scanning and skimming may help the two processes become concrete for students.

Strategies for Teaching Keywords

Integrate vocabulary and the concept of keywords into the instructional day. (See Chapter 7). Develop students' awareness that different people use different words to describe the same thing. Students must use the same words the writer uses in order to locate his or her information. Keywords are frequently nouns. So begin by randomly challenging students to use other words for nouns they encounter during the school day. At times brainstorm to see what other words students might use to replace the original noun. At other times consult a thesaurus for assistance or examples.

Have students underline the keyword in the assignment before they begin to work. Students may be challenged to create a graphic organizer when the assignment requires location of a lot of information. The organizer, as suggested by Eisenberg and Berkowitz (114), may identify the keywords found within the assignment. Under each of the keywords contained in the assignment the student may list other words authors may have used when writing about the original keyword (see Figure 9.5).

Assignment	Identify and describe five aspects of Southern life during the Civil War.		
Keywords found in assignment	South or Southern	Life	Civil War
Other words authors may use instead of keywords in assignment	■ Southern states ■ Confederacy ■ Confederate States of America ■ Virginia, Georgia, Tennessee, etc.	■ Culture ■ Living ■ Customs ■ Way of life ■ Traditions ■ Society ■ Family ■ Clothing ■ Hobbies ■ Religious practice	■ War Between the States

Figure 9.5 Keyword Organizer

Provide intense practice in identifying keywords. Prepare a list of questions. Use showdown (see Chapter 8) or another game format and challenge students to identify the keywords in the questions. Ask students, "How did you know that was the keyword?" Having students verbalize their thinking, e.g. the keyword is usually a noun, may be helpful for students who struggle with identification.

Strategies for Teaching Text Aids, Conventions, or Features

Teach students the concept of text aids. Students need to understand what text aids, features, or conventions are before they can be expected to use them. Lesson Plan 9.2 Text Aids, Features, or Conventions: The What & Why is one example of a lesson designed to provide students the information needed to both recognize and use these features to locate information.

Provide opportunities to use aids to locate information. Model as you think aloud using aids for students. Then provide opportunities for guided and independent practice using aids. Learning will be facilitated if the practice opportunities are in context or authentic, i. e. using the aids to find information actually needed to solve a problem.

Start with the familiar. First have students locate aids within familiar sources such as the textbook. Then make connections between the aids in the familiar sources and those found in new sources such as almanacs, the Internet, etc.

Strategies for Teaching Internet Skills

Model. Use a projection device and think aloud as you search for information on the Internet. Ask students to either scan for a specific letter or skim for a specific word and then raise their hand when they find it. Ask students to identify how they found the information, e.g. used the index or menu, looked at the picture, etc.

Make comparisons between print and Internet sources. Have students use both electronic and print reference sources and then compare.

1. Prepare a set of questions to be answered using reference sources such as dictionaries, encyclopedias, almanacs, and atlases. Students must verify the answer using one of the sources even if they believe they know the answer.
2. Divide the class into two groups. The first group answers the questions using print sources while the second group answers the questions using electronic sources.
3. At the end of 10 or 15 minutes ask students to count how many questions they answered. The groups switch. The first group now uses electronic sources and the second group uses print sources.
4. After another 10 or 15 minutes, ask students to count how many questions they answered. Create a chart comparing the number of questions answered using print sources with the number of questions answered using electronic sources.
5. Break the class into pairs or groups and have each complete a Venn diagram or chart comparing use of print sources with use of electronic sources. For instance, when using a print source the problem solver must scan for the keyword, but when using an electronic source the source scans for you. When using either electronic or print sources the problem solver must identify the keywords and use, or read, the information. Both electronic and print sources use text aids.
6. Prepare a class chart, using student input, of advantages and disadvantages of both print and electronic sources.

LESSON TITLE: TEXT AIDS, FEATURES, OR CONVENTIONS: THE WHAT & WHY

Grade Level: 3rd-5th	Time Frame: ■ One 30- or 45-minute session
Content Objective: Communication Arts: ■ Reading nonfiction text ■ Writing nonfiction text	**Information Literacy Objective/Big6 Objective:** ■ Practice use of the steps of the problem solving process ■ Location and Access: specifically scanning

Materials and Sources:
- Textbooks
- Examples of reference, nonfiction, and fiction books
- Electronic sources (optional)
- Document camera and/or projector (optional)

PLAN

Problem:
- Hold up a nonfiction book containing lots of information: Do you think it would take you long to find important information, one specific fact you need, in this book?
- Would you like to be able to find information faster? Did you know authors of information or nonfiction books frequently put in aids to make it easier to find information? Would that make it easier to find that one specific fact?

Task Definition:
- What is our task? *To be able to find information quickly in nonfiction or information books by using the aids authors provide.*

Information Seeking Strategies:
- What sources can we use? *Textbook, nonfiction books, reference books such as encyclopedias, electronic sources, prior knowledge.*

Location and Access:
- Have students get their textbooks. Ask five or six students to go to shelves and each pull a nonfiction book or reference book. Ask two students to go to shelves and each pull a fiction book.
- How will we find the information in these sources? That is what we are going to be learning today.

Use of Information:
- If we talk about types of books, there are basically two broad genres. What are they? *fiction and nonfiction.* What is the purpose of fiction? *To entertain. It tells a story. It has a beginning, middle, and end.* Briefly share two fiction books students brought. Demonstrate how it is difficult to make sense of the words in the book by opening it to the middle and starting to read.
- What about nonfiction? What is its purpose? *To inform.* How can we access the information in a nonfiction book? *Open a nonfiction book in the middle and begin reading.* Does it make sense? Do we need to start reading at the beginning for the book to make sense? *We could access information that way. Could read from cover-to-cover. Also could scan and skim to find specific information that is needed.*

- Scanning and skimming are especially helpful when you are completing research and may not have time to read all the books containing information from cover-to-cover. What do you scan and skim? The text or paragraphs? Maybe. Authors try to make it easier to find information by including text aids or features or conventions which can be used to locate specific information.

- What are these aids? You probably already know. You just may not know that you know!

- Let's think about aids. Aids help us, right? If you have trouble seeing, glasses aid you. If you have trouble hearing, you might use a hearing aid. What aids might you use if you have trouble walking? *cane, crutches, walker, wheelchair, braces.* If trying to find information in a book, there are also aids. Authors include these aids to help us . . . *find information.*

- Is there ever more than one word used to describe the same thing, e.g. dog, mutt, puppy, canine? The same is true of aids. They are sometimes called conventions or text features. Have you heard those terms before? Some people call them text conventions because like other text conventions, such as commas and periods, they help communicate the information in the book to the reader. Some people call them text features because you find them in almost all nonfiction books so they are features of nonfiction genre. Kind of like having a beginning, middle, and end is a feature of most fiction books.

- Borrow a textbook from one of the students. That student may look at the textbook with his neighbor. Use a document camera if available or simply hold up the text: Let's look at some text aids. Let's start with your textbook. Raise your hand if you think you are going to recognize some of these.*

- Open the text and point out aids, such as index, chapter titles, headings, pictures, charts, graphs, bold or highlighted words, etc. As each is pointed out and page number provided so that students may see the aid, ask students to identify the aid by name: Look on page 10, top right corner, is that an aid? What is that called? Look at the back of book, page 276. Is that an aid? What is that called? Create a t-chart listing the aids which students identify. As you list the aids on the chart, record all the text aids on the left side of chart and all the graphic aids on the right side.

- Use a projection device and display a variety of aids from both print and electronic sources. Add each aid to the list if it is new or point out what it is called if it is already on the list.

- After students have been introduced to the desired aids, ask: Have you wondered why I created a two-column chart instead of one? Do you notice any common feature about all the aids listed on one side or the other? *One side is all text aids and the other is all graphic.* Is it easier to remember each item on our list or to remember text and graphic? *Text and graphic.* When we use one word to label several others it is called chunking. It can be a powerful tool to help us make connections. Connections may help us store and retrieve information (see Chapter 3).

Option for introducing if students have some familiarity with text aids. Use instead of textbook: Can you think of some text aids which help locate information in books? Brainstorm a class chart of aids, include two columns—one for text and one for graphic.

Synthesis:

- Students use the aids when they need to locate information to solve problems.

Note: Students, even though able to find and name aids, may not automatically use aids when looking for information. Teachers and library media specialists need to prompt students to do so.

Evaluation:

- Product: What are aids? What two other words may be used to identify aids? What is the purpose of aids?

- Process: Did it help to look at a variety of sources and identify the same aids in each? What will synthesis look like if you use the information you learned today? Is it important to be able to identify table of contents, pictures, indexes, etc. as aids? Why?

LESSON TITLE: IDENTIFYING THE BEST SOURCE AND LOCATING INFORMATION

Grade Level: 3rd-5th	**Time Frame:** ■ One 30- to 45-minute session
Content Objective: ■ Any content (example is explorers)	**Information Literacy Objective/Big6 Objective:** ■ Practice using the steps of the problem solving process ■ Information Seeking Strategies & Location and Access

Materials and Sources:

■ Six or seven sets of questions about content

■ Questions should require use of a variety of sources to answer

■ The set should contain about 10 different questions

■ See sample questions

PLAN

Note: This lesson was taught by the library media specialist but with minor changes could be taught by the classroom teacher.

Problem:

■ In a conversation with your teacher, she indicated you were studying about America's earliest explorers. When I told her I had some questions about explorers, she volunteered you to find the answers for me!

■ Given enough time I am sure you can find the answers to my questions. However, I am an impatient person and I want to know now! Plus your teacher says she can only let you have about 30 minutes to find the answers to my questions. So we are going to make this a team challenge and see which team can find the most answers in our allotted time.

Task Definition:

■ What is our task? *To answer library media specialist's questions and to do so as quickly as possible, winning the team challenge.*

■ What information is needed? *Answer.* Yes. But I also want to make sure it is an accurate answer. What can you do to help me know your answer is correct? *cite the source.* You only need to include the title and the page number. I am also interested in your finding the answer as quickly as possible. I think if you identify the keywords in your question you will be able to find the answer faster. So what else do I want you to do? *keywords.* You can simply underline those.

■ Randomly call on two or three students to identify the task, including all three pieces of information which need to be included with the question. *keywords underlined, answer, and title and page number of source.* Unless all three pieces of information are included, the question is not considered answered.

Information Seeking Strategies:

- While the information may be found in several different sources, there is usually one source which is faster or easier to use. In fact I want to encourage you to work smarter and not harder, so I will give you a bonus point if you access the answer using the **best** source.
- Ask students to brainstorm list of possible sources. Make sure the needed sources are on the list. In this example possible sources will include the dictionary, thesaurus, encyclopedia, almanac, and atlas.

Optional depending upon level of information seeking strategies of the students: Do you need to know what type of information is in each of these sources to know if it is a good source? Do you know? *If student response indicates students need review, create a two-column class chart with type of source in left column and keywords which identify the type of information found in each source in the right column. See sample below:*

Location and Access:	
Source	**Type of info**
Atlas	Maps
Dictionary	Definitions

- If a class chart is created, a third column may be added listing the call number of each source.
- What is the process for finding information within the source? *Scan or skim for keywords using the text aids.* Discuss the process if needed.

Use of Information:

- Give each pair of students a question. Ask each student to write their name on the paper.
- Randomly call on one or two students to again identify the task including underlining the keyword, writing the answer, and citing source title and page.
- After you have an answer, bring your card to me. If all parts are included, you will receive one point. If you used the best source, you will get another point.
- You will also receive another question and the opportunity to earn more points.
- *Note:* Remind students:
  - This is a team challenge; the questions need to be answered with input from all members of the team.
  - Library Walk and Library Talk are required. Consequence of not using Library Walk and Library Talk: Team must be seated and count to 10. If team feels they can remember Library Walk and Library Talk they may resume competition. Repeated failure to use Library Walk and Library Talk may result in the team being seated for the duration of the competition.

Synthesis:

Team answers question, returns answer to the library media specialist, and receives another question.
Team with the most points at the end of competition wins the challenge.

Evaluation:

- Product:

- Library media specialist evaluates product with students as answer is turned in. At the end of the session, ask: Show me how many points your team earned. Students show how many points by showing that number of fingers. One point for each correct answer (answer, keywords underlined, and source cited) plus one point if best source used. Acknowledge the winner of the challenge. Allow that team to be the first to line up when leaving the library.

- Process:

  - Have students discuss within their team: What worked well? What should you have done differently?

  - Randomly call on students to share. Explain students' task to them as the sharing occurs: If you are called upon, your task is to share with class. If you are not called upon, your task is to compare what is said with what you did and decide if it this information would help you.

  - It also is beneficial to ask the team who answered the most questions: What worked for you? And to ask the team which did not do as well: What would you do differently next time?

Note: It is suggested this activity be repeated, possibly with different content questions, until students become efficient at identifying sources and locating information within the sources. If this is the second or third time students have completed the challenge, ask: What did you do differently? How did that work for you? Anything you would differently if we repeated again?

Sample questions:

- Pizarro explored this country whose neighbors include Ecuador, Brazil, Bolivia, and Chili. What is the country? (atlas)

- What area did Cortes conquer? (encyclopedia)

- Cabeza was appointed governor but was a failure and the colonists disposed him. What does dispose mean? (dictionary)

- Desoto became known as a "courageous explorer." How else can I say this? (thesaurus)

- This Portuguese explorer sailed for Spain in 1519-20 discovering straits now named after him. Who was he? (almanac)

Culminating Lesson

A lesson allowing students to identify the best source and then locate the information within that source may serve as a good culminating activity. This activity may help students synthesize or put the individual pieces of the problem solving process back within the process. Lesson Plan 9.3 provides one such lesson. The questions in the sample lesson relate to explorers of the Americas. To make the lesson an authentic problem solving opportunity, the content of the questions should reflect the content recently studied or soon to be studied in either science or social studies.

Finding enough information was the challenge of location and access during the twentieth century. That challenge has changed with the entry of computers, mass media, satellites, and the Internet. Today it is difficult not to find too much information. Students of today, who will be the citizens and workers of tomorrow, must meet this challenge. They must become adept at locating and accessing information and be able to do so in an efficient and timely manner. As teachers and library media specialists, you already spend time locating and accessing information. The challenge you face is to teach the process you use to your students.

Works Cited

Eisenberg, Michael and Robert Berkowitz. *Teaching Information & Technology Skills: The Big6 in Elementary Schools.* Worthington, OH: Linworth Publishing, Incorporated, 1999.

Eisenberg, Michael and Robert Berkowitz. *Teaching Information & Technology Skills: The Big6 in Secondary Schools.* Worthington, OH: Linworth Publishing, Incorporated, 2000.

The BIG 6

CHAPTER 10
USE OF INFORMATION

What Is Use of Information?

Use of information is one of the most difficult steps in the problem solving process. It entails activities which are often mentally challenging. Use of information is the link between the located information and the finished product. It requires the problem solver to engage with the information and extract the information deemed important by the task. The needed information falls into one of two categories:

- Old or prior information gathered from the long-term memory via connections

- New information gathered via reading, listening, or seeing from other sources such as parents, teachers, textbooks, dictionaries, or encyclopedias

Both the processes of engaging and extracting are complex. To master the skills used to engage or absorb information into the brain, such as making connections, reading, listening, and seeing, requires practice. Mastery of these skills does not just happen naturally or without effort. Another challenge in using information is extracting the important information. To extract the needed information, the problem solver must identify what is important. It is often difficult to select all of the important information and only the important information when so much is absorbed into the brain. It is easy to become overwhelmed by the amount of information and miss needed information or lose focus and extract information which is not needed.

Why Is Use of Information Important?

It is not possible to synthesize or solve a problem unless information is used. Use of information may be challenging. Because of the importance and complexity of this step, it is especially important to focus on the individual skills required to effectively use information. Focusing on the individual skills results in the skills becoming more concrete and easier to practice and master.

An analogy comparing rain drops to information may help students understand the need to use information, or to engage and extract.

> Imagine standing outside in the rain trying to catch raindrops in a bucket. Hundreds of raindrops are coming at you. You cannot possibly catch every rain drop. You may catch those hitting your head by holding the bucket over your head, or those falling right in front of you by holding the bucket in front of you. Imagine each raindrop is a piece of information. You cannot possibly catch every piece of information. But if you know which pieces of information are needed (Big6 #1), either those falling on your head or those falling in front of you, you may hold out your bucket and catch the pieces needed to solve your problem.

The ability to engage and extract information impacts our ability to problem solve. Sharing the following thoughts and examples may help students understand the importance of perfecting their skills in using information.

> **The amount of information with which we are bombarded signals the importance of extracting information**. Every second of every hour of every day our senses are showered with information. The amount of information continues to increase as the technological age of the twenty-first century is entered. More information is received than humanly possible to process (Jansen 4). The amount of information bombarding our senses makes it more important than ever for problem solvers to be able to quickly engage and then extract only the needed information.
>
> **Extracting skills help turn 20 pages of information into two pages**. Once the task and needed information are identified (Big6 #1), it is possible to extract, or filter, specific information out of all of the information that is received. By filtering information, 20 pages may be compacted to two pages. This filtered information, or two pages, may be used to solve the problem and all of the other information, the other 18 pages, may be disregarded.
>
> **It is easier to use information when the process is concrete and well defined**. The following experience with 4th graders illustrates the importance of understanding the use of information process. The students' task was to answer four or five questions about a story the class read. In observing various groups, it became evident that all of the groups skipped the second question, which asked students to summarize the story. When students were asked why that question was skipped, the answer was almost unanimously because it was a difficult question. With one group of students the teacher paused and asked, "Could you tell me what happened at the beginning of the story? What happened next? What happened at the end of the story?" Students eagerly and easily answered the questions. The teacher then said, "You just summarized the story."

The students looked wide-eyed at each other and the teacher. In this case the students possessed the ability to use the information. They were unable to identify the information needed because the process was unclear to them. Once the process became concrete students found it easy to use the information.

Information must be absorbed into the brain during the engage process via the senses. Typically in the school setting this means the student must read, if text, or listen, if oral. If the information is in text form, there is no other way to use the information unless it is read. If the information is in oral form, there is no other way to use the information unless the problem solver listens. Recognizing these facts may help motivate students to become better readers and listeners.

Extracting information may make test preparation easier and less time consuming. This is true only if students have developed the skills to successfully extract the important information. Sharing the following experience with 5th graders may help your students understand the importance of extracting information. The day before a social studies test the teacher had the following discussion with her students.

"Tomorrow you have a test over the content in Chapter 5. Which information would you rather use to study for the test (she held up both sources for students to see): the 25 pages in Chapter 5 of your textbook or your one page of notes or outline of Chapter 5?" The majority of students indicated they would prefer to use the information in the text. The teacher, assuming students would prefer to study one page rather than 25 pages, was surprised. She asked, "Why?" The students responded, "Sometimes I leave out important information when I outline or take notes." "Sometimes I don't write the information in a way that makes sense to me." These answers identified a use of information problem: students had difficulty extracting information or taking notes. Instead of trying to improve their note taking skills their solution was to use the original source or text. The teacher pointed out, "Yes, the text does have all of the needed information but it also contains information that is not needed. By using the text you are requiring yourself to spend more time and learn information you do not need. This may work for you. But have you thought about what will happen when you go on to high school and college? How many of you think you may be going to college? Did you know that at the high school and college level instead of 25 pages, tests may include content from 200 or 300 pages? Do you think you will be able to use the text to study for these tests?" After this discussion students recognized the importance of becoming effective with information extraction. Students were provided opportunities to practice focusing on identifying the important information and writing so the extracted information made sense to them (See Chapter 14, Notetaking).

The ability to extract information can reduce the amount of time spent reading. At one time a standard assignment in school was to read the chapter. The expectation was that the student would read every word and commit to memory all the information in the chapter. Knowledge of how the brain functions indicates this was a very difficult task (Wolfe 90). The truth is sometimes it may be necessary to read every page of a chapter or article to use the important or needed information and at other times it is only necessary to read portions. Students who understand this and can determine how much reading is required are in a position to take control of their learning, make decisions, and make the most effective use of their time. It is necessary to identify what information is needed (Big6 #1) to know what portions of text need to be read. As guide and coach, the teacher should help students, using established goals and objectives, identify what information is important. Once students are aware of what information is needed, the student needs to first skim to locate the information and then read and extract the information. To establish a need to identify what text needed to be read, one teacher had the following discussion with her students:

Before starting a new unit of instruction, the teacher held up a copy of the textbook and opened it to the chapter containing information that was to be studied. She asked students, "There are 25 pages in this chapter. How many pages do you need to read? Do you need to read the entire chapter?" The majority of students responded, "yes." The teacher then asked, "Why?" The students responded they needed to read the entire chapter so they would not miss any important information. The teacher asked, "What if all of the information in the text is not important? What if you knew what information was needed or important?" Students suggested they could identify the information needed (Big6 #1), skim to locate that information, (Big6 #3) and read just those portions of the text (Big6 #4). At this point students were ready for guided practice building their skill to identify what information or text needed to be read.

Tips and Strategies to Help Students Develop Use of Information Skills

Tips and Strategies to Develop Engaging and Extracting Skills

Have students create pictures or nonlinguistic representations of information extracted. Part of using information is understanding the concept or information. One method of increasing understanding is to challenge students to create a nonlinguistic representation of the information (Marzano 73). To create a drawing of the concept or information, the student must have an understanding of the information.

Remind students to separate processes into steps. First you find the information (Big6 #3). Then you use or read the information (Big6 #4). You must engage or read (Big6 #4.1) before you can extract (Big6 #4.2).

Make students accountable for their learning. Ask students to evaluate. For instance, students are using information in a text. When students are engaged or reading it will be quiet. If the classroom is noisy, guide students as they evaluate. "What is your task? How can you engage or get the information from the text to your brain? What will it look like and sound like if you are engaged? Are you engaged?"

Stress the importance of task definition. Remind students that identifying the important information requires knowing what the task is and what information is needed.

Teach students note taking strategies. When students take notes they are using information (Big6 #4). See Chapter 14 for specific tips and strategies on note taking.

Tips and Strategies to Improve Engaging Skills

Visualize engagement. Make students conscious of what engaging looks and sounds like, e.g. reading, listening, or seeing. If you are not engaged then you are not learning.

Self-monitoring. Encourage students to monitor behavior. Ask students to evaluate their behavior to make sure they are engaging. For instance, "Evaluate. Are you engaged? Are you listening? Are you reading? Are you watching?"

Tips and Strategies to Improve Extracting Skills

Encourage use of note taking organizers. Creating and using organizers, such as a web, t-chart, or Venn diagram, aids in extracting information. The organizer may assist in identifying the important information and also make it easier to record information in a manner which makes sense and can be understood later.

Provide direct instruction. Utilize direct instruction designed to teach extracting skills such as summarizing and comparing.

Monitor notes. Examine the information students extract, or their notes, to ensure students:

- extract only the important information
- extract phrases or words instead of complete sentences
- can make sense of what they have extracted

Teach a process to extract from print. When students begin to extract information from text, have them mark out and underline on the text copy and transfer important or extracted information to a note taking organizer. This will require making a copy of the text for students to mark on. Instead of making copies of the text, you may give each student a blank transparency and a transparency marker. The transparency can be placed over the text and students could underline and mark on it.

Teach a process to extract from an electronic source. If an electronic source is being used as the text, model for students cutting the words that are not important.

Scaffold extracting instruction. Identify levels of extracting skills. Move up the scaffold as students master the previous skill. See Figure 10.1 for suggestions for teaching skills using a scaffold which moves from extracting direct quotes, extracting words and phrases, and finally summarizing or paraphrasing the phrases.

Citation Tips and Strategies

Preventing Plagiarism

A concern when students do research is plagiarism and failure to give proper credit for information used. Thanks to the Internet it is now easier to ascertain if students have copied work. However, this is still a time-consuming activity which leaves both teachers and students with negative feelings and does nothing to promote our initial purpose for giving research assignments—student learning.

There is an alternative. Consider the old adage: *an ounce of prevention is worth a pound of cure*. Instead of reacting to student plagiarism, it is possible to become proactive and take steps to prevent plagiarism from happening. Perhaps the first step to preventing plagiarism is to consider why students plagiarize. Students may plagiarize because:

Teaching Extracting Skills

Scaffolding instruction provides support and aids in student mastery by sequencing instruction from simple to complex. Below is a suggested scaffold for teaching students to extract or pull important or needed information.

A three-step scaffold for extracting (Big6 #4.2) follows. Students must complete each of the steps prior to #4.2 before actually extracting information:

Steps to complete prior to extracting information:
1.1 Identify the task.
1.2 Identify the information needed and keywords.
2.0 Identify the source to be used.
3.1 Locate the source.
3.2 Scan and skim for keywords using text aids.
4.1 Engage or read the information.
4.2 *Extract the important or needed information.*

Assuming students have completed Big6, #1—#3, they are ready to begin reading (Big6 #4.1) When important or needed information is identified, students are ready to use one of the strategies below to pull or extract the needed information:

Step 1: Direct Quotes.
- Students identify sentences in the source which include the needed information.
- The sentences are copied, exactly as they appear in the text.
- Quotation marks are placed around these exact quotes.
- The page number cited should be recorded. If more than one source is used, the title of the source should also be included.
- Students should be able to identify this as a *direct quote.*
- *Rationale:* This is a logical starting place when beginning to extract information as it is easier to copy than to paraphrase or summarize. It may also lead to a better understanding of quotations (Eisenberg 84).

Step 2: Extract Important words and Phrases.
- The next skill to focus on is the ability to extract, from sentences, the words and phrases which provide the needed information.
- Trash & Treasure, created by Barbara Jansen, is a powerful strategy which makes the process of extracting the important words or phrases very concrete for students.
- To teach Trash & Treasure Jansen suggests:

  "Demonstrate this concept (Trash & Treasure) using a projected image of an encyclopedia article or section. The students should each have a copy of the article so they can follow along and practice the technique.
    1. *Show a prepared question, including the underlined keywords and list of related words.*
    2. *Skim the article for essential points of access (skim text features for keywords) until you locate the appropriate heading or section.*
    3. *Place a slash at the end of the first sentence and read it. Ask "Does this sentence answer the question?"*
    4. *If the answer is no, tell the students that this sentence is "trash" to them. Go on to the next sentence, placing a slash at the end.*
    5. *If the answer is yes, underline the first phrase and ask if that phrase answers the question. If the answer is no, underline the next phrase and repeat the question.*
    6. *If the answer is yes, read that phrase word-by-word, asking which words are needed to answer the question—treasure words. Circle those words, and then write them in the appropriate place on the projected data chart or whichever organizer the students are using. Those that do not answer the question are trash words. Continue phrase by phrase and word by word until the end of the sentence. Count the words in the sentence and then count the treasure words. Students are very impressed when you say, "The sentence has 17 words and I only needed to write four of them. I don't know about you, but I would rather write four than 17!"*

7. Demonstrate the process again, allowing the students to practice, using copies of the article. Allow students to independently practice a few times before they begin their own research. The library media specialist and teacher should monitor each student's work, reteaching as necessary." (Jansen, pp. 109-110).

- Suggestions for mastering Trash & Treasure:
  - Let students practice extracting treasure from some of the direct quotes from previous assignments, Step 1.
  - After introducing Trash & Treasure, have students write only extracted or treasure words and phrases when answering questions.
  - Initially students need to read each individual word and decide if it is trash or treasure. As skills are refined, it may be possible to read a phrase and circle the treasure without looking at each individual word.
  - Reiterate:
    - The task or information needed must be identified *before* treasure can be found.
    - Words showing quantity such as some, more, or all are usually treasure.
    - A specific piece of information may be trash when solving one problem and treasure when solving another.
- Trash & Treasure or extracting pluses and minuses:
  - Minus: It requires time and effort to extract the important words.
  - Plus: You do not have to write as many words.
  - Plus: At some point before synthesis the words must be read. By reading and extracting during use (Big6 #4) speeds up synthesis (Big6 #5)

Step 3: Summarize or paraphrase using the extracted words.

- Identify need to summarize or paraphrase:
  - Does your treasure make sense to you? Will it still make sense next week or next month? What if you handed your notes to a stranger? Would they be able to make sense of them? Do they communicate the information?
  - This evaluation may help students recognize information may be communicated more easily and accurately if extracted or treasure words are put back within complete sentences.
- Model and guide students in constructing complete sentences from extracted words and substituted words when appropriate.
- Reiterate:
  - Words can only be substituted when they do not change the meaning of the information. Sometimes a word can be substituted without changing the meaning, at other times it is impossible to substitute. For instance, it might be possible to substitute *reasons* or *motives* for *causes* and not change the meaning. However, finding a word to substitute for *slavery* might be difficult.
  - Initially, it is helpful to write the treasure or extracted information, prior to summarizing or paraphrasing. As skills are refined, it may be possible to mentally extract the treasure instead of writing it down.

Example of "Treasure" or Extracted Information	**Example of Information Paraphrased or Summarized from Treasure**
Civil War	
- Started 1864	- The American Civil War began in 1864.
- North = union	- The northern states were called the Union.
- South = confederacy	- The southern states were called the Confederacy.
- Issues: slavery, states' rights,	- Two of the causes of this war were slavery and states' rights

Figure 10.1 Teaching Extracting Skills

1. It is obviously easier to copy someone else's words than to process and use our own words.
2. It is not easy to summarize and paraphrase. For many students these skills are rather vague. It is difficult, if not impossible, to read and then put material into their own words.
3. Students, the majority of which are novice writers, are asked to paraphrase the words of professional writers. The words in the sources used by students are written by professional writers. No matter how hard a student works trying to reword or summarize these words it probably will not sound as good as the original. Who wants to do all that work when the results are not as good as what you started with? Copying may be seen as one way of guaranteeing good writing.
4. Students may not understand how to give credit to others for their work or may find it a difficult process.
5. Students may not comprehend the seriousness of plagiarism. In reality plagiarism is stealing. Many students, while they may know this, do not truly understand or recognize it.

Teachers, equipped with a better understanding of why students plagiarize, are in the position to create assignments and provide instruction minimizing the likelihood of plagiarism. The following strategies may discourage plagiarism and encourage students to create their own work resulting in increased learning:

Design research problems which require students to manipulate or reformat the information found. For example, requiring students to compare and contrast, create a time-line, write a letter, or write using the voice of the person or object being researched require students to reformat information. See Chapter 6 for additional examples. To copy assignments of this nature requires more work on the student's part. It may even be impossible.

Reassure students you do not expect their writing to sound like that of a professional. Remind students that "If you were a professional writer, you would not need to be in school spending time on learning to write. One of the purposes of the assignment is to provide you the opportunity to practice and improve your writing skills. If you copy you cheat yourself of that opportunity."

Provide students direct instruction so that summarizing, paraphrasing, and using direct quotes become concrete skills students master. See Figure 10.1 for ideas of scaffolding instruction moving from direct quotes to paraphrasing and summarizing.

Encourage citation. Encourage students to respect the work of others and provide them the skills needed to give credit when they decide to use another's work.

Why Do Sources Need to Be Cited?

There are at least three reasons for students to cite sources. Share with students that by citing sources they:

■ **Prove information is accurate**. For instance, you are reading a report about the American bald eagle. It says the eagle is eight feet long. Do you believe that? If the author has cited sources, it is possible to find that information again and prove it is correct or incorrect. Citing sources lends strength to your work. It allows others to

Task Definition:

- Our task is to learn how to cite sources.

Use of Information:

- **What information to include?**

What is the purpose of citing sources?

To enable others to locate the information in the original source.

What information is needed to be able to locate a source and information in the source?

Guide students to identify: title, author, publisher, date of publication, city of publication, page number. For information found on the Internet, the URL.

If students suggest using the call number: Reinforce the call number would work to locate information in local library, but call numbers may vary from library to library, e.g. some libraries use Library of Congress numbers instead of Dewey Decimal.

Note: Because creating a list of sources cited may be overwhelming for younger students, consider having students begin by including only the title and page number.

- *In what order should information be included?*

How do you think we should arrange that information?

After students make suggestions, share with students while there is generally agreement on what information to include, there is no one right style. Mention MLA and APA as two examples of acceptable style. Help students realize the right style for their report will be whatever their teacher requires. If the teacher does not require a specific style, the student may choose any acceptable style.

Note: It is also helpful for students to realize all styles tend to separate each piece of information with some form of punctuation, e.g. comma, colon, period.

Synthesis:

- *Provide students a cheat sheet of an acceptable style. The sheet should include entries for various formats, such as books and Web sites. Including both the information to be included and a sample entry is helpful.*

- *Students may refer to, or copy from, the cheat sheet when writing citations for the sources they use.*

Note: The idea of being able to legally cheat will delight students. At the same time using the cheat sheet will help them develop the skills needed to accurately cite sources.

Figure 10.2 How Do We Cite Sources?

verify that it is correct. By the way, the eagle's **wing span** may be eight feet (World Book 3). It appears our writer needs to polish paraphrasing skills.

- **Allow readers to find more information**. For instance, what if you write a really good report? A report so interesting your teacher and your readers want to know more about your topic? By citing your source you make it easy for your audience to find more information.

- **Give credit to and acknowledge the person whose work has been used**. For instance, assume Mrs. Jones, your teacher, shares your paper with other classes. As she shares she lets students assume she is responsible for the information being shared. How do you feel? Angry? Sad? Frustrated? You may experience some negative feelings. Now assume that when Mrs. Jones shares your paper with other classes she says "Class, I want to share the work of *your name*." How do you feel? Proud? Happy? You are likely to experience positive feelings. Citing sources allows you to give credit and thanks to the people whose work and ideas you borrowed. That is only fair. Is it not?

- If you need another reason to cite sources, then remember there are copyright laws which make it illegal to use other people's work without giving credit.

Once students understand the teacher is not just torturing them, that valid reasons exist for citing sources, they are ready to learn how to cite. For elementary students it is preferable to focus on the mechanics of citing rather than the specifics of formatting. See Figure 10.2 for a strategy which introduces and explains the information needed to cite.

Students' success in mastering the mechanics of citing sources may be aided if the teacher:

- Models citing sources both orally and in writing.

- Requires students to cite sources in class discussions, e.g. the teacher said, the text said.

- Utilizes daily assignments as practice opportunities. For instance, when students submit daily assignments, require them to cite the source, e.g. the textbook, the teacher, prior knowledge, parents, etc. The citation may be as simple as writing the source at a specified location on the paper or even using a stamp provided by the teacher. (See Chapter 9 for more details on using stamps to cite sources.)

Use of information is one of the most difficult and important steps in the problem solving process. Teachers and library media specialists may assist students in mastering the process by helping students visualize what it looks like to engage and extract information. In addition, direct skills instruction, along with opportunities to practice, help the step become visible and concrete for students.

Works Cited

"Eagles." *World Book Encyclopedia*. 2007 ed.

Eisenberg, Michael and Robert Berkowitz. *Teaching Information & Technology Skills: The Big6 in Elementary Schools*. Worthington, OH: Linworth Publishing, Inc., 1999.

Jansen, Barbara A. *The Big6 in Middle School, Teaching Information and Communications Technology Skills*. Columbus, OH: Linworth Publishing, Inc., 2007.

Marzano, Robert J., Debra J. Pickering, and Jane E. Pollock. *Classroom Instruction That Works, Research-Based Strategies for Increasing Student Achievement*. Alexandria, VA: Association for Supervision and Curriculum Development, 2001.

Wolfe, Patricia. *Brain Matters, Translating Research into Classroom Practice*. Alexandria, VA: Association for Supervision and Curriculum Development, 2001.

CHAPTER 11
SYNTHESIS

What Is Synthesis?

Synthesis is the reason for problem solving. It is in this fifth step of our problem solving process that the problem is solved or the solution found. As students and teachers, you may not be familiar with the term *synthesis,* but you are familiar with what synthesis looks like. For example, synthesis occurs anytime students:

- answer questions orally
- write a research paper
- make a poster
- give a speech
- take a spelling test
- complete a mandated test

Synthesis is the one step of the problem solving process which is almost never omitted. For without synthesis our problem is not solved or completed. Synthesis involves organizing information and communicating the solution of the problem. Organization may be very simple, e.g. answering a question in class, or very extensive, e.g. preparing a research paper. While synthesis often involves writing or speaking, it varies depending upon the problem being solved. When synthesis results in creation of an electronic format, such as a video or PowerPoint, an opportunity for authentic integration of technology occurs. The quality of synthesis hinges upon the problem solver's organization and communication skills.

Why Is Synthesis Important?

Synthesis must happen if our problems are to be solved. It is frequently the sole means used to judge what students learn in today's schools. For example, the answer to a question asked in class, the answers on a test, or a speech given. Synthesis is often the basis upon which grades are assigned and success measured. It is important for students to develop the skills required to successfully synthesize because of the emphasis placed upon synthesis.

Effective and efficient synthesis requires the abilities to organize information and then to communicate that information. Organizational skills, such as outlining or webbing, are required if students are to present the solution in a logical or easily understood manner. Organizational skills also allow students to utilize time to synthesize as quickly as possible. It is possible for students to work out an effective solution but not be able to convey the solution. This is where oral and written skills come in to play. For instance, Johnny may know the answer to a math problem is 24 or two dozen. But if Johnny writes 24 dozen he did not communicate properly. Or perhaps Johnny writes 24 on his paper but the person evaluating his work does not see the 24 because Johnny's paper is so messy or his handwriting is not legible.

The need for organizational skills and speaking and writing skills become a reality when students understand the purpose of synthesis. When students understand that the purpose of synthesis is to communicate the solution, it becomes a concrete process. This understanding may motivate students to learn the skills and also aid in improving the skills. For example, assume Candy understands the only way she can communicate her answer is by the words she writes. This knowledge is likely to motivate her to improve her writing. Knowing the purpose for which she is writing may also help her improve writing skills.

Tips and Strategies to Help Students Synthesize More Effectively

Strategies to Improve Synthesis

Refer back to the task. Synthesis results in the problem being solved or the task completed. Questions about what synthesis should look like may be resolved by referring back to task definition (Big6 #1).

Provide authentic problems. Authentic problems may motivate, increase connections, and result in a higher level of learning. Provide authentic problems to solve, rather than just assignments to complete. The following examples illustrate the difference between authentic problems and assignments:

- *Authentic problem.* You are going to take a walk through nature (the walk may either be a real or simulated walk with the teacher providing pictures of sites along the way). You will be required to describe the land forms you see along the way. Page 54 of your workbook describes types of land forms you may see on your walk.

- *Assignment.* Page 54 of your workbook describes the types of land forms; complete that page.

In both cases the student will complete or synthesize the questions on page 54 of the workbook. Synthesis of the assignment only requires the answers be written on the workbook page (knowledge level). Synthesis of the authentic problem is not completed until students can use the information on page 54 to describe the landforms encountered along the walk (application level). A higher level of learning will occur when students synthesize the problem rather than the assignment (Bloom 201-207). The problem also gives students an authentic reason to complete the workbook. In order to identify the land forms students need to read the workbook page (Big6 #4, Use) and a write their answers (Big6 #5, Synthesis). The purpose of completing the workbook page for the assignment is simply because the teacher requires it. Students may be more motivated to complete the workbook page to solve the problem than because the teacher has asked it.

Address objectives. Synthesis should directly address the objectives of the lesson. Evaluate to be sure synthesis addresses the objectives being taught. For instance, the stated objective for a 3rd grade class is to learn what a mountain, lake, river, and desert are. The activity designed for synthesis in the workbook involves students drawing a line between two columns. Column One identifies a land feature such as a mountain or river. Column Two names an example of a landform in the U.S. such as Rocky, Mississippi, Mojave. Synthesis, in this instance, will not meet the stated objective. Drawing a line from the landform to the example only ensures students know an example of the landform. It does not ensure they know what each land form is.

Consider level of learning. The level of learning is impacted by the type of synthesis. For instance:

- If the topic is landforms, synthesis may be matching a landform with a definition, identifying landforms as students take a walk, or creating a diorama.

- If the topic is Famous Historical Figures, students may choose 10 people and identify the major contribution of each or write a five-page paper on one individual.

- If the topic is Dewey Decimal, students may recite the numbers and categories or find books on the shelves using the Dewey Decimal system.

In each of these instances the level of learning varies based upon the form of synthesis. Students benefit when teachers and library media specialists consciously consider the level of learning desirable for student success. For example, a group of students who had been taught to use Venn diagrams and t-charts were given a task comparing two items. The majority of students wrote the comparison in paragraph style rather than using the Venn diagram or the t-chart which are much better organizational strategies for comparison. Students obviously did not reach the desired level of learning. Utilization of the verbs in Bloom's taxonomy (Bloom 201-207), when determining the format of synthesis, makes it possible to help students reach the desired level of learning. See Chapter 6 for additional information.

Provide authentic audiences. Sharing synthesis of the product with a real audience may enhance the power of the lesson. Solving the problem becomes more purposeful and motivating when students know their solution will be shared with a real audience. Provide opportunities for students to share their work with real audiences, such as other students, staff, or parents. There are a variety of methods to reach these real audiences, such as:

- Have students share their work with a classmate.

- Invite another class to visit your classroom and either display students' work or allow students to share their work orally.

- Share students' work, with their permission, within your class or with another class.

- Post students' work in the hall.

- Publish students' work in a newsletter.

- Share work through a living museum where each student becomes an exhibit. They become the person or object researched. Students orally share with museum visitors as they view the exhibits.

- Have a writers' celebration where students choose one of their writings to display. Invite parents and others to visit the celebration, read the students' work, and make positive comments on the writing.

Strategies for Organizing

The amount of organization required depends upon the amount and type of information needed to solve the problem. Very little organization is required for many of the problems students must solve. For example, find the time of the next basketball practice, answer a question the teacher asks, or find a favorite book in the library.

The ability to organize information, however, is essential when the problem being solved requires either a large quantity of information or complex information. Information, depending upon the content, may usually be organized into one of the following formats:

- chronology such as a timeline or sequence

- cause and effect

- comparison of similarities and differences

- categories or web

- pros and cons

- questions and answers

Let students experience organization. Eisenberg suggests students experience how information may be organized. This may be done by dividing your class into groups of four or five students each. Give each group a packet of 10 to 20 pictures randomly clipped from magazines. The students' task is to group or organize the pictures. Allow students to determine how they will group the various pictures without any teacher input. Then share with the class how the pictures were organized or grouped (Eisenberg and Berkowitz 140). The resulting groupings typically provide examples of the various organizational strategies, e.g. timeline, web, cause and effect. This is an effective way to help students develop an awareness of the variety of ways information may be organized.

Utilize a note taking organizer. The use of a note taking organizer may be helpful when it is essential to organize information. Scaffold instruction. Teachers or library media specialists may initially provide students with an organizer. As students develop needed skills they should design their own note taking organizers. The type of organizer used will depend upon the type of information needed. For instance, the organizer may consist of a web if information is organized by categories or a timeline if information is sequential. Students enter the information as it is extracted (Big6 #4). As students move to synthesis (Big6 #5), they have already begun to organize information.

Use notebook paper as a note taking organizer. My favorite note taking organizer is easy to create and makes the process of organization very concrete. To create the note taking organizer, simply write one question to be answered through research at the top of a piece of lined notebook paper. If there are five questions to research, then you will need six pieces of paper. You will have one page for each question plus one additional page for sources. The sources page will include a numbered list of each source used with appropriate bibliographical information. As information is extracted, it is recorded on the appropriate piece of paper. Each fact is written as a separate, bulleted fact. The number of the source, taken from the numbered list of sources, is recorded beside the fact. This method makes it easy to quickly glance over the notes and determine when all questions are answered.

This method of organization is also very user friendly during the synthesis or writing stage of problem solving. The notebook papers may be quickly sorted according to the order questions will be included in the rough draft. With the notebook papers in correct order, the student selects all notes on one topic or question. The bulleted facts on these pages are cut apart. Next the student physically places each fact where it best fits within this section and then tapes the cut items back together in the correct order. This process of cutting and taping is continued for each question or topic until all information is arranged in the order to be included in the final report. At this point the student is ready to begin writing the rough draft. Because organization of the information is complete, the student needs to focus only on the writing process and communicating with the audience.

Electronic note taking organizers. Computer programs, such as word processors and spreadsheets, also deserve consideration as possible note taking organizers. The ability of these tools to organize information makes them valuable to students. For instance, cutting and pasting becomes an easy task when using word processing software and spreadsheets can be used to quickly and easily sort data or information.

Strategies for Communicating

It is possible to have the correct answer to a problem and still fail to synthesize. Synthesis is not complete until the answer or solution is communicated. How, and to whom, the solution is communicated varies with each problem. Communication, however, usually involves speaking and writing. Helping students develop these skills may lead to improved communication.

Successful communication is also facilitated when students understand the importance of communicating the solution and develop the ability to identify whether the communication will be one-way, problem solver to audience, or two-way, problem solver to audience to problem solver. In the classroom, the student usually verbalizes or writes the answer in an effort to communicate the answer to the teacher. Further communication, in the form of questions and answers, may be needed if the answer is not communicated successfully the first time, e.g. the teacher cannot read the student's writing, cannot hear the student's answer, or does not understand what the student wrote. This two-way communication ensures the audience understands the solution. In other instances, two-way communication is not possible and the student must successfully communicate the solution the first time, e.g. state mandated tests which are graded at a central location. Teaching students to evaluate their answers, e.g. does the answer make sense or does it say what I want it to say, may raise the level of synthesis when students have only one chance to communicate.

Determining the Form of Synthesis

The method of communicating the solution or the form of synthesis varies. In some situations the form synthesis takes will be a foregone conclusion. For instance, if the teacher asks a question during class discussion the obvious form of synthesis is an oral response. In other situations, successful synthesis may take several different forms, e.g. either a written report, a journal, or a PowerPoint presentation may be used to solve the problem. When possible allow students to choose what the final product will look like. When the teacher determines what synthesis will look like, the teacher is doing the thinking and learning. When students decide they must do the thinking and learning. Discussions, which engage students in identifying and choosing valid forms, may help students become effective and efficient with synthesis. One such method is to have students brainstorm possible forms synthesis may take and then allow them to choose from the proposed forms.

The form synthesis takes (see Figure 11.1) is limited only by the imagination of the problem solver. Access to technology has enhanced the possibilities of what syntheses might look like. Forms of synthesis which utilize technology are **bolded** in Figure 11.1. Many of the other forms of synthesis, e.g. banner, pamphlet, or graph, may also be completed using technology.

The following table contains (in alphabetical order) some possible forms of synthesis:			
Advertisement	Flow Chart	Model	Speech
Banner	Game	Newspaper Article	**Spreadsheet (i.e. Excel®)**
Baseball Cards	Graph	Outline	Storyboard
Book	Graphic	Poster	Test
Book Jacket	Headlines	**PowerPoint® or Electronic Slide Show**	Time Capsule
Brochure or Pamphlet	Historical Document	Puzzles	Time Line
Chart or Table	Journal Entry	*Report* **(using word processor)**	Venn Diagram
Collage	Labeled Diagram	Riddles	*Video*
Diorama	Letter	Scrapbook	**Web Page**
Flip Chart	Mobile	Story	

Figure 11.1 Synthesis Forms

Using technology to synthesize is an authentic use of technology and a powerful learning opportunity to master technology skills as well.

The fifth step in the problem solving process, synthesis, is a step which all students have experienced. The challenge to teachers and library media specialists is to raise student awareness of this step so students may be more deliberate in organizing and sharing the results of their solutions.

Works Cited

Bloom, Benjamin S. *Taxonomy of Educational Objectives, Handbook One.* New York: Allyn & Bacon, 1984.

Eisenberg, Michael and Berkowitz, Robert. *Teaching Information & Technology Skills: The Big6 in Secondary Schools.* Worthington, OH: Linworth Publishing, Inc., 2000.

CHAPTER 12
EVALUATION

What Is Evaluation?

Evaluation involves identifying the strengths and weaknesses of problem solving. Some of the terms used to talk about evaluation include assessment, reflection, review, study, feedback, and grades. Evaluation is the sixth and final step in the Big6 problem solving process. Many effective problem solvers, however, find themselves evaluating throughout the process as well as when the problem is solved. Evaluation may have a greater impact on long-term learning than any other step of the process.

Eisenberg and Berkowitz break evaluation into two components: judging the result or effectiveness; and judging the process or efficiency (Eisenberg and Berkowitz 19). In the school setting, results or effectiveness usually are evaluated. In fact most grades are based upon the teacher's evaluation of the result or product. It is important that students also be given the opportunity to evaluate the product, as this step allows time to reflect upon content which has been learned and to correct any misunderstandings.

Evaluation of efficiency or process provides problem solvers the opportunity to perfect their problem solving process. As synthesis (Big6 #5) is necessary to provide a solution to the problem, and evaluation of product or results provides the needed grade, these steps are seldom skipped. If instructional time is short, evaluation of process is often the step in the process which is omitted. Before omitting this step, it is important to consider its potential to help students improve their problem solving skills. The importance of improving the problem solving process becomes evident when you consider:

- A particular product will normally be completed only once.
- The process will be completed every time a problem is solved.

Evaluation may be formal, such as rubrics and written reflections, or informal, such as an oral question-and-answer format. It is important to remember, regardless of the evaluation format, the problem solving process is not complete until evaluation occurs. Evaluation needs to become an automatic part of problem solving for students.

Accurate student evaluation does not simply happen. It requires practice and teacher or library media specialist guidance. Examples of student evaluations, prior to instruction and after instruction, illustrate the potential of accurate student evaluation of process (see Figure 12.1). Example 1 is typical of initial student evaluations prior to instruction and does not yield much useful knowledge. Example 2 illustrates the type of valuable student insight possible when students have been taught to be effective evaluators. The self-awareness illustrated in Example 2 has the potential of positively impacting student achievement.

Example 1: 2nd grade students with no evaluation experience.

A workbook page required 2nd grade students to answer the following three questions evaluating the work they had completed on the workbook page.

Question 1: How did you do on Step 1?
Student Response: I did fine.

Question 2: How did you do on Step 2?
Student Response: I worked hard.

Question 3: Does your answer make sense? Why?
Student Response: Because it has to make sense.

Example 2: 4th grade students with evaluation experience.

4th grade students were asked to evaluate after using Big6 to solve math word problems.

Question: Evaluate. What are your strengths and weaknesses when using the Big6 process to solve math word problems?

Student 1 Response: I am bad at synthesizing because we almost always get division and I am not good at division. I am good at identifying my task and information needed because it is on my paper (paper contains the problem).

Student 2 Response: I am good at doing what's my task and synthesize. My weakest link is evaluate and sometimes use.

Student 3 Response: My strongest piece in Big6 is #5 Solving because solving is just like a math problem and math is my strongest subject. My weakest piece in Big6 is #1.2 finding what information I need and how to word it.

Figure 12.1 Accurate Evaluation

Why Is Evaluation Important?

A college professor posed the following question to a group of students ready to embark upon their teaching careers. *Will you have 25 years of experience, or one year of experience 25 times?* One factor which allows individuals to change and broaden experience, experience 25 years versus one year 25 times, is evaluation. Another way of saying this is the idiom, *If you always do what you have always done, you will always get what you have always gotten.* Change and growth are results of evaluation. Conscious evaluation can lead to the development of focused practice designed to build upon strengths. Focused practice results in more effective and efficient learning than relying upon trial-and-error or hit-and-miss practice.

Evaluation is a learned skill and leads to more effective and efficient learning. Eisenberg (Eisenberg and Berkowitz 23) suggests that teachers and library media specialists remind students the goal in school is to do as well as possible, with as little time and effort as possible. Effective evaluation skills are key in reaching that goal as illustrated by the following examples. Students, in both instances, were guided by the teacher and library media specialist. Sharing these examples may help students understand the importance of effective evaluation.

Example One

Fifth grade students were assigned to groups and given the task of finding the name of Native American tribes, the language spoken, and type of housing for specific United States regions, such as the Southwest. Information was to be written in crayon on a U.S. map provided by the teacher. Students were given one class period to gather the information and enter it on their section of the map. At the end of the class period students were asked to evaluate: How did you do? Did you complete your task? The teacher and the library media specialist evaluated projects with *thumbs up* as all groups found at least one tribe and most found three tribes in their region. Student evaluations, however, were *thumbs down*. When asked why they felt the task was not completed, students answered they did not find *all* of the tribes and their writing on the map was messy. After a discussion, which included a review of the task and the limited time available for completion of the task, students were asked to evaluate again. This time students evaluated with a *thumbs up*.

Example Two

Fourth grade students were told that if they planned it and prepared it they could have a class luau. After discussion, students divided themselves into four teams by topic: what to eat, what to wear, what to do, and what it will look like. The class visited the library to gather information. Time was called after the teacher noticed each group had three or four ideas for their topic. Students appeared flustered. They voiced concern they had not finished using information (Big6 # 4). The teacher asked students how much time they had for their luau and how many ideas they could use during that limited time. Students grew thoughtful as the teacher asked students to evaluate if they had enough information to plan and prepare the luau. Students voiced the opinion that with three or four ideas they were ready to begin synthesis. In fact, any more time spent using information would be a waste.

Evaluation is one strategy students may use to increase achievement without investing a lot of additional time and effort. Students who evaluate before turning in assignments tend to catch silly mistakes resulting in higher achievement. Students who evaluate returned assignments and tests maximize their learning. Compare two students who take a test and get the test back after the teacher has evaluated it.

Student A looks at the letter grade and then tosses the test in the trash can. Student B looks at the test and evaluates which items were answered correctly, locates the incorrect test items and identifies the correct answer, and checks for other errors such as leaving items blank and forgetting to write name on test. Student A has learned nothing since turning in the test. Student B, on the other hand, has increased knowledge and test-taking abilities through evaluation.

Why Self-Evaluation?

Teachers spend a large portion of time evaluating students. Teacher evaluation is necessary in the school setting. When teachers evaluate:

- grades are obtained and recorded. Grades are still required in most of today's schools.
- the teacher identifies the strengths and weaknesses of the students. This information is needed to help the teacher develop activities and strategies designed to build upon strengths and strengthen weaknesses.

While teacher evaluation is helpful to students, self-evaluation may have a greater potential to impact student learning. Remember learning is not something teachers can do for students, but rather something students must do for themselves (Chapter 3). An important step toward accepting responsibility for learning occurs when students evaluate their own work. Student achievement may also be positively impacted by self-evaluation as:

Self-evaluation results in student awareness of strengths and weaknesses. Knowledge of successes and failures, or strengths and weaknesses, makes it possible to focus practice on the specific needs of the learner. Self-evaluation is preferable to teacher evaluation because:

- when teachers evaluate, students may not gather the knowledge of their own strengths and weaknesses
- teachers must focus upon an entire class while the student may focus all time and effort upon improving his or her skills
- practicing evaluation helps students develop effective evaluation skills

Self-evaluation is less threatening than teacher evaluation. To tell ourselves we are weak in a specific area is less threatening than to have another person tell us. People often become defensive when evaluated by others. Maslow's hierarchy, which identifies safety as a basic human need, explains this (Maslow 370). Our feeling of safety may be violated when others are pointing out our weaknesses. It is natural to focus upon protecting ourselves and not on improving our skills when we feel threatened.

Self-evaluation leads to more active learning. Students are actively engaged and involved in their learning when they evaluate themselves. Engagement results in a deeper understanding of what learning involves. This understanding in turn leads to students accepting more responsibility for their learning. Students who evaluate themselves tend to assume control and take responsibility for their own learning thus becoming active participants. The teacher becomes the coach, guide, facilitator, or the person the student turns to for assistance.

Sometimes teachers and library media specialists voice concern over having enough time to let students evaluate. Additional time is needed to teach students to be effective evaluators. As a vital skill for lifelong learners, however, there is a responsibility to teach this skill. On the positive side, once students become effective evaluators and take on more of the responsibility for evaluation, the teacher will save time.

Tips and Strategies to Help Students Become More Effective and Efficient Evaluators

Evaluating Product and Process

Utilize evaluation and problem solving instead of lecturing or nagging. Utilize instances when students are not good problem solvers as opportunities to practice and develop evaluation skills. Rather than getting frustrated or upset when students exhibit poor problem solving skills, require students to solve the resulting problem. Have students evaluate after the new problem has been solved. This strategy allows students to experience the consequences of poor problem solving and provides practice to improve problem solving skills. What this strategy may look like in the classroom is illustrated in the following two examples:

In this first example, students have problems with location and access (Big6 #3). At the end of class, the teacher has asked students to put worksheets in a safe place to be completed the next day. The next day several students have trouble locating their worksheets. The teacher asks students: How can you solve this problem? One student suggests the teacher provide another copy of the worksheet. The teacher points out that only one worksheet per student is available because resources are limited. Students decide if the worksheet cannot be found, they need to get a piece of notebook paper and use a classmate's worksheet as the *source* of information. When *using the information* students will need to copy both the information from the worksheet and their answer. The teacher asks students to evaluate after the assignment is completed: Did it take longer to complete the assignment if you had lost your worksheet? Some students indicated it really did not take long to write the needed information on the notebook paper. The teacher asked: Although you were able to complete the assignment quickly, could you have completed the work in less time with your worksheet? Could you have had some *free time*? What can you do next time so your paper will not be lost? The discussion helped students develop a specific plan for keeping worksheets and important papers.

The second example reflects poor task definition on the part of students. Directions on a student worksheet indicate students should write one synonym and one antonym for each word listed on the worksheet. As the teacher observes students completing the assignment, she notes many write two or three words instead of the one required. The teacher asks students to evaluate after the assignment is completed: How many words did you write? How many words were you required to write? Did it take more time to write two or three words rather than the one required? Did you spend more time than needed on this assignment? Did you spend the extra time because of poor task definition? How can you save time on assignments in the future?

In both examples the teacher required students to accept responsibility for problem solving. Poor problem solving was turned into a positive learning experience rather than a lecturing session. This strategy resulted in authentic problem solving practice. The additional time required to solve the problem and evaluate may be recouped in the future when students are able to identify their task (Big6 #1), and locate and access information (Big6 #3) as a result of this practice.

Require students to evaluate. Teachers often evaluate for students rather than insist on student evaluation. What may result is a learned helplessness. Students fail to evaluate because teachers do it for them. Students fail to recognize problems or weaknesses and are not motivated to solve the problem or strengthen their weaknesses because they do not evaluate. This would be acceptable if the teacher could solve the problem for the student. Learning, however, is something students must do for themselves. Here is an example of how learned helplessness may result, along with a suggestion to actively engage the student in evaluating:

A group of teachers are discussing a student who is experiencing some learning problems. One of the teachers comments she has noticed the student has a hard time with directions. The other teachers all agree with this evaluation. The teachers' evaluation has led to the identification of a problem solving weakness, task definition. Our student, unfortunately, is unaware he has problems with task definition because he has not evaluated. He has left that step to the teacher. At this point does he have incentive to focus on task definition (Big6 #1) and following directions? Can his achievement improve without effort on his part?

Teacher guidance at this point may be the key to improving the student's achievement. By posing questions for the student to answer, the student may be guided to successfully evaluate and identify his weakness. In this example, the questions might include: Have you thought much about directions? Do you have a hard time following directions? Why do you think that is? Do you think you would be more successful if it was easier to follow directions? Would you like me to help you with some strategies? The resulting student evaluation allows the student to recognize a problem exists, creates a desire to solve the problem, and encourages use of problem solving skills to solve the problem.

Ensure that all students are engaged and evaluating by requiring students to give immediate feedback. Ask students evaluation questions. Require students to share their evaluation or response using the pre-determined signals. Possible signals include:

- thumbs up for yes, thumbs down for no, thumbs sideways for maybe or I don't know
- the deaf symbols for yes and no
- smiley faces for yes, frowns for no

Provide consequences which encourage evaluation. Consequences help motivate. Students may be encouraged to evaluate and do so more effectively when they know there will be consequences based upon evaluation. It is important students be aware of possible consequences of evaluation, such as grade points lost or earned, prior to being asked to evaluate. Consequences for evaluating may be provided by:

Give a separate grade for student evaluation. Perhaps the assignment is worth 25 points. Add an additional 5 points for evaluation to make the paper worth 30 points. The 5 points may be determined by specific criteria, e.g. 1 point is earned for having name on paper, 1 point is earned if no answers are skipped.

Have students evaluate papers for errors immediately before turning in an assignment. If errors are found, but time is not available to correct the errors, bonus points may be given for finding them.

Deduct a predetermined number of points when students obviously fail to evaluate, e.g. no name on paper, blanks left, etc.

Have students complete a rubric or scoring guide before turning in major assignments. Give bonus points if student evaluation matches teacher evaluation.

Provide students credit for evaluating returned tests by correcting wrong answers and explaining process errors. For instance, students might earn a bonus point if they identify process errors such as failing to read a question correctly, or not communicating an answer, and then identify what they will do differently next time. Prior to the next test, ask students to list what they need to do differently to improve test scores. Credit may be given if students are able to create such a list or if the list is used.

Build credit for completing evaluation into major projects. To earn these points students might be required to:

- evaluate at specific points in the process. For instance, after completion of task definition and identification of needed information ask students to reflect upon what they did, how it worked for them, and what they might do differently next time.

- keep a log of actions taken in completing the project. After the project is complete have students evaluate steps taken, strengths and weaknesses.

- require a written evaluation of the project after it is complete. Initially the teacher or library media specialist will probably provide questions to guide students. Focus of the evaluation may be on what worked and what needs to be done differently next time.

Evaluating Product

Teachers have a great deal of experience in evaluation of result or effectiveness. The focus of Big6, however, is upon student evaluation. Some strategies which may help students successfully evaluate product include:

Require students to complete a rubric or scoring guide.

Ask students to evaluate their own work and then exchange papers with other students in the class. Students evaluate the assignment and then return it to its owner. The owner then examines his paper, noting additional corrections, additions, or deletions. Students are provided time to reflect upon their initial evaluation and any changes they need to make the next time they evaluate.

Challenge students to develop criteria for evaluation. Give an assignment. Have students, work as whole group or in small groups, and develop evaluation criteria for the assignment.

Evaluate completed assignments with the class. Remove names from completed assignments and display using a projection device such as an overhead or document camera. Ask students to evaluate the assignment. Focus the evaluation on what the student may want to do the same next time and what the student would want to do differently. This strategy works best in classrooms where a supportive environment exists and students view making errors as part of the learning process.

Utilize research buddies or peer editing. Research buddies assist each other through the process of task identification, information seeking strategies, location and access, and use. Peer editors evaluate each others work during the synthesis step and offer suggestions for improving the product. A cooperative classroom atmosphere enhances the effectiveness of both strategies.

Evaluating Process

Present evaluation as specific, concrete questions and actions. Effective evaluators know what questions to ask as they evaluate. When questions are specific and concrete, student achievement may be positively impacted. Some strategies that may be used to guide students as they begin to question and evaluate include:

Develop, through class input and teacher guidance, a list of questions students may answer to evaluate completed work. For instance: 1) Reread the original task. Did you complete the task? 2) Does your answer make sense? 3) Did you communicate your answer? 4) Can some read and understand your answer? Post the list and encourage students to answer each question before assignments are submitted. When students use this type of list they may catch many of their own mistakes and develop the habit of evaluating.

The teacher may need to pose questions as students begin to evaluate. Students, as their expertise increases, should be able to ask their own questions. Questions should be very specific, especially at the beginning stages of evaluation (see Figure 12.2). Rather than asking a general question such as: Did you look over your paper? ask specific questions such as: Do you have your name on your paper? Did you answer every question? Will someone be able to read your writing?

Ask students to identify strengths and weaknesses and likes and dislikes. One goal of evaluation is to become familiar with both our abilities and our preferences. This knowledge empowers the problem solver to take control of problem solving. It allows practice time to be spent on building strengths and strengthening weaknesses. It allows the problem solver to choose those activities which are most enjoyable. For instance, the recognition that use of information is difficult because of poor reading skills allows the learner to take control and focus on improving reading skills. A student who realizes location and access of information is enjoyable may be able to volunteer to locate information when jobs are assigned. Knowledge of likes and dislikes may be used by students to motivate themselves to become effective problem solvers: I really do not like use of information (Big6 #4), but as soon as I get this done I can synthesize (Big6 #5), which I do like. I really do not like to locate information within sources, so I am going to learn all I can about this part of the process so I can locate the information quickly and spend less time on something I do not like to do.

After completion of a project, ask students to complete a written evaluation of each of the steps in the Big6 process. After students complete the written evaluation, ask them to identify the steps which were most frustrating and those which were most fun and why. This activity may lead students to a better understanding of their abilities and preferences.

Model evaluation for students. Teachers and library media specialists spend their days evaluating. Most evaluation takes place in the form of internal, non-verbal evaluation. Thinking aloud provides students the opportunity to observe how to evaluate and the importance of evaluation. An added benefit of thinking aloud is the opportunity for students to understand why teachers and library media specialists make certain decisions.

Suggested Evaluation Questions

Questions about:
- Product or effectiveness: What was your task? Did you complete it?
- Process or efficiency: What worked well for you? What would you do differently next time?

Multiple choice questions:
How well did you do on your project?
- Great! I did my best work.
- Pretty well. I almost did my best work.
- Not very well. I could do better next time.
- I did not try and did not do my best.

Open-ended questions:
- What did you do well?
- What do you need or want to work on next time?
- I did a good job when . . .
- I could have done a better job by . . .
- What did I learn how to do that I can use again? e.g. how to use the index of a book, search the Internet.
- What would you do differently next time?

Questions designed to improve state-mandated test scores:
- Did you communicate your answer?
- Can someone read and understand your answer?

Questions identifying preferences:
- What was your favorite part of the project? What did you like best?
- What was your least favorite part of the project?
- What part was the hardest for you? Why?
- What part was the easiest for you? Why?

Questions about group interaction or cooperative learning:
- Did you work well with your partner?
- Did you share the work load evenly? How?
- Did you treat each other with respect?
- Name a contribution each member brought to the team.
- When we disagreed, we solved the problem by . . .
- What was the best part of working as a team?
- What was the hardest part of working as a team?

Questions identifying specific strengths and weaknesses:
- What did you do that really helped you in your research?
- What could you improve on the next time you do a research project?
- Which part of the process would you describe as your weakest link? Why?
- In which part of the process do you excel?

Figure 12.2 Suggested Evaluation Questions

Questions about each step in the Big6 process:

Task Definition
- Did you define your task properly?
- Did you identify all the needed information or treasure?
- Did you identify the keywords describing the information needed?
- Did you follow your guiding questions to answer the essential question?

Information Seeking Strategies
- Did you identify all the useful resources?
- Did you select the best resources to use?

Location and Access
- Did you use advanced search methods?
- Did you have trouble locating any sources?
- Did you have trouble locating the information in the sources?
- Did you skim and scan rather than read?
- Did you use text aids to locate the information faster?

Use of Information
- Did you spend enough time reading and learning material?
- Did you take good notes, extracting the important information?
- Did you use a note taking organizer?
- Did you write only phrases in your notes?
- Did your notes make sense to you?
- Did you use Trash & Treasure?
- Did you cite your sources?

Synthesis
- How well did you organize your material?
- How well did you plan your presentation?
- Did you choose the best presentation method?
- Did you put the information in your own words?
- Was your product interesting and visually appealing?
- Did your final product match your task definition?

Evaluation
- What did you do well?
- What would you want to do better next time?

Figure 12.2 Suggested Evaluation Questions

This is what it might sound like as the teacher thinks aloud or models evaluation in the classroom:

My task was to finish the math lesson before lunch. How did I do? I did not get the lesson completed. We needed about 10 minutes. Next time I think I can save time if two or three student helpers hand out papers while I answer questions.

Practice evaluation of process throughout the day. Utilize the problems students solve throughout the day, behavior and transition as well as daily lessons, to provide opportunities to practice evaluation. A few examples of what this might look like in the classroom follow:

It is time to go to art class and students have been asked to get their art boxes and line up. When students have lined up the teacher might ask: What was our task? Evaluate. How did we do? What should we do differently next time?

A student is running to get in line. Instead of directing the student to walk, the teacher or library media specialist stops the student and asks: What is your task? Evaluate. How are you doing? The student evaluates and identifies the problem. The student may then be asked if he or she can solve the problem.

At random times throughout the day, stop and ask students questions such as:

- Where are we in the problem solving process, which step are we currently completing? What is your task (Big6 #1.1)?
- What information do you need (Big6 #1.2)?
- What source are you using (Big6 #2)?
- Have you located your source (Big6 #3.1)?
- Have you located the information within the source (Big6 #3.2)?
- Are you engaged and using information (Big6 #4.1)?
- Are you extracting information (Big6 #4.2)?
- Have you solved or synthesized yet (Big6 #5)?
- Did you evaluate product (Big6 #6.1)?
- Did you evaluate process (Big6 #6.2)?"

Students may randomly be called on to answer. If the question is a yes or no variety, students may show thumbs up and thumbs down. This strategy allows students to be caught using Big6 to solve authentic problems. It provides guided practice of evaluation skills, strengthens understanding of the problem solving process, and increases familiarity of vocabulary.

Provide a scaffold to support students as they develop questioning skills. Teaching evaluation skills begins when the teacher or library media specialist asks questions and students respond. Gradually students ask their own questions. An example of what this scaffolding might look like over a period of time in a classroom is described on the following page. The students' task in this example is to evaluate work before it is submitted:

Stage One: The teacher and students work together to create a specific laundry list of questions students should answer before work is submitted to the teacher, e.g. Is your name on your paper? Is your writing legible? Did you answer all questions? Before work is submitted, the teacher or library media specialist asks students to evaluate and answer each of the questions on the laundry list.

Stage Two: Students are directed to locate their laundry list. They are reminded that before they submit their paper they need to evaluate their work based on each of the questions on the laundry list.

Stage Three: Students receive a prompt, such as: Remember to evaluate your work using your laundry list.

Stage Four: Students automatically evaluate work before turning it in.

Evaluation has the potential to positively impact student achievement. Increased content learning may result from evaluation. Evaluation is also a valuable tool for improving problem solving process skills as it actively engages students in the identification of strengths and weaknesses. It is important for students to develop and use the necessary skills to evaluate their own product and process.

Works Cited

Eisenberg, Michael. "Evaluation—Checking It All Out." *Library Media Connection* 24 (November 2005): 23.

Eisenberg, Michael and Berkowitz, Robert. *Teaching Information & Technology Skills: The Big6 in Elementary Schools.* Worthington, OH: Linworth Publishing, Company, 1999.

Maslow, A.H. "A Theory of Human Motivation," *Psychological Review,* 50, 370-396, 1943.

PART 4

The BIG 6

PLUGGING IN THE BIG6 PROBLEM SOLVING PROCESS

This section provides activities and lessons which integrate the Big6 problem solving process into existing classroom activities and content. These activities and lessons may be used "as is" or as a basis to create even more effective and efficient learning opportunities for your students. The activities and lessons are offered in recognition of the power of integrating process with content (helping students make connections), and the importance of practice or repetition in aiding learning. Integrating the Big6 problem solving into existing classroom activities enables students to improve their problem solving or information literacy skills. It also utilizes the limited amount of instructional time more effectively.

CHAPTER 13
APPLYING THE BIG6
TO RESEARCH PROBLEMS

R esearch is typically one of the first uses associated with the Big6 problem solving process. As awareness and knowledge of the Big6 process grows, users begin to realize Big6 is more than a research process. It may be used to solve many types of problems including personal problems. The Big6 problem solving process, however, remains a very effective tool for solving research problems.

How Do I Introduce the Big6 as a Research Strategy?

To introduce the Big6 process to students who have little experience in research is usually straightforward.

> The teacher or library media specialist may present the research problem to be solved and ask students: Do we need information to solve this problem? I have a plan I use anytime I need to use information. It is like a recipe. It guides me through all the steps so I can quickly and easily find the information I need and solve my problem. Would you like me to share my process or recipe with you? At this point the teacher or library media specialist may introduce the steps of Big6 and model for students what it looks like to solve a similar research problem using Big6. After modeling, the teacher or library media specialist guides students as they solve their research problem using the Big6 steps. Remember to verbalize and use the vocabulary so the process becomes concrete and familiar to students.

To introduce the Big6 to students who have prior research experience, but no Big6 experience, a slightly different approach may be taken. These students will have acquired some of the skills needed to access, evaluate, and use information. Students will be more ready to accept and learn to use the Big6 process if the teacher or library media specialist takes time to validate the skills students already possess. To begin explain the purpose of Big6 is not to replace the knowledge students already have about solving information problems. The purpose of Big6 is to first plug the research skills previously mastered into an organized process and then to fill in any existing gaps in the process (see Figures 13.1 and 13.2). The examples in both figures are designed to use with students who have previous research experience as they validate students' prior knowledge, introduce the Big6 process, and help plug existing skills into the

---

Pose a research problem students might be expected to solve.
- For instance, write a three-page report about one explorer to the New World.

Ask students to think about how they would solve this problem.
- What will you do? Write down the steps you would take to solve this problem.

Introduce the idea of a problem solving process or strategy.
- Did you know others have done what I just asked you to do? They have written the steps needed to solve problems like this.
- Most of the steps these people have identified are similar. That really is not too surprising, since the steps are being used to solve the same type of problem.
- The vocabulary or terminology used to describe the steps is different. That is not too surprising either, since there are lots of words that mean the same thing.
- The process that is my favorite is called Big6. Can you guess how many steps it has?
- I like it because of the vocabulary. It is rather generic vocabulary and so I can use it for research, to solve math word problems, conduct science experiments, write social studies reports, and even to solve personal problems.

Share the six steps and have students compare to their process.
- Name the six steps of Big6.
- Ask students to compare how many of their steps match the Big6 steps.
- Discuss what each step looks like when solving the problem you posed to students.

Discuss results of comparison.
- Ask students to count how many of their steps matched the Big6 steps.
- Have students share by holding up one finger for each step in Big6 which matched their process.
- Go through each of the six steps asking students to raise their hand if they had identified that step.
- Or randomly call on students to identify which of the Big6 steps they had written down. For instance, a student might report "Two of my steps were the same as Big6. I wrote I would decide what information I needed for my report (Task Definition) and what source I would use to find that information (Information Seeking Strategies)."

Discuss potential of Big6 to guide problem solving.
- Do you already use some of the steps in Big6? Do you use all of the steps?
- Do the steps seem logical to you?
- Do you think it would be helpful to use the Big6 steps to guide you through the process of completing research? Why?
- Reiterate that Big6 can fill in any gaps they may have in their research process.
- Big6 can help you proceed step-by-step through the process so steps are not skipped or left out.

Figure 13.1 Compare Student Research Process with Big6 Process

Comparison of Faulty Research Process with Big6 Process

Ask participants to think back to reports or research completed in the past.

Share your own previous research experience:

- When I think back to college and the research completed, papers written, I have really negative memories. I really struggled with the research process.
- I would like to share with you the way I tackled research or the way not to research. As I share my research process, I want you to reflect on your own research process and if you did what I did just blurt out, "I did that!"
- I doubt if any of you will be able to say, "I did that!" to every step. I hope you were not as ineffective as I was. Here goes . . .
- I used to go to the library and find as many sources as I could possibly find, some were just sort of about my topic. There was not as much information available then as there is today.
- I never read all the sources because by the time I found them I had run out of time.
- I did take notes, but I wrote some of the notes in complete sentences and some in phrases. I put all the notes from one source on one piece of paper. I wrote on every line, scribbled out, and wrote up and around and into the margins.
- When I got ready to write my paper, I would remember a note I had taken, or information I needed. But I would spend what felt like hours trying to find that one piece of information again.
- I would write my 20-page paper and then go back and create an outline. The only reason I bothered with an outline was because it was required and I lost points if I did not have one!
- When I created the bibliography, I would almost always have to go back to the library one more time because I had failed to get the name of a publisher or a page number, or some piece of information needed for the reference.

Identify the Big6 steps as you model what your research would have looked like with Big6:

- That is how I used to do research before I learned Big6. It wasn't very efficient or effective was it?
- I would like to walk you through what that research would have looked like if I had used Big6 then as I do today.

Task Definition (Big6 #1)

- I start by identifying my task and the information needed or the questions I need to answer. These questions are my outline!

Information Seeking Strategies (Big6 #2)

- I identify the best sources, rather than using every source I can find.

Location and Access (Big6 #3)

- I scan and skim to find my keywords using text aids.

Use of Information (Big6 #4)

- I write one question at the top each sheet of note taking paper. As I begin reading or

Figure 13.2 Compare of Faulty Research Process with Big6 Process

using information I record the needed information or answer to my question on the appropriate sheet. I bullet each fact and leave space before and after it. I write only phrases and not complete sentences.

- ■ I use a separate sheet to write down complete bibliographic information from a source before I begin taking notes. I number each source on this list. On my questions pages I write the number of the source used.

Synthesis (Big6 #5)

- ■ When it is time to write my report, I layout each separate sheet in the order I want to include it in my report. I cut apart each bulleted fact on each page. Put the facts in order and then tape them back together. When I begin writing my rough draft all I have to do is follow the order I have created and write the phrases in complete sentences.

Evaluate (Big6 #6)

- ■ Before turning in my paper I evaluate by:
  - ■ Rereading my task and making sure I have completed the task.
  - ■ Examining my paper to make sure it can be read and understood. Appropriate labels, spacing, etc.
  - ■ Rereading my paper to make sure it communicates what I want to communicate.

Ask students to compare and evaluate how you used to do research with research using Big6.

- • By the time you have finished solving the problem using Big6, it will be obvious to a majority of your students how much simpler research is using Big6.

Note: Preparing and using visuals which illustrate each of the steps talked about in both processes may help students better visualize the processes. For instance a visual of every book you can find as compared to one with only three or four books, notes which are written in complete sentences and extremely sloppy as compared to notes with questions at the top of the page, bullets, and phrases rather than complete sentences.

Figure 13.2 Compare of Faulty Research Process with Big6 Process

process. If students have received little, if any, previous instruction in the research process, the example in Figure 13.2 may be especially effective.

What Might Big6 Research Look Like with Primary Students?

Primary students can do research. These students will, however, need more support because of shorter attention spans and limited use skills (Big6 #4), such as reading; and synthesis skills, such as writing.

Research Topics

A simple, yet effective, method of introducing younger students to research and the Big6 process is to use questions which crop up during class discussions. The teacher or library media specialist may utilize such questions to model the use of Big6 to find the answer or solve the problem (see Lesson Plan 13.1).

Authors, whose books the class has read, are also a good topic to use as you model and guide younger students in the use of the Big6 problem solving process. The resulting research project could be a single session studying one author or a series of sessions in which several authors are studied. This type of research may promote understanding of the Big6 process and build student enthusiasm for reading and writing as students become familiar with the authors of some of their favorite books (see Lesson Plan 13.2).

Use of Mnemonics

Students in the early grades, with guidance, may also complete more traditional research projects using Big6. The use of a mnemonic, such as www.use, works well to help younger students remember the steps of the problem solving process.

What is my task? Task Definition
What source can I use? Information Seeking Strategy
Where can I find the information? Location and Access:
Use of Information
Synthesis
Evaluation

Sample Research Project

One example of what a research project for primary students might look like is given in Lesson Plan 13.3. The content used in the sample research project is animal classification. It is important, when research projects are designed, to utilize the content students in that particular grade are required to study. In this way the instructional time required for completion of the project will meet a variety of learning goals, e.g. content, problem solving or information literacy, reading, writing, etc. To adapt the sample lesson plan for different content, keep the Big6 framework and substitute the desired content where the animal content appears. Other research projects for primary grades may be found in Chapter 18, *Science and the Big6*, and Chapter 19, *Social Studies and the Big6*.

LESSON PLAN 13.1

LESSON TITLE: ANSWERING A SIMPLE RESEARCH QUESTION

Grade Level: K-2nd	**Time Frame:** ■ One 30-minute session
Content Objective: ■ The topic of the question being asked	**Information Literacy Objective/Big6 Objective:** ■ Modeling the 6 steps of Big6

Materials and Sources:
- Student-generated content question
- Source of information about that content
- If available a projection device

PLAN

Problem:
- As content is studied in the classroom, students typically have questions. These questions are used in this lesson to model using the six steps of problem solving to find the answer. The teacher or library media specialist simply solves the problem. He or she thinks aloud through the process as the answer is found or the problem solved.

Task Definition (What):
- Identify the question for the class. Student questions I solved include: How old was Martin Luther King when he died? How do penguins get from their bellies to their feet on ice? How big is the earth? What are the Christmas customs of people in Antarctica?
- Identify the keywords, or important words, which will help find the answer.

Information Seeking Strategies (What):
- Brainstorm for students possible sources, such as books or the Internet. Choose one and tell students why that source was chosen. Verbalize for students that *prior knowledge* must also be used.

Location and Access (Where):
- Think aloud as the source is located: I am going to the Reference Collection because that is where encyclopedias are kept.
- Think aloud as you identify how the source is arranged and whether guide words and/or the index/menu will be used to locate information.
- Think aloud as you scan or skim for the keywords. Identify the text aids, such as headings or bold words, you use to locate the information within the text.

Use of Information:

- Ask students to help use the information. Repeat the question for students. Ask them to raise their hand when they hear the needed information or treasure.
- Begin reading the previously located information. Mention reading or listening are the only possible ways to get the information into the brain.
- Think aloud as information is extracted from the text and from prior knowledge to answer the question.

Synthesis:

- Tell students the answer or write it on the board or note taking form.

Evaluation:

Have students help you with an oral evaluation. Ask:

- Product: Did we solve our problem or find our answer?
- Process: Did the process I used help me find the answer? How many things did I do at one time? That is right, only one. Did I read when I was locating information or did I scan and skim? Was there a time when I had to read to solve the problem? Do you think this process will help me the next time I need to answer a question? Would this process work if I used the teacher, or parent, as a source?

Note: How do penguins get from their bellies to their feet on the slick ice? While students watched and listened, I unsuccessfully tried to locate the information needed to answer this question within the library and then on the Internet. Finally, a Web site with an "Ask the Expert" feature was located. Students, with my assistance, composed and sent an e-mail to the expert asking the question. The next time the class visited the library, the expert's reply was shared with students, providing the answer to the question. For the curious: It seems the penguin plants his beak in the ice and then uses his feet to walk towards his beak until he can reach a standing position. Many thanks to the expert!

LESSON PLAN 13.2

LESSON TITLE: AUTHOR STUDY

Grade Level: K–2nd	**Time Frame:** ■ One 30-minute session

Content Objective: Communication Arts: ■ Authors and genre	■ Book selection ■ Writing	**Information Literacy Objective/Big6 Objective:** ■ Modeling the 6 steps of Big6

Materials and Sources:

- Names of authors to be studied
- Books by the authors and their location in the library

- Internet with projector
- Portions of this lesson must be completed in the library

PLAN

Problem:

- Students read many stories in the classroom. The authors of these stories provide an authentic and engaging topic for research conducted by either the teacher or the library media specialist. As students learn about the authors they become real people for the students. A few favorite authors of students at this age include Jan Brett, Audrey Wood, and Eric Carle.

Task Definition (What):

- I understand that you just read, *(title of book)* by *(author)* in the classroom. Evaluate, did you like that story? *Thumbs up/thumbs down.* Would you like to read other books by this author? Would you like me to show you where you can find these books in the library? Would you like to know more about the author? *Most kindergarten and 1st grade students will be excited.*

Information Seeking Strategies (What):

- I will be your source to find where the author's books are in the library. But what source do you think we could use to find out more about the author? *Students normally identify the Internet as a good source.*

Location and Access (Where):

- Hold up one book by the author. Ask: In which collection do you think we will find this book? *Easy or Everybody collection because it is a picture book.*
- Ask a student to lead you to that collection in the library. Then ask: On what shelf do you think we will find this book? There are lots of shelves and I really do not want to have to look on all of them to find this book.
- What do we need to know to identify what shelf? *The author's last name.* Tell students the author's last name and then again ask: Which shelf? After students identify the shelf (A, C, B, etc.) lead the group to that shelf.
- Ask students to sit around the area. Pull the books found on the shelf by that author and hold up one at a time. Ask students to raise their hand if they have read this book. You might ask students: Do you think these people who have already read the book will be a good source to help me decide if I want to read the book?

Evaluation:

- Evaluate Product: Our task was to locate other books by our author. Have we done that? *Thumbs up/thumbs down.* Our second task was to find out more about the author; have we done that? *Thumbs up/thumbs down.*

Information Seeking Strategy (What):

- Ask students: What source were we going to use? *Internet*

Location and Access (Where):

- Ask one student to lead the group to the site of Internet access. Students follow and take seat in that area.
- Model and think aloud as the favorite author is located on the Internet.
Note: I created a Web page as part of the library Web page with links to various authors' Web pages. Authors' names were listed in alphabetic order by last name. Students were asked to scan and raise their hand when the first letter of the author's last name was found. After the first or second time, even kindergartners were able to look at the Web page menu or index and identify where to click to obtain the information.
- Model skimming text features (bold, menu choices, headings, etc.) to find information about the author. Read some of the menu choices on the author's Web site to students and ask them to identify what part of the Web site they would like to visit.
Note: Students typically like to see pictures of the author, know where they live, and to read anything the author had written about himself or herself or about writing.

Use of Information:

- Discuss graphics and text found and share with students.
Note: In one class students were discussing where they could get ideas for their writing. Whenever an author was studied, the class would search to see if the author had included any information about where he or she got ideas for writing. Almost every author did. This information was recorded on a two-column chart, e.g. Author/Where I Get My Ideas. The chart was shared with the classroom teacher who used it in writing instruction.

Synthesis:

- When the teacher arrived in the library to pick up the class, students were randomly called on to tell: a) which author was studied, b) where books by the author were found, and c) one or two interesting facts about the author.
- Students found and checked out books by these familiar authors during regular visits to the library to check out books.

Evaluation:

Ask students to do a thumbs up/thumbs down:

- Product: Did we find other books by the author? Will you be able to find them when you return to the library? Did we find out more about our author? Tell me something you learned.
- Process: Did it help to identify our task or to know what we were going to do? Did our source work, e.g. going to the shelves, using the Internet? Could you find the author Web site again? Could you find another author on our Web link? Did we read all the text on the Web page? Was it faster to skim than read everything? Did we find the information we wanted that way?

From *Teaching Elementary Information Literacy Skills with the Big6™* by **Joyce Needham**. Columbus, OH: Linworth Publishing, Inc. Copyright © 2009.

LESSON PLAN 13.3

LESSON TITLE: CLASSIFICATION OF ANIMALS

Grade Level: 1st-3rd	Time Frame:
	■ About 12 30-minute sessions if all work is completed at school

Content Objective:	Information Literacy Objective
■ Science: Animal classes: birds, fish, reptiles, amphibians, mammals	■ Practice using the steps in the problem solving process
	■ Use of information: note taking

Materials and Sources:

■ Nonfiction books, one for each of the above animal classes

■ Chart paper for KW (what we know and what we want to know)—one sheet for each classification

■ File folders and book pockets or envelopes

■ Paper for completing report

■ Cards for note taking

PLAN

Problem:

■ Ask students: Raise your hand if you like animals. What if I told you our next science topic is animals? Are you excited? What if I told you that instead of listening to me, you were going to be able to use books from the library to find out about animals? That you were going to be able to write a report . . . just like the 4th and 5th graders?

■ Introduce the idea of a problem solving process: If I asked you to bake a cake, would it help you if I gave you a recipe as well as the ingredients? Well, I have a recipe for solving problems or research. There are six steps in my process and so it is called Big6.

Task Definition (What):

■ Ask: How many steps are there? The first step is called task definition. Write on chart, #1 What is my task? What do I need to know?

■ We humans like to classify things or label things. It makes it easier to understand and think about that way. For instance, we label or classify colors: red, green, yellow, blue, etc. We label or classify students: 1st grade, 3rd grade, kindergarten, etc.

■ Did you know we classify animals? One way we label or classify animals is based on whether they have a backbone. If they have a backbone they are called . . . Get ready for this . . . This is a really big word . . . I am not sure 1st graders are ready for it . . . vertebrates. If an animal has a backbone, it called a vertebrate. There are five different types of animals that are vertebrates. They are . . . I bet you will know these . . . Fish, Mammals, Birds, Amphibians, and Reptiles.

■ Our task is to write a report about each one of these classes of animals. You will be working with a group. I get to decide who is in your group. I will tell you who you are working with later. How many reports do we need? *Five.* So how many groups will we need? *Five.* Very good.

■ Randomly call on five different students to write one of the classes to be studied on the chart paper under #1.

- Create a KW, or what we know and what we want to know, chart. Ask: Do you already know something about these classes? Give each group one piece of chart paper with one class of animal written on the top. Each group also needs one crayon that is a different color. Ask each group to write what they know and what they want to know on the chart. Rotate papers so each group has a different chart. With the same crayon used before, have students write what they know or what they want to know about this class of animal. Repeat until each group has had an opportunity to write on each of the five classes.

- Post these KW charts. Let students use the charts to develop a class list of four questions to be answered with student research. Possible questions might be: Where they live, their covering, what they eat, and fun facts. These questions identify what information is needed.

- Divide the class into five groups. Each group may draw to determine the class of animal they will be researching. Teacher grouping allows for students with varying abilities to be placed together so all students experience success.

Information Seeking Strategies (What):
- On chart write, #2 What sources can I use? Have students brainstorm possible sources. Let each student who has an idea come up and add it to the chart.
- Discuss pros and cons of each source. Discussion might include: it is too hard to read, we do not have access, it has pictures, it is easy to read, etc.
- Select the best source. Guide students to select nonfiction books because they are accessible, accurate, and available.
- Students might also be encouraged to search for sources at home with the help of Mom and Dad.

Location and Access (Where):
- On chart write, #3 Where can I find the information?
- Hand each group a book about their class of animal. Ask: Have you located the source of your information?
- Ask students how they can find the information within the book. Guide students in understanding that every word in the book does not need to be read to locate the information. Model skimming or scanning for keywords, such as: eat, dine, covering, skin, fur, feathers, places like desert, forest. Also model using text aids to locate keywords.
- Refer students back to the questions they are trying to answer and give students time to find answers to their questions. Students may put a sticky note on the page where important information is found.

Use of Information:
- On the chart, write #4 Use It! Read and pull the important information.
- Give each team a blank file folder with either four envelopes or four book pockets.
- Each team should create their note taking organizer. In the center of the file folder draw a circle and write the animal classification, e.g. mammal, fish, etc. Then glue the envelopes or book pockets, one in each corner. On each book pocket/envelope write one of the four questions. Draw a line from the center circle to the book pocket/envelopes. Draw a rectangle to record source. See sample on next page.

Chapter 13: Applying the Big6 to Research Problems 155

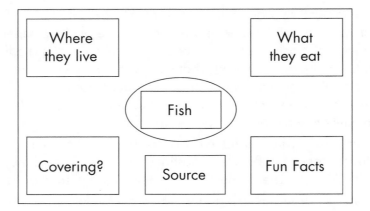

- Share process of using information with students: To use the information we need to get it into our brain. What is the only way to get text into our brain? *Read.* After you read, you need to pull or extract the important information. Remember, what is important is what answers our four questions. The important information will only be phrases, not complete sentences. You may want to highlight or underline the information as you find it. You will copy important information on the index cards and place each card in the appropriate pocket.

- Model using information: reading, underlining or highlighting, copying onto cards. Also model recording the source of the information: title and page number. Make sure students understand when copying they should copy every letter of the word so it will be spelled correctly (see Chapter 14).

- Ask students: How will you know when you have all the information you need? *There will be at least one card in each envelope/book pocket.*

Synthesis:

- On chart, write #5 Synthesis. Make It!

- This is another big word, but it just means complete the task or solve the problem. We have all the information now, but is it ready to be shared with others?

- What if I took my notes and wrote them in complete sentences? Would other students be able to read and know what I learned? Could Mr./Miss (principal) know what we learned? What if we put a picture of our animal at the top of the page? Would that make it even better?

- What we need to do then is synthesize or make our report. Remind students of the writing process, i.e. rough draft first, then revise, then edit, and finally publish on final paper.

- Have each group decide who will draw the picture.

- *Note:* Students should write rough draft using only notes as the source.

Evaluation:

- Have each group complete a written evaluation form which asks questions that evaluate both product and process. Use of faces, smiling or frowning, works well with younger students.

- Questions to be included on the evaluation could include:
    - Product: What did you learn? List facts or information.
    - Process: How did we do on our project? What did we do well this time? What could we do better next time? What did we like best about doing this project? Did Big6, our recipe, help us?

What Might Big6 Research Look Like with Intermediate Students?

Modeling and Guiding

A good place to start is to introduce students to all six steps of the Big6 problem solving process. Guide students through the six steps of the process as they attempt their first research project. Once students become familiar with the process, they should be expected to independently follow the six steps.

All the major skills students need to effectively and efficiently research may be included within the context of Big6. A useful strategy, in addition to utilizing each of the six steps, is to identify one or two of the Little 12 skills which are especially important to a particular research problem. Instruction would target these identified skills. For instance, the teacher or library media specialist may wish to focus on what information is needed (Big6 #1.2) and extracting information (Big6 #4.2) to help students focus on note taking skills. With another project the focus may be on location and access (Big6 #3). Students would focus on quickly and efficiently locating information by improving scanning and skimming skills and use of text features. Students may be more successful in understanding when and how to use the skills when taught within the framework of the Big6.

Incorporating Choice

Research on learning (Chapter 3) verifies choice can be a key component to engage students. The ability to make good choices is hindered when students have limited prior knowledge. For this reason it is suggested students initially be given limited choices. To begin, limit students' choice to only one or two steps in the research process, e.g. choice of form synthesis takes or choice of sources to be used. Limited choice within that step is also suggested the first time students are allowed choice. For instance, rather than making the form of synthesis an open ended choice, give students three or four choices of acceptable forms. Creation of a class generated list of possible choices is a strategy which allows students more involvement while still providing teacher guidance. Students may then choose from the generated list rather than being told by the teacher they must write a paper. Many opportunities for student choice exist within research projects (see Figure 13.3).

Task Definition:
- Choice of topic
- Choice of questions or information included in the report

Use of Information:
- Choice of which source to use

Synthesis:
- Choice of form for presentation of the information

Evaluation:
- Class-generated rubric. Let students, as a class, determine the requirements of the project.

Figure 13.3 Opportunities for Choice

Sample Research Project

What might a research project for the intermediate grades look like? Lesson Plan 13.4 provides one sample of an intermediate research project. Additional research projects are presented in Chapters 18, *Science and Big6*, and Chapter 19, *Social Studies and Big6*. It is important when research projects are designed to utilize the content which students in that particular grade are required to study. In this way, the instructional time required for completion of the project will be meeting a variety of learning goals, e.g. content, information literacy, reading, writing, etc. To adapt the sample lesson plan for different content, keep the Big6 framework and substitute the desired content where the Civil War content appears.

Tips and Strategies to Strengthen Students' Research Skills

Demand students focus on one step of the process at a time. Research is a process like tying a shoe or riding a bike. Processes involve more than one step to complete. Students are encouraged to focus on mastery of each step when the process is broken into component pieces.

A more thorough understanding of the process occurs when students focus on each individual step. Students may still have a tendency to multi-task and focus upon finishing the process rather than upon mastering each step. You may motivate students if you explain how mastery of each step leads to mastery of the entire process, which leads to solving problems in an easier and faster manner. Another strategy which may encourage students to focus on individual steps is to include in the final project grade credit for completion of each step. For instance, the final grade may include credit for identifying the questions (Big6 #1.2), listing possible sources (Big6 #2.1), taking notes with phrases only (Big6 #4.2), and completing an evaluation (Big6 #6) as well as for synthesis (Big6 #5).

Guide students in developing questioning skills. Questioning is an important skill for problem solvers to develop. Guided practice and repetition, as with other skills, are valuable tools to assist in the development of questioning skills. Provide students the opportunity to construct and evaluate questions during task definition. It is important for students to realize the questions written may serve as a guide for the research to be completed. It is possible that, as students use information (Big6 #4), additional questions will be generated. It is also possible that students will be unable to locate (Big6 #3) answers to all of the initial questions. Students should know it is acceptable to add and delete questions from the research unless the teacher says otherwise. Remember Big6 is not linear. It is not unusual to work through the process and arrive at use of information (Big6 #4) only to evaluate (Big6 #6) and need to revisit task definition (Big6 #1).

Develop ability to write and identify questions at various levels of learning. Provide students a research or study topic. Ask students to write questions they want answered on the topic. Questions should be written on sticky notes, one question per note. Post chart paper at the front of the room with the various levels of questions the teacher desires to be included, e.g. knowledge level questions only, evaluation level questions only, a combination of levels (Bloom 201-207). Discuss the levels of questions and the type of questions which would fit within each level. Ask students to attach their sticky note questions on the appropriate chart. After all questions are attached, have students evaluate, e.g. are there questions at each level, are additional questions needed at any level, are there are too many questions at a particular level? Develop a class set of questions from the charts.

LESSON PLAN 13.4

LESSON TITLE: CIVIL WAR STUDY

Grade Level: 4th and 5th	Time Frame:
	■ About 12 sessions with all work completed at school

Content Objective:	Information Literacy Objective/Big6 Objective:
■ Civil War	■ Practice use of the steps in the problem solving process.
	■ Evaluation: Accurate student evaluation

Materials and Sources:
- ■ Nonfiction books on civil war
- ■ Civil War Web sites
- ■ Encyclopedias
- ■ Note taking organizer

PLAN

Problem:

- ■ Did you know in our country we once had a war where people in one state fought people in another state? Actually people from the same state fought each other. Some brothers fought each other. That is right. It was called the Civil War. Would you like to know more about the war?

- ■ Instead of my telling you all about the war, would you rather learn about the war on your own and share what you learn with the class?

Task Definition (What):

- ■ What is our task? *To learn about the Civil War and share this information with our class.*

- ■ What information do you think we need to find or research? What questions do you have? Students brainstorm and create a class list of questions. The teacher may guide and direct students in developing relevant and reasonable questions. If there are specific content or curriculum requirements, make sure those are included.

- ■ We have a list of 15 questions. If you notice, I have highlighted five questions. These five questions are ones the state or school district requires you to be able to answer. Everyone must include answers to those in your project. You may pick and choose from the other questions. Require students answer a specific number of questions in their research.

- ■ Questions generated may include: What were the political, social, and economic causes of the war? How were soldiers drafted? What weapons were used? How was the country divided? How did our state fight? When did the war begin and end? Who were the key leaders on both sides? How did the war affect the country? Casualties—how many people died? What changes took place in our state because of the war? What ended the war? How were minorities treated?

- ■ You need to decide how you will share your information with the class. What are some formats that might work? Brainstorm a list of possible ways to synthesize. Mark out any that students may not use. Keep this chart posted for students to refer to it.

Information Seeking Strategies (What):

- Obviously we are going to need information from sources other than our prior knowledge. What are some sources which might be helpful? Brainstorm a list with students. Discuss pros and cons and mark off any sources not considered appropriate.

- Allow students to choose which sources to use. Requiring a specified number of sources is sometimes desirable.

Location and Access (Where):

- Visit the library and have students locate all possible sources.

- Remind students that to locate the information within the source they need to skim and scan to find keywords using text features.

- Revisit questions (task definition) and develop class list of keywords that may be helpful.

- Model scanning, skimming, and reading. Have students identify which is best strategy to locate information. *Scanning and skimming.*

- As you model point out text features that will be helpful—guide words if book is arranged alphabetically, index if arranged in another manner, or menu if using Web site.

Use of Information:

- Provide students with a note taking organizer, such as folded data chart with columns for questions and answers, individual sheets of paper with one question written at the top, note cards, file folder with envelope for each question, etc. (see Chapter 14).

- Remind students of the process of using information: First you must get the information into your brain or engage. What will that look like? *Reading.* Next you must pull or extract the important or needed information. Where will you record this important information? *Note taking organizer.* What will it look like on the organizer? *Phrases and source cited.*

- Students begin the process of locating information and using information.

- Conduct mini lessons, or short lessons addressing specific weaknesses observed as students are using information, as needed. For instance, if several students are having difficulty finding the answer to one question, teach a lesson sharing where to find the information or addressing the answer to the question. If students are having difficulty extracting information or taking notes, conduct a short lesson.

Note: Students in Jeannie Ratcliff's class (Springfield Public Schools elementary teacher) selected a research buddy. Each buddy was responsible for his or her own project. If either buddy had a question about the process or product, he or she would consult with his buddy before approaching Mrs. Ratcliff for assistance. Often students were able to solve their own problems. Buddies also looked out for each other. If in the process of researching they found information their buddy needed, they shared that information.

Synthesis:

- Ask students to refer back to list of possible formats for synthesis. Students may be allowed to choose any format from the list or be given three or four choices from those on the list.

- Students create projects using the selected format and present to the class.

Note: Projects created in one 4th/5th grade class included: traditional written reports, dioramas, brochures, tri-fold displays, posters, oral reports, booklets, and journals.

Evaluation:

- Product:

  - Develop a rubric to evaluate product. Teacher may create or it may be created with student input.

  - Have students' complete rubric and submit with project. You might choose to give bonus points if the student does an accurate job of evaluating the project.

  - A rubric for this project might include: creativity/originality, required questions answered, other questions answered, accurate information, clear and focused, presenter is prepared, sources included.

- Process:

  - Have students complete and submit with the project a written evaluation of the process.

  - Questions might include: Which of the Big6 steps was easiest for you? Which was the hardest? What did you like best about doing this project? What did you learn that will help you the next time you complete research?

From *Teaching Elementary Information Literacy Skills with the Big6™* by **Joyce Needham**. Columbus, OH: Linworth Publishing, Inc. Copyright © 2009.

Provide opportunities to generate and organize questions. Give students a research topic. Have each student write at least three questions they think should be answered with the research. Write one question per sticky note. Randomly call on individual students to read a question. Ask the class to identify the category that the question fits within. For instance, if the topic is famous Americans, the categories might include personal life and accomplishments. Post chart paper. As categories are suggested, write the category on the chart paper and have students place all their questions which fit within that category on the paper. Continue randomly calling on students until all student questions are placed on the chart paper. Guide students in evaluation by asking: Is there any other information we would want to include? Do we have categories which are logical? At this point the teacher may guide students to ensure all required content will be included in the questions. The identified questions may also be used to discuss what type of information is needed and what sources might provide the needed information. Remind students prior knowledge may also be needed, especially with higher level questions.

Provide instruction and practice locating and accessing information. When locating information within text it is necessary to scan or skim for keywords using the available text features. This is a very concrete process, yet for many students and adults these skills remain rather vague or shadowy. Instruction (see Chapter 9) may make these skills concrete, visible, and doable for the student.

Require student evaluation, not just teacher evaluation. Students need to evaluate their own work in order to know how to improve. The ability to evaluate product empowers students to understand what a quality product looks like. Ask students to identify how they will know they have a good product. Use this student input and have the class develop a rubric to be used to evaluate the product. Ability to evaluate process leads to improved problem solving skills. Students who take time to reflect upon their process skills may be empowered to work smarter and not harder.

Research and Big6 go together like soup and sandwich or a horse and carriage. They complement each other. By utilizing the Big6 process to complete research, students are provided an opportunity to learn:

- content such as science or social studies
- information literacy or problem solving skills
- the communication arts skills: reading, listening, speaking, and writing

While research may require a significant amount of time, the power of learning in this manner, coupled with the number of learning objectives addressed and the motivational possibilities, make it a powerful learning activity.

Works Cited

Bloom, Benjamin S. *Taxonomy of Educational Objectives, Handbook One.* New York: Allyn & Bacon, 1984.

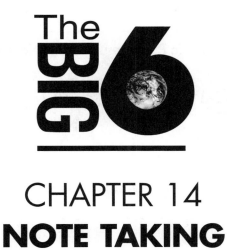

The BIG6

CHAPTER 14
NOTE TAKING

- After five days of lecture over Colonial America, students complete a test.

- Using at least three references, students write a three-page paper comparing two explorers of the New World.

- Yesterday students were asked to read about volcanoes in their science book, today they have a pop quiz over volcanoes.

What is the connection between these three assignments? Each relies upon successful note taking skills. Note taking is the ability to gather information, from a variety of sources, and store it in such a way it may be used later. It is also a skill which may be taught within the framework of Big6.

What Is Note Taking

Within the Big6 problem solving process, note taking is completed when using the information (Big6 #4). More specifically, note taking engages the brain to access information and then extract or gather the important information: information about Colonial America, information about two explorers of the New World, or information about volcanoes. While what is important changes from problem to problem, it can always be identified by the task (Big6 #1). The process of extracting or gathering information may be referred to as note taking when the problem solver records the information found. Note taking frequently involves the need to summarize information. Marzano refers to note taking and summarizing as "two of the most useful academic skills students can have" (Marzano 29).

Note taking involves accessing information by reading or listening, then extracting the important information, and finally recording it (see Figure 14.1).

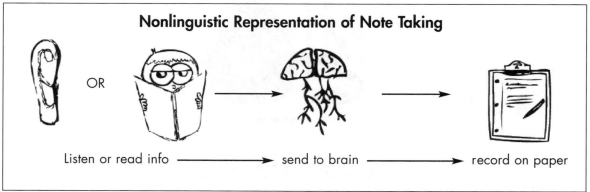

Nonlinguistic Representation of Note Taking

OR

Listen or read info ⟶ send to brain ⟶ record on paper

* *Clipart used with permission of Izuno Design*

Figure 14.1 Nonlinguistic Representation of Note Taking

During the note taking process, the information must pass from the source, either text or oral, to the brain and then to the notes. Students often try to shortcut the process by going directly from the source to the notes. An indication information is not being filtered through the brain is notes which are written in complete sentences or copied directly from the source. Successful note taking requires information to be transferred from the source to the brain and then to notes.

It is important to distinguish that note taking is using information (Big6 #4) not synthesizing (Big6 #5). Note taking in and of itself does not solve the problem; however, it does make it possible to solve the problem or synthesize (Big6 #5). Direct instruction may help students master the challenging process of transferring information to and from the brain.

Note taking skills are required for two of the most common problems students are asked to solve: taking tests and completing research. Sometimes students are asked to take notes from teacher lecture or class discussion. At other times students are expected to take notes from textbooks and reference sources. The note taking process is the same whether notes are taken from an oral or a print source. The only difference is in what source is being used (Big6 #2).

Why Is Note Taking Instruction Important?

Use of information is perhaps the most difficult step in problem solving. Nevertheless, it may have the greatest impact upon thinking and learning. Students who master note taking improve their ability to access and extract information thus being more successful users of information.

Effective note taking may make learning faster and easier. Students are able to engage their minds to access information and extract the important information when they master note taking skills. Taking good notes enables students to study notes rather than reread hundreds of pages in preparation for tests. It empowers the student to produce a quality research product with minimum effort. Good notes speed up the organization and sharing of information (Big6 #5).

At some point students must think, or engage, and extract the important information. Separating use (Big6 #4) from locating the information (Big6 #3) and synthesizing (Big6 #5) simplifies the problem solving. It allows the problem solver to focus on one step at a time.

Taking good notes does not just happen, it requires specific skills. For many students these skills are unclear. It is an indication students are not comprehending note taking skills when they are observed:

- attempting to reread entire chapters the night before a test instead of studying a few pages of notes
- copying complete sentences from the source and then rereading these entire sentences to synthesize when completing research

Tips and Strategies for Teaching Successful Note Taking

Note taking skills can be broken into three parts:

- accessing information from print or oral sources
- identifying and extracting important information
- recording the important information

Specific tips and strategies for each of the specific skills follow:

Accessing Information from Print and Oral Sources

Reading and listening skills are key to successful note taking. The problem solver must read to access information from print sources. The problem solver must listen to access information from oral sources. Instruction designed to improve reading and listening skills is essential. It is also crucial students understand why these skills are important, i.e. without reading and listening, it is not possible to access the information.

Identifying and Extracting Important Information

The second step of note taking is to identify and extract the important information. This is not an easy task. It requires students to focus only on the important information, know what information is important, and identify the important information. A better understanding of what each step looks like, along with possible strategies, may allow the teacher or library media specialist to guide students more successfully.

Focus only on the important information. Students often attempt to extract all or most of the information presented. At other times students are sidetracked by interesting information which is not important for the defined task. Students need to be like those who sign for the hearing impaired, signing or recording only the words necessary to communicate the important information. Successful note taking requires concentration on the important information only.

Know what information is important or the treasure. The task determines what information is important. The problem solver, therefore, needs to have the task clearly in mind before starting to extract information. To identify what is important is difficult for elementary students as they have limited prior knowledge. Especially during the elementary years, the teacher or library media specialist should assume responsibility for presenting the problem in a manner which promotes student recognition of the important information. The task, as illustrated in Figure 14.2, has great impact upon what information is important. Extract information using the three scenarios to experience the impact of the task.

ARTICLE

The Wilson's Creek Battle took place just outside of Springfield, Missouri, on August 10, 1861, a mere four months after the firing on Fort Sumter and the beginning of the Civil War. It was the first major battle west of the Mississippi River.

Union troops, under the leadership of Brigadier General Nathaniel Lyon, were camped at Springfield, Missouri. Southern troops, under the command of Brigadier General Ben McCulloch, approached.

The Union forces struck first attacking the Confederate Calvary at about 5:00 a.m. The Confederates attacked the Union line three times during the day withdrawing after the third attack at about 11:00 a.m. Lyon was killed during the battle. The Union soldiers, exhausted and low in ammunition, were ordered back to Springfield.

The Battle, recorded as a Confederate victory, gave the South control of southwest Missouri.

Task One: Use the information in the above article to identify the important information.

Important information for Task One:

How does your list of important information compare to the following list?

- Springfield, Missouri
- August 10, 1861
- North led by Lyon
- South led by McCulloch
- First major battle west of Mississippi River
- Union troops attacked first
- Confederates attacked three times
- General Lyon died
- Confederate victory
- Confederacy controlled southwest Missouri

Task Two: Use the above article to determine if Wilson's Creek was one of the first or one of the last battles of the Civil War.

Important Information for Task Two: Compare your treasure or important information with that listed below:

August 10, 1861, a mere four months after . . . the beginning of the Civil War.

Task Three: Use the above article to determine the outcome of the Battle of Wilson's Creek

---

Important Information for Task Three: Compare your treasure or important information with that listed below:

Confederate victory
Confederacy controlled southwest Missouri

Figure 14.2 Wilson's Creek Battle

In the first scenario, the task does not identify what information is important. Therefore, all facts became important. In the second and third scenarios, the task is clearly identified, allowing the problem solver to focus and extract only the information which is important. In the last two scenarios, the problem solver knows the needed information: Scenario 2, whether the battle was fought at the beginning or at the end of the war, and Scenario 3, the outcome. Knowing what information is needed allows the problem solver to extract less information. In Scenario 2 it is not necessary to read the last three paragraphs of the article. Clearly, task definition makes it easier and faster to extract the needed information.

You may be thinking all of the information in the article is important. If so, you may choose to have your student read the entire article. As a matter of semantics, do you want your students to read or know? Keep in mind reading is part of using information (Big6 #4) which leads to synthesis (Big6 #5) or knowing. Determining the content, or what information is important, for students is both your right and responsibility as a teacher. If you determine all of the information is important, then pose a problem for students reflecting that all the information as important. For instance, you might ask students: Who fought in the Battle of Wilson's Creek? When and where was the battle fought? What were the actions of the armies involved and what was the outcome of the battle? Spelling out what information is important supports elementary students by enabling them to extract the needed information and to begin developing the skills needed to determine independently what is important.

One of the most effective methods to identify what information is important is to return to Big6 #1, What is your task and what information do you need. The information needed is the important information. Students initially need teacher support in order to identify what information is important. The following strategies may help students identify what information is needed:

Pose questions. As the teacher or library media specialist, pose questions for students to answer as they listen in class or read from the text book.

Identify needed information. Provide students a list of what information is needed (Big6 #1.2). This list may help students focus on identifying and extracting only the important information or the treasure. The list may be created by students, the teacher, or cooperatively by both.

Students create questions. Require students, as part of task definition, to list the questions they hope to answer when conducting research. This initial list of questions serves to remind students of the important information they seek. These initial questions may be changed and adapted based upon the information found.

Use prior knowledge. Help students develop a habit of using prior knowledge to assist in locating the important information. To use prior knowledge when engaged, as you listen or read, enhances the ability to locate the information. An example of how prior knowledge may be used to solve a problem exists in Figure 14.2. The problem solver learns the Battle of Wilson's Creek was fought on August 10, 1861. By using prior knowledge the learner would know the war lasted four years and began on April 12, 1861. The use of this prior knowledge would enable the learner to reason that the battle was one of the first battles.

Who, what, when, where, and how. Teach students to think in terms of who, what, when, where, and how as an aid to determine what information is important in situations where specific questions are not posed.

Writers and speaker's clues. Raise student awareness of the clues speakers and writers often include which help identify the information they consider important. For instance, in oral presentations the speaker might identify the treasure or important information by:

- writing the information on the board
- repeating the information
- emphasizing the information by tone of voice and gesture
- spending more time on the information
- giving word clues, such as . . . the first reason or . . . in conclusion
- giving summaries at the end of class or a review at the beginning of class

Authors often provide clues to the important information within their writing by use of:

- headings
- graphics such as pictures, charts, and graphs
- bold and italic print

Identify the important information. The note taker is now ready to identify the important information. Extraction of the important information is facilitated by the exclusive focus on finding important information and awareness of what is important. Barbara Jansen's Trash & Treasure method of note taking, briefly described in Figure 10.1, is a very user-friendly strategy for identifying the important information (Jansen 109). You may wish to use the word *treasure* to identify important information if you teach students the Trash & Treasure method.

Recording the Important Information

The final step in note taking is to record the important information. It is essential students understand the writing required during note taking (Big6 #4) serves a different purpose than the writing required during the synthesis step (Big6 #5). The writings will look considerably different because they serve different purposes. The purpose of writing during synthesis is to communicate to others the information or solution to our problem. The purpose of writing during note taking or use (Big6 #4) is to communicate to the note taker the information which may be used to solve the problem, typically to study for a test or to write a research paper.

Notes taken during the research process should include citation information. Bibliographic information which identifies the source of the information is important and should be included in notes. One method of allowing students to work smarter, not harder is to encourage them to write the bibliographic information from a source once and to assign a number to each source. If a source is cited a second time, the note taker need only record the number assigned the source and the page cited. Time may also be saved when the same information is found in more than one source. Suggest students find the original copy of the information and add the citation for the second source rather than re-copy information. This saves time and increases the validity of students' work. For more information on citing sources see Chapter 10.

Reflecting upon the purpose of taking notes, the following behaviors may lead to good notes:

Write Phrases

Good notes contain only phrases. Writing phrases, instead of complete sentences, saves time in taking notes and also in using notes. It also requires that the student be engaged and identify the important information. In order to leave out some words and replace others, the student will need to access prior knowledge and the written or oral source of the information.

Notes Which Can Be Read

One test notes must pass is: Do the notes make sense to me? Notes are written to be used by the note taker, not by any other. To be useful the note taker must be able to use the notes or read and make sense of them. Useful notes:

- are written legibly so the note taker can read them
- are organized in a logical order so they make sense to the note taker
- use words and phrases that can be understood

Organize Notes

There are many different ways to organize notes. Organization depends upon the content and the preferences of the note taker. For instance, when notes are taken during research, it is advantageous to use a form which allows information about one question or topic to be grouped together. This organizational format allows information to be easily sorted and reorganized when synthesizing. Jason may decide to take notes on notebook paper, placing a bullet in front of each fact and leaving space before and after. Joanna, on the other hand, may prefer to use index cards writing one fact on each card. Both methods of organization will be effective as they allow for the easy sorting and reorganization of information.

Some organizational formats include:

- index cards
- outlines
- webs
- two-column notes
- data charts or tables

You may wish to introduce students to a variety of note taking formats. Allow students to practice each of the formats as it is introduced. After practicing several formats, students may benefit from being given a choice between two or three appropriate formats. Students should eventually be allowed and encouraged to select the format which best suits their style of note taking and the content.

Scaffold for Teaching Note Taking

As with any process scaffolding is suggested. Begin by modeling. Then guide before you expect students to independently practice. What might each level of the scaffold look like when teaching note taking? Some suggested strategies for modeling and guiding follow:

Modeling

Provide students with teacher-prepared notes. Allowing students to compare the original text with the notes provided by the teacher may increase student ability to identify the important information.

Take notes with your students. Pose a problem or identify what information is needed (Big6 #1). Then ask students to listen as you read to them. Students should raise their hand if they hear important information. Call on students to identify the important information. Record the words or phrases identified as important on a teacher-designed note taking form. This strategy works well with younger students because the teacher assists with the reading and writing skills which students are just beginning to develop. It may actually motivate students to improve their reading and writing skills. Adapt the strategy to more fully engage older students by allowing them to read and write.

Model the process of copying words and phrases into notes. Use chart paper and create a form for taking notes. Display the source or text being used on an overhead projector or electronic projection device. Ask students: Do you think these words I need to copy are spelled correctly? Would it be easier to copy the words with correct spelling now or to look up spelling in a dictionary later? Most students will acknowledge it is easier to copy correct spelling now. Use the index finger on one hand to keep your place in the text while writing with the other. Think aloud as you model copying the word letter by letter rather than as a word, e.g. copy the letters, l e a r n i n g, instead of the word, learning. Explain to students: If I do not know how to spell a word, I say each letter in the word and copy letter by letter. Not only will I get the spelling correct by copying a letter at a time, but I can actually copy faster because I do know each letter.

Guiding

Present students with incomplete notes. Prepare a set of notes over a lecture or from a text and then blank out some of the words or phrases. As students read or listen they are to identify the treasure and fill in the blanks. The access to some of the treasure simplifies the note taking.

Create a note taking table. Prepare questions which when answered will provide the needed information. Write one question in each cell in the first column. Create a second column with blank cells. As students read or listen they fill in the blank cells with the needed information or the answers to the questions.

Provide independent practice followed by student evaluation. Give students text, a highlighter, and the task or information needed (Big6 #1). Have students highlight the words and phrases they think are important. After students highlight, permit them to evaluate the highlighted text by comparing it with the teacher or library media specialist's highlighted text. Discuss reasons for similarities and differences in the notes.

Evaluate as a whole class after guided note taking. Some students will find it difficult to identify the important information. Evaluate as a whole class group after students have individually taken notes. Expose students to the thinking of their peers by calling upon students and asking them to share: Why did you write that? Why did you not include . . . ? Forcing students to reflect may help them experience the thinking necessary to identify treasure.

Practice note taking using timed reading and writing. Provide students with text and challenge them to read and extract the important information during a specified length of time. Follow the reading with a specified amount of time for students to write notes without referring back to the text. For instance, students may be given five minutes to read and three minutes to write. Next provide students the opportunity to evaluate and reflect upon their efforts, taking time to identify strengths and weaknesses.

Practice closed book note taking. Provide students a task, a text, and a note taking form. Students then engage and extract the important information from the text, following the rule that if you are writing, the book must be closed. Evaluation should follow the note taking activity. A round-table share is one method of evaluating. Have students, working as teams of four, compare the notes they took, and identify all of the different facts they have recorded. Next move from team to team as one member stands and identifies a fact or important information recorded. All students put a check by the fact if it is recorded on their paper. That fact will not be shared again. Continue to move from team to team until all of the information students have recorded is shared with the class. At this point students can evaluate their note taking process by answering such questions as: Did you extract most of the facts or treasure? Could you read your notes, were they legible? Did what you wrote make sense to you? Did you record the information accurately? Both the closed book note taking and the timed reading and writing strategies force students to transfer information to the brain before putting it down on paper.

Independent Practice

When students are ready to begin independent note taking practice, teachers or library media specialists may employ the following strategies to encourage students to improve their note taking efforts:

Require all rough drafts be written using only notes. Do not allow students to have access to the original text or source when they are writing a rough draft. Allow students to take notes, go back to the original source, and edit or add to notes if they find notes are inadequate. After students feel notes are accurate and complete, the original source may be put away, and students may resume work on the rough draft using only their notes. If students must refer back to the original source to edit notes, ask them to evaluate: Did it require more time to go back to the original source? Why did you have to go back to the original source? What can you do so the next time you do not have to go back to the original source? The time students take to evaluate helps them understand why note taking is important and what is required to improve their skills.

Give credit or a grade for notes. There is a tendency for students to associate the importance of a particular skill with its impact upon their grade, e.g. If I get a grade on this skill then it is an important skill and I need to learn it. The grade or credit assigned may be simple or complex. For instance, the student may receive 10 points on a 100-point research assignment if notes are turned in. Or the teacher may design a note taking rubric evaluating specific skills such as legibility, words and phrases rather than complete sentences, spelling, organization, number of pieces of important information identified, etc. Remember the problem solver is the person who ultimately needs to be aware of strengths and weaknesses regardless of how a grade or credit is assigned. For this reason, focus on evaluation methods which allow students to obtain this information. Methods which allow students to evaluate without adding a great investment of your time are also preferable.

Note taking remains a vague and complicated process for many students. The importance of note taking is recognized when we think of its impact upon test preparation and research. It is possible to identify and teach specific skills that may help students' master note taking by making this process of engaging and extracting information very concrete and visible. Students may improve their note taking skills and, through repetition and practice, become more effective problem solvers if these skills are taught within the Big6 framework.

Works Cited

Jansen, Barbara A. *The Big6 in Middle School, Teaching Information and Communications Technology Skills.* Columbus, OH: Linworth Publishing, Inc., 2007.

Marzano, Robert J., Debra J. Pickering, and Jane E. Pollock. *Classroom Instruction That Works, Research-Based Strategies for Increasing Student Achievement.* Alexandria, VA: Association for Supervision and Curriculum Development, 2001.

The BIG 6

CHAPTER 15
ANSWERING QUESTIONS FROM THE TEXT AND TEST TAKING

Should Students Answer Questions from Text?

At one time students in classrooms across the nation were asked to *read the chapter and answer the questions* as a learning strategy. Based upon information now available about learning (see Chapter 3) many teachers have abandoned this strategy. This might be a good time to remember the old saying, *Don't throw the baby out with the bathwater.* Instead of throwing out the strategy, it may be possible to revise its implementation making it an effective strategy, i.e. keep the baby and add fresh water. Consider the power of reading and questioning. Reading enables students to engage and access information. It is an extremely powerful learning strategy for lifelong learners. Questioning inherently creates problems to be solved and engages students. The ability to answer questions is important for continued learning and success. Effective practice of these two powerful strategies should lead to increased student achievement.

The weakness with this traditional assignment may exist in its implementation. For instance, as a classroom teacher, I expected students to read the entire chapter without any input as to what information in the chapter was important or without any guidance. Students were then expected to answer all of the questions at the end of the chapter. Whether those questions identified important information was not considered. The expectation was students, after reading and answering questions, would know all of the information in the chapter. This expectation was probably not realistic based upon what we now know from brain-based learning research (see Chapter 3).

Suggestions for implementing this strategy more efficiently include:

First identify what information is important for the students to know. Textbooks are written by professional writers. These writers usually create well-written questions which relate to what the writer considers important. Once the teacher identifies the information students need to gather from the text, existing questions may be read with the purpose of identifying those relevant to the important information. Students should be expected to answer only those questions. Additional questions may be added by the teacher, if needed, to ensure students identify all relevant information. Students should be presented with these questions (Big6 #1) prior to reading (Big6 #4,), i.e. instead of reading for the purpose of reading, students are now reading for the purpose of gathering specified information.

Make reading and answering questions one of many strategies used to teach. When reading and answering questions was prevalent, teachers did not have access to much of the knowledge now available about the learning process or the multitude of strategies which exist today. Teachers often had to rely upon reading and answering questions, lecturing, and the occasional research to teach students. Today we have access to many teaching strategies and understand the importance of utilizing many different strategies when teaching. Using a variety of strategies enables teachers to reach more students more effectively.

Provide the opportunity for students to read from many different sources. Prior to the information explosion, it was common for the textbook to contain all of the information or content students needed to know on a particular subject. With the rapid increase in—and the accessibility of—information, the textbook is no longer the only source. It is possible, and desirable, that students read from other sources such as newspapers, nonfiction books, magazine articles, instruction manuals, and the Internet. The strategy of reading and answering questions can effectively be applied to any print source. To be effective, however, it is important students be provided guidance as to what information they are seeking before they begin to read.

Can the Big6 be Applied to Answer Questions?

Perhaps you already noticed the pieces of the Big6 process involved in reading and answering questions (see Figure 15.1).

The power of using Big6 to answer questions lies in methodically answering the questions by focusing on one small step at a time. For instance, students concentrate on identifying the task (Big6 #1.1) and then focus on identifying what information is needed to solve the task (Big6 #1.2). They focus on identifying possible sources (Big6 #2.1) and then determine which source is best (Big6 # 2.2). Students are able to efficiently complete each step by focusing on one small step at a time. As students repeat the process, each step and the entire process becomes automatic. Many of the individual skills teachers identify as important may be mastered as a result of students mastering the Big6 process. For instance, students gain understanding of:

- keywords and main ideas as they identify the task

- nonfiction text features as they locate information

- importance of reading and listening as they access information

- note taking and summarizing skills as they use the information and engage and extract

Answering Questions from Text

1. **Task Definition:**

1.1 **What is the task?**
   - To answer the questions using the textbook.

1.2 **What information do I need?**
   - Read the questions and identify the keywords of each. For instance if the question is "**When** was the **Civil War** fought?" Then **when Civil War** are keywords to help locate the answer to the question. Read all questions and note keywords.

2. **Information Seeking Strategies. What source can I use?**
   - Textbook. In a typical classroom the teacher identifies the source for the student.
   - Prior knowledge will also be needed.

3. **Location and Access. Where is the source and where is the information?**
   - Find the textbook.
   - Find the information within the text: Skim or scan for keywords using text aids.
   - The teacher may assist by:
     - Making sure students know:
       - How to scan matching letters and skim matching words (See Chapter 9)
       - What the keywords are as identified in Task Definition, Step 1.2
       - How to identify and utilize text features
     - Encouraging effective habits:
       - Resist tendency to read prior to scanning and skimming
       - Utilize index or guide words, followed by other text aids before searching in paragraphs

4. **Use of Information.**

4.1 **Engage.**
   - If the information is in the text, you must either *read* or *listen* as someone reads the text to you.

4.2 **Extract.**
   - Extract only the needed or important information as identified in task definition, 1.2. The information needed to answer the questions.

5. **Synthesis.**
   - Write the answers to the questions.
   - Include the page number on which information was found for evaluation purposes and to create a habit of citing sources.
   - Teacher should determine and let students know if answers need to be written in complete sentences or phrases. For example, do students need practice in writing complete thoughts or sentences? Or will the answers be used to study for test? If that is the case writing phrases will make the information easier to use. Form of answers may vary from one assignment to another based upon student needs.

Figure 15.1 Answering Questions from Text

6. **Evaluation.**

6.1 **Product.**
- Possible evaluation methods:
    - Turn in paper and teacher grades or evaluates.
    - Evaluate answers using teacher's correct answers.
- Advantages to self-evaluation:
    - Frequently when the teacher does the evaluation or grading students do not bother to go back and identify the specific errors made and so they learn incorrect information.
    - It requires a smaller investment of teacher time.
- Teacher options:
    - If grades are needed for the assignment: A possible solution to this need for a grade is to simply give students points for completion of the assignment. A quick walk around the room can identify those students who did not complete the assignment.
    - If concerned about accurate student evaluation: The teacher may collect and evaluate for correct grading assignments after the students have made corrections. Points may be given to those who successfully correct their papers, encouraging accurate evaluation.

6.2 **Process.**
- Did you:
    - Identify the task? Identify the keywords?
    - Remember to use prior knowledge?
    - Use the text aids to help you locate keywords?
    - Did you read after locating the keywords?
    - Write your answers so they made sense? Include page number?
    - Did you evaluate the product? The process?
    - Which step was easiest for you? Why?
    - Which step was hardest for you? Why?
- Importance: While you will not be answering the same questions again, you will most likely be answering other questions from other texts in the future. Evaluating each step within the Big6 process may help you be more efficient and effective at answering questions.
- Example of impact of evaluating process:
    - Jenny was answering a multiple choice question from a reading selection. She identified keywords in each of the possible *answers* to the question. Locating one of the keywords in the reading she selected the choice containing that keyword as the answer.
    - It turned out to be the wrong answer. Jenny decided scanning did not work and she would simply read everything.
    - Jenny did not effectively evaluate process. If she had, she would have identified two process errors:
        - Keywords are normally found in the *question*, not in possible *answers* to the question.
        - After information is located by scanning (Big6 #3), it must be read or used (Big6 #4).

Note: Writing page numbers during synthesis makes it easy to go back to the text and evaluate why a specific question is answered incorrectly. For example, did I read and extract incorrectly, did I fail to locate the information, etc.

Figure 15.1 Answering Questions from Text continued

The familiarity with the text, which results from using it as a source when answering questions, leads students to be more effective users of text. For instance, when students are familiar with text they may recognize that the order in which questions are asked in text frequently matches the order in which information is introduced in the text. They may comprehend that the writing strategies introduced by their teacher—begin paragraphs with a topic sentence and end with a summary statement—are used by the authors of their textbooks and reference books. With this comprehension comes the ability to locate information more quickly by skimming the first and last sentences of paragraphs rather than skimming the entire paragraph. This familiarity with text, and the skill it brings, is especially important considering the large amount of information high school and college students are exposed to in textbooks and reference sources. It is also important as students take mandated tests requiring they answer questions from the provided text.

What About the Big6 and Test Scores?

I had the opportunity to experience the power of Big6 when applied to answering test questions several years ago. Sitting in the first faculty meeting in a new school, the principal handed out a sample social studies test similar to the new state-mandated test (DESE 1998). Staff was asked to take the test so they might better relate to what students faced with the mandated tests. Being new to the staff, I wanted to make a good impression. To have the respect of peers is important to both students and adults. Additional stress existed because of my poor social studies background. Armed with the Big6 problem solving process and limited content knowledge, I tackled the problem (see Figure 15.2).

Test Item:
How have territorial boundaries in the Western part of the country changed since the days of the Oregon Trail wagon trains? Include at least one specific example of a boundary change in your answer. (Test item included a map of the western U.S. and the Oregon Trail in 1850.)

Applying Big6
#1: Task Definition: Reading the problem, the words in bold identify the task.
How have territorial boundaries in the Western part of the country ***changed since the days of*** the ***Oregon Trail*** wagon trains? Include ***at least one specific example of a boundary change*** in your answer.

#2 Information Seeking Strategy: The test item and prior knowledge may be used as sources.

#4 Use of Information: Looking at the map, even with limited knowledge, problem solver is able to recognize that Washington state did not exist in 1850. It was part of the Oregon Territory.

#5 Synthesis: Problem solver wrote: The Oregon Territory has been divided into several states. For instance Washington state now exists in the northwestern corner of what was the Oregon Territory and the state of Oregon is sandwiched between Washington state and California.

Figure 15.2 Social Studies Test Item

The principal presented the correct answer and asked how many people answered it correctly. Only two hands were raised, mine and that of the 5th grade teacher who taught the content. During discussion, it was obvious many teachers were more knowledgeable than I on the topic of westward expansion and geography. However, only two people correctly identified the task. While others provided accurate information, they did not solve the problem, which was to identify how territorial boundaries changed and to provide an example. Big6 enabled me to correctly identify the task and successfully use my limited knowledge. It was not until much later in the year staff learned of my limited social studies knowledge, and by that time they were impressed with what Big6 could do for their students.

This experience reveals two parts to successful test performance: knowledge and the ability to communicate that knowledge. The knowledge part consists mainly of facts, such as how many planets are in our solar system, what were causes of the Civil War, etc. The ability to communicate that knowledge requires students to:

- identify what knowledge is being asked for (Big 6 #1)
- access and use (Big6 #3 and #4) that knowledge
- solve the problem or answer the question (Big6 #5)
- evaluate (Big6 #6) if the knowledge has actually been communicated

Mastery of knowledge alone will not guarantee success in a testing situation. Using Big6 provides students the tools needed to successfully communicate and fully utilize any knowledge possessed in a testing situation.

The current push for accountability in our schools has resulted in the implementation of mandated tests. These tests are designed to measure the success of our students and therefore the success of our schools. Much emphasis is placed upon test performance because state and federal funding of schools may be tied to the test results.

Teachers and schools are working hard to improve test scores. In some situations schools are teaching to the test. Curriculum is determined by the content of the test rather than the identified skills and content needs of students. If the test utilizes multiple choice questions, then students are exposed to multiple choice questions during instruction. If the test requires students to create a graphic organizer or answer in a complete sentence, then students practice creating graphic organizers and writing in complete sentences in the classroom. The strategies often are used without considering whether it is the most logical or valuable strategy to assist in student learning. In other situations, students are provided huge laundry lists of do's and don'ts when taking the test. For instance, always write your answer in complete sentences, repeat the question in your answer, underline the keywords, etc. Both approaches may be likened to putting a band aid on a leak in a dam. Just as a band aid is applied to the recognized weakness or leak, another leak is spotted. While student performance may improve, the approach either opens educators to public criticism for teaching to the test or leads to stressed students who struggle to memorize an unconnected list of test taking tips. Big6 allows students to tackle test questions through a logical step-by-step process, a problem solving process. It allows students to think and determine the best way to communicate their answer. It is much easier to master, because it is a sequence or process, rather than a list of unconnected skills to be memorized. Students are required to think and problem solve as they work their way through the Big6 steps. When faced with new or unfamiliar problems, they have a familiar strategy to rely upon.

The power of Big6 as a strategy to help students communicate their knowledge may be observed in the following elementary school situation.

In order to measure growth in reading ability, students take a test at the beginning of the year and at the end of the year. At the beginning of the year, all students took a paper-and-pencil test. The decision was made to transition from paper-and-pencil to a computerized reading assessment. Students would take the test electronically at the end of the year. The scores of the first few classes to use the computerized test were not as high as anticipated. In fact, some students actually scored lower on the end-of-year test. One 1st grade teacher concluded the change in format may be affecting students' ability to communicate their knowledge. She scheduled a session with her class in the computer lab prior to administering the reading assessment. During that session she utilized Big6 to help her students solve the problem of transitioning to another format for the reading test (see Figure 15.3).

---

1. **Task Definition: What is your task?**

To answer the questions using the reading selection.

---

2. **Information Seeking Strategies. What source will you be using?**

Our source will be our prior knowledge and the computer.

---

3. **Location and Access. Where is the source and the information in the source?**

If information is not on your computer screen anymore, can you go back and look at it? How can you locate this information?
Answer: Yes, it can be accessed by using the arrow keys.

---

4. **Use of Information.**

If you were taking the test on paper how would you keep from losing your place?
Answer: By using our finger to move along under the text.

Can you do that on the computer screen?
Answer: Yes

What if you are reading from paper and you don't know a word? What strategies do you use?
Answer: Chunk it, sound it out, etc.

Can you use those strategies if you are reading from the computer monitor?
Answer: Yes

---

5. **Synthesis.**

If you are taking a test with paper and pencil, how do you mark your answer?
Answer: Fill in the bubble.

If you are taking the test with the computer, you do not have a pencil, so how do you mark your answer?
Answer: Typing the letter or clicking

---

6. **Evaluation.**

What do you do to evaluate or check your work before turning in a paper and pencil test?
Answer: Go back and check to make sure all blanks are filled in and if there is time reread the question and check to see if the answer makes sense.

Can you do that on an electronic test?
Answer: Yes

Figure 15.3 Connecting Electronic Testing to Paper and Pencil Testing

This teacher realized the ability to communicate is necessary if students are to show all the knowledge they learn. Using Big6 as a strategy, the teacher helped students make connections (see Chapter 3) between test taking using a print source and test taking using an electronic source (Big6 #2, Information Seeking Strategies). She helped students communicate what they knew. You may be wondering if the use of Big6 made a difference. It turns out the reading scores of the students in this teacher's class were among the highest in the building.

How Can Students Be Taught to Utilize Big6 in Test Taking?

Students will become familiar with the Big6 steps if they are provided opportunities to practice the process throughout the school year. Teachers and library media specialists may help students transfer skills to test taking by intentionally making connections between answering a question from text and answering a question on a test (see Figure 15.4).

Some specific examples of what it might look like as students use Big6 when taking tests follow:

Task Definition

Active task definition helps students reduce the task to its simplest form making it easier to keep the problem in mind. Students are able to reduce the number of words used to describe the task when they ask: What is my task? What do I need to do? For instance, in the following boxed text, students would only need to store the words in bold. Rather than storing 10 to 15 words to identify the task, students need store only five or six words to remember the task.

Fill in the **bubble** beside the **best answer** to each question.
On the lines below, **copy** these **sentences** and **use** the **correct capital letters**.
Read each sentence. Read the word choices. **Circle** the **word** that **best completes** each **sentence**. *[Note: While reading is not identified as part of the task, it is necessary to read in order to circle the word which best completes the sentence or to solve the problem. Reading is the means to an end, rather than the end. It is the use or engage step (Big6 #4) rather than the synthesis step (Big6 #5).]*

Reading Selection Questions

Big6 changes the focus from reading to gather all the information in a selection to reading for a more specific purpose. Big6 makes the process of answering questions systematic. Students focus their energy on one step at a time, logically proceeding from one step to the next. Prior to reading the selection, students identify the task (Big6 #1). They read the directions and questions to be answered to identify the information needed and possible keywords (Big6 #1.2). They scan and skim to locate the needed information (Big6 #3). They begin to read (Big6 #4) with a specific target in mind, finding the answer to the question.

Comparison of Answering Questions from Text to Answering Questions on Tests

Answering Questions from Text	Answering Questions on Tests
1. Task Definition: *It is helpful for students to recognize reading is not the task . . . it is part of the process (step 4, use of information, engage). No points are given for reading; the purpose for reading is to find the answer.*	
What is the task? ■ To answer the questions using the textbook. **What information do I need?** ■ Read the questions and identify the keywords of each.	**What is the task?** ■ To answer the questions on the test. ■ Read the questions and identify the keywords of each.
2. Information Seeking Strategies. What source can I use? *Acknowledging prior knowledge as a source encourages students to retrieve needed information.*	
■ Textbook ■ Prior Knowledge	■ Test ■ Prior Knowledge
3. Location and Access. Where is the source and where is the information?	
■ Find the textbook. ■ Find the information within the text: Skim or scan for keywords using text aids.	■ Find the test. ■ Find the information within the test: Skim and scan for keywords using text aids.
4. Use of Information.	
4.1 Engage. ■ If the information is in the text, you must either *read* or *listen* as someone reads the text to you. **4.2 Extract.** ■ Extract only the needed or important information as identified in task definition, 1.2. The information needed to answer the questions.	**4.2 Engage.** ■ Read the information in the text. **4.2 Extract.** ■ Extract only the needed or important information as identified in task definition, 1.2. The information needed to answer the questions.
5. Synthesis.	
■ Write the answers to the questions. ■ Include the page number on which information was found for evaluation purposes and to create a habit of citing sources.	■ Write the answers to the test questions.
6. Evaluation. *If students have practiced and acquired a habit of evaluation, it may positively impact student test scores.*	

Product.
■ Check accuracy of answers
 	
Process. Did you:
■ Identify the task? Identify the keywords?
■ Remember to use prior knowledge?
■ Use the text aids to help you locate keywords?
■ Did you read after locating the keywords?
■ Write your answers so they made sense? Include page number?
■ Did you evaluate the product? The process?
	Product.
	■ Reread the task (Big6 #1) and check to make sure you have answered the question.
	Process.
	■ Have you answered all questions, e.g. no blanks on test.
	■ Have you communicated your answer:
	  ■ Can it be read?
	  ■ Does it make sense?

From *Teaching Elementary Information Literacy Skills with the Big6™* by **Joyce Needham**. Columbus, OH: Linworth Publishing, Inc. Copyright © 2009.

Figure 15.4 Comparison of Answering Questions from Text to Answering Questions on Tests

*Words in **bold** identify the task. <u>Underlined</u> words identify keywords.*

Directions: Circle the letter beside the best answer for each question.

1. **How** are **teddy bears** <u>different</u> **from real bears?**
   a. Teddy bears may be brown, black, or white.
   b. Teddy bears are furry.
   c. Teddy bears are toys.

2. What could be **another** <u>title</u> for this story?
   a. Bears at home.
   b. A Walk in the Woods.
   c. All About Bears

3. **Which** <u>word</u> comes <u>first</u> **in alphabetical order?**
   a. woods
   b. bears
   c. toys

Figure 15.5 Sample Reading Selection Questions

Secondary Social Studies Item

The British economist John Maynard Keynes developed a radical new economic theory. According to his theory, during times of depression, government spending could create jobs through a program of public works. Explain how applying this theory might help (1) the unemployed, (2) businesses, and (3) the government.

Applying the steps of Big6 to solve the problem:

1. **What is my task? (Task Definition)**
   ▪ Explain how economic theory helps: unemployed, businesses, and government

2. **What source can I use? (Information Seeking Strategies)**
   ▪ As with all test items, the test item itself and prior knowledge.

3. **Where are the source and the information? (Location and Access)**
   ▪ Prior knowledge: make connections to retrieve information.
   ▪ Use text features and skim for keywords.

4. **Use of Information: Engage or read and extract the important information**
   ▪ Government spending can create jobs through public works.

5. **Synthesis:**
   ▪ Unemployed: Will benefit because jobs will be available.
   ▪ Businesses: Will benefit because people employed to fill the jobs will now have money to spend at these businesses increasing business profit.
   ▪ Government: The government (people) will have these public works to use. Since people are now working, they will be paying taxes resulting in more money for the government.

6. **Evaluation:**
   ▪ Did I solve the problem?
   ▪ Did Big6 help me locate and use limited knowledge?

Figure 15.6 Sample Test Item

For example, using the directions and questions in Figure 15.5 , the student would:

- Read the directions and questions to identify the task as identified by the bold words (Big6 #1.1).

- Identify the keywords or information needed to answer the questions as shown by underlining (Big6 #1.2).

- Identify the source needed to find the information (Big6 #2). In a testing situation, the student has only two possible sources: the test itself and prior knowledge. For instance, in Figure 15.5 Questions 1 and 3 require only prior knowledge as the source. There is no need for students to read the selection to find the answer. Question 2, however, requires students to use both prior knowledge and the selection as sources.

- Locate the selection and skim and scan to find the keywords (Big6 #3).

- After keywords are located, begin to read for the specific purpose of finding the answer to the questions (Big6 #4). In this example, students only need focus on finding another title for the story.

Maximum Use of Limited Knowledge

Through task definition, the problem is reduced to its simplest terms and the knowledge needed to solve the problem becomes visible. This makes it easier for the problem solver to apply knowledge. Task definition may assist the problem solver in effectively using knowledge (see Figure 15.6) (DESE 2001).

After reading this test item the immediate reaction is typically: I cannot answer this question. I do not know the answer. A majority of problem solvers find, after applying the Big6 steps, they can solve the problem.

Information problems are being solved whenever questions are answered. Sometimes those questions are asked by teachers and are answered using text as the source, e.g. answer the question at the end of the chapter. At other times, those questions are asked on tests and are answered using prior knowledge as the source. In either case, the questions represent problems. As such, using the Big6 process may help learners successfully answer the questions or solve the problems. The basic difference between answering questions from text and answering questions on tests is the source (Big6 #2) used.

It is important for students to be aware that the same skills, the Big6 steps, are used to answer questions from the text or to answer questions on a test. This awareness provides students the opportunity to consciously practice Big6 on daily assignments as they answer questions from text. With the knowledge that the same process, Big6, may be used to answer questions on tests, the problem solving skills mastered during daily practice may easily be transferred to improve test performance.

Works Cited

Missouri Department of Elementary and Secondary Education (DESE). *Preview of the New Missouri Assessment Program, Grade 4 Social Studies "Sampler."* Jefferson City, MO: 1998.

Missouri Department of Elementary and Secondary Education (DESE). *Released Secondary Social Studies Item.* 2001. <http://www.dese.mo.gov./divimprove/assess/Released_Items/archives/ss_archive/2001/ss11scoreguide.2001.pdf>.

CHAPTER 16
CLASSROOM MANAGEMENT AND THE BIG6

How Can Classroom Management Be Used as an Opportunity to Teach the Big6?

Every teacher and library media specialist is charged with teaching specific curriculum or content. A crucial factor which affects the success of that instruction is classroom management. Classroom management involves establishing routines and procedures for daily learning activities and creation of a brain friendly environment where learning may take place.

Classroom management also provides a unique opportunity to teach students the Big6 in an authentic problem solving situation. A typical school day provides many opportunities for students to solve problems related to classroom management, e.g. transitioning from one activity to another, moving from one location to another, gathering needed materials, or displaying the behavior needed to allow others to learn. Each of these problems provides a valuable opportunity for students to practice problem solving skills. The majority of students understand these problems. As a result, when the Big6 is used to solve the problems, students are able to focus on the process rather than the problem. This makes classroom management a valuable opportunity to master problem solving.

Implementation of Big6 in the classroom also allows students to take responsibility for their learning. Students are encouraged to think as the teacher or library media specialist poses questions rather than gives directions. In a typical classroom, the teacher often does the thinking and then tells students what to do. When Big6 is implemented as a classroom management strategy, the teacher poses the problem and allows the student to think and solve the problem. The teacher is there to guide and direct students as needed.

The problems, however, belong to students and it is their responsibility to solve them. Implementation of Big6 as the basis of the classroom management system also provides added bonuses in the areas of:

Time. Implementing any strategy initially requires an investment of time. Big6 requires little, if any, extra time after it has been implemented. It is possible that implementation of Big6 may even result in saving time as students begin to automatically solve classroom management problems and teachers do not have to continually repeat directions for students.

Safe environment. Self-assessment or evaluation is not as threatening as teacher evaluation. Students tend to be defensive when the teacher tells them what to do or corrects their actions. When others evaluate, we tend to feel threatened or under attack. In this situation, our focus is on protecting ourselves and not on solving problems. When students take responsibility and evaluate themselves, the focus tends to shift to solving the problem.

Responsibility shift. The teacher's responsibility for classroom management lessens as students accept responsibility for classroom behavior and procedures. Learning may actually flourish as teachers have more time to devote to teaching responsibilities.

What Does Classroom Management Look Like Using the Big6?

In classrooms that implement problem solving as a classroom management tool, the teacher asks rather then tells. Students solve the problems without being told by the teacher. Students are conscious of what their problem is (Big6 #1) and continuously assess or evaluate (Big6 #6) if they are accurately solving classroom routines, procedures, and behavior. The teacher asks questions to guide and direct students when they have difficulty solving problems independently. The students think about what they should be doing and how they should behave. In this situation, the teacher is able to focus on how to best help students learn the prescribed curriculum. There are differences between the traditional teacher-directed class and the Big6 teacher-questioning class (see Figure 16.1).

How Important Are Consequences and Consistency?

Learning is something each individual must do for himself or herself. Others may guide and direct, but the individual ultimately makes the learning happen. For this reason, it is especially important that students assume responsibility for their learning. Two factors which have a direct impact on students' willingness to accept responsibility are consequences and consistency. For some students, it is necessary to experience the consequences of poor problem solving in order to be convinced to improve problem solving skills.

Teachers and library media specialists, perhaps because of their concern for students, often try to minimize the consequences of poor problem solving or make the consequences less painful for the student. Minimizing consequences for the student may result in less immediate pain for the student. It may, however, lead to more pain in the future if the student does not focus on being a better problem solver.

A better solution may be to let students experience the consequences of their problem solving, both good and bad, and to require students to evaluate their problem solving, thus recognizing the behavior or lack of behavior and the resulting consequences. Knowledge of the cause for poor problem solving empowers students to improve. This

Comparison of Teacher Directing to Teacher Questioning

Teacher Directing	Teacher Questioning
Example 1: Teacher observes a student running in the hall.	
Teacher gives directive: Stop running!	<ul><li>Teacher stops student and asks (Task Definition #1): What is your task? What are you supposed to be doing?</li><li>Student responds: e.g. going to library, going to bathroom, etc.</li><li>Teacher asks student (Evaluate #6): Evaluate. How are you doing? Can you fix the problem? Thank you.</li><li>Student proceeds to walk down the hall to library, bathroom, etc.</li></ul> ***JaDene Denniston,*** *Big6 Certified Trainer, first suggested this strategy.*
Evaluate	
Was there a problem? Who solved the problem or assumed responsibility in each approach? Who is doing the thinking (identifying the problem and deciding how to solve)? In which approach is the student more likely to be positive or negative about the encounter with the teacher?	
Example 2: An 11th grade student in advanced geometry class completes an assignment. Holding up the completed assignment he asks the teacher, "Where do I put this?" The student wants the teacher to be his source of information, (Big6 #2)	
<ul><li>Teacher says, You need to put it in the plastic tray on my desk.</li><li>Teacher thinks, I've only told you that 30 times this year. You are supposed to be smart! Student may be lucky if he does not get a lecture or sarcastic response from teacher.</li></ul>	<ul><li>Teacher asks: Where do you put it?</li><li>Student is forced to access prior knowledge rather than use the teacher as the source. Student solves problem.</li></ul> **Posing a problem and also providing direct instruction in problem solving:** <ul><li>Teacher says: Should the source (Information Seeking Strategies, Big6 #2) of that information be me or you, your prior knowledge? Where should you put that paper? Don't you feel powerful when you solve your own problems?</li><li>Student solves the problem and a lesson on Information Seeking Strategies has been taught.</li></ul>
Evaluate	
Which approach leaves student and teacher both feeling more positive? Which approach requires the student to take responsibility for his learning? Which approach allows the teacher the opportunity to guide the student in perfecting his problem solving process?	

From ***Teaching Elementary Information Literacy Skills with the Big6™*** by **Joyce Needham**. Columbus, OH: Linworth Publishing, Inc. Copyright © 2009.

Figure 16.1 Comparison of Directing to Questioning

knowledge, along with experiencing consequences of poor problem solving, may motivate students to take action and improve their problem solving.

Love and Logic's Jim Fay and David Funk point out " . . . when kids actually see the connection between their behavior and what happened as a result of that behavior, they learn" (Fay and Funk 130). In other words, if students suffer the consequences of their poor problem solving they may learn to be better problem solvers. Consequences of poor problem solving typically are painful. However, consequences faced as elementary students, such as missing a field trip or receiving a poor grade, will normally be less painful and life altering than those which poor problem solvers face as teenagers and adults, e.g. expulsion from school or losing a driver's license. It seems logical then to help students become effective problem solvers as soon as possible, even if they must suffer the consequences of their poor problem solving in order to learn.

Consistency of consequences may also facilitate learning. It is more likely students will make the connection between their actions and the consequences if they consistently experience the consequences of their problem solving. Accepting this responsibility empowers students to take action and become better problem solvers. If there are consequences at times and not at other times, students may fail to make connections and rationalize it is not their problem solving causing the consequences. They may place blame on other people or other factors. This will diminish the possibility of students taking action to become more effective problem solvers.

The following examples may illustrate the importance of consistency and consequences and provide ideas for integrating Big6 to improve poor problem solving:

In our first example students in a high school did not read and follow directions on assignments. As a result, or consequence, they began to receive low grades. Parents, concerned about the poor grades, began to call teachers.

At this point teachers identified the problem as poor task definition (Big6 #1). Teachers assumed responsibility for the students' inability to identify their task. Teachers began to read assignments and identify the tasks for students since students could not, or would not, read directions. Students' grades did improve as a result of the teachers' efforts. Teachers had, however, inadvertently taken away the consequences and the motivation for students to improve their task definition skills. Though bored and unengaged, students were content to let the teachers solve the problem. They did not attempt to improve their ability to read and follow written directions, a necessary skill for successful students and workers.

In this situation the teachers were doing their best. They were frustrated with reading assignments to students and felt overworked. Teachers were in fact working harder than their students because they were solving the problem. So what might it have looked like if the teachers integrated Big6 to solve the problem of poor task definition? The teachers might have posed a problem to students:

We are concerned with low grades on assignments. Your parents are concerned. We know, both your parents and I, that the grades do not indicate your ability. After studying the situation we believe the poor grades are a result of not following directions or failure to identify your task. For instance, the directions may say underline and we find you circling. Or the directions may say to list and explain and you only list. Do you agree this might be the problem? How important is it for you to develop the skills to read and follow directions? Think about your schooling to date. Are you expected to read and accept more responsibility for identifying your task as a high school student than as an elementary school student? Middle school student? What do you think will happen as you progress to the college level? What about as workers? Do you think your parents ever have to read and follow directions at work? When paying taxes? Obtaining auto licenses? Paying bills? We agree. The ability to follow directions is very important.

Now the teacher is ready to integrate Big6 and pose the problem (Big6 #1) to students: How can you improve your ability to read and follow directions? As students take responsibility for the problem, the teachers may guide students to find and use strategies (Big6 #2, 3, 4, and 5) to improve task definition. Students may be motivated to evaluate (Big6 #6) and determine why they did not identify the task correctly if poor grades are identified as a consequence of poor task definition. Phone calls from parents may be turned into opportunities to gain parental support by explaining the problem to parents, sharing strategies, and asking parents to help their children to be better problem solvers.

In this second example, a library policy on overdue books conflicted with a classroom reading strategy which required students to have library books. The library policy stated if any library material was overdue nothing else could be checked out until the original material was returned or payment received. The classroom reading strategy utilized book clubs, or groups of students with similar reading skills, who selected and read books from the library paperback collection. Students read a prescribed number of pages from the book and then discussed with classmates. The conflict arose when students who needed to check out books for their book club had overdue library materials. The library media specialist and the classroom teacher conferred about the dilemma.

If students were allowed to check out another library book, there were no consequences for failing to return books on time. If the students did not have books, they would fall behind in their book clubs. The teacher and the library media specialist wanted students to solve their own problems and suffer the consequences of poor problem solving, but they did not want those consequences to impact student learning.

The teacher identified a solution. Students with unreturned materials would not be allowed to check out books. Students who fell behind because they could not check out a book were required to catch up once the book was checked out. Often this meant giving up recess or having extra homework. With this solution, the student retained responsibility for solving the problem and faced the consequences of poor problem solving behavior.

The library media specialist added another piece to the solution. To help students become better problem solvers, the process was made visible for students. Instead of just refusing to let students check out if they had overdue materials, she verbalized the problem solving steps for students: Suzie, what is your problem? Why can't you check out the book you need for reading (Big6 #1, Task Definition)? After Suzie acknowledged the failure to return her library book, the library media specialist would ask Suzie: Evaluate. How well did you solve this problem? What could you do differently next time (Big6 #6, Evaluation)? The library media specialist then guided students as she suggested strategies to help students return books on time, such as having one place where the library book is always kept, asking Mom to help you remember to return it, or writing yourself a reminder note.

The majority of students who had overdue library materials were able to either return materials or pay for them and in turn catch up on the reading assignment. Students with overdues, whose finances were limited, were provided the opportunity to pay for materials by working in the library before or after school or during recesses. Very few students had to face this problem more than once and the library did not lose library materials.

How Do I Implement the Big6 into Classroom Management?

Implementation of Big6 will require a change in habits. As a teacher or library media specialist, you already have a system for classroom management. Because of the frequency of classroom management issues, implementation of the system is probably a habit. Something you do without conscious thought, much like you might drive to school each day on autopilot (see Chapter 3). Replacing classroom management habits with new habits that integrate Big6 will require conscious thought and repetition. Eventually, however, these new habits will replace the old and become automatic. Remember, as a result of integrating Big6, students will be provided opportunities to practice and perfect their problem solving skills in a supportive environment with the teacher available to guide.

Successful integration of Big6 is more likely if the teacher or library media specialist take into account each of the following:

- establishing concrete expectations
- making the process visible by using Big6 vocabulary
- scaffolding by modeling and guiding before expecting independent practice
- providing students opportunities to evaluate
- posing questions, perhaps the most important factor

Establish Concrete Behavior Expectations

The introduction of this book referred to three parts of learning: what is being learned, why it is being learned, and how it will be learned. Students are frequently told how to behave without knowledge of what is expected and why. Big6 step number one, task definition, provides the opportunity to ensure students know what they are to learn and why. The objective of classroom management is to establish routines, procedures, and behaviors producing an environment to ensure maximum learning. The task is to create a brain-friendly environment. Students may begin, with this understanding of what classroom management is and the purpose for it, to take an active part in problem solving and creating the desired environment.

Classroom management may be facilitated when concrete behavior expectations are established and shared with students. Rather than creation of a laundry list of acceptable behaviors, expectations may be condensed into one or two words or one statement. For instance, the only expectation in the library or classroom is:

- Safety and courtesy
- Respect for both others and things or property
- You may feel free to do anything you wish as long as it does not create a problem for anyone else

There are similarities between all three expectations. Each focuses on what students should do. Each is relatively short and easy to remember. Each requires the student to be the problem solver and decide if specific behaviors are acceptable. Each provides authentic problem solving practice. Consider the issue of talking in the library. Instead of the teacher or library media specialist telling students they must use a quiet voice in the library, students must ask themselves: What type of voice is necessary if there is no one else in the library? What type of voice is necessary if the library media specialist is reading a story to a class or explaining how to locate sources? The establishment of behavior expectations begins the integration of Big6 and encourages students to take responsibility for their behavior.

Make the Process Visible

The goal of classroom management is for students to independently solve classroom procedure and behavior problems. In order to independently solve problems, students must be aware of the steps of problem solving. An effective strategy is to verbalize the steps of problem solving using Big6 vocabulary. All of the steps of Big6 are utilized when students solve classroom management problems. There are, however, two steps which are essential when guiding students through the process. These two steps are task definition (Big6 #1) and evaluation (Big6 #6). These can be verbalized by asking students: What is your task? Evaluate. How are you doing? The problem solving process becomes visible and students are encouraged to accept the responsibility for solving the problems when these two steps are verbalized.

Scaffold Instruction

Modeling, followed by guided practice, is an effective strategy to help students learn and use Big6 independently to solve classroom procedure and behavior problems.

Scaffolding Classroom Routines and Procedures

The following illustrates one method of helping students learn classroom routines and procedures by scaffolding instruction.

Modeling Classroom Routines and Procedures
The first time a routine or procedure is used, the process needs to be modeled as students are guided through it. For instance, if the task is to turn papers or assignments in, it might look like this:

1. Any time you turn a paper in you need to put your full name, last name first, in the top right hand corner. Please do that now.

2. When I collect papers, the person at the back of the room should pass his or her paper forward to the classmate in front of him or her. That classmate in turn passes both papers to the classmate sitting in front of him or her. This continues until all the papers are passed to the first person in each row. Please pass your papers forward now.

3. The first person in the front left row will pick up papers from others in the front row and put them in the blue *In* box on my desk. Please do that now.

Guiding Classroom Routines and Procedures
The next time the procedure is used you will want to evaluate if students follow the proper procedure. If students successfully complete the procedure, provide feedback indicating the procedure was followed correctly and remind students this is the procedure for turning in papers for the rest of the year. If students did not successfully follow the procedure, guide or direct students as they repeat the procedure. This is what it might look like as the teacher guides students through the evaluation process by asking:

- What do you need to include on your paper before turning it in?
- Where do you write your name?
- Who passes their paper first?
- When does the second person in the row pass his or her paper?
- Who gathers the papers from the first person in each row?
- Where does that person put the papers?

Each time the procedure is used, over the next few days, students need to evaluate: How did we do with passing in our papers? Did we follow the procedure correctly? Do we need to do anything differently? The teacher should guide students in successful completion of the procedure if it is not being followed correctly.

Independent Practice of Routines and Procedures
Students should master the procedure within a short period of time. Once students master this process the teacher will only need to direct students to: Turn in your papers. Within a short amount of time, students will be able to solve the problem unconsciously or using autopilot (see Chapter 6). Valuable instructional time will be saved and students will be provided an opportunity to problem solve every time they are asked to turn in a paper. They will also have benefited from the opportunity to use Big6 while having the support of their teacher.

Scaffolding Behavior

A glimpse of what scaffolding might look like when the problem is a student behavior follows.

Modeling Behavior
Initially, the teacher will walk students through each step of the process:
1. Pose the problem: Some students find it difficult to think and learn when there is a lot of noise. Right now our classroom is very loud.
2. Ask students to identify the task: What do we need to do?
3. Guide students, if necessary, until they identify the task: We need to decrease the noise level of the classroom. (Task Definition #1)
4. Ask students what source can be used to access needed information: prior knowledge (Information Seeking Strategies #2)
5. Ask students to solve the problem. It might be necessary to discuss with students specific actions which will solve the problem, e.g. if everyone whispers, only talk about the assignment. (Use and Synthesis #4 and #5)
6. Ask students to evaluate after they have solved or attempted to solve the problem: Did you solve the problem? What did you do that worked? What would you do differently next time? (Evaluation #6)

Guiding Behavior
As behavior problems arise in the classroom, instead of directing students and telling students what to do, the teacher may guide the students to solve the problem by using each of the six steps as students are prompted:
1. What is our problem? Students should be able to identify the problem that noise affects the ability to learn. (Task Definition #1)

2. What sources can be used to help you solve this classroom management problem? Are you using prior knowledge successfully? If not, do you need me to be your source?

3. Would you solve that problem for me? What will it look like or sound like if you are solving the problem? (Use and Synthesis #4 and #5)

4. How did you do? Did you solve the problem? (Evaluate #6)

Independent Practice of Behavior
Many students will be able to independently monitor their behavior and solve any potential problems at this point. Other students, with less self-discipline, may always require some prompting. Eventually prompting may only require the teacher to ask the student to evaluate (Big6 #6).

Pose Problems

Teachers either tell students what to do or they prompt and ask. When teachers tell, they do the thinking and problem solving. When teachers prompt or ask, students are required to do the thinking and problem solving. At first glance it may appear easier to tell students what to do in regard to classroom procedures and behavior. For instance, telling students to sit down or open your book to page 114 is easier than prompting or asking students: What do we need to do before we start class? Open your book to the section on simple machines. Unfortunately, as long as you tell students, they will rely on you, because they are not getting any practice thinking or taking responsibility for their problems. When the teacher does the telling, she will have to tell on day 1, day 20, and maybe even on day 120. On the other hand, if the teacher prompts, students eventually rely upon themselves as the source. When this happens students begin to tell themselves and the teacher is not required to either tell or ask. This saves the teacher time and effort and also requires students to take responsibility for solving their own problems.

The first step in posing problems, for many teachers and library media specialists, is breaking the habit of telling or directing. Remember changing habits requires conscious thought and repetition. The benefits derived by both students and teachers, when students are the problem solvers, may provide the motivation to change habits. Seeing examples of asking, instead of telling (see Figure 16.2), may facilitate your change of habits.

Provide Opportunities for Student Evaluation

Before a problem may be solved it must first be recognized as a problem. Evaluation raises awareness that problems exist. When the existing problems are student problems, such as poor behavior choices or failing to follow established routines, students need to be aware of the problems. Student evaluation is, therefore, important. The questions relative to common classroom routines and procedures and classroom behavior identified in Figure 16.2 may be helpful as you encourage students to evaluate.

Telling vs. Questioning

Teacher telling and directing (Teacher thinking)	Teacher posing problems and prompting (Big6 #1 Task Definition) (Student thinking)	Providing opportunities for Student Evaluation (Big6 #6)
Stand in a straight line, stop talking, and keep your hands to yourself.	It is time to leave the library. What do you need to do?	Evaluate. How are you doing? What do you need to do to fix the problem? Can you do that?
Take a seat in the story nook.	We have a story to share today. Where do you think we need to go? Would you go there please?	Evaluate. Did we solve our problem? Are we in the right place? Did we get here safely and courteously?
Put your name on your paper.	■ I am going to be collecting these, recording grades, and returning them to you. What do you think is the first thing you need to do? ■ How will I know this is your paper?	■ After a few weeks, you should be able to go directly to evaluation. ■ If I collect this paper will I be able to return it to you? Record a grade for you? If not, can you fix that problem?
■ Write the answers to the questions in your journal. ■ Make sure to include the page number you found the answer on and write in complete sentences.	■ We need to answer some questions from our text. Would you get the materials you need to do so. ■ If I want to check where you found your answer, what do you need to include? ■ I also will need to read and understand your answers (without referring back to the book); what do you need to do? *NOTE: Students may or may not need to write in complete sentences as long as answer makes sense without text. The student has to think and determine what the answer will look like.*	Evaluate: ■ Do you have your answers written in the journal? ■ Did you include the number of the page on which the answer was found? ■ Do your answers make sense?
Take your textbook home tonight.	You have a social studies test or an assignment due tomorrow. Do you need to take anything home tonight?	Evaluate. Do have the source you need to complete your social studies assignment?
Be quiet.	What is your task? If you are talking are you solving your problem?	Evaluate. I am listening. Do I hear people solving their problem?
Answer questions 1-5 on page 200.	■ You need to know about classification of animals. Where will you find	Evaluate. ■ Did you find the information on animal classification?

Figure 16.2 Telling vs. Questioning

	information in your text on animal classification? Answer the questions in that section to help you learn about animal classification. ■ You need to know about . . . complete the questions on that topic in your text.	■ Did you find the questions you need to answer? ■ Did you use text features to help you find the questions quickly? ■ Which features did you use? ■ Did you answer the questions?
Walk please. Stop running. Keep your hands to yourself.	Are you being safe? Are you being courteous? Is it safe if you are running? Can you fix the problem?	Evaluate. Have you fixed the problem?
Why are you running? Don't you have any sense? Stop running.	Stop. Evaluate. Are you being safe? Can you be safe? Will you? Thank you so much because I know if you tell me you will do something I can trust you to do it.	Evaluate. What is your task? How are you doing?
I see a lot of people sitting around not reading. You were supposed to bring something to read or get something to read.	What was your task? Are you reading? Do you have something to read?	Evaluate. Are you reading? Why not? What do you need to do to solve your problem?

Transitioning from one activity or one class to another:

Get your art box and line up.	It is time for art. What do you need? What do you need to do?	Evaluate. Are you ready to go to art?
Put away your math. Clean off your desk and get your science textbooks.	It's time for science. What do you need to do?	Evaluate. Are you ready? What do you need?
Get your blue folder, pencil, and paper and get ready for reading.	It is time for reading. Are you ready?	Evaluate. Are you ready for reading? Do you have your materials?
Stand up, push your chair in.	It is . . . lunch time. Let's get ready.	Evaluate. Were we safe getting up? Were we courteous? Are chairs pushed in? If I have to push chairs in for you is that courteous?
Sit down and be quiet.	It is time for class to begin. What do you need to do? Can you show me that you are ready?	Evaluate: Are you ready to begin class?
Any transition:	Our task is ____. Would you solve that problem for me?	Evaluate. How did we do? What do we need to do differently next time?

Student asks, "How do you spell . . . afraid?"

Don't ask me. Look it up in the dictionary.	What source can you use?	Evaluate. Did you find the source? Did you find the word?

Figure 16.2 Telling vs. Questioning continued

Students talking when they should be reading.		
Stop talking.	What is your task? Using information? Engaging? What is the only way to engage?	Evaluate. Are you engaging? Will you?
Students talking when they should be working independently.		
Stop talking. You don't need to talk.	What source should you be using? Your brain or prior knowledge? If you are talking are you using your prior knowledge?	Evaluate. Do you need to talk to use that source? Does talking make it more difficult to use your source?
Students are following along as one student reads. The student reading is reading too fast . . . calling words but not taking the time necessary to comprehend.		
Slow down.	Are you comprehending or understanding what you are reading? What do we need to do to better understand? Slow down?	Evaluate. How are we doing?
Students need to answer questions on a study guide.		
<ul><li>Close books.</li><li>Get study guides out to page 3.</li><li>We have five questions.</li><li>Teacher reads question one and shows it on overhead.</li><li>One student raises her hand.</li><li>The teacher calls on her to answer.</li><li>The teacher writes the answer on the overhead.</li><li>Write the answer on your study guide.</li></ul>	<ul><li>Teacher identifies the topic and asks students to locate the page needed in the study guide.</li><li>Teacher calls upon student to read the question. Gives students think time and then randomly calls on a student to give answer.</li><li>Students are allowed a few minutes to write the answer on their study guide. Teacher observes to see all are on task.</li></ul>	Evaluate: <ul><li>Did you find the correct page in the study guide?</li><li>How did you do that?</li><li>Were you able to write the answers on your study guide?</li></ul>

Figure 16.2 Telling vs. Questioning continued

Establishing a Classroom Management System Utilizing Big6

| Content objective: | Classroom management/behavior |

Content objective: Classroom management/behavior

Information Literacy objective: Application of Big6 problem solving process

Time Requirement: About 10 to 15 minutes to introduce and then integrated into all classes and planned activities.

Rationale: For years the author had four rules for students when they were in the library. One year as part of end-of year student evaluation, students were asked to name the four rules. The majority of students could not. A light bulb turned on: That might be why students did not always follow the rules. How could they follow a rule they did not remember? Further reflection resulted in realization that students were given rules in the classroom in art, in music, in p.e., in the cafeteria, on the playground, etc. As an adult the number of rules was staggering. Making an effort to simplify, library expectations were condensed to two: Safe and Courteous.* When students remembered those two expectations, they found they were usually ok in all their classes without having to remember a lot of sets of rules. *NOTE: The author felt she must be on the right track when her new cell phone greeted her with: Be safe. Be courteous.*

Task Definition:

- At the beginning of the school year, introduce or review the two rules or expectations. Students must be SAFE and they must be COURTEOUS. It is important to make sure younger students understand the meaning of both safe and courteous.
- Discuss WHY the two rules are necessary and give examples of students not being safe and courteous, followed by examples of safe and courteous behavior.
- Encourage students to share the expectations with their parents most of whom will be pleased the school is reinforcing what they expect of their children.

ISS and L&A:

- Post several Safe and Courteous signs throughout the classroom.
- Initially the teacher or library media specialist acts as a source, verbalizing and pointing to signs, when students need to be reminded or guided to be safe and courteous.
- Soon the class may act as a source: What are our two rules?
- Eventually each student is expected to be a source being able to verbalize the two rules and knowing what they look like and sound like.

Synthesis:

What it sounds like in the classroom: Task Definition (Big6 #1) followed by Evaluation (Big6 #6)

With the entire class, if several students are having difficulty:

Teacher: What are the only 2 things expected of you in the classroom or library?

Student: Be safe and Be courteous.

Teacher: Evaluate. How is our class doing?

Student: Thumbs up/thumbs down.

If thumbs down:

Teacher: Can we fix this problem? Do you need me to fix this problem?

Most students choose to solve the problem themselves.

With an individual student who is having difficulty:

Teacher: There are only two rules in the library. What are they?

Evaluate. Are you being safe? Are you being courteous?

After the student acknowledges there is a problem:

Figure 16.3 Establishing a Classroom Management System Utilizing Big6

Teacher: CAN you be safe and courteous? WILL you be safe and courteous?

Students normally say yes.

Teacher: Good. Because I know that if you tell me you will be safe and courteous I can count on you or trust you. Can't I?

If a student has trouble evaluating objectively, an offer to work with them during recess to make sure they understand safe and courteous usually jogs their memory.

---

*Other teachers have used:

- Respect. Respect for others and for things.
- You are free to do anything you want as long as it does not create a problem for anyone else.
- Create your own.

Figure 16.3 Establishing a Classroom Management System Utilizing Big6 continued

Addressing Faulty Behavior

Background: You have introduced students to the classroom or library expectations. In this example the expectation is: Respect: Respect for others and respect for things. You have evaluated and find that while most students are showing respect there are a number who are not. Because of the number of students who need to be reminded of respect, you decide another lesson is needed. After sharing the problem with students you guide them through the Big6 problem solving process. This is what that lesson might look like:

The print that is italicized is how the students might respond.

Task Definition:

Teacher: What is our task when we are checking out books?

Check out books with respect. Respect for books and for others.

Teacher: What do you think it should look like and sound like when we check out?

—Shelves left in good order so others can find books.

—Quiet talking so we do not disturb others.

Evaluate:

Teacher: Evaluate by doing thumbs up or thumbs down how you think we are doing:

Are we leaving shelves in good order?

—A few of us are having problems. But overall we are doing a good job with keeping books in order.

Teacher: Are we talking quietly so we do not disturb others?

No, we are pretty loud. Students in the hall can probably hear us. You have to talk really loud to be heard above our voices.

Task Definition:

Teacher: To use quiet talking so we do not disturb others.

Information Seeking Strategies:

Teacher: What sources can we use?

—Mrs. Smith, the teacher

—ourselves

Figure 16.4 Addressing Faulty Behavior

Use of Information:

Teacher: Let's brainstorm how we might solve our problem.

—*We could have no talking. Absolutely quiet.*

—*We could have Mrs. Smith act as a monitor or police and make sure we use quiet voices.*

—*We could monitor ourselves.*

Teacher: Which would you rather try? Let's discuss.

—*No talking does not sound like any fun.*

—*If Mrs. Smith has to act as monitor she cannot be checking out our books. So we would have to wait and all get in line to check out at one time. That means we would have to stand in line longer. Mrs. Smith wouldn't be available to help us because she would be busy monitoring and checking out books.*

—*We could monitor ourselves. It hasn't worked too well yet. Are we mature enough to monitor ourselves?*

Teacher: What if a student doesn't use a quiet voice? Should there be consequences? For that student or the entire class? What might some consequences be?

—*Time out? The person being loud would have to go to table and sit down. Count to 10 or 20. If after counting person felt they could monitor themselves they could get back up and check out.*

—*If you still had problems being quiet, you wouldn't be able to select a book or to check out a book.*

Teacher: Let's vote. How do we want to monitor our noise during check out?

—*Students will probably decide to self monitor.*

Teacher: If this does not work, then who will have to monitor?

—*Mrs. Smith will have to monitor.*

Teacher: What about consequences? Thumbs up if you think our consequences are fair. Thumbs down if you don't think they are fair.

—*Majority of students will agree they are fair.*

Synthesis:

During checkout time, the students and Mrs. Smith will be listening for quiet voices.

Students will attempt to each monitor themselves.

If a student is not quiet, they will have to sit down and count.

If they still do not monitor themselves they will lose the privilege of checking out a book.

Evaluation:

After checkout session, Mrs. Smith will help students evaluate using thumbs up and thumbs down.

Teacher: How did we do? Did we have quiet voices?

If yes . . . Celebrate with a library hurrah (hands in air waving but no sound!) and continue self-monitoring next week.

If no . . . Next week Mrs. Smith will have to monitor and students will have to wait and then stand in line to check out books.

Figure 16.4 Addressing Faulty Behavior continued

How to Begin Integration of Big6 into Classroom Management

Integration of Big6 into your classroom management system will initially require an investment of time. Time is required to introduce the management system to students and then to model and guide students as they master classroom routines and procedures and classroom behavior. Less time will be required once students master the classroom management system. In fact, the time devoted to classroom management once students master the system may be less than the teacher currently spends on management. One approach to introducing Big6 as a classroom management strategy is presented in Figure 16.3.

One lesson may be all that is required to introduce students to the use of Big6 with classroom management. The teacher or library media specialist should evaluate and devote additional lessons if needed. These additional lessons (see Figure 16.4) should focus on development of task definition and evaluation skills, which lead students to effectively follow classroom routines and procedures and display classroom behavior.

Effective classroom management is critical if teachers and library media specialists are to make the most of their limited time with students. With the integration of Big6 into the classroom management system, it is possible to create a brain-friendly environment where little time needs to be devoted to classroom routines and procedures and classroom behavior. In addition, integration of Big6 into the classroom management system provides valuable opportunities for students to practice and develop their problem solving skills by solving authentic problems.

Works Cited

Denniston, JaDene, Certified Big6 Trainer. Conversation with Author. August, 2001.
Fay, Jim and David Funk. *Teaching with Love and Logic, Taking Control of the Classroom.* U.S.: The Love and Logic Press, 1995.

CHAPTER 17
MATH AND THE BIG6

One of the biggest math challenges for students is the dreaded *word problem*. You may be wondering what this has to do with Big6. The challenge cited is word **problems** and the Big6 is a **problem solving process**. Could Big6 possibly help solve word problems? The connection between word problems and the Big6 problem solving process was first suggested by Janell Bagwell, an elementary principal and former classroom teacher. She challenged me to tackle those dreaded math word problems using the Big6 steps.

What Does the Big6 Look Like Applied to Math Word Problems?

Figure 17.1 Big6 Organizer for Math Problems explains the steps of applying the Big6 process to math word problems.

1. What is my task and what information do I need? (Task Definition)
Read the problem to find the task and to identify the information needed to solve the problem.
2. What sources will I use? (Information Seeking Strategies)
The sources for solving math problems are usually the same. The problem solver is limited to his prior knowledge and the problem itself if it is a test situation. In practice sessions within the classroom the math text, teacher, parent, or classmate may also be available.
3. Where are the sources and the information? (Location and Access)
Location is typically not a problem for students. Teachers normally make the sources accessible. However awareness of this step can facilitate future problem solving and aid in retrieving needed information from prior knowledge.
4. Use the information
Engage (or read) and extract treasure. The treasure with math problems is the information needed (Step 1) and the math strategy needed.
5. Synthesize
Solve the problem.

6. Evaluate
 ■ Evaluate the product:
    ■ *Reread my task: Have I completed my task or solved my problem?*
    ■ *Is my answer reasonable?*
    ■ *Have I communicated my answer?*
    ■ *Can someone else find and read my answer?*
    ■ *Did I label the numbers in my answer using treasure words?*
    ■ *Did I explain my thinking?*
 ■ Evaluate the process:
    ■ *What part of the process was easiest for me?*
    ■ *What part was the hardest?*
    ■ *Did I know the math concepts?*

From **Teaching Elementary Information Literacy Skills with the Big6™** by **Joyce Needham**. Columbus, OH: Linworth Publishing, Inc. Copyright © 2009.

Figure 17.1 Big6 Organizer for Math Problems

Here is the problem.

On Friday, October 15, Tom and Julie went to the pet store. They saw 15 fish which were Tom's favorite pet and 19 dogs which were Julie's favorite pet. They also saw 4 snakes, 18 cats, and 3 lizards. How many more dogs than snakes did they see?

Now let's Big6 the problem (see Figure 17.2 on the following page). Following each of the six steps allows us to solve our math problem in a logical, sequential manner.

Big6 Math Organizer--How Many More Dogs Than Snakes

1. What is my task?

1.1 Task: How many more dogs than snakes did they see?

On Friday, October 15, Tom and Julie went to the pet store. They saw 15 fish, Tom's favorite pet, and 19 dogs, Julie's favorite pet. They also saw 4 snakes, 18 cats, and 3 lizards. **How many more dogs than snakes did they see?**

1.2 What information do I need to solve the problem?
How many dogs.
How many snakes.

2. What sources will I use?
The problem.
My prior knowledge (my brain).

3. Where are the sources and the information?
The sources are here: the problem is in front of me and my brain is in my head.

4. Use the information
Engage and extract treasure (information needed from 1.2) and math strategy .
How many dogs.
How many snakes.

Treasure: 19 dogs   4 snakes

On Friday, October 15, Tom and Julie went to the pet store. They saw 15 fish, Tom's favorite pet, and **19 dogs**, Julie's favorite pet. They also saw **4 snakes**, 18 cats, and 3 lizards. How many more dogs than snakes did they see?

Strategy: Using prior knowledge as my source I decide the math strategy I need is subtraction.

5. Synthesize or solve

$$\begin{array}{r} 19 \text{ dogs} \\ -\ 4 \text{ snakes} \\ \hline 15 \text{ more dogs than snakes} \end{array}$$

6. Evaluate

- Evaluate the Product:

Reread my task: How many more dogs than snakes? Have I solved my problem? Yes
Is my answer reasonable? Yes 15 seems reasonable if there were almost 20 dogs and only 4 snakes.
Have I communicated my answer?

- Can someone else read and find my answer? *Yes, I think so.*

- Did I label the numbers in my answer using treasure words? *Yes*

- Did I explain my thinking if I needed to? *My thinking should be clear because I identified the numbers. It did not ask me to explain as a separate task.*

- Evaluate the Process:

  What part of the process was easiest for me? *Solving was easiest for me.*

  What part was the hardest? *Identifying what information was needed was the hardest part for me.*

  Did I know the math concepts? *I did know that subtraction was the strategy needed and I knew how to subtract.*

From *Teaching Elementary Information Literacy Skills with the Big6™* by **Joyce Needham**. Columbus, OH: Linworth Publishing, Inc. Copyright © 2009.

Figure 17.2 Big6 Math Organizer–How Many More Dogs Than Snakes

Try the process one more time with a more complicated problem. Here is the problem.

> Jack has a marble collection. Half of it is blue because that is his favorite color to collect. One-fourth is red, and the remaining fourth is yellow. He will not tell anyone exactly how many marbles are in his collection but he says he has more than 10. However, his collection box will hold no more than 25. Draw and label one possible solution for Jack's marble mystery. Explain how you know this could be a possible answer.

Try to Big6 the problem using the organizer, Figure 17.1. To check your solution, see Figure 17.3.

Big6 Math Organizer—Marbles

1.1 What is my task
Reading the problem I find the task is to <u>draw and label one possible solution and to explain.</u>

Jack has a marble collection. Half of it is blue because that is his favorite color to collect. One-fourth is red, and the remaining fourth is yellow. He will not tell anyone exactly how many marbles are in his collection but he says he has more than 10. However, his collection box will hold no more than 25. <u>Draw and label one possible solution</u> for Jack's marble mystery. <u>Explain</u> how you know this could be a possible answer.

1.2 What information do I need to solve the problem?

How many marbles total (more than and less than)?

How many blue marbles?

How many red marbles?

How many yellow marbles?

2. What sources may I use?
The problem.
My prior knowledge.

3. Where are the sources and the information?
The sources are here: the problem is in front of me and my brain is in my head.

4. Use the information
Engage and extract treasure (information needed from 1.2) and math strategy.
Rereading information needed 1.2 reminds me of my treasure.

How many marbles total (more than and less than)?

How many blue marbles?

How many red marbles?

How many yellow marbles?

Treasure:
½ are blue, ¼ red, ¼ yellow
Total marbles = More than 10, no more than 25

Jack has a marble collection. **Half** of it is **blue** because that is his favorite color to collect. **One fourth is red**, and the **remaining fourth is yellow**. He will not tell anyone exactly how many marbles are in his collection but he says he has **more than 10**. However, his collection box will hold **no more than 25**. Draw and label one possible solution for Jack's marble mystery. Explain how you know this could be a possible answer.

Strategy:
Using prior knowledge I decide the math approach strategy of guess and test will work.

5.   Synthesize or solve

I think I will try 15.

- 15 is more than 10 and less than 25. That works. $\frac{1}{2}$ of 15 is 7.5. That will not work because I cannot divide a marble. Therefore my solution must be an even number.

- I think I will try 16. 16 is more than 10 and less than 25. $\frac{1}{2}$ of 16 is 8. 8 marbles could be blue. $\frac{1}{4}$ of 16 is 4. 4 marbles could be red and 4 marbles could be yellow. 8 + 4 + 4 = 16. So this could be a possible answer.

6.   Evaluate

- Evaluate the Product:

   Reread my task and evaluate to see if I solved the problem. Draw and label one possible solution and to explain. I did not draw, label or explain.

(It is important to remember that Big6 is not always linear. In this case, I need to go back to step 5 synthesis and then return to step 6 evaluate.

5.   Synthesize and solve (again)

- I think I will try 16. 16 is more than 10 and less than 25. $\frac{1}{2}$ of 16 is 8. 8 marbles could be blue. $\frac{1}{4}$ of 16 is 4. 4 marbles could be red and 4 marbles could be yellow. 8 + 4 + 4 = 16. So this could be a possible answer.

8 blue marbles

4 red marbles

4 yellow marbles

Explanation: If Jack had 16 marbles he would have more than 10 and less than 25. If 8 marbles were blue that would equal $\frac{1}{2}$ of his collection. 4 red and 4 yellow marbles would each equal $\frac{1}{4}$ of his collection.
(Notice highlighted words. Using treasure words make it faster and easier to explain.)

6.   Evaluate

- Evaluate the Product:
   Reread my task. <u>Draw and label one possible solution and explain.</u> Have I solved my problem? *Yes*
   Is my answer reasonable? *Rereading my explanation I think my answer is reasonable.*
   Have I communicated my answer?

- Can someone else find and read my answer? *Yes, but I might want to circle the answer to make it even easier to find.*

- Did I label the numbers in my answer using treasure words? *Yes*

- Did I explain my thinking? *Yes*

- Evaluate the Process:
   What part of the process was easiest for me?
   What part was the hardest?
   Did I know the math concepts?

From *Teaching Elementary Information Literacy Skills with the Big6™* by **Joyce Needham**. Columbus, OH: Linworth Publishing, Inc. Copyright © 2009.

Figure 17.3 Big6 Math Organizer—Marbles

Using the Big6 may help students conquer those dreaded word problems. How does it help? The answer lies in a question once asked during a staff development session. The question was: How do you eat an elephant? The answer: One bite at a time. By taking one bite at a time it is possible to tackle and solve difficult problems. Breaking the problem solving process into small steps makes the process concrete and visible. This enables students to apply each of the steps to solve math problems much as a cook uses a recipe (see Chapter 3).

What Basic Math Concepts Can Develop Through the Use of Big6?

Use of the Big6 process may also lead to a deeper understanding of the math process. A group of 4th grade students identified several math concepts (see Figure 17.4) after using Big6 to solve math word problems.

Task Definition: What is my task? ■ The task is usually stated at the end of the problem. ■ Since the task is often a question, scanning for a question mark (?) can help find the task. ■ To solve a problem you must take action, so scanning for verbs or action words can help find the task.
Task Definition: What information do I need? ■ Identifying information needed to solve problems is important, but also difficult. ■ To identify information needed requires using prior knowledge as well as the problem. ■ Visualizing the problem (drawing) can help me figure out what information is needed.
Information Seeking Strategies: ■ The problem and prior knowledge are almost always the sources needed. ■ Knowing whether to use the problem or prior knowledge for each step is hard but is important.
Location and Access: ■ Locating sources is almost always a no-brainer with math problems. ■ Locating information within prior knowledge (retrieval) is an important skill. ■ While location and access are pretty easy when solving math problems, it can be challenging when solving other types of problems, i.e. researching a topic or finding a telephone number in a directory.
Use of Information: ■ Going back and rereading the task makes it easier to identify and extract the needed information. ■ To identify which math strategy to use, prior knowledge is a source. ■ To choose which math strategy to use, I must recall all the different strategies AND why the strategy is used.
Synthesis: ■ Synthesis and solving the problem are synonymous. ■ At this step I just need to use the treasure numbers and apply the math strategy.
Evaluation: ■ Rereading the problem helps evaluate the product. "Did I complete my task?" ■ Evaluating helps catch "silly mistakes", i.e. failing to communicate the answer because I did not label numbers or answers that do not make sense (100 – 20 = 120) because of careless mistakes. ■ Reflecting on the process helps me solve my next problem faster and easier.

Figure 17.4 Math Concepts

The concepts were student-discovered during the problem solving process and not teacher-told. There is a greater possibility the learning will become a permanent part of the students' schema due to the connections students made as this learning occurred (see Chapter 3). These concepts will be valuable to students as they continue solving math problems.

How Can I Guide My Students to Use Big6 to Solve Math Problems?

Begin by reviewing what is known about teaching processes:

- Break the process into small steps
- Go from simple to complex
- Model and guide prior to providing independent practice
- Use the power of repetition (see Chapter 4 for more about teaching process)

Keeping these criteria in mind, the following sequence of learning strategies can be effective:

1. Verbalize and ensure that students **know** the following:

   - **What are we are learning?** We are learning to master the problem solving process to enable us to solve word problems with little conscious effort, i.e. autopilot, much as we solve 2 + 2 and 5 − 3.

   - **Why do we need the Big6 process?** Breaking process into small steps and consciously using the steps, i.e. manual drive, is the best way to **master a process** and to **solve difficult problems** or brain-busters.

2. The following analogy may help students understand <u>what</u> and <u>why</u>.

A typical 10-month-old child has to consciously practice the steps in walking (balance, foot up, foot forward, foot down, left foot, right foot, etc.). He must use manual drive. At around 15 months of age, when we refer to the child as a toddler, he is in the process of learning or mastering the process of walking. Although he can walk, he is still a bit clumsy and falls frequently. Sometimes he functions on autopilot, but at other times he must revert to manual drive. By the time the child is age 3 or 4 he has mastered the process of walking and can do so on autopilot with no conscious thought to the process. However, when faced with difficult situations, such as walking with a new pair of shoes, walking on ice, walking with a brace the child may still find it helpful to give conscious thought to the process.

Perhaps you have mastered the process of walking. However, when the process involved is solving problems you may be like the 10- or 15-month-old child. You are beginning to learn the process of problem solving or you have learned part of the process. Giving conscious thought to the process may enable you to master the process. Once the process is mastered, you will solve math problems on autopilot, especially those no-brainers or easy problems. However you may find switching back to manual drive, which requires you to know the steps in the process, helpful when faced with brain-buster problems.

3. **Solve simple problems**

   Begin by using the process to solve simple problems. This allows students to focus on the process. Once the process is learned, students will be ready to tackle more difficult problems. I discovered, through experience, the importance of beginning with simple math problems. Students were given difficult word problems to solve the first time Big6 was used to teach problem solving. This required students to learn the process while trying to solve brain-buster problems. Students were successful in solving the problems; however, they associated the difficulty of the problems with the process (Big6). Based upon that experience, the following sequence may work better:

   - Have students tackle a difficult word problem without the aid of Big6.

   - Model using the Big6 to solve that same problem. Students will be eager to learn the process after witnessing the power of the Big6.

   - Use simple word problems, no-brainers, to help students learn the six steps and practice the process.

   - Finally, apply the Big6 to those brain-buster problems.

4. **TSE or Plan-Do-Review for Younger Students**

   If you teach younger students, kindergartners and 1st graders, you may wish to introduce only three of the six steps in the Big6, for instance TSE:

   T = Task
   S = Solve or synthesize
   E = Evaluate

   The remaining three steps may be added after students master TSE. Another option is to use the Super Three, or Plan-Do-Review, (Eisenberg and Berkowitz 21). One advantage of beginning with TSE is the vocabulary will always stay the same. Students simply add to existing vocabulary rather than learning new terminology as they progress to all six steps of the process.

5. **Using a Big6 organizer**

   Require students to complete a Big6 organizer as the math word problem is solved. Using an organizer (see Figure 17.5) may guide students while making each step of the process visible and concrete. The organizer also ensures repetition of each of the steps. Repetition is a powerful learning strategy.

6. **Scaffold learning**

   - Begin by modeling. Solve one or two problems completing a Big6 organizer as your students observe. Use a projection device such as an overhead projector.

   - Move to guided practice by randomly calling on individual students to complete each step of the process. As your students verbalize the information needed, record it on the Big6 organizer.

   - Provide students with opportunities for guided practice. *Note:* Solving problems using an organizer is a labor intensive activity. It is important students be frequently reminded that they are *only expected to use the organizer until they learn the process.* To help motivate students you might verbalize: The sooner we learn the process, the sooner we may abandon the organizer. Remind students that once the process is mastered they might still want to use the organizer when faced with a brain-buster.

Big6 Math Organizer

1. Task Definition: 1.1 What is my task? (visualize)   1.2 What information do I need to solve the problem?
2. Information Seeking Strategies: What sources will I use?
3. Location and Access: Where are the sources and the information?
4. Use the information: What is the treasure?   What math strategy can I use?
5. Synthesize: Solve the problem.

6. Evaluate:
■ Evaluate the Product:
   Reread my task: Have I completed my task? . . . solved my problem?
   Is my answer reasonable?
   Have I communicated my answer?
      ■ Can someone else find and read my answer?
      ■ Did I label the numbers in my answer using treasure words?
      ■ Did I explain my thinking if I needed to?
■ Evaluate the Process:
   What part of the process was easiest for me?
   What part was the hardest?
   Did I know the math concepts?

Figure 17.5 Big6 Math Organizer

7. **Using a mnemonic**

As students master the individual steps, the organizer may be taken away and students encouraged to use a mnemonic (see Figure 17.6) to remember the steps. The student may write the mnemonic at the top of his paper to guide him through the problem solving process. Remember, the goal is to help students master the process, to learn the process so well it becomes automatic or invisible. Students who master the process will not normally need the mnemonic. However, it remains a helpful strategy when faced with difficult problems.

Mnemonic 1:

TIL USE (Eisenberg)

Task Definition
Information Seeking Strategies
Location and Access

Use of Information
Synthesis
Evaluation

Mnemonic 2:

www.use (Needham)

What is my task and what information do I need?
What source can I use?
Where is the source and the information?
Use the information
Synthesis
Evaluation

I found www.use easy for elementary students to remember (see Chapter 1 for more information). Students familiarity with Web addresses make www. easy for students to remember. Also at this age what, what, where are logical and therefore user friendly.

Figure 17.6 Mnemonics

Strategies That May Be Used to Address Specific Weaknesses

When Students Have Difficulty Breaking the Process into Small Steps

Provide practice in which students solve only one step of the problem before passing it to another group. For instance, one group would solve step 1 with problem A, step 2 with problem B, etc.

Supplies or materials needed:

- One math word problem for each group
- One piece of chart paper for each group
- Markers

Process:

- Divide the class into groups of 3 or 4 students each. Five groups work well. Give each group a different problem and chart paper. Group A has problem 1, group B has problem 2, etc.

- Ask each group to complete only one step:

Rounds	Step to be completed
Round 1	1.1 What is my task?
Round 2	1.2 What information is needed?
Discuss 2 & 3	What sources can I use and where are the sources and information?
Round 3	4 Use, extract treasure information
Round 4	4 Use, extract math strategy
Round 5	5 Synthesize or solve

- After a step is completed, guide the class in evaluating that step. After evaluating, rotate the problem and chart paper to the next group. Figure 17.7 illustrates which problem

	Group A	Group B	Group C	Group D	Group E
Round 1	Problem 1	Problem 2	Problem 3	Problem 4	Problem 5
Round 2	Problem 5	Problem 1	Problem 2	Problem 3	Problem 4
Round 3	Problem 4	Problem 5	Problem 1	Problem 2	Problem 3
Round 4	Problem 3	Problem 4	Problem 5	Problem 1	Problem 2
Round 5	Problem 2	Problem 3	Problem 4	Problem 5	Problem 1

Figure 17.7 Rotation

each group will be working on in the various rounds.

- End the exercise by posting all chart papers. Ask students to do a final evaluation of the process, e.g., What did we do well? What will we want to do differently next time? Figure 17.8 illustrates the process following one problem as it moves from group to group through the rounds.

When Students Have Difficulty Identifying the Task or Information Needed

Teach students to visualize. Help them to create a nonlinguistic representation of the problem (Marzano 73). Visualization can make the abstract concrete. As the student visualizes the problem, he will connect to prior knowledge. For instance, our problem is to determine how much money we would get back from $1 if we bought an apple for 30 cents and a banana for 25 cents. As the child visualizes, he might see himself or his parents standing at the cash register handing a $1 bill to the clerk. An apple and a banana would be on the counter. This picture allows the child to connect to prior knowledge. He would see the clerk adding the total of all the items purchased, his parents giving money to the clerk, and the clerk handing money back to his parents. Accessing this prior knowledge will help the stu-

Problem: Josie buys a stereo system through a television ad. She makes three payments of $79.95 each to pay for it. She also pays $12.50 for shipping. **What is** the **total** cost of the **stereo system?**
Round 1, Group 1. Task Definition, 1.1, **What** is my task? Underline and restate the task. Evaluate and pass problem and chart paper. The problem is to find the total cost of the stereo system.

Round 2, Group 2. Task Definition, 1.2, What information is needed?
 List information needed on chart paper. Evaluate and pass problem and chart paper.
The needed information or treasure is
    ■ How many payments?
    ■ Amount of each payment?
    ■ Any additional costs?

Information Seeking Strategy, 2, & Location and Access, 3. Randomly call on students to verbalize but do not pass papers. Sources needed are prior knowledge and the problem. The sources are located here. Prior knowledge in brain and the problem in front of student.
Round 3, Group 3. Use of Information, extract treasure. Circle or rewrite the treasure. Evaluate and pass problem and chart paper. Treasure has been identified as how many payments, the amount of each payment, and any additional costs. Rereading the problem the treasure is located. 3 payments each payment was $79.95 and there was additional cost of $12.50 for shipping
Round 4, Group 4. Use of Information, extract or determine the strategy needed. List the math strategy or strategies needed. Evaluate and pass problem and chart paper. First multiply or add, and then add.
Round 5, Group 5. Synthesize or Solve the problem. Students should be able to solve the problem using only chart paper. Evaluate and post the chart paper. $79.95 x 3 = $239.85 $239.85 + $12.50 = $252.35

Figure 17.8 Following One Problem through the Process

dent identify the task and what information is needed to solve the problem.

One helpful approach when teaching students to visualize follows:

1. Present a problem to students

2. During task definition, identify two or three keywords in the problem

3. Do a nonlinguistic drawing of the keywords or the problem

4. Proceed through the rest of the problem solving process

5. After you have modeled two or three problems, it is time to provide guided practice for your students. Randomly call on students to identify the keywords and do a nonlinguistic drawing as the class solves two or three problems together.

6. Students should now be ready to practice solving problems independently.

7. Remember, the purpose of solving these problems is to practice visualizing the problem. So be sure to evaluate both the identification of keywords and the nonlinguistic drawings. Figure 17.9 illustrates what students' visualization might look like.

Sample One	
Problem	Karen spent 60 minutes practicing the piano. Tell how much time she spent on practice in hours.
Keywords	Piano Minutes/hours
Nonlinguistic representation	 60 minutes in hour
Sample Two	
Problem	Molly buys a dogwood tree that costs $85. She also buys a bag of soil for $7 and a bag of mulch to spread around the tree after it is planted for $8. How much did she spend all together?
Keywords	Dogwood tree Bag of dirt Bag of mulch
Nonlinguistic representation	
*Clipart used with permission of *Izuno Design*	

From *Teaching Elementary Information Literacy Skills with the Big6™* by **Joyce Needham**. Columbus, OH: Linworth Publishing, Inc. Copyright © 2009.

Figure 17.9 Using Drawing and Visualization

The nonlinguistic drawings should be done quickly. The task is to identify keywords and create a drawing to help identify the problem and information needed. The task is not to create a work of art. You may need to remind some students of the task.

When this strategy was used with 4th graders, teacher observation suggested that the visualization helped students solve problems. This observation was supported by the responses students made when asked to evaluate the helpfulness of visualizing:

■ Now I can do some problems in a snap

■ It makes it clearer to me

■ It gives you an idea of what the information is

When Math Strategies Are the Weakness

Develop a math strategy bank. Students frequently have knowledge of a variety of math strategies, but have difficulty extracting the needed strategy. Recalling the needed strategies may be a problem because strategies are not stored in a logical manner in long-term memory. The problem may also be that students do not know why the strategy is used. Creating a math strategy bank can assist students in selecting the strategy needed. Figure 17.10, developed by 4th grade teacher Laura Mullins and myself, illustrates one way to organize math strategies.

As the teacher, you may choose to present the strategy bank to your class. Another option is to lead your students as they create their own chart by identifying and classifying strategies. Either way the strategy bank may be used as a guide by students when deciding which strategy is needed to solve the problem (Step #4). Eventually information will be transferred to prior knowledge and the guide will not be necessary. Figure 17.11 illustrates what it might look like if you lead your class in constructing their own strategy bank.

Start with blank chart paper and pose the problem or task for students:
We have learned many strategies for solving math problems. Some are computation strategies like adding and subtracting. Others help us approach the problem such as looking for a pattern or working backward.
One reason word problems can be difficult is because they do not tell us what math strategy to use. We must reach into our brain and retrieve the strategy we need to use from all those strategies we have stored. Our problem is two-fold. First we must recall the different strategies. Secondly deciding which strategy to use by identifying why each is used.
Do you think if we created a list of all the strategies we know it would be helpful in identifying the needed strategy? Would you want to be 30 years old and pull out your list of strategies to solve a math problem? Do you think if we create it, use it now, we might be able to store that information in our brain and use prior knowledge instead of a chart when we are 30?
What if instead of just listing the strategies we categorized them as to why we would use them? Would that make the chart easier to use? Easier to remember?
O.K., let's start with just our own brains as the source and see what we can create. What other source could we use if we need to? That is right, we could use our math book.
Let's think categories first. You might have students determine categories, e.g. "What categories do you think we need?" Or you might direct, e.g. "The categories I have thought of are . . . Do you agree? Do you see anything I missed?" At this point you would have student call out strategies and identify the category the strategy would fall under.

Figure 17.11 Creating a Math Strategy Bank

When Students Need to Strengthen Their Evaluation Skills

Provide practice evaluating. Two possible strategies follow.

Strategy 1

Have students practice evaluating student responses.

Supplies:

- one word problem
- organizer or mnemonic
- paper and pencil for each student

Math Strategy Bank

Getting Started:
- Do I need a strategy or am I just **interpreting** information?
- Does this problem require **multi-steps**?

Do I need an _organizational_ strategy? "Do I need to organize the information or treasure?"
- Make a list?
- Make a drawing (picture, array, etc.)?
- Make a table or chart?
- Make a graph?
- Make a Venn Diagram?

Do I need an _approach_ strategy? "How can I get started solving the problem?"
- Do I see a **pattern?**
- Do I need to work **backward?**
- Can I solve a **simpler problem first?**
- Should I **guess, test it, and revise** until I get the answer?

What _computation_ strategy do I need? "Are there keywords that tell me the operation?"
- Add

  How many total? How many in all? Find the sum. How many altogether. Plus, Add.
- Subtract

  The difference. How much less? How many more/much more? How many are left? Compare. Minus. Subtract.
- Multiply

  Find the product. How many times?
- Divide

  Find the quotient. How many in each . . . ? How can it be spread out equally? How many groups will you have/can you make/can you break into?

Still stuck?
Go back, is there another strategy you could use?

*Created by Laura Mullins and Joyce Needham

From *Teaching Elementary Information Literacy Skills with the Big6™* by **Joyce Needham**. Columbus, OH: Linworth Publishing, Inc. Copyright © 2009.

Figure 17.10 Math Strategy Bank

Process:

1. Have all students solve the same problem using the organizer or mnemonic.

2. Collect student work.

3. Separate the responses for each step, e.g. all the task definitions together.

4. Display the responses for each step, anonymously, using overhead or projection device. You might begin by displaying all student responses to task definition (Big6 #1.1).

5. Ask students to evaluate each response with thumbs up for yes, thumbs down for no, or thumbs sideways for maybe or not sure. For 1.1 Task Definition you might ask students: Is this the task?

6. Continue practicing evaluation through each of the steps in the process.

7. Display responses identifying the needed information (Big6 #1.2). Ask students to evaluate: Is this the information needed?

8. Display responses to Use of Information (Big6 #3) extracting the treasure. Ask students to: Evaluate, Is this the treasure?

9. Display responses to Use of Information (Big6 #3) extracting the strategy. Ask students to: Evaluate, Will this strategy work?

10. Display solution or synthesis (Big6 #5). Ask students to: Evaluate, Is the problem solved? Is the answer reasonable? Has the answer been communicated? Has work been explained?

     This repetitive practice helps students become more accurate evaluators. In addition, as students see the responses of classmates, they understand that making mistakes is part of the learning process. Through our mistakes we learn. Using the process and solving problems without making mistakes indicates mastery. To continue practice would be a waste of our time.

Strategy 2

Have students explain their problem solving process to the class and then challenge the class to evaluate both product and process.

Supplies:

- 1 word problem
- chart paper for each group
- marker for each group

Process:

1. Break class into groups.

2. Have each group solve the same problem on chart paper using mnemonic.

3. The whole class meets after problems have been solved.

4. Have each group explain each step of the process they used to solve the problem to the entire class: Our task was . . . The information we needed was . . . .

5. Students in the audience may ask questions of the group presenting. They might ask: Is that a 2 or a 3? What is that 9? Is it the number of dogs or the number of cats?

6. Students may also randomly be called upon to evaluate the problem solving process used by the group. For instance, a student might evaluate by saying: You identified your problems correctly. Are you sure you selected the correct math strategy?

This strategy provides additional evaluation practice for students and also provides feedback from peers which can be very powerful.

When Students Are Ready to Move to the Next Level

Provide opportunities to identify strengths and weaknesses and build upon them.

Strategy 1

Help students determine the strengths and weaknesses in their problem solving process through self-evaluation or teacher conferences.

Approximately six weeks into applying Big6 to math problems, 4th grade students were asked to identify the steps of the process that were easy for them and the steps that were difficult (see Figure 17.12). Rather than being vague, such as I just cannot solve math problems, responses were more specific. This knowledge of specific strengths and weaknesses was used by students to identify the next steps to becoming better problem solvers, such as practicing division or visualizing.

Evaluations made by 4th grade students after about six weeks of practice using Big6 as a strategy to solve math word problems:
I am good at doing "what's my task" and "synthesis." My weakest link is "evaluate" and sometimes "use."
I think the hardest part of Big6 is when I solve. I think solving is hard for me because the solution sometimes is something I don't understand or I have trouble with, like I have trouble with division and I sometimes need to practice my eights and fours in multiplication. I think the easiest part of Big6 is when I do my task. I think doing my task is easiest for me because I understand what I am supposed to do.
Deciding on a strategy and solving are the hardest for me. I am not good at deciding on a strategy but sometimes when it says, "find the total" then that is easy.
My strongest piece in Big6 is #5 Solving because solving is just like a math problem and math is my strongest subject. My weakest piece in Big6 is #1, part 2, finding what information I need and how to word it.
I am bad at synthesizing because we almost always get division and I am not good at division. I am good at my task and what I need to know because it is on my paper. I think Big6 really helps me.
Weller 4th Grade Students

Figure 17.12 Student Evaluations

Strategy 2

Provide diagnostic or prescriptive drills for students.

Instead of practicing each step of the problem solving process, provide students opportunities for extensive practice on the step which is weak. Observing a typical basketball practice session may illustrate what diagnostic practice looks like. In one area we may see the player who has difficulty making free throws standing at the free throw line and shooting 50 free throws. In another area his teammate who has trouble keeping up in a fast-pace game is running extra wind-sprints to build his stamina. The coach is observing the practice and guiding the athletes to ensure the process is practiced accurately.

To apply that same concept to problem solving, the student would practice just his weakest step in the process (see Figure 17.13). For instance, if the weakness was task definition the student would perhaps tackle five problems, but he would only identify the task for each problem. He would not complete any of the other steps. If his weakness was identifying treasure, he would be given a problem with the task and information needed identified. He would only practice locating the treasure. Practicing only the weakest step, rather than the entire process, allows students to make greater gains with less time invested.

The Big6 can provide an effective strategy for solving those dreaded word problems. Solving problems by engaging in each of the steps provides students a framework for identifying weaknesses and provides opportunities to employ specific actions to improve weak skills.

Works Cited

Eisenberg, Michael and Robert Berkowitz. *Teaching Information & Technology Skills: The Big6 in Elementary Schools.* Worthington, OH: Linworth Publishing Company, 1999.

Marzano, Robert J., Debra J. Pickering, and Jane E. Pollock. *Classroom Instruction That Works, Research-Based Strategies for Increasing Student Achievement.* Alexandria, VA: Association for Supervision and Curriculum Development, 2001.

Sample Diagnostic Practice

Example of what prescriptive or diagnostic practice might look like:
If task definition (What is my task) is weakness:
Problem 1: There are 4 shelves with scarves. Three shelves have 26 scarves on each shelf. The fourth shelf has 24 scarves. How many scarves are there on all the shelves? *WHAT task am I asked to do?*
Problem 2: The store charges $4 for gift-wrapping. They wrapped 13 gifts in the morning and 22 gifts in the afternoon. How much money did the store make on gift-wrapping? *WHAT task am I asked to do?*
If task definition (What information is needed) is weakness:
Problem 1: My task: Total number of scarves on all shelves. *WHAT information is needed to solve the problem?*
Problem 2: My task: How much money did the store make on gift-wrapping? *WHAT information is needed to solve the problem?*
If use of information (find the treasure) is weakness:
Problem 1: There are 4 shelves with scarves. Three shelves have 26 scarves on each shelf. The fourth shelf has 24 scarves. How many scarves are there on all the shelves? My treasure will be: number of shelves and number of scarves on each shelf Record or write treasure:
Problem 2: The store charges $4 for gift-wrapping. They wrapped 13 gifts in the morning and 22 gifts in the afternoon. How much money did the store make on gift-wrapping? My treasure will be: number of packages wrapped and cost to wrap each package. *Record or write treasure:*
If use of information (what math strategy do I need) is weakness:
Problem 1: My task: Total number of scarves on all shelves. My treasure: 3 shelves with 26 scarves on each and 1 shelf with 24 scarves. *Decide on strategy and write:*
Problem 3: My task: How much money did the store make on gift-wrapping? My treasure: 13 gifts wrapped in morning, 22 gifts wrapped in afternoon, and $4 to wrap each gift. *Decide on strategy and write:*
If synthesis (or solving) is weakness:

Figure 17.13 Sample Diagnostic Practice

Problem 1:
My task: Total number of scarves on all shelves.
My treasure: 3 shelves with 26 scarves on each and 1 shelf with 24 scarves.
My strategy: Add
Solve or synthesize:

Problem 2:
My task: How much money did the store make on gift-wrapping?
My treasure: 13 gifts wrapped in morning, 22 gifts wrapped in afternoon and $4 to wrap each present.
My strategy: Add and multiply
Solve or synthesize:

If evaluation is weakness:

Problem 1:
My task: Total number of scarves on all shelves.
Synthesis (answer):   26 shelf 1
                             26 shelf 2
                             26 shelf 3
                             24 shelf 4
                             74 scarves total

Evaluate:
Reread my task. Have I completed my work?
Does my answer make sense?
Can I/did I explain using treasure words?
Have I communicated my answer? Can someone else READ and UNDERSTAND my answer?

Problem 2:
My task: How much money did the store make on gift-wrapping?
Synthesis (answer)

13 gifts wrapped in the morning	35 gifts wrapped
22 gifts wrapped in the afternoon	$ 4 cost to wrap each gift
35 gifts wrapped	$140 made wrapping gifts

Evaluate:
Reread my task. Have I completed my work?
Does my answer make sense?
Can I/did I explain using treasure words?
Have I communicated my answer? Can someone else READ and UNDERSTAND my answer?

Figure 17.13 Sample Diagnostic Practice continued

CHAPTER 18
SCIENCE AND THE BIG6

Where Does the Big6 Fit into the Science Curriculum?

The body of knowledge we call science encompasses information about both the natural world around us and manmade objects. This body of knowledge exists because of the study, observation, and problem solving efforts of thousands of individuals. These individuals, or scientists, have utilized scientific inquiry in their efforts to understand and explain our world.

A review of the Science Content Standards, published by the National Academy of Sciences (NAS), reveals two content areas which overlap with the Big6 problem solving process: Science as Inquiry and Science and Technology (6). Both content areas involve problem solving processes. The basic difference in the two content areas or problem solving processes is the goal. Scientific inquiry is problem solving designed to understand the natural world. Technological design is problem solving designed to modify the natural world to meet human needs. (NAS 24) Both processes share steps with the Big6 problem solving process (see Figure 18.1).

A comparison of the three problem solving processes reveals that while terminology may differ, the processes are basically the same. The Big6 steps not specifically named in scientific inquiry and technological design are implied in those processes. It is possible, when teaching science content, to connect the Big6 process with either scientific inquiry or technological design. Making connections between these problem solving processes enables students to reach a deeper understanding of problem solving.

Problem Solving	Science as Inquiry	Science and Technology
Big6 Steps	**Full Scientific Inquiry (NAS, 123)**	**Technological Design (NAS, 137-138)**
Task Definition ■ Identify task ■ Identify information needed	Asking a simple question.	Identifying a simple problem.
Information Seeking Strategies ■ Identify possible sources ■ Select the best source		
Location and Access ■ Locate the source ■ Locate the information within the source		
Use of Information ■ Engage ■ Extract	Completing an investigation.	Proposing a solution. Implementing proposed solutions.
Synthesis ■ Organize ■ Present	Answering the question. Presenting the results to others.	Communicating a problem, design, and solution.
Evaluation ■ Product ■ Process		Evaluating a product or design.

A review of the Science Content Standards published by the National Academy of Sciences (p. 6) reveals two content areas which overlap with the Big6 problem solving process: science as inquiry and science and technology. Full scientific inquiry, within science as inquiry, is defined as asking a simple question (Big6 #1), completing an investigation (Big6 #3), answering the question (Big6 #5), and presenting the results to others (Big6 #5). Abilities of technological design, within science and technology, include identifying an individual problem (Big6 #1), proposing a probable solution, implementing the solution (Big6 #5), evaluating the solution (Big6 #6), and communicating the results (Big6 #5).

Figure 18.1 Problem Solving and Science

Utilizing a problem solving process to study science content provides students authentic problem solving practice. To validate the power of solving authentic problems to increase learning, think back to your days in school. Specifically think back to the time you spent in science classes. Based upon those reflections do you recall any specific daily lessons, e.g. lectures, discussions, text readings? Do you recall any problem solving lessons which required research papers, projects, or science experiments, e.g. completing a leaf collection, dissecting a frog, creating a science fair project? More than likely, if you recalled those science classes, your memories involved the problem solving lessons which required your active engagement, e.g. labs, experiments, projects. These lessons required you to solve authentic problems using a problem solving process. They integrated problem solving with content and provided the opportunity to master content and develop problem solving skills at the same time.

When students, already familiar with the Big6 process, are introduced to scientific inquiry, they are able to make connections (see Figure 18.2) which may lead to deeper understanding of both processes. Any time students complete an experiment, or scientific inquiry, there exists an opportunity to integrate Big6 and strengthen understanding of both processes. The student planner presented in Figure 18.2 may be used to help students successfully complete scientific experiments and become more familiar with the Big6 steps.

Big6 Steps	Science Process	Student Plan
#1 Task Definition (What is my task?)	Identify and state problem or question.	
#2 Information Seeking Strategies (What sources?)	What sources (including materials) do I need?	
#3 Location and Access (Where is source/info?)	Where are the sources?	
#4 Use of Information	Formulate a hypothesis (predict outcome). Design a procedure (list my steps). Conduct experiment and gather data (observe, measure, collect).	
#5 Synthesis	Report data (tables, graphs, charts). Draw conclusions (interpret data).	
#6 Evaluate	▪ Does my conclusion address my hypothesis? ▪ Is my experiment valid? Can it be repeated?	
Created by Laura Mullins, Traci Zay, and Joyce Needham		

From *Teaching Elementary Information Literacy Skills with the Big6™* by **Joyce Needham**. Columbus, OH: Linworth Publishing, Inc. Copyright © 2009.

Figure 18.2 Scientific Inquiry and Big6 Planner

Sample Lessons Integrating the Big6 Problem Solving Process and Science Content

Combining science content with the problem solving process provides unlimited teaching opportunities. Several sample lesson plans are included in this chapter to facilitate integration of science content and the problem solving process. These lessons may be taught by the classroom teacher alone. A better scenario, if you believe the two-heads-are-better-than-one philosophy, might be the classroom teacher and library media specialist collaborating to team teach the lessons. The classroom teacher may bring expert knowledge of content and specific students. The library media specialist may bring expert knowledge of the problem solving process and sources. This pooling of talents and sharing of responsibilities may lead to greater student success as well as professional support.

The content of the sample lesson plans is based upon the standards identified by the National Academy of Science (103) as the content students should know, understand,

Science Content Standards as identified by the National Academy of Sciences (104)
Unifying Concepts and Processes Science as Inquiry Physical Science Life Science Earth and Space Science Science and Technology Science in Personal and Social Perspectives History and Nature of Science

Figure 18.3 Science Content Standards

and be able to do in the field of science (see Figure 18.3).

Each general content area and a more specific content goal is identified for each lesson plan. Sample lesson plans are provided for both primary students, grades k-2, and intermediate students, grades 3-5.

The science content in each of the sample lesson plans is presented as a problem. This means each lesson provides an opportunity to practice problem solving skills. The Big6 process may become visible if each step is verbalized as the problem is solved. Use of a Big6 organizer, completed by the teacher or student, is another method of making the process visible to students. Figure 4.1 (Chapter 4) provides an example of a Big6 organizer.

Depending upon the lesson, students may focus on the entire process or on one or two specific steps or problem solving skills significant to the particular problem. Specific suggestions for evaluation of process are included in the sample lesson plans. Teachers and library media specialists may also choose to refer to Chapter 12 for additional suggestions for evaluating.

Through problem solving, each lesson addresses either Science as Inquiry or Science and Technology content standards. In addition, each sample lesson involves authentic reading and writing practice which provides students opportunities to improve these vital skills.

Students need to master science concepts. Developing problem solving skills is also important. Integration of science content and problem solving instruction allows for more efficient use of limited instructional time. For instance, if science and problem solving are taught separately during a 30-minute period of instruction, students could receive 15 minutes of science content and 15 minutes of problem solving. By integrating instruction, students could receive 30 minutes of science content and 30 minutes of problem solving instruction. Another positive result of integration is the creation of authentic learning situations, e.g. students use problem solving for a real purpose, not just to learn the process. In addition, most integrated lessons incorporate instruction in communication arts processes such as reading, writing, listening, and speaking. Integrating instruction of all these important skills within one authentic learning situation utilizes limited instructional time and leads to powerful learning opportunities.

LESSON PLAN 18.1

LESSON TITLE: PROPERTIES OF OBJECTS: COMPARING, SORTING, AND DESCRIBING

Grade Level: K-2nd	**Time Frame:** ■ One 20- to 30-minute session
Content Objective: Physical Science: ■ K-4th Properties of objects and materials	**Information Literacy Objective:** ■ Practice steps of the problem solving process

Materials and Sources:

■ A collection of objects exhibiting a variety of properties (different sizes, weights, shapes, colors, temperatures, and made from a variety of paper, wood, and metal). Every object should share one property with at least one other object in the collection, e.g. at least two objects should be of the same size or temperature.

PLAN

Problem:

■ Scientists look closely at the world around us. They observe. As they observe they begin to compare and sort and describe. Through their work scientists are able to explain a lot about the world in which we live. For instance, because of the work of scientists we know that although the climate or temperature varies throughout our world each climate has seasons. Those seasons have similarities. Winter is the coldest. Spring is the wettest. Those seasons follow in the same order throughout the world. Fall is followed by winter which is followed by spring which is followed by summer.

■ Would you like to be a scientist? Would you like to observe, compare, sort, and describe the world around you? I have some objects found in our world that I would like to know more about. Would you like to practice being a scientist and help me?

Task Definition (What):

■ What is our task? *To learn more about these objects by observing them, then comparing, sorting, and describing them.*

■ Could we solve our problem if: We all observe. One person selects two or three objects which are alike in some way. Another person describes the selected objects and tells how they are alike. Would that work?

■ What information is needed (Big6 #1.2)? How might you group objects or how might objects be alike? *Let students look at the objects you have collected and brainstorm a list of properties. Compare the brainstormed list with the properties of objects (sizes, weights, shapes, colors, temperatures, and what they are made of such as paper, wood, or metal). Add to the list any properties students did not identify.*

Information Seeking Strategies (What):

■ What sources will we use? *The objects, our list of properties, our eyes as we observe, and our prior knowledge.*

Location and Access (Where):

■ Have you located all the sources?

Use of Information and Synthesis:

- Ask all students to observe. Students are specifically looking for properties which the objects have in common or which are shared. For instance: Do you see two or three objects which are the same size? . . . the same shape? . . . made of the same material?

Randomly call on one student to select two or three items (compare and sort) from the collection of objects.

Allow think time.

Randomly call on another student to describe the property which the objects have in common or to share how the objects were sorted.

Evaluation:

- Product:
    - Do you know more about objects now?
    - Take away the list of properties and ask students to recall the properties using prior knowledge.
- Process:
    - Have students complete and submit with the project a written evaluation of the process.
    - Did we act as scientists? Explain.
    - Did we use Big6 or our problem solving process to solve this problem?
    - What might we want to do differently next time?

LESSON PLAN 18.2

LESSON TITLE: LIFE CYCLES

Grade Level: K-1st	**Time Frame:** ■ One 30-minute session
Content Objective: Life Science ■ K-5th Life Cycles of Organisms	**Information Literacy Objective:** ■ Practice steps of the problem solving process ■ Ability to recognize problems

Materials and Sources:

■ *The Caterpillar and Pollywog* by Jack Kent
■ Cards depicting the life cycle of a frog (four cards each with one picture of the life cycle)
■ Cards depicting the life cycle of a butterfly (four cards each with one picture of the life cycle)
■ Pictures may be obtained from Enchanted Learning Web site:
<http://www.enchantedlearning.com>

PLAN

Problem:

■ I have a book about a caterpillar and a pollywog I would like to share with you. The caterpillar and the pollywog have something in common or something they share. As you listen to the story would you help me figure out what that something is? Don't shout out. We will talk about it when we finish our story.
■ Read *The Caterpillar and the Pollywog.*

Task Definition (What):

■ What was our problem? What did the caterpillar and the pollywog have in common? How were they the same? *Students should identify that both animals changed.* When animals change as they grow it is called life cycle. *Write life cycle for students to see.* The book showed the stages or steps the caterpillar and the pollywog went through in their life cycle. Can you put those stages in order?

Information Seeking Strategies (What):

■ What source can we use to solve our problem? I have these pictures which show the four stages of each animal. What other source do you need? *Students should identify prior knowledge or what they know as source.* Would you like to have not just your prior knowledge to use but that of your classmates, too? O.K., let's work as partners.

Use of Information:

■ Divide class into eight groups. Give each group a card with a picture of one phase of the life cycle of either the frog or the butterfly. Ask students to decide which animal is shown on their group's card. Then ask which of the four stages of the life cycle their card illustrates: first, second, third, or fourth.

Synthesis:

■ Use cooperative strategy, Line Up. Complete a line for the life cycle of each animal. For instance: Let's start with the life cycle of the frog. Look at your card. If you think you have the first a stage of the frog's life, bring your card and line up. Second stage? Continue until the entire life cycle of the frog is illustrated by the line up. Follow the same procedure for the butterfly.

Alternate Use and Synthesis:

■ Randomly give each of four children one of the cards representing a stage of the life cycle for the frog. Ask those children to line up in sequential order, or first, second, etc. Do the same with the butterfly. Repeat process until all students have a chance to participate in the line up and until students line up accurately.

Evaluation:

■ Product: Can we identify the four stages of the frog' life cycle? Can we identify the four stages of the butterfly's life cycle?

■ Process: How did your group do using the information? When we were lining up were students courteous? Did you like the line up? Which activity would you like to repeat? Was the book a good source of information?

From *Teaching Elementary Information Literacy Skills with the Big6™* by **Joyce Needham**. Columbus, OH: Linworth Publishing, Inc. Copyright © 2009.

LESSON PLAN 18.3

LESSON TITLE: DINOSAUR REPORT

Grade Level: K-2nd	**Time Frame:** Approx. 5 sessions ■ One 15- to 30-minute session intro ■ Three 1-hour sessions for centers (three or four students per center, each center 20 minutes, three centers each day). ■ One 15- to 30-minute session follow up
Content Objective: Life Science ■ K-4th Characteristics of Organisms and Environments • Could be used with any content	**Information Literacy Objective:** ■ Practice steps of the problem solving process • Synthesis: creating a report to share info.

Materials and Sources:

- Approximately 6-10 dinosaur books. Books should:
  - identify the type of dinosaur, e.g. t-rex, stegosaurus, etc.
  - include drawings of the dinosaur
  - include some text about the dinosaur
- Paper for student to create report. Include space for name of dinosaur, picture of dinosaur, and room to write two or three sentences. See sample at the end of lesson plan
- Parent or other helpers to read to students.

PLAN

Problem:

- Do you like dinosaurs? Would you like to learn more about them? Would you like to research a dinosaur? Write a report about the dinosaur?
- Do you have older brothers? . . . sisters? . . . friends? We are going to use the steps those older students use to write reports. Do you think you can do that?

Task Definition (What):

- You will choose a dinosaur, draw a picture of that dinosaur, and write a sentence or two about your dinosaur using the information you find in a book.
- Have students repeat task to you.

Information Seeking Strategies (What):

- Share books (hold books up and scan while students watch) with students and ask: Could you use this book to find information or facts about your dinosaur? Could you write a sentence or two using those facts? Could you use the pictures to help you draw a picture of your dinosaur?

Use of Information:

- When students come to the library, they select one dinosaur for their report. Adult reads paragraph about the dinosaur. Student then tells adult the one or two sentences he wants to write about his dinosaur. The sentence needs to include information obtained by looking at the picture of the dinosaur or from the text. Since this is a report, the source of the information should be the book rather than the student's prior knowledge.

Synthesis:

- Depending upon ability, the student may either write his sentence on the report form or the adult can write the sentence on scrap paper and the student may copy it onto the report form.

- As one adult will be working with three or four students at one time, it is helpful to have one or two students begin to draw their dinosaur while the adult reads and helps another student to prepare his sentence. As this child begins to write, the adult can help the next student by reading.

- After reports are complete, display the reports with the caption: Kindergarten Dinosaur Research.

Evaluation:

It is important to have a follow-up session for the purpose of evaluation after reports are completed and posted.

- Product: Remind students that their task was to complete a report or research on a dinosaur. Have students indicate, via thumbs up/thumbs down, if they completed the project. Ask students to evaluate again via thumbs: How do you feel about the picture you drew for the report? . . . about the sentence or sentences you wrote? Were your parents impressed with your report?

- Process:

   - Remind students they used the same steps or process to create their report that older boys and girls use. So, when you get older, will you have to learn a new process or can you use this process which you are already familiar with?

   - Guide students through the steps of Big6 and ask them to evaluate if the steps worked for them:

      - Did you think about what your task (#1) was: to create a report of one dinosaur with a picture and a sentence? Did it help you to think about your task? Did you need to draw two pictures? *No.* Did you need to make a clay dinosaur? *Of course not.* Did you need to write at least one sentence? *Yes.*

      - Did you choose a source (#2) for your report? *Yes.* What was your source? *A book from the table in the library.*

      - Did you locate or find (#3) the source and the information within the source?

      - Did you use (#4) the information? Look at the picture to know how to draw your picture? Listen or read to know what information to include in your sentence? Did it help to have the adult read to you?

      - Did you synthesize (#5) or complete your report? Did you write your own sentence? . . . Did the helper write your sentence for you to copy? . . . Did the helper write some of the words from your sentence for you to copy? Did that help you?

      - Are we evaluating (#6) now? Are we thinking what we did right and what we need to do differently next time?

      - We just did the same thing high school and college students do when they have projects and reports to complete. Will we do this dinosaur report again? *Probably not.* Do you think you will be asked to learn about other topics and subjects and write a report? *Probably.* Will these steps help you do a good job the next time?

Name of Dinosaur

_____

_____

_____

_____

_____

_____
(student's name)

LESSON PLAN 18.4

LESSON TITLE: CLASS ANIMAL BOOK

Grade Level: K-2nd	Time Frame: ■ Five 30-minute sessions
Content Objective: Life Science ■ K-5th Characteristics of organisms and environments	**Information Literacy Objective:** ■ Practice steps of the problem solving process ■ Synthesis: creating a report to share info.

Materials and Sources:

- One nonfiction book about each animal to be included in student's book. An encyclopedia article may be substituted for younger students. The nonfiction book needs to include at least one picture of the animal.
- Scanner to digitize the pictures of animals which students draw
- Digital camera to take picture of the students
- PowerPoint or software to create book
- Note taking organizer, including place to cite source. See sample organizer following evaluation.
- 4th or 5th grade class to buddy with 1st graders and assist when "using" information
- Crayons or markers to draw pictures

PLAN

Session One:

Problems:

- Your teacher tells me you have been studying living and nonliving things. She thought you might be interested in learning more about living things. Is she right? What do you think about learning more about living things and then creating a class book with all that information? You could be the authors and illustrators?

Task Definition (What):

- What is our task? *To create a class book about living things.*
- Guide students in designing the book. One format possibility: Students, working in pairs, select an animal and create one page for the class book. Include on the page: name of the animal, drawing of the animal, four to five facts about the animal, picture and names of the student authors and illustrators, and names of the 4th or 5th grade buddies who assist.
- Let each pair of students choose the animal they want to study and write about. Lay out nonfiction books about a variety of animals or let students go to the shelves and select an animal by selecting a book from that section. Create a chart indicating each pair of students and the animal to be studied.
- Let students brainstorm the information they might like to find about their animal, e.g. what it eats, where it lives. Remind students that unless the teacher says they must include a specific piece of information, they are the authors and may choose what they find interesting.

Information Seeking Strategies (What):

■ How can we learn more about animals? What are some possible sources of information? After brainstorming a list, guide students in selecting books as the best source this time because they will contain all the needed information and are easy to access in the library. Also, since we are creating a book, studying the format of books will be helpful.

Location and Access (Where):

■ Pull an appropriate book for each pair of students. Think aloud: These books are all nonfiction. They have the same Dewey number.

■ Show students where this call number is located in the library, enabling them to find the books in the future.

■ Model for students locating the information within the book by skimming and using text features such as the headings, index, pictures, charts, etc.

■ Let students skim their books and use sticky notes to mark text or graphics they want to use.

Session One:
Use of Information:

■ Have both 1st graders and older buddies together for this session.

■ Explain the task to 4th and 5th graders: You know how to take notes, but this is pretty new for your 1st grade buddies so I need you to help them. What we have to do now is use the information. Remember, this means we need to take information in the book, send it to our brains, think about it, and extract or pull out the information we want to include on our page in the book.

■ Can we just copy from this published book into our book? That is called plagiarism and it is breaking the law, plus it is not nice. (See Chapter for 10 for more information on citing sources.) Can we read the book, put facts in our own words, and include in our book?

■ I find notes make it easier to use my own words. When I take notes or filter information from the book to my brain and then to my paper, I only use the important or treasure words. So I write phrases, or one or two words. It is important, though, that what I write makes sense to me. It doesn't have to make sense to anyone else, just me.

■ Model taking notes using the same note taking organizer students are using. Review with a few questions: Do you write complete sentences? Do you write just the important words? Who do the notes have to make sense to?

■ Model by showing students how to use their index finger as a pointer under the word to be copied. Also model copying letter by letter those words students are unsure of how to spell. Ask: Will I want the words in my book spelled correctly? Are the words in the text spelled correctly? Is it easier to copy them correctly now, letter by letter, or to go back later and use a dictionary to spell correctly?

■ 1st graders and their buddies work together reading and taking notes. Add names of buddies to the list of 1st grade pairs and animals.

Sessions Three and Four:
Synthesis:

■ Once we write our pages, we need to put all the pages together to form a book. Would you like me to do that? I will be your editor and publisher.

■ Other than your pages, what else do we need to make our book complete? Title page? List of sources? As editor I can use your note taking organizer to create list of sources. What about title? Can you help me create it now?

- Guide students in completing title page including title, authors and illustrators, and copyright date.
- Now we need to each complete our page. What needs to go on our page? *Text, picture of animal, picture of authors and illustrators, names of assistants.* As editor I can take care of names of assistants. Can you take care of the text and picture of the animal?
- Students are now ready to create the text for their pages. Model, using the note taking organizer, turning phrases in notes into complete sentences for the book. For this age group, creating a bulleted list, instead of paragraphs, may be more appropriate.
- We only need one picture. So you might decide which partner is the illustrator and have that person draw the picture while the other partner writes the rough draft. You might both want to draw a picture and then decide which to include in the book. As editor I can decide for you.
- That covers everything except picture of authors and illustrators. What if, while you are working, I call you, one set of partners at a time, and take your picture? Will we have everything we need to complete our book?
- Students complete rough draft and picture of the animal. Teacher calls one pair at a time to take photo.
- The final step is for the teacher or library media specialist to input all information into PowerPoint. One slide per page and print for students. Other possibilities would be to have a volunteer help with creating the PowerPoint, or work with the technology teacher who might have students key in text, older students scan, etc.

Session Five:
- After books are published, present one copy to each child.

Evaluation:
- Product and Process: Have students complete an oral or written evaluation of both the product and the process.

NOTE TAKING ORGANIZER
Name of 1st graders:
Name of 4th/5th grader:
Name of animal:
Write interesting facts about your animal. One fact in each square. Write ONLY the important or treasure words. Do NOT write complete sentences. 1st grader: decides what facts   4th/5th grader: write the facts
Title of source and page numbers

From *Teaching Elementary Information Literacy Skills with the Big6™* by **Joyce Needham**. Columbus, OH: Linworth Publishing, Inc. Copyright © 2009.

LESSON PLAN 18.5

LESSON TITLE: AN AUSTRALIAN RAINFOREST LIVING MUSEUM

Grade Level: 2nd – 4th

Time Frame:
- Seven 30-minute sessions
    - 1 session: intro and task definition
    - 2 sessions: complete note taking organizer
    - 1 session: complete fill-in report form
    - 1 session: complete visual
    - 1 longer session: living museum
    - 1 short session: evaluate

Content Objective:
Life Science
- K – 4th Organisms and environments

Information Literacy Objective:
- Practice steps of the problem solving process
- Use of Information: Note taking
- ISS and L&A: Using an electronic source
- Evaluation: Evaluating accurately

Materials and Sources:
- List of plants and animals living in Australian rainforests. Include five or six from each area: fish, mammals, birds, reptiles, insects, plants. Suggested Web site to access information: Rainforest-Australia: http://rainforest-australia.com/
- Pictures of and information about plants and animals from the Internet
- Note taking organizers, one for plants and one for animals
- Fill in blank report form. Sample follows the end of the lesson plan
- Materials to make model of plant or animal

PLAN

Problem:
- One objective in second grade is to study rainforests. I thought instead of just reading about rainforests, it might be fun to create a rainforest … or at least make the animals and plants that live in a rainforest. What do you think?"

Task Definition (What):
- What is our task? *To create a rainforest by creating models of animals and plants that are found in the rainforest.*
- Guide students to determine what information is needed about plants and animals. (Place this info on note taking organizer). Suggested questions:

Plants (Must answer question with *, choose 1 of the other 3 questions.)
*Where does it live (floor, under storey, canopy)? May need to infer. *What does it look like (include size)? What eats it? Is it helpful (to man or animals)? How has it adapted to survive? *I think it is interesting that …

Animals (Must answer question with *, choose 1 of the other 3 questions.)

*Where does it live (floor, under storey, canopy)? May need to infer.
*What does it look like (include size)?
*What does it eat?
What eats it?
What is its life like (social behavior)?
How has it adapted to survive?
*I think it is interesting that …

■ Provide a list of possible plants and animals to study. Ask each student to use the list and write first and second choices on a slip of paper. If two or more students choose the same animal randomly draw one. Let the other student have his/her second choice if possible.
■ Create list of research assignments.

Information Seeking Strategies (What):
■ We are going to use the Internet as our source because we want you to practice locating information on web pages.
■ Provide students with web address and/or make link to Web site on home page or desktop.

Location & Access (Where):
■ Project the Internet site while you model locating the Web site and skimming text features (menu choices, headings, bold, pictures, etc.) to locate the information needed.
■ Working with small groups of students, have students access Web site, their plant and or animal, skim to locate needed information, and then print the information.

Use of Information:
■ Provide each student a note taking organizer (plant or animal).
■ Project the Internet site while you model finding the important words/phrases or treasure and copy information onto the note taking organizer.
■ Students complete the note taking organizer using the information previously printed.

Synthesis:
■ Provide each student with a fill-in report form. Sample at end of the lesson plan.
■ Model using the note taking organizer to complete fill-in report form.
■ Students use note taking organizer and complete report.
■ Students create a visual using material of their choice. Can make picture or model.
■ Set up Living Museum. Mark the three layers of the rainforest and have students take their model and report to the appropriate area. Place a sticker on hand.
■ Invite other classes to visit the rainforest museum. As students walk through they can press the sticker to hear the information contained in the student report.

Note: Museum may be very simple with just the three layers marked and the models made by students or it may be very elaborate using empty carpet rolls for trees, green construction paper and crepe paper for leaves and vines, blue paper for water, etc.

Evaluation:

- Product: Create a rubric including all the information to be included (see task definition). Have students mark the rubric before turning in the report. The teacher should also complete the rubric and return to students. Students who accurately evaluated may be given bonus points. All students should study the rubric to compare their evaluation with the teacher's evaluation.

- Process: Have short session with students to evaluate process. Evaluation may be completed by individual students, by small groups of students, or orally with teacher leading evaluation. Develop questions to evaluate each of the six steps in the process. Questions might include:
    - Did knowing what information you needed make it easier or harder to complete your report? (Big6 #1)
    - Did you like using the Internet? How is using the Internet different than using a book? (Big6 #2)
    - If I gave you a web address today could you find it? Name some text features that helped you locate the information you needed on the Web site. Are these found in books or text? (Big6 #3)
    - Do you have to read before you take notes? Did you spell correctly when you copied your notes? Did you only include phrases in your notes? (Big6 #4)
    - Which did you like best: completing report or making model? What would you do differently next time? (Big6 #5)
    - Why are we taking time to look back at the process or to look at what we did? Will this process be helpful the next time we need to find information for a project or report? (Big6 #6)

RAINFOREST REPORT

(Draw or paste picture of animal or plant)

An Australian Rainforest Report By

The _____ is a plant/animal which lives mainly in the _____ layer of the rainforest. You can see by looking at my picture that_____

_____

I think it is interesting that_____

_____

From *Teaching Elementary Information Literacy Skills with the Big6™* by **Joyce Needham**. Columbus, OH: Linworth Publishing, Inc. Copyright © 2009.

LESSON PLAN 18.6

LESSON TITLE: OBJECTS IN THE SKY

Grade Level: 1st-3rd	**Time Frame:** ■ One 30- to 40-minute session
Content Objective: Earth and Space Science ■ K-4th Objects in the Sky	**Information Literacy Objective:** ■ Practice steps of the problem solving process ■ Information Seeking Strategies: Internet sources

Materials and Sources:

■ Electronic slide show or PowerPoint of pictures including sky, or sky with clouds, airplane, hot air balloon, stars, sun, bird, and moon
■ Set of printed pictures (one set for each team) with the different phrases of the moon, i.e. new moon, waxing crescent, first quarter, waxing gibbous, full moon, waning gibbous, waning crescent. Pictures should be in random order.

Note: Pictures may be obtained from electronic sources. Be careful of copyright issues.

PLAN

Problem:

■ Do you ever look up at the sky? Do you see objects in the sky? Do you see the same objects day and night or different objects? Are the objects man-made, natural, or both? Do you know? I have some pictures of objects in the sky. I thought it might be fun to see how many of them we can identify. Would you like to do that? What if we issue a challenge, e.g. boys vs. girls, tallest vs. shortest, birthdays Jan.-June vs. July-Dec., those wearing tennis shoes vs. those wearing other shoes, etc.

Task Definition (What):

■ What is our task? *Identify objects in the sky and facts about the object.*
■ For each picture we will ask one team to identify:
    ■ what the object is
    ■ whether it is found in the night sky or during the day
    ■ whether it is natural or man-made
■ A team can earn 3 points for each picture.
■ We will take turns, e.g. first girls' chance to earn 3 points and then boys' chance to earn 3 points.
■ Final challenge: Put the phases of the moon in the correct order. Your team can earn 6 points for putting the phases in the correct order, plus 1 point for each phase labeled.

Information Seeking Strategies (What):

■ What source will we be using? *Pictures, both electronic and print, prior knowledge, and classmates' prior knowledge.*

Use of Information and Synthesis:

- Remind students of the behavior expectations while playing the game, e.g. must be safe and courteous. If students fail to comply, stop, wait until all are safe and quiet and then continue. Remind students play has halted because someone is not being safe or courteous. This will help students solve behavior problems.

- Show a picture of one object. Call on one team member to identify what the object is, the next team member to tell when it is seen, and a third member to identify if it is natural or man-made. Move to the next team for the next object, again allowing each team member to answer one question. Either the teacher may keep score or appoint a member of the class to keep score. After all the pictures in the slide show are viewed, give each team a print copy of the phases of the moon and one minute to place them in order and name each phase of the moon.

Evaluation:

- Product: Did we identify the objects in the sky? Which team named the most objects?
- Process: Did you like using the pictures to identify the objects? Did you like playing the game? What might we want to do differently next time?

From *Teaching Elementary Information Literacy Skills with the Big6™* by **Joyce Needham**. Columbus, OH: Linworth Publishing, Inc. Copyright © 2009.

LESSON PLAN 18.7

LESSON TITLE: CREATING OUR SAFETY RULES

Grade Level: K-4th

Time Frame:
- One 30- or 45-minute session

Content Objective:
Science in Personal and Social Perspective
- K-5th Personal Health

Information Literacy Objective:
- Practice steps of the problem solving process
- Information Seeking Strategies: prior knowledge
- Recognition of problems

Materials and Sources:
- *Officer Buckle and Gloria* by Peggy Rathman
- Construction paper to create safety signs
- Markers or crayons

PLAN

Problem:
- I have an award-winning book I'd like to share with you.
- Read *Office Buckle and Gloria.* Ask students to identify what problem Officer Buckle and Gloria were trying to solve at school.

Task Definition (What):
- How can we make *our* school a safer school? Guide students to decide to create and post safety signs around the school.

Information Seeking Strategies (What):
- What source can we use to determine what signs we need? Guide students to recognize they know how to be safe and they know their school, so prior knowledge is a good source.

Location and Access (Where):
- Where is your prior knowledge? Students point to head.
- How can we get the information from our head to paper? Guide students to recognize they need to think and extract information.

Use of Information:
- Discuss how talking can sometimes help us make connections and pull information from our prior knowledge. Ask students to talk with a partner and think of two or three things students need to do to be safe at school.
- Each student needs to select at least one safety tip to include on a sign.

Synthesis:
- Distribute construction paper to students. Have students create *safety sign.*

- Students might be given choice of:
    - crayons or markers to create sign
    - shape of sign (rectangle, square, star, oval, etc.)
- Have student post safety signs around school in appropriate places.

Evaluation:

During next class session ask students to evaluate:

- Product: Did we create signs and post them? Did we make our school a safer place? What signs do you think were especially important to remind students?
- Process: Did we identify our problem? Did we choose a good source? Should we have used another source, e.g. asked the teacher or principal? Did it help to find information in our brain by talking to a partner? What did you like about the sign you prepared? What would you do differently if I asked you to make another sign today?

From *Teaching Elementary Information Literacy Skills with the Big6™* by **Joyce Needham**. Columbus, OH: Linworth Publishing, Inc. Copyright © 2009.

LESSON PLAN 18.8

LESSON TITLE: SIMPLE MACHINES AND WESTWARD EXPANSION

Grade Level: 5th	Time Frame:
	▪ One or two 30-minute sessions

Content Objective:	Information Literacy Objective:
Physical Science:	▪ Practice steps of the problem solving process
▪ 5th -8th Motion and Forces	▪ Information Seeking Strategies: Use of Internet as source
Social Studies:	
▪ History, Westward Expansion	▪ Location and Access: Practice scanning and skimming on the Internet

Materials and Sources:

- Internet Web site identifying or listing tools pioneers packed for their travels west <http://library.thinkquest.org/6400/> is a very good site if available
- Create a worksheet for students to complete, include: the Web address for information about pioneers, the six types of simple tools (may wish to let students gather this information), and a blank chart for students to complete. A sample chart follows:

Simple Machine	Parts of or samples of
Lever	Hinges, balance i.e. paddle, screwdriver, scissors (2 levers)
Wheel	Cogs, axle, bearings i.e. watch, doorknob
Pulley	Ropes i.e. elevator, ski lift, sails
Wedge	i.e. axe, a doorstop
Screw	Spring
Inclined plane	i.e. seesaw

Tool	Simple Machine

PLAN

Problem:

- Pioneers traveled west to settle new lands. When they reached their destination, after weeks of traveling in a covered wagon, could they check into a hotel? Stop by McDonalds or a fast food restaurant for meals? Or did they have to camp out until they could build their homes and barns? Prepare their own food? Clear their own land and plant their fields? What did the pioneers have to take with them to do all this work? *Tools.*

Task Definition (What):

- This is your challenge: You have studied tools. Your task is to list the tools the pioneers took with them on their westward journey and to identify those which are simple machines. You need to say if the tool is a simple machine and also identify it as one of the six simple machines we studied.

Information Seeking Strategies (What):

- Web site identifying tools pioneers took with them. If <http://library.thinkquest.org/6400/> is available it is a valuable resource. To find the items pioneers took with them in their travels click on *Pioneers*.
- Students will need to use a list of simple machines and prior knowledge as sources to complete the worksheet.

Location and Access (Where):

- Discuss with students how the ability to locate information quickly can save time and effort in completing assignments. Remind students of the power of practice in building skills. Challenge students to practice scanning and skimming to locate the information quickly.

Use of Information:

- Reading and extracting to identify the tools taken.
- Using information, from the worksheet or prior knowledge, to identify and classify simple machines.

Synthesis:

- Completing the worksheet.
- Creating a class chart which identifies all of the simple machines found.
- Strategy: Group students into teams of four. Each team compares and creates a list of all of the simple machines found. Round robin share with each team reporting one simple machine found. Record each machine on the class chart. Continue until the chart lists all of the simple machines found.

Evaluation:

- Product:
    - Did we identify the tools pioneers took with them? Were we able to identify what type of simple machine the tools were?
    - Working in partners, without looking at notes or the chart and using only prior knowledge, ask students to identify the six types of simple machines and then to list tools taken by pioneers.
- Process: Were you able to find the suggested Web site? How did you do with locating information? What strategies did you use to find information, i.e. read, skim, scan? Did you use prior knowledge as a source? Explain?

LESSON TITLE: ANIMAL CLASSIFICATION RIDDLE STEP BOOK

Grade Level: 3rd-5th	Time Frame:
	■ One initial 30- or 40-minute session to introduce
	■ Additional sessions may be used to complete book or it may be completed as a homework assignment

Content Objective:	Information Literacy Objective:
Life Science:	■ Practice the steps of the problem solving process
■ K-4th characteristics of organisms	■ Information Seeking Strategy: Selection of the best source
■ 5th-8th diversity and adaptations of organisms	■ Location and Access: Independent practice locating and accessing information

Materials and Sources:

- Three pieces of 12-inch by 18-inch construction paper for each student to be used as the pages of the book
- Pens and markers
- Books, Internet, or other sources of information about animals. Sources need to identify the five classifications of vertebrate and examples of animals within each classification.

PLAN

Problem:

- One learning goal this year is to learn about and classify animals. The study of animals is probably not new to you as I know other grades also study animals. That gave me an idea. What if instead of just learning about animals, we use the information learned to write animal books? We could read our books with students in lower grades as they study animals. Do you like that idea?

- I was trying to think of the kind of books younger students might enjoy. What do you think about riddles? Do you like riddle books? Do you think younger students might? Here were my thoughts: We need to learn about the five classes of vertebrate animals. So what if we create a riddle book including five riddles. A riddle for one animal in each of the five classes of vertebrates? You could each choose the animals you want to include so long as you have one animal from each class. Do you like that idea?

- Share a model of what a riddle book might look like. For each animal the front of the page will include a picture, name of the animal, and a clue which will help identify the animal classification. The answer to the riddle or identity of the class, e.g. mammal, reptile, etc., will be written on the back of the page. The book should include a title page and on the back of the title page sources used should be cited.

- The format of the book is called a step book as each successive page extends a step or an inch below the preceding page. Create the book by folding the three pieces of construction paper. Fold one sheet forming a 1-inch overlap, fold the second forming a 2-inch overlap, and the third to form a 3-inch overlap. Insert the page with 2-inch overlap in the middle of the page with 3-inch overlap. Next insert the page with 1-inch overlap in the middle of the 2-inch overlap. Staple at the fold. An illustration of what the book looks like follows:

Which Class of Vertebrate Am I?
Snake
Monkey
Frog
Cardinal
Trout

On the back of each page the class is identified.

Additional Sessions for completion of the project:

- Students may independently use Big6 to create books or the teacher may guide students through the process depending upon prior knowledge. In either instance requiring students to complete a Big6 organizer, like the sample at the end of lesson plan, may help students increase understanding of the process and also provide a means of assessing the students understanding of the process.

- The book may actually be completed as a homework assignment without any additional sessions if students work independently. A disadvantage of creating the book as a homework assignment is the inability of the teacher or library media specialist to observe students. Observing students in the process of solving a problem allows the teacher to identify problem solving weaknesses and provide valuable guidance.

From *Teaching Elementary Information Literacy Skills with the Big6™* by **Joyce Needham**. Columbus, OH: Linworth Publishing, Inc. Copyright © 2009.

Organizer for Animal Classification Riddle Book

1. What (Task Definition) ■ Task? ■ Info?	■ The task is to create a riddle book. The book will have riddles about five animals, one from each of the five classifications of vertebrate. ■ The information needed will include: five animals (one from each class), five pictures (drawn or photocopied), a clue for each animal that will help the reader identify the class of vertebrate.
2. What (Information Seeking Strategies) ■ Source?	■ Prior knowledge to select and classify animals ■ Nonfiction books ■ Internet for pictures ■ Encyclopedia (Teacher Note: If possible, allow students to choose source to use.)
3. Where (Location and Access) ■ Source where? ■ Info where?	■ The source will be found . . . ■ The information will be found by scanning and skimming for keywords using text sources. (Teacher Note: Monitor, if possible, offering assistance when needed.)
4. Use the information ■ Engage (read, listen, see) ■ Trash and Treasure	■ Create an organizer to gather information. ■ Identify the five animals to be included in the book. ■ Engage and extract at least one characteristic that could be used as a clue to the animal's classification and a picture of the animal.
5. Synthesize ■ Complete the task!	■ Create the book. 　■ Draw, print, or copy picture of each animal. 　■ Write clues for each animal. 　■ Write title page, page with sources cited, and front and back page of each animal.
6. Evaluate ■ Product? ■ Process?	■ Evaluate product and process by completing the teacher-provided rubric. (Teacher Note: Create a rubric evaluating both: ■ *Product: pictures, clues, title page, sources identified, neatness, writing, etc.* ■ *Process: Was it easy or difficult to follow the Big6 steps, did the steps save you time and effort, what would you do differently next time, etc.?)*

LESSON TITLE: INTERNET SCAVENGER HUNT: EARTHQUAKES AND VOLCANOES

Grade Level: 3rd-5th	**Time Frame:** ■ One 30- to 40-minute session
Content Objective: Earth and Space Science: ■ K-4th Changes in earth and sky ■ 5th-8th Structure of the earth systems	**Information Literacy Objective:** ■ Practice the steps of the problem solving process ■ Task Definition: Identifying keywords ■ Location and Access: Scanning and skimming to locate information on the Internet

Materials and Sources:

■ Pre-selected Web sites. Some sites which students might find interesting and informative include:

- ■ USGS Earthquake Hazards Program: <www.earthquakes.usgs.gov>
- ■ USGS Volcano Hazards Program: <www.volcanoes.usgs.gov>
- ■ Understanding Earthquakes: <http://projects.crustal.ucsb.edu/understanding/>
- ■ Volcano World: <http://volcano.und.edu/>

■ Teacher created scavenger hunt. Guide students to scan and quickly locate the information by identifying the menu or index choices, headings, and bold words which need to be selected at each site. It is suggested you verify accuracy of Web addresses and text features before each scavenger hunt because of the frequency with which Web sites change. A sample scavenger hunt is found at the end of this lesson plan.

PLAN

Problem:

■ One of our science objectives is to learn about volcanoes and earthquakes.

■ Do you think we can find any information about volcanoes and earthquakes on the Internet? *Yes.* I agree there is a tremendous amount of information available on the Internet. In fact, when using the Internet, I often find myself spending lots of time locating and accessing the information I need. Do you ever have that problem?

■ What do you think? Would you like to see if we can combine learning about volcanoes and earthquakes with polishing our location and access skills? Do you think we could do that if we went on an Internet scavenger hunt? I can create a scavenger hunt, or questions, and you could answer using information you find on the Internet.

■ You could each work with a partner and we could see which pair of students could find the most information in the shortest amount of time.

Task Definition (What):

■ What is your task? *Go on an Internet scavenger hunt to find information as quickly as possible.*

- What information do you need? *Answers to the questions on the scavenger hunt that teacher or library media specialist has prepared.* What can you do to quickly find the information on the Internet? *Identify the task by reading the questions on the scavenger hunt and identify keywords.* Provide assistance with identification of keywords if necessary.

Information Seeking Strategies (What):

- What source will you be using? *Internet sites selected by teacher.*

Location and Access (Where):

- How will you locate the source or Internet site? Explain to students how they can access these Web sites, e.g. using an Internet search engine, typing in URL, selecting from home page index, etc.
- Will you be reading or scanning and skimming to locate the information? *Scanning and skimming.*
- What will you scan and skim? *Scan the menu, or index, and other available text aids such as headings, bold text, and graphics. Skim the text once found.*
- What will you be scanning and skimming to find? *The keywords provided at the beginning of each question on the scavenger hunt and the keywords determined from the question itself.*

Use of Information:

- What will it look like when you use the information? *We will be reading and extracting, or pulling, the important information from the text.*

Synthesis:

- How will you synthesize? *By writing the correct answer on the handout.*

Evaluation:

- Product:
  - After completion of the scavenger hunt, have students check their papers and determine the number of correct answers.
  - Identify the winners of the scavenger hunt or those who found the most information.
- Process:
  - Ask those students finding the most correct answers to share some of the strategies which worked for them.
  - Ask the rest of the class to evaluate: Did you use the strategies? Do you think the strategies might have helped you be more successful?
  - Using student input, create a class list of do's and don'ts for using the Internet to quickly find information.

Sample Scavenger Hunt:
Volcanoes and Earthquakes

(Teacher Note: Scavenger Web sites were posted on school Web site by title and students simply selected the identified site. Students were also guided to scan, match letter by letter, or skim, match the word.)

1. a Click on **Understanding Earthquakes** *(scan)*
   b. Click on Rebound *(scan)*
   c. Read paragraph three and then view ANIMATION.
   d. After viewing the animation explain—
   e. What causes an earthquake *(skim)*_____

2. a. Click on **Understanding Earthquakes** *(scan)*
   b. Click on Earthquake Quiz *(scan)*
   c. Circle the correct answer to each of the following questions:
      1. North America, Asia, or South America *(skim)*
      2. Stay inside or go outside *(skim)*
      3. Alaska, Arkansas, California, Hawaii, Missouri, Montana, Nevada, Idaho, Washington, all of the preceding
      4. China, Great Britain, Japan, United States

3. a. Click on USGS Earthquake Hazards *(scan)*
   b. Click on Latest Quakes *(scan)*
   c. Click on USA *(scan)*
   d. Click on All Earthquakes List *(scan)*
   e. Complete the following chart with information from the last three BIG (magnitude = 3.0 or greater) earthquakes. *(skim)*

Date	Magnitude	Location

LESSON TITLE: PLANETS BROCHURE

Grade Level: 3rd-5th	Time Frame:
	■ Two sessions to complete Big6 #1-3
	■ One class session for use #4
	■ Three sessions for synthesis and evaluation #5 & 6

Content Objective:	Information Literacy Objective:
Earth and Space Science:	■ Practice using the steps of the problem solving process.
■ 5th -8th Earth in the Solar System	■ Information Seeking Strategies : Criteria for selecting best source

Materials and Sources:
- Note taking organizer
- Paper for final brochure
- Teacher or library media specialist created rubric
- Sources: nonfiction books, science textbook, encyclopedia, pre-selected Internet sites

PLAN

Problem:
- Show students some sample four-page brochures for tourist locations, e.g. San Francisco, Disney World, Silver Dollar City, etc. Ask: When someone wants to encourage us to visit a place, they will frequently create a brochure describing the place and all the fun things you can do on a visit to that location. The brochure uses facts and information but also lots of graphics or pictures. Do you think it might be fun to create a brochure?
- Our next topic in science is the planets in our solar system. Have you ever thought what it might be like if you could visit Mars? Or Saturn? Would that be cool?
- What if . . . we pretended you could visit a planet and created travel brochures for the planets?

Task Definition (What):
- What is our task? *Study the planets in our solar system and create a brochure about one planet.*
    - Each student will create a brochure about one planet.
    - After brochures are created, students can trade and collect a brochure from each planet.
- Guide students to design a four-page brochure using four pieces of chart paper and science objectives. For instance:
    - Page 1: Identify the planet. Drawing of the planet or drawing of all of the planets identifying the planet's place in the galaxy.

- Page 2: Facts about the planet. Might include: size compared to earth, atmosphere, number of moons, identifying features such as rings. Identify source of information.
  - Page 3: Student choice. New and exciting information the student learned about the planet. Might include your weight and age on the planet. May be found by searching for weight and age at <www.exploratorium.edu>.
  - Page 4: Fun Page. Create a crossword, word search, fill-in-the-blank, etc. for classmates to complete. Include answer in small print, upside down, at the bottom of the page.
- Let students draw to determine which planet to research. If you have 25 students then create 25 slips of paper each having the name of one planet, e.g. write 2 planets' names twice or on 4 slips of paper, and write the other 7 planets' names 3 times or on 21 slips of papers.

Information Seeking Strategies (What):

- Have students brainstorm possible sources. Sources might include textbook, nonfiction books, encyclopedias, or selected Internet sites.
- Randomly ask students to choose one possible source and tell why they would or would not use that source, e.g. easy to find or locate, hard to read, etc.
- If copyright date is not mentioned, hold up a source which is at least five years old. Ask students: Would this be a good source?
- Mention the date of publication and read from the book information now known to be inaccurate. Ask students: Do you agree with what I read? Do you think that is a fact?
- Explain why wrong information might be in the book: Space exploration is ongoing. With new technologies and studies we learn more each day. Sometimes we learn that what we thought was fact is wrong.
- So . . . is the date or age of the source important for this project? Would the copyright date be important if you were doing a report about . . . George Washington? . . . the invention of the first airplane? Guide students to realize the copyright date may or may not be important based upon what topic is being researched.
- Select the best source. Teacher may allow students to choose the source they wish to use from an acceptable list (student choice encourages engagement), or teacher may specifiy which source is to be used. If teacher selects, it is good to let students know why you are requiring they use a specific source. For example: The encyclopedia is a valuable source of information and one, as a 3rd grader, you need to know how to use. I want you to use it for this project so you will learn how to use it quickly and easily. Or: Because we are going to be using our information during our computer time, I want you to use these Web sites on the Internet, instead of a book or encyclopedia.

Location and Access (Where):

- Model locating information within a source. Pick a topic and have students identify keywords which might help you locate the needed information. Model scanning and skimming for keywords using available text features such as index or menu, headings, bold or highlighted text (see Chapter 9). Help students experience locating or finding information (Big6 #3) as a separate step to be completed before using information or reading (Big6 #4). The research process may speed up when students complete each step separately.

Session Three:
Use of Information:

- Provide students with note taking organizers, one for each of the four pages of the brochure.

■ Model Trash and Treasure note taking (see Chapter 10). Also model citing the source. Students read and take notes.

Sessions Four through Six:
Synthesis:

■ Model drafting your notes from previous lesson into complete sentences.

■ Students write rough draft of all four pages of the brochure.

■ Allow time for students to revise and edit their work.

Evaluation:

■ Provide students a rubric.

■ Ask students to evaluate or compare their brochure with expectations identified on the rubric.

Synthesis:

■ Students create brochure.

■ Make multiple copies of the finished brochures for student trading.

■ Display all the different brochures and allow students to move about the room looking at each.

■ Students gather all the copies of their brochure.

■ Students are given another task: At the end of this last session you need to have a brochure from each of the nine planets. How can this happen?

■ Suggest students move around the room, using library voices and library walk, and trade until they have a complete set of brochures.

■ How will we know when everyone is done? What if . . . as soon as you complete your collection you take a seat?

Evaluation:

■ Product: Do you have a complete set of brochures?

■ Process: Group students in teams of four and ask them to discuss: What worked well in completing the brochure? What was difficult about the project? What part was the most fun? What part was the hardest? What did you learn that will help you with your next project? After discussion within teams, ask each team to share one reflection with the entire group.

(Teacher Note: It is important for students to be aware of each step in the process and to complete one step before beginning the next if they are to learn the process as well as the content. This can be encouraged by including points on the rubric for completion of each step of the process and by requiring students to turn in work after each step, e.g. turn in notes, rough draft, revision, edited copy, final copy.)

LESSON PLAN 18.12

LESSON TITLE: NECESSITY IS THE MOTHER OF INVENTION

Grade Level: 1st-5th	Time Frame:
	■ One 30- or 40-minute session

Content Objective:	Information Literacy Objective:
Science in Personal and Social Perspectives:	■ Practice the steps of the problem solving process
■ K-5th Science and Technology in Local Challenges	■ Making connections between problem solving processes: Big6 and technological design
History and Nature of Science:	
■ K-4th Science as a Human Endeavor	
Science and Technology:	
■ K-5th Abilities of Technological Design	

Materials and Sources:

■ Samples of a few problems and inventions which solved the problem, e.g. a mass of computer wires and conduit to hide and protect the wires, a lot of remotes and a remote box designed to hold three or more remotes, or hand-held cellular phone and photo of cellular phone built into a car

■ Chart paper

PLAN

Problem:

■ Think about science. What is science? How does technology fit within science?

■ Discuss science, as observation and understanding of the natural world, and technology, as modifying the natural world to make man's life easier and better.

■ Identify the people who solve these problems as inventors.

■ Share a couple of problems and examples of inventions created to solve the problems. Examples of problems might include:

   ■ Problem: the mass of wires required for electronics such as computers, televisions, stereos

   ■ Invention: conduit designed to manage these wires

   ■ Problem: the number of remote controls which may be needed for a home theatre (television, stereo, DVD, satellite, etc.)

   ■ Solution: Remote boxes or organizers designed to keep remotes together and safe

   ■ Problem: the number of auto accidents because people are holding, dialing, messaging, talking etc. on cell phones

   ■ Solution: cellular phones built into cars designed to make cell phone use hands free and safer when in a vehicle

■ Ask students to brainstorm some problems and technological solutions, e.g. cases to protect Game Boys, suitcases with wheels making them easier to move. Ask: Have we solved all of man's problems? Is there anything left for inventors to invent? Would you like to be an inventor today? What if we identify some problems faced by mankind, by you, by me, by the world? Do you think you could think of possible solutions to those problems? Would you like to try?

Task Definition (What):

- What is our task today? *To identify problems faced by mankind and think of possible solutions to those problems or ideas for inventions.*

Information Seeking Strategies (What):

- What sources can we use to identify problems? *Our prior knowledge, classmates, teacher.* Once you identify the problem you will probably use prior knowledge to help invent a solution but could you also access information from books and the Internet?

Location and Access (Where):

- Let's locate our prior knowledge first.

Use of Information:

- Give students time to individually think about problems faced at school or at home and create a list. Have students, working in groups, share lists and create a group list of problems. Bring students back together as a class and create one class list of problems that need to be solved, e.g. losing lunch money, keeping school papers organized, forgetting assignments, losing papers, etc.

- Ask students to select one or more problems from the brainstormed list and focus on a solution or invention to the problem. Students may choose to work independently or in small groups. Groups or partners should be determined based upon common interest in a specific problem. Allow time for students to generate ideas.

Location and Access:

- Students may need to access factual information about their need or problem or possible inventions. Assist students as needed as they locate the source, e.g. book or Internet, and access the information via scanning and skimming for keywords using text features.

Synthesis:

- Students create a print copy of their problem or need and a bulleted list of possible inventions or solutions. Students may opt to choose one invention or solution for further investigation.

- Students share their lists with class either orally, via a poster or an electronic slide show.

Evaluation:

Following the sharing of ideas and inventions:

- Product:
    - Did we identify some problems which need to be solved? Did we have some viable ideas for solutions or inventions?
    - The class may vote to select their favorite invention or the best invention idea. Criteria may be established to judge, e.g. does it solve the problem, is it a reasonable or practical invention?

- Process: Did we use Big6 or did we use technological design or did we use both? Explain. Did the process help us? If we wanted to make this idea a reality would the process help us?

From *Teaching Elementary Information Literacy Skills with the Big6™* by **Joyce Needham**. Columbus, OH: Linworth Publishing, Inc. Copyright © 2009.

LESSON PLAN 18.13

LESSON TITLE: INVENTIONS AND OUR LIFE

Grade Level: 3rd-5th

Time Frame:
- Three 30-minute sessions

Content Objective:
- Content Standard Science in Personal and Social Perspectives, K-5 Science and Technology in Local Challenges
- Content Standard History and Nature of Science, K-5 Science as a Human Endeavor
- Communication Arts: Fact and Opinion

Information Literacy Objective:
- Practice using the steps of the problem solving process
- Information Seeking Strategies: Sources of facts and opinions
- Location and Access: Locating information in encyclopedia

Materials and Sources:
- Encyclopedia

PLAN

First Session:
Problem:

- Technology has caused lots of changes in our world. People do not always agree if these changes have been good or bad. For instance: Technology is responsible for the creation of video games. Some people think video games are entertaining and fun and that they help develop manual dexterity and quick reflexes. Others would argue they are time wasters, that kids are not reading as much because of them, and they are causing carpal tunnel syndrome. Same invention, different opinions. In reality most things are not totally good or bad, but both good and bad. There are pros and cons.

- Being able to see both sides of an issue is an important skill. A skill we might want to spend some time on improving. I thought one fun way to improve our ability to see both sides would be to have class debates. Some students will point out the good or positive effects of a specific invention and others will point out the negative effects. We could let the rest of the class vote, based on our arguments or facts, whether they feel the inventions are more positive or negative. What do you think?

- There is one more piece of information about these inventions which might be important to us. As we study different periods of history and try to understand why certain events happened, do you think it would be helpful to know what life was like? If they had access to television? Traveled in cars or on horses? What if you created a timeline of the inventions or placed them in the order they were invented. Could you begin to visualize or see what life was like at different times in the past?"

Task Definition (What):

- What is our task? *To debate the good and bad of some specific inventions and to put those inventions on a time line.*

- Model for students what the debate will look like. Select an invention such as electricity. Ask students: Do you agree this invention is . . . or does . . . (*Identify what the invention is or does.*) Present the pros or good points of the invention. Present the cons or negatives of the invention. To present pros and cons you may opt to get a partner to do the opposing side or you may role play and verbally and physically become another person to do the opposing view. For instance, the teacher standing on the left may model the pro argument while the principal standing on the right gives the con argument. After the debate ask students to decide if the invention has more pros or more cons. Ask: Do you feel comfortable with what our task will look like?

- Identify four inventions to be debated. Inventions debated might include gas motor, telephone, television, personal computers, and cellular phones.
- Ask students to create a timeline of the invention you modeled and the other four, i.e. which invention was first, second, etc. Collect these predicted timelines.
- Ask students to identify what information is needed to solve the problem:
    - What does the invention do (fact)?
    - When was the invention made (for timeline creation)?
    - Positive effects of the invention upon the world (opinion supported by fact)?
    - Negative effects of the invention upon the world (opinion supported by fact)?
- Acknowledge that two types of information will be needed: fact and opinion. Discuss the difference between fact and opinion and the important part facts should play in forming opinions.
- Divide the class into eight groups. Two groups will have the same invention, one group will do the pro argument and one will do the con argument. Both groups will prepare pro and con arguments. After using information, groups will draw to see which has the pro and which has the con side.
- Let each group draw to determine which invention.

Session Two:
Information Seeking Strategies (What):
- Tell students: I think we need two sources to solve our problem: prior knowledge and an encyclopedia article.
- What kind of information will we get from the encyclopedia article? *Facts*
- What source do we use to get the opinions? *prior knowledge and the facts*

Location and Access (Where):
- Model choosing the correct volume of the encyclopedia and using the guide words to locate the information.

Use of Information:
- Students read and extract: what the invention is or does and when it was created.
- Students utilize facts and prior knowledge in an effort to list the good points and bad points of the inventions.

Synthesis:
- Give each student a timeline organizer. Call on each group to share the date their invention was created as students enter the year and invention in their organizer.
- Return student timeline predictions; celebrate those who put the inventions in the correct order.

Session Three:
Use of Information:

- Have each group draw to determine which side they will be presenting, pro or con.

- Provide a few minutes for students to organize. Suggest three positive or three negative effects of the invention be presented.

Synthesis:

- For each invention have the positive and the negative impacts shared. You may have students pick a number to see which side presents first.

- Have the class choose and vote: I think this invention has more positive effects than negative or I think this invention has more negative effects than positive.

Product: Do you have a better concept of how long these inventions have been with us? Could you identify the order in which the inventions were made? Did we discover positive and negative effects of each invention? Do you agree there are usually two sides to an issue? Both good and bad?

Process: How did the process work for us? Did you have to use the encyclopedia and prior knowledge? Did you use facts and opinions? Was it harder to gather facts or form opinions? Did you like the debate format of solving the problem? What was your favorite part of the process? Which part was the hardest?

From *Teaching Elementary Information Literacy Skills with the Big6™* by **Joyce Needham**. Columbus, OH: Linworth Publishing, Inc. Copyright © 2009.

LESSON PLAN 18.14

LESSON TITLE: INVENTION TIMELINE

Grade Level: 3rd-5th	**Time Frame:** ■ Four 30-minute sessions

Content Objective: History and Nature of Science: ■ K-4th and 5th-8th Science as a human endeavor ■ 5th-8th History of science	**Information Literacy Objective:** ■ Practice steps of the problem solving process ■ Information Seeking Strategies: Internet ■ Use of Information: Citing sources ■ Synthesis: PowerPoint

Materials and Sources:
■ Selected Internet sites. Might include:
  ■ MIT Inventor of the Week
  ■ Invent Now National Inventors Hall of Fame
  ■ Smithsonian's Spotlight
■ List of inventions and inventors
■ Note taking organizer
■ PowerPoint or electronic slide
■ Step-by-step written directions for saving pictures and for creating a PowerPoint slide
• Teacher created rubric
■ String or yarn to create timeline
■ Years to label timeline (optional)

PLAN

Problem:
■ Think for a moment about science and technology. You might think in terms of Dewey's classification of science in the 500s and technology or applied science in the 600s. Science focuses upon the world around us. Applied science or technology focuses upon changing that world to make life better or easier for mankind. With that in mind look around the room. Do you see examples of science? *Students might identify the air they are breathing, themselves, trees or sky they may see through the windows.* Do you see any examples of applied science or technology? *Students will have a multitude of items to list: their clothing, the floor, the walls, the shelves, the books, the computers, the lights, etc.* Think all of those things you just mentioned. Would you say you are surrounded more by our natural world, science, or by applied science and technology? Have all those items you just mentioned been invented or created? Who was responsible for inventing them? *Men and women.* Would you be interested in learning more about inventions and about the people who invented them?

■ Which do you think came first magazines or newspapers? . . . lights or electricity? . . . fans, or air conditioners? . . . computers or telephone answering machines? Are you curious?

■ I was thinking, how could we combine learning to use some of this technology with satisfying our curiosity about some inventions, such as when it was invented, who invented it, etc.?

What if . . . we each took an invention, researched it, created a PowerPoint slide, and put all our slides in a timeline?

Task Definition (What):

- What is our task? *Create a timeline of inventions. The timeline will consist of slides we create for our invention.*
- Will it be easier for others to understand our timeline if each slide uses the same format? Share sample slide (sample found at end of this lesson plan.) Ask students for any changes they would like to make in the sample.
- Using the modified slide, identify the information needed. May include: name of invention, year of the invention, picture of the invention, name of inventor, picture of inventor, and source.
- Have students choose invention from the provided list of inventions and inventors. If more than one student chooses the same invention, ask a student not involved to tell you a number between 1 and 10. Ask each student who wants the same invention to pick a number. The student who is closest gets his or her choice of invention. Other students may use the list to choose another invention.

Information Seeking Strategies (What):

- What sources will we need to find information on inventions? Use teacher selected Web sites. Cite reasons for teacher selection rather than students searching for sites, e.g. amount of time available and reliability of sites.
- Will we need a source to help us learn to create a slide? A teacher could be the source, however, when we are in the computer lab there will be a whole class of students and only one or two teachers. Ask: What if you had printed directions for use? If you can read and follow these directions will it be faster and easier for you to complete your slide?

Location and Access (Where):

- Share with students where they may access computers, e.g. classroom, computer lab, library, home.
- Model for students how to access pre-selected Web sites. Possibilities might be using favorites, clicking on links from the home page, or typing in addresses.
- Model accessing information from a Web site by entering keyword, name of invention or name of inventor (last name first), and letting the Web site search for the information needed.

Use of Information:

- Provide students a note taking organizer and model use of the organizer to extract treasure or needed information. The organizer may be similar to sample slide found at end of lesson plan.
- Model following the provided print directions to save pictures of inventor and invention. Be sure to include directions telling students where to save pictures, e.g. desktop, My Pictures, etc.
- Model citing an Internet source. What information should be included and where that information may be found.
- After the teacher models, the students should use print directions and complete note taking organizer, cite their source, and save pictures of both the invention and the inventor.

Synthesis:

Synthesis of slide:

- Provide written directions for creating the slide, including importing saved pictures and typing facts from note taking organizer.
- Model creation of a sample slide.

- Students, using written directions, create and print their slide.
- Once all files have been created and printed, use a line up with each student representing their invention. Line up may be by year of invention, type of invention, birth date of inventor, etc.

Synthesis of timeline:

- Create a timeline on wall in classroom or hallway by attaching line of string or yarn. Adding years to the timeline is optional.
- With printed slide in hand and using the year invention was created, have students group themselves by centuries, e.g. 1800s, 1900s, 2000s, etc.
- Once sorted by century have each group of students line up by decade, e.g. 1910s, 1920s, 1930s, etc.
- Finally have students within each decade line up by year, e.g, 1910, 1911, 1912, etc.
- Beginning with the earliest invention, have students, one at a time, attach their slide to the timeline. Each student, as the slide is attached to the timeline, shares the name of invention, inventor, and any other information teacher has designated.

Teacher Note: The timeline may be used to help students develop a sense of time, identify how inventions may have built upon each other (electricity lead to electric lights, etc.) and to make connections between inventions and historical events and lifestyle of that era. The teacher may also opt to compile all student slides into one electronic slide presentation.

Evaluation:

- Product:
  - Have students complete teacher prepared rubric.
  - Students may also be asked to name two or three inventions and identify which came first, second, etc.
- Process: May be written or oral and include such questions as: Did you solve your problem? Did the slide present all the information we wanted to share? Did the timeline help you become aware of the sequence of inventions? Did the written directions work for you? With those directions could you go to a computer now and create a slide? . . . save and import a picture? . . . access a Web site? . . . cite a source? What was your favorite part of the project? What would you want to do differently next time?

Invention Timeline: Sample Format PowerPoint Slide	
Year:_____	
Name of Invention	Name of Inventor
Picture of Invention	*Picture of Invention*
Source: Name of Web page. Available at: (include Web address). Date accessed.	

Works Cited

Enchanted Learning. 25 February 2008 <http://www.enchantedlearning.com/Home.html>.

Exploratorium the Museum of Science Art and Human Perception. 25 February 2008 <http://www.exploratorium.edu>.

Invent Now, National Inventors Hall of Fame. 25 February 2008 <http://www.invent.org/hall_of_fame/1_1_search.asp>.

MIT Inventor of the Week Archives. 25 February 2008 <http://web.mit.edu/invent/i-archive.html>.

National Research Council, National Academy of Sciences (NAS). *National Science Education Standards.* Washington, D.C.: National Academy Press, 1996.

Pioneers. 25 February 2008 <http://library.thinkquest.org/6400>.

Rainforest-Australia. 25 February 2008 <http://rainforest-australia.com>.

Smithsonian's Spotlight: Biography, Inventors. 25 February 2008 <http://www.smithsonianeducation.org/spotlight/start.html>.

USGS Earthquake Hazards Program, Earthquakes for Kids. 25 February 2008 <http://earthquake.usgs.gov/learning/kids/http://earthquake.usgs.gov/Pro>.

USGS Volcano Hazards Program. 25 February 2008 <http://volcanoes.usgs.gov>.

Understanding Earthquakes. 25 February 2008 <http://projects.crustal.ucsb.edu/understanding>.Volcano World. 25 February 2008 <http://volcano.und.edu>.

CHAPTER 19
SOCIAL STUDIES
AND THE BIG6

Where Do Problems and the Big6 Fit Within Social Studies?

Social studies in most elementary schools includes geography, history, civics, government, economics, and multicultural awareness. The National Council for the Social Studies (NCSS) identifies (148-149) essential social studies skills (see Figure 19.1). Examination of these skills reveals several connections to Big6 problem solving and information literacy skills.

The NCSS proposes "these skill categories should not be seen as a fragmented list of things that students and teacher should do. Rather, they should be used as an interconnected framework in which one skill is dependent upon and enriched by all other skills. All together are necessary for a program of excellence (8)." There is a connection between these essential social studies skills and the Big6 process. This connection makes it possible to integrate social studies content and problem solving. This may be accomplished by posing social studies content as problems and then using Big6 to solve the problems. This approach to teaching social studies is further supported by NCSS's belief that powerful social studies teaching is both integrative and integrated. It is integrative in treatment of topics and across time and space. It integrates knowledge, skills, beliefs, values, and attitudes to actions. It also integrates the effective use of technology (164-166).

Integrating the content of social studies within the steps of Big6 provides students opportunities to practice solving authentic problems. For instance: Why did the U.S. have a Civil War? What is the difference between a need and a want? How is our President elected? What role did Thomas Jefferson play in the development of our country? By using the Big6 to solve these and other content problems, students learn important social studies content and also become more efficient and effective problem solvers.

Social Studies Skills and Big6 Skills

Social Studies Essential Skills	Big6 Problem Solving Steps
Acquiring Information:	
■ Reading Skills: comprehension, vocabulary, and rate of reading.	■ 3.1 Use of Information, Engage
■ Study skills: find information and arrange information in usable forms.	■ 3. Location and Access ■ 5.1 Synthesis, Organize
■ Reference and Information-Search Skills: the library; special references; maps, globes, and graphics; and community resources.	■ 2. Information Seeking Strategies
■ Technical Skills Unique to Electronic Devices: computer and telephone; and television information networks.	■ 2. Information Seeking Strategies ■ 5. Synthesis
Organizing and Using Information:	
■ Thinking Skills: classify information, interpret information, analyze information, summarize information, synthesize information, and evaluate information.	■ 3. Use of Information ■ 5. Synthesis
■ Decision-Making Skills	■ 1. Task Definition ■ 5. Synthesis
■ Metacognitive Skills	■ 6. Evaluation
Interpersonal Relationships and Social Participation:	
■ Personal Skills	■ 5.1 Synthesis, Communicate
■ Group Interaction Skills	
■ Social and Political Participation Skills	

From *Teaching Elementary Information Literacy Skills with the Big6™* by **Joyce Needham**. Columbus, OH: Linworth Publishing, Inc. Copyright © 2009.

Figure 19.1 Social Studies Skills and Big6 Skills

Creating Integrated Social Studies Lessons

Begin first with content. Identify the social studies content to be taught and the specific student learning objective. For our example the content is the American Revolutionary War. Our students' learning objective is to explain the American Revolution, including the perspectives of patriots and loyalists.

Pose a problem. With content and objective identified, the next step is to pose a problem students can solve. Solving the problem needs to result in students being able to meet their learning goal, or for our example, to explain the American Revolution, including the perspectives of patriots and loyalists. Brainstorming works well when determining the problem to pose. It is even more powerful when the classroom teacher, library media specialist, technology teacher, art teacher, etc. may all brainstorm and work together to guide students to solve the problem. For our example our problem might be:

> The year is 1777. You are a colonist. Realizing that you are living in a time when history is being made, you decide to keep a journal for your descendents. Please share your journal entry which explains what is happening in your world right now.

To provide different perspectives of the war, have students draw or select different backgrounds as represented by:

- patriot or a loyalist
- colony in which they live
- career or role

Completed journal entries may be shared anonymously and students challenged to determine whether the writer is a patriot or a loyalist. Students may also try to determine where the colonist lived, e.g. which colony, city or rural, and their career, such as merchant, soldier, plantation owner, statesman, woman, slave, or child.

Integrate Big6 process. At this point consider each of the steps of the Big6 and focus upon specific skills within the process that are needed to study the content. One method for integrating Big6 is to pose the problem and talk through each of the steps of Big6 as you solve the problem (see Figure 19.2).

Once the problem has been determined, think through the Big6 steps. This will allow you to identify those steps that may be more difficult for students. Students may be offered assistance as they work through these steps. For instance, students completing our example may find it difficult to identify the information needed (Big6 #1.2) and to synthesize the point of view (Big6 #5). Students might benefit if the teacher, with student guidance, creates a chart identifying the information needed. It might also be helpful if the teacher models writing from different perspectives prior to the students attempt to synthesize the journal entry.

Integrate other processes. The problem now integrates social studies content and Big6 skills. Even more powerful learning may occur, however, if the problem is analyzed and other skills are integrated or identified. For instance, problems frequently require use of reading and writing skills. Some even present a need to learn and use a specific reading or writing skill. Consider our example, which requires students to include point of view or

American Revolution Journal Entry

	The following is what it might look like as the teacher or library media specialist plans the lesson by first identifying the problem and then addressing each of the six steps in the process.
Problem:	The year is 1777. You are a colonist. Realizing that you are living in a time when history is being made, you decide to keep a journal for your descendents. Please share your journal entry explaining what is happening in your world right now. So different perspectives of the war will be provided, students either draw or choose: ■ to be either a patriot or a loyalist ■ a specific colony in which they live, e.g. New York, Georgia, Virginia, Pennsylvania, etc. ■ a specific role, e.g. farmer, merchant, soldier, plantation owner, statesman, woman, slave, child After all journal entries have been created they may be shared anonymously and students challenged to determine whether the writer is a patriot or a loyalist. May also try to determine the role of the author and where he or she lives.
Task Definition (What):	Task: Write a journal entry explaining the revolutionary war. The entry will vary depending upon if for or against the war, where you live, and role. What information is needed: Create class list of information needed. Might include: facts about what the war was, causes of the war, what the British felt, what the colonists felt, what life was like in the colonies, what life was like for men (merchant, farmer, plantation owner, and statesman), women, children, slaves. Identify keywords that may help locate information.
Information Seeking Strategies (What):	Brainstorm possible sources. Don't forget social studies textbook as source. Internet as a possible source?
Location and Access (Where):	Depending upon source, identify where sources are located. Depending upon student skills, either model or guide students to: scan or skim for keywords using text features.
Use of Information:	Read the information and extract the important information or the treasure. Prepare a note taking organizer.
Synthesis:	Write a journal entry. Remember entry must reflect where you live, your role, and whether you are a loyalist or a patriot.
Evaluation:	
• **Product:**	■ Prepare a rubric. Give grade for accurate evaluation. ■ Evaluate success in expressing perspective of loyalist or patriot as journal entries are read aloud.
• **Process:**	■ Prepare a written reflection form. See samples in Chapter 12.

Figure 19.2 American Revolution Journal Entry

perspective within the writing. This problem provides an opportunity to teach this writing skill and provide authentic practice.

Problems may also provide the opportunity to integrate other skills, such as technology, art, and music. In our example students may integrate art by edging the journal entry or by illustrating it. The art teacher may take advantage of this opportunity by teaching a specific skill which students then use in their journal entry. Technology skills may also be integrated by requiring students to use the Internet to access information. As students use the Internet, they may develop successful search strategies and utilize the text features of the Web sites.

The final steps before instruction begins are to identify and gather materials needed and to establish a timeline for the lesson.

Integrating Problem Solving into Existing Lessons

You may have social studies lessons you have previously planned and taught. If that is the case, rather than beginning from scratch, you may choose to integrate Big6 into those existing lessons. To integrate, begin by examining these existing lessons. It is likely that the problem solving process is already embedded within the lesson. For instance, as you examine the lessons can you identify a task, sources to be used, etc.? If this is true you have already been using Big6 in your teaching.

Your task now is to move to the next level and teach the process. Teaching the process may be facilitated if you:

1. Make sure students know they are going to learn a problem solving process.

2. Post the steps in the process.

3. Pencil the Big6 terminology in on your existing lesson plan.

4. Verbalize those steps, making the process visible to students as the problem is solved:

   - What will it sound like?

   - What is our problem?

   - What sources can you use?

   - Have you located the information?

   - You should now be using the information. Are you engaged? . . . reading? . . . listening?

   - Have you extracted the needed information?

   - Can you solve your problem or synthesize?

   - Evaluate. Did you complete your task?

   - Did the process guide you through the problem solving?

5. Work together to solve problems and encourage students to use the Big6 terminology and identify the steps of the process.

6. Provide students with opportunities to use the Big6 process independently to solve their problems.

Sample Lessons Integrating Big6 and Social Studies

There is an old saying; a picture is worth a thousand words. Based upon the belief that for teachers the picture is a lesson plan, the remainder of this chapter is dedicated to sample lesson plans. The lesson plans are organized first according to the discipline the lesson addresses, e.g. history or geography, and then by grade level, primary or intermediate.

The social studies theme identified by the NCSS is labeled (15). Each lesson plan has a component of reading and writing which may be utilized to provide authentic practice of those skills. In addition, many lessons provide opportunities to integrate technology skills either through location skills (Big6 #3) or synthesis (Big6 #5).

Motivators

The sample lessons utilize a variety of motivators to encourage student engagement such as use of stories, questioning, timelines, people, and games.

Stories or Literature

Literature or stories help students make connections to new learning. A wealth of well-written and finely illustrated historical fiction picture books exist today. Students enjoy the opportunity to learn history content, practice problem solving, improve reading skills, and develop a love of reading when these books are used. (See Appendix B)

Questions

Young students, especially, are full of questions. The Big6 steps may be utilized to find the answers to these burning questions. Big6 encourages student engagement, exposes students to the problem solving process, and provides the desired answers simultaneously. (See Lesson Plan 13.1)

Timelines

A thorough understanding of history relies upon development of a sense of time. Sense of time is often a difficult concept for elementary students. Ask elementary students how old their teacher is and the answer will probably vary from 19 years old to 80 years old. The age of the teacher in question may actually be 30 years of age. I have experienced students express both surprise that I was alive when Martin Luther King, Jr. lived and dismay I did not know Abraham Lincoln. Timelines help historical events and people become concrete and may lead to developing the concept of time. Physically placing events and names of people on a line at a specific date helps make the concept of time visible. It may also help students see connections between various events and people leading to increased understanding of cause and effect upon history. Giving students the opportunity to personalize their timeline by adding birth dates of people known to the students, e.g. parents or grandparents, may result in the concept of time becoming even more concrete. (See Lesson Plan 19.7)

Skills

The sample lesson plans present a variety of skills which may be taught using the problem solving process:

- knowledge of primary and secondary sources
- familiarity with the variety of sources available in our environment such as telephone directories and various agencies
- consciousness of when enough information has been gathered
- questioning skills
- the ability to locate information in a variety of sources quickly and easily

Time Requirements

Lessons which integrate Big6, as evidenced by these sample lesson plans, may be intense, time-consuming research projects or short, simple questions to be answered. The sample lessons may be used in their entirety or as a starting point from which teachers may develop lessons to fit the specific needs of students.

Integrating the Big6 problem solving process is one strategy for teaching both social studies content, such as geography and history, and the essential skills of social studies, such as acquiring and organizing information. The resulting lessons are logical, authentic problem solving opportunities which encourage student engagement.

Some characteristics of successful student learning identified by research on learning (see Chapter 3) include student engagement, making connections between new and old learning, and learning in context or when a need exists. Posing problems for students to solve using social studies content utilizes those characteristics to create a learning environment which encourages successful learning. Such instruction may result in increased learning within a decreased amount of instructional time.

The integrated approach to teaching social studies may also provide a larger segment of time to be devoted to a lesson. With integration it is possible, and likely, that one lesson incorporates learning goals from several subject areas, i.e. social studies, reading, writing, information literacy or problem solving, and technology. Combining the teaching time of the included subject areas produces a larger segment of time for students to master skills. For instance, if a typical schedule provides 30 minutes of instruction each for reading, writing, social studies, information literacy or library, and technology, it is possible to devote $2^1/_2$ hours to solving the problem or learning the goals by teaching skills from each curriculum area in one lesson.

The problem solving approach to teaching social studies offers another significant benefit. With this approach students become the problem solvers. In their role of problem solvers, students assume responsibility for their learning. As learning is something students must do for themselves, rather than something teachers or library media specialists can do for them, this has a tremendous impact upon student learning.

Works Cited

American Revolution.org. 28 February 2008
        <http://www.americanrevolution.org//revere.html>.
Spy Letters of the American Revolution. 28 February 2008
        <http://www.si.umich.edu/SPIES/index-people.html>.
Task Force of the National Council for the Social Studies (NCSS). *Curriculum Standards for Social Studies, Expectations in Excellence.* Washington, D.C.: National Council for the Social Studies, 1994.

LESSON PLAN 19.1

LESSON TITLE: USING PICTURE BOOKS TO TEACH SOCIAL STUDIES

Grade Level: 1st-5th	**Time Frame:** ■ Six 30-minute session
Content Objective: History ■ Social Studies Theme: Time, Continuity, and Change	**Information Literacy Objective:** ■ Practice using the steps of the problem solving process ■ Information Seeking Strategies: Picture books as sources

Materials and Sources:

■ A picture book based upon the historical event to be studied *(See Appendix B for suggested list of picture books relating to specific historical events)*

■ Factual source of information about the historical event, e.g. nonfiction book, encyclopedia, textbook, etc.

PLAN

Problem:

■ There are many picture books which mention historical events and real people. We know these books are fiction or make believe. Does that mean everything in the story is make believe? Is it possible to learn real facts from a fiction story? As you listen to this story see if you can identify any facts.

Task Definition (What):

■ Identify the historical event to which the book refers. Depending upon the students' prior knowledge, and your purpose in using the book, you may or may not choose to discuss the historical event before reading the book to the class.

■ What is your task? *To identify the historical event which really did happen and to identify any facts about that historical event.*

Note: Depending upon age of students and available instructional time you may opt to guide the whole group in identifying facts or have students independently research to determine facts.

Information Seeking Strategies (What):

■ What sources will we need? *Picture book and prior knowledge about the historical event.*

Location and Access (Where):

■ Location and access of the information in the book is a no-brainer for this activity. Students need to listen to access the needed information as the book is read. Accessing prior knowledge may be more difficult. Remember, asking questions and making connections may help students recall prior knowledge about the event.

Use of Information:

■ On a chart write any information from the picture book which students believe to be factual.

- At this point, depending upon instructional needs of students and available time, choose one of the following options:

  - The teacher or library media specialist identifies the correct information: Proceed to Synthesis (Big6 #5).

    or

  - Students research to determine which information is true: Return to Information Seeking Strategies (Big6 #2)

Information Seeking Strategies (What):

- What sources can we use? *Nonfiction books, encyclopedia, or Internet with information about the historical event.*

Location and Access (Where):

- Locate the sources and skim and scan to find the information pertaining to the information listed on the class chart.

Use of Information:

- Read the information in the nonfiction books and compare it with information written on the chart.

Synthesis:

- Identify those pieces of information which are factual on the chart. For instance, facts may be highlighted or a line may be drawn through any incorrect information.

Evaluation: Oral evaluation

- Product: Did the book contain some facts about the historical event? Did we identify the factual or true information in the story? Do you think the author researched the event before writing the book?

- Process: What part of the process was easiest for you? What part of the process was most difficult? What did you learn about accessing information and using information that will help the next time you have this task of identifying the facts?

From *Teaching Elementary Information Literacy Skills with the Big6™* by **Joyce Needham**. Columbus, OH: Linworth Publishing, Inc. Copyright © 2009.

LESSON TITLE: LANDFORMS BOOK AND GAME

Grade Level: 1st-3rd	**Time Frame:** ■ Six 30-minute sessions

Content Objective: Geography—Landforms (desert, rain forest, river, mountain, island, peninsula) ■ Social Studies Theme: People, Places, and Environment ■ Communication Arts: Write and illustrate a book	**Information Literacy Objective:** ■ Practice using the steps of the problem solving process ■ Task Definition: Identifying keyword ■ Information Seeking Strategies: Using electronic sources ■ Location and Access: Modeling use of search engine and scanning and skimming to locate information

Materials and Sources:
- An Internet search engine (used to locate definitions and pictures)
- Computer and video projector
- Class note taking organizer to write definition of each landform
- Page template: Include line to identify or label landform at top of page, space for picture, followed by lines at bottom for writing summary
- Construction paper to be used as folder and then as book cover
- Pictures for Showdown
- Questions for Showdown

PLAN

Session One:
Problem:

- I am going to name some landforms. As I name each I want you visualize or get a mental picture of the landform. Name several landforms: mountain, desert, etc. Ask: Were you able to visualize? Do you think if we spent some time studying landforms you might get a clearer or better picture?

- I've been thinking. Is there a way we could combine our study of landforms and improve our writing skills? What if . . . you were to write a book about landforms? Would that help you learn about landforms? Work on your writing skills? Would you like to write a book?

- So what do you think? Can we write a book about landforms? Will it help us reach our learning goals? Would it be fun?"

Task Definition (What):

- What is your task? *To create a book about landforms.*
- What information will we need? Guide students to determine:
    - landforms to be included: desert, rainforest, river, mountain, island, peninsula
    - each landform will be one page in the book

- each page will need the name of the landform, drawing of the landform, and description or definition of the landform
    - title page and table of contents page will be needed
    - source will need to be cited

Information Seeking Strategies (What):

- What source could we use to help us write our book? Will our book be fiction or nonfiction? Will it have facts or a story? Where might we find our facts?
- Let students brainstorm possible sources. Help them identify using a computer to access the Internet as a possible source. Ask: Would you like to use the Internet?

Location and Access (Where):

- Model finding needed information for the first landform, e.g. desert. First locate a search engine. Ask: What keyword will help us find the information needed? *Desert.* What information do we want about the landform? *Definition.* In the search box type the keywords, e.g. desert definition. When the search is completed select the choice which provides Web definitions for desert.

Use of Information:

- With younger students, read two or three definitions as students listen. With older students, call on individual students to read as classmates listen. Randomly call on a student to use this information and verbalize a one or two sentence definition or description of the landform. Record sentence(s) on chart for entire class. Also make note of the source used on the class chart.

Synthesis:

- Using page templates, each student should write the name of the landform and either copy the sentence from the class chart or write their own sentence using the information from the source. Student should also note the source of the information.

Sessions Two through Four
Location and Access (Where):

- Return to search engine. Search for images using the landform as a keyword, e.g. desert.

Use of Information:

- Students use prior knowledge and pictures found on the Internet to decide how they will draw the landform.

Synthesis:

- Students draw a picture of the landform, e.g. desert, on page template.

Location and Access, Use of Information, and Synthesis:

- Repeat locating, using, and writing description of the landform and locating and drawing a picture of the landform until each page of the book is completed or all six landforms are studied. Students should be able to complete two pages in their landforms book in one session.
- At the end of the first session, provide students with a sheet of construction paper, folded in half, to be used as a folder for storing pages.

Fifth Session:
Evaluation:

- Product:
- Students locate folder with pages and work completed to date. Because of student absences and differences in abilities some students may not have completed all pages.   Students evaluate product, or work in folder, to determine if their pages are complete: Do you have all six pages? . . . an illustration on each page? . . . a description on each page? . . . the landform labeled? Is each page neat and easy to read? etc.

Use of Information and Synthesis:

- Students complete any unfinished pages. If information is needed to complete the pages, students use other students' finished pages as a *source*. Student needs to locate others whose pages are complete and ask permission to borrow that page.

Note: This encourages students to take responsibility for locating the needed information and reinforces the need to seek permission when borrowing ideas or information from another.

- Type the title page for the book using the computer and projector as students dictate what to include and suggest format.
- Pose question: How do you want to organize your book? Guide students to decide on table of contents, with pages in alphabetic order and numbered. Have students again dictate as you type table of contents page.
- Book is completed as students:
  - Arrange pages of book in alphabetic order
  - Number the pages
  - Pick up copy of the title page and contents page created with teacher assistance
  - Bind the book using the construction paper folder.

Evaluation:

- Product:
- Students again evaluate product: Do you have all six pages? . . . an illustration on each page? . . . a description on each page? . . . the landform labeled? Is each page neat and easy to read? Do you have a book cover? . . . title page? . . . table of contents? . . . are pages numbered correctly?"

Final Session: Evaluation of process and product

- **Process:** How did Big6 work for us? Did you know what you needed to do each time you came to the library? Did the pictures and definitions we found on the Internet help? Will it get easier to solve your problems as you become a better reader?"
- **Product:** As a culminating activity, and final evaluation of product, students compete in a **Showdown of Landforms:**
  - Divide class into two teams.
  - One student from each team faces the teacher who shows a picture of a landform and asks a question.
  - The first person to say the correct answer stays. The person who did not answer first is replaced by the next person on his or her team.
  - The game continues with the new person and the person who gave the correct answer. The student who responds first with an accurate answer stays until failing to give the

first accurate answer.

- Content of the showdown consists of students naming or identifying the landform after either:
    - looking at a picture of one of the landforms (may be printed from Internet)
    - listening to the description of the landform, or
    - listening to an example of the landform, e.g. Rockies or Mississippi
- The teacher judges who responds first with correct answer. In case of tie, another question is asked.

Note: Explaining rules and purpose of game prior to beginning play helps create a friendly learning environment. For example, the teacher may say: When you go to a ball game who decides if rules are broken? The umpire or referee. Do they sometimes make mistakes? Do you have to accept those mistakes? Today I am going to be the referee. So who decides who answers correctly: you or me? I'll try not to make any mistakes, but I may. Just remember. Why are we playing this game? That's right—to learn and to have fun. Is it any fun if someone gets upset or angry?

From *Teaching Elementary Information Literacy Skills with the Big6™* by **Joyce Needham**. Columbus, OH: Linworth Publishing, Inc. Copyright © 2009.

LESSON PLAN 19.3

LESSON TITLE: CLASS LUAU

Grade Level: 3rd-5th	**Time Frame:** ■ Three 30-minute sessions

Content Objective: Geography ■ Social Studies Theme: People, Places, and Environments ■ Multicultural Awareness	**Information Literacy Objective:** ■ Practice using the steps of the problem solving process ■ Task Definition: Recognizing amount of information needed ■ Information Seeking Strategies: Selection of best source ■ Location and Access: Identifying text feature to use, e.g. index or guide words and using keywords to scan/skim

Materials and Sources:
■ Sources of information about luaus
■ Items identified in above sources

PLAN

Session One:
Problem:

■ In studying about the Pacific states you learned about luaus. Do you think it would be fun to attend a luau? We can't go to Hawaii, but could we gather information, plan, and have a luau here at school?

Task Definition (What):

■ What is our task? *To have a luau.*

■ What information do we need? Create a class chart identifying the categories of information needed. List might include: activities or what to do, what to wear, what to eat, what it looks like or decorations.

■ After we gather the information needed, how might we plan our luau? Guide students to think of committees or groups of students, each taking responsibility for one area.

■ Group students according to information they will gather to prepare the luau.

Information Seeking Strategies (What):

■ Create a brainstormed list of what sources can be used.

■ Allow students to choose the source they think best.

■ Move from group to group asking students to identify which source they will use.

Location and Access (Where):

■ As each group identifies which source they will use, ask the class to identify where the source will be located in the library.

- Ask: What text features do you use to locate information in a book? *Index or guide words.* How do you know whether to use index or guide words? *Determine how the book is organized. Alphabetical order or some other order.* If it is arranged in alphabetical order which feature do you use? *Guide words.* If it is arranged in some other order by subject or chronology what feature do you use? *Index.* What is another word for index if using the Internet or an electronic source? *Menu.*

- Ask: Will you read or scan/skim to find the information needed? *Scan or skim.* What will you be scanning or skimming for? *Keywords, e.g. luau, food, entertainment.* Which do you scan/skim first? Text or text features? *Text features.*

- Students locate sources and access needed information.

Session Two:
Use of Information:

- After information is located ask: Do you need to record this information? Do you need to write in complete sentences? Do you need to use your best handwriting? Is it O.K. to just jot down important phrases?

- Students record the information found.

- What is the next step? *Committees need to meet and decide what materials are needed for our luau and what will happen at the luau.*

- Committees meet to make plans and provide teacher a list of needed materials.

Note: No more than 10 or 15 minutes should be required once information is found in a source. Efficient problem solving is facilitated when students learn that more is not always better. One class learned this lesson through the luau project. When the class was told to put away sources after about 15 minutes, they began to panic. They objected indicating they still needed the sources because all the information available had not been used. The teacher asked students: Evaluate. How much time do we have for our luau? So how many pieces of information do you probably need? If we have all the information needed, is it a good idea to spend more time gathering more information? Students decided only two or three pieces of information were needed and that they no longer needed or wanted to spend more time with the sources.

Session Three:
Synthesis:

- Set up and attend the luau.

Note: This project provides a good opportunity for students to be creative. For instance, plastic garbage bags cut into strips can substitute for grass skirts.

Evaluation:

- Following the luau, a short session, 10 minutes or so, is required for evaluation.

- Product: Did we have a luau? Was it an authentic luau? Did the luau help us learn more about the culture of the Hawaiians? Was it fun?

- Process: Did Big6 help us solve our problem? Did we use the process so we did not work any harder than we needed to? Did we use the process so we solved the problem as quickly as possible? What did you learn about problem solving that will help you the next time you have a problem to solve?

LESSON PLAN 19.4

LESSON TITLE: LEARNING ABOUT OUR STATE

Grade Level: 3rd-5th	**Time Frame:** ■ One 45-minute session

Content Objective: Geography ■ Social Studies Theme: People, Places, and Environments ■ Communication Arts: Letter writing (e-mail or snail mail) and telephone calls	**Information Literacy Objective:** ■ Practice using the six steps of the problem solving process ■ Information Seeking Strategy: Knowledge of sources: *World Almanac* and state Chamber of Commerce and Tourism Departments

Materials and Sources:
- *World Almanac*
- Note taking organizer
- One envelope and one stamp for each student, telephone access, or Internet access

PLAN

Problem:

- This lesson is designed to be completed six to eight weeks prior to studying states in the United States. The unit of study about the states should involve each student selecting a specific state for in-depth study and a preparing a project to share the information learned, e.g. report, 3-D model of the state, tri-fold display, scrapbook page, etc.

- When we begin our study of states, you are going to need information about your state. If you have access to information in a variety of formats: pictures, charts, graphs, etc. it will make your project more interesting. Books might have those types of information, but will you be able to cut the information out of a book and display it in your project?

- Our problem is locating sources which provide pictures that may be placed in our projects. The Internet is a possibility. Are printer ink cartridges expensive? Would we need ink to print materials from the Internet?

Task Definition (What):

- What is your task? *To locate information about our state in an inexpensive source, providing lots of different formats.*

- Would it help you find information if you knew which state you were researching?

- Let students select state. If two students opt to research the same state, draw to determine who gets first choice.

- What information is needed to contact source and get information? Create a class list identifying needed information such as: address, Web address, and telephone number of source, name and address to which information should be sent, date by which information is needed, why information is needed, and what information is needed. Use this information to create a note taking organizer for students.

Information Seeking Strategies (What):

- What source might we use? Brainstorm a list: books, Internet, encyclopedias, videos.
- Have students evaluate, based upon assignment, if any of these sources meet their needs.

- Introduce the state as a source: Have you thought about using the state as the source? If you could visit the state, take pictures, talk to people, etc. would that be using the state as a source? Is it possible for us to do that? There is another way we can access information from the state without leaving our classroom. Each state has either a Chamber of Commerce and or Tourism Division. These agencies provide information about the state to people interested in visiting the state, moving to the state, or even opening a business in the state. You can usually access this information from these agencies through the Internet, but then you would have to print it. Expensive. These agencies also provide this information in the form of brochures and packets of information. They will send this information to you at no charge. You can write, call, or e-mail to request this information. Would this meet our needs? Can we afford the information? Could we cut information out of brochures and pamphlets?

- What information do you need to contact this source? *Web address is needed to e-mail; telephone number is needed to call. Address is needed to write.* Where could we find those? Does anyone know a reference source that will give me the Web address, telephone number, or address? Introduce the *World Almanac.*

Location and Access (Where):

- Think aloud as you identify the collection and call number of the *World Almanac* and go to the shelf to locate the book.

- What do you think our keyword will be? *Name of state, e.g. Missouri.* Where do you think you should look for the keyword . . . what text feature? The book is organized by subject. *Index.* Here is a hint: The information we need is usually found on the first page listed under the state's name.

Use of Information:

- Model reading and extracting the Web address, telephone number, and address, and recording it on the note taking organizer.

- Provide each student a copy of the note taking organizer.

Location and Access and Use of Information:

- If a class set of almanacs is available, each student should locate their state in the *World Almanac* and record the Web address, telephone number, and address.

- If a class set of almanacs is unavailable, provide each group of four or five students a copy of the almanac and ask them to assist each other as each locates and records the needed information.

Use of Information:

- Meet with class and provide other information needed to complete the note taking organizer.

- Each student should e-mail, call, or write the Tourism Department or Chamber of Commerce requesting information when the note taking organizer is complete.

- Students should note on their note taking organizer the date contact was made or letter was mailed.

Synthesis:

- Synthesis will be completed when information is received from the state.

Evaluation:

- Product: Did you send your e-mail or letter or make telephone call? Did you get a response from the state? Did you receive the information you requested?

- Process: Were you able to locate the needed Web address, address, or telephone number in the almanac? Did you remember the format for writing a letter? Did you complete your telephone call in a clear, organized manner? Did your e-mail follow the format of a letter? How was it different? What was your favorite part of this project? What was your least favorite part?

From *Teaching Elementary Information Literacy Skills with the Big6™* by **Joyce Needham**. Columbus, OH: Linworth Publishing, Inc. Copyright © 2009.

LESSON PLAN 19.5

LESSON TITLE: CREATING A STATE SCRAPBOOK
This lesson could be the project utilizing the information located in the previous lesson.

Grade Level: 3rd-5th	**Time Frame:** ■ Four or five 30-minute sessions
Content Objective: Geography ■ Social Studies Theme: People, Places, Environments	**Information Literacy Objective:** ■ Practice using the steps of the problem solving process ■ Use of Information: Note taking

Materials and Sources:

- Internet, nonfiction books, encyclopedias, or information from Chamber of Commerce or Tourism Department
- Note taking organizer, include place to identify title and page of source used
- Completed note taking organizer showing samples of good and poor note taking
- One piece of construction paper to be used as scrapbook page
- Rubric

PLAN

Problem:

- We live in the United States. While we live in *name state of residence* and probably know quite a lot about it, there are 49 other states. Do you think as citizens of the United States we need to know about those other states?
- How can we learn about the states? Could we read about all the states? . . . watch videos on all the states? . . . write reports about all the states? Are there any other ways to learn? What if we each became an expert on one state? What if we created one page, a scrapbook page, about that state? If all the pages were bound in a *Scrapbook of the United States* and we used that as a source, would that be a fun and effective way to learn about the states?

Task Definition (What):

- What is our task? *To create a class scrapbook of the United States by each class member researching one state and creating one page of the scrapbook.*
- Is it a good idea for two students to scrapbook the same state? Remember we have a total of 50 states.
- Have students draw for state or sign up for the state they wish to research. If two students choose to research the same state, draw to see who gets first choice.
- Since all the scrapbook pages will go into one book, do we want some consistency in the pages? Maybe the same information? What information do you want to include in our scrapbook?
- Create a class chart of information to be included. Use this information to create the note taking organizer. Information could include: name of state, map or outline of the state, capitol, major cities, major rivers, major landforms, state flower, song, flag, tree, motto, population, major industries, climate, number of senators, number of representatives, interesting facts, etc.

Information Seeking Strategies (What):

- Brainstorm possible sources and select the best.
- If available, students may use information gathered from the Chamber of Commerce and State Tourism Department.

Location and Access (Where):

- Guide students as they locate sources and the information within the sources.
- Provide mini lessons as needed. For instance, if students have difficulty locating books, model using the library catalog to locate call numbers and go to the shelf to locate the book. If students have difficulty quickly locating information within the source, model scanning and skimming for keywords using text features.

Use of Information:

- Provide students with note taking organizer.
- Depending upon students' skills, you may wish to model engaging (reading) and extracting information from the text. Make sure students know they must read if they are to engage. Assist students as they extract the important information.
- Provide students samples, some good and some bad, of completed note taking organizers. Identify, with students, samples of good note taking, e.g. source cited, phrases only, makes sense, can be read, is complete, etc.
- Students engage or read and complete note taking organizer by extracting important information.

Synthesis:

- Students create scrapbook page using note taking organizer and any graphic material. Graphic material may be obtained from Chamber of Commerce and State Tourism Department, printed from Internet, or drawn. Remind students to cite source. Scrapbook page should be completed without using any of the original sources—only the note taking organizer should be used.

Evaluation:

Create a rubric which evaluates both product and process. Students should use rubric to evaluate scrapbook page prior to turning it in.

- Product: Include both information to be included on the scrapbook page, such as the state flower and state motto, and presentation requirements, such as neatness and aesthetic appeal.
- Process: Include questions such as: What part was easiest for you? What part was most difficult? What would you do differently next time?

From *Teaching Elementary Information Literacy Skills with the Big6™* by **Joyce Needham**. Columbus, OH: Linworth Publishing, Inc. Copyright © 2009.

LESSON TITLE: EXPLORING OUR CITY

Grade Level: 3rd-5th	Time Frame:
	■ Two one-hour sessions plus brief evaluation session

Content Objective:	Information Literacy Objective:
Government and Geography ■ Social Studies Theme: Power, Authority, and Governance	■ Practice the steps of the problem solving process ■ Information Seeking Strategies: Familiarity with a variety of sources ■ Location and Access: Practice locating information within a variety of sources

Materials and Sources:
- Materials for eight centers, see list below
- Eight volunteer parents and older students to assist at each center
- Rotation schedule

PLAN

Problem:
- Are you a citizen of the United States? . . . the state of _____ (state in which student lives)? . . . the city of _____ (city in which students live)? As a citizen do you have certain rights? What about responsibilities? As a citizen is it important that you be familiar with your country, state, and city? Do you think there is any thing about your city you do not know? How can you find out more about your city? Where can you find information?

Task Definition (What):
- What is your task or your challenge? *To learn as much as I can about my city by learning about and using a variety of sources.*
- How can we do that? What if . . . we set up eight centers or stations? Each center will have a different source and different information. Could you visit each center to find information about your city and to use the source to do so? Would you learn more about your city by visiting these centers or stations? Would you learn about more sources?

Information Seeking Strategies (What):
Sources to be used at the centers and information to be gathered from each includes:
- *World Almanac*: Worksheet with questions about governor of city, city population, etc.
- Local telephone directory: Worksheet listing a variety of city agencies for which students locate phone numbers.
- Local newspaper: One issue containing article about city council members, pending legislation, etc. Worksheet with questions pertaining to contents of article.
- City map: Include a list of various parks, buildings, services, areas which students may locate on the map.

- Broadcast of City Council Meeting: Worksheet requiring students to identify the procedure of making a bill a law and to identify the order of the meeting, e.g. roll call, reading of minutes, first readings, committee reports, etc.
- List of city departments and responsibilities of each which may be obtained from the city. Worksheet designed as a matching exercise for students.
- Internet: Worksheet to be completed including facts about city such as services offered, e.g. hospitals and schools, cost of housing, and names of employers and how many people they employ.
- Internet: Worksheet to be completed with tourist information.

Location and Access (Where):

- Set up each center with two or three copies of the source and copies of the worksheet for each student. Centers may be set up in the library or classroom. It is desirable to have volunteers, either parents or "expert" students at center to assist.
- Remind students to skim and scan for keywords using features of the book to locate information quickly.

Use of Information and Synthesis:

- Divide class into eight teams. Each team rotates through four centers on the first day and through the final four centers on the second day. Each rotation is 15 minutes.
- Teacher keeps time and directs students from center to center.
- As students visit each center, they complete the accompanying worksheet. Worksheets are taken along when students travel to the next center.

Evaluation:

- Product: Have students write all the facts they learned about the city. Discuss.
- Process: Did you learn about your city by visiting each center? Did you learn about a variety of sources? Did you learn to use those sources? What did you like best about completing the centers? What did you like least about the centers?

From *Teaching Elementary Information Literacy Skills with the Big6™* by **Joyce Needham**. Columbus, OH: Linworth Publishing, Inc. Copyright © 2009.

LESSON TITLE: HISTORY TIMELINE

Grade Level: 3rd-5th	**Time Frame:** ■ Two 30-minute sessions
Content Objective: History ■ Social Studies Theme: Time, Continuity, and Change	**Information Literacy Objective:** ■ Practice using the steps of the problem solving process ■ Information Seeking Strategies: primary and secondary sources

Materials and Sources:
- Timeline of U.S. (see sample at end of the lesson plan)
- Parents, family members, or family friends

PLAN

Problem:

- Think. What is history? What sources can you use to study history? Share, or have another adult share, their stories or memories of historical events such as 9/11, Iraq War, Vietnam, first satellite, whatever event the speaker experienced.

- Did you enjoy hearing those stories? Did you realize you were just listening to history? History consists of stories of people who lived before us. Some hundreds and hundreds of years ago. Some yesterday. Some of the history only affects a small group and so that history or story is only passed down to a small group of people affected by the event. For instance, a marriage in your family or a new business coming to town. Other events affect a large portion of our country, and are remembered by an entire region or nation. Have you experienced any events that will be remembered by our nation? *Election of a president, Hurricane Katrina, Iraq War, war on terrorism, etc.* Could you learn about our country's history from your parents? . . . from grandparents? . . . from great-grandparents? Would you like to know what was happening in the United States during your grandparents' lives? When their parents were young? Would it be easier to visualize and understand this history if you created a timeline?

Task Definition (What):

- I challenge you to create a timeline using your family as a source to learn about U.S. history. To learn about our country's history and to visualize life as your ancestors lived it, e.g. what wars they experienced, what new discoveries were made, or who was president.

Information Seeking Strategies (What):

- What sources can you use to find information on past events or history? *Talk to people who experienced, books, Internet.*
- Relatives who actually experienced these events and share those experiences with you would be considered primary (first) sources.
- Books and Internet articles written by someone who did not experience the event but spoke to others who did and read about it in other books and then wrote would be considered secondary sources.
- For this project, let's use primary sources.

Location and Access (Where):

■ The sources will be people. Family members or family friends. These people will need to be located and asked questions via oral or written interviews.

Use of Information and Synthesis:

■ Using a timeline students need to:
  ■ identify and label the birth year of the family member or friend interviewed and birth years of any other family members which are known
  ■ identify the date of historical events discussed
  ■ record a title or keyword identifying each historical event added to the timeline
  ■ take additional notes as desired to help remember details learned

Use of Information:

■ Extract at least one story or historical event from interviews with family members or family friends to share with classmates.

Synthesis:

■ Share one story or historical event with the class. Students may share randomly with a partner, with the entire class, within a group of students who have a story about the same historical event, etc.

■ Throughout the year students should monitor content studied and add appropriate information to the timeline. Information which might be added could include names of presidents, inventions, additional historical events as studied.

■ Refer students to their timeline to make connections as historical events are studied during the year. For instance, how old was your father when ____ was president? Was your grandfather alive during the Vietnam War?

Evaluation:

Evaluation may be quick oral questioning with students indicating thumbs up or thumbs down. Sample questions might include:

■ Product: Do you have a sense of what history is? Do you know at least one source that can be used to study history? How interested are you in learning about history? Were you able to add birth dates to your timeline?

■ Process: Was your relative a good source? Would a book, secondary source, be a better source? Why? Did you enjoy learning about the event from your relative? What have you learned about primary sources? Is the timeline a good way to organize history? Why?

Sample Timeline

Event	Year	Date of Relative's Birth and Major Life Events
Election of U.S. President	2008	
	2007	Ayla, granddaughter born Jordan and Joyce retired from teaching
	2006	
Hurricane Katrina, New Orleans	2005	
George W. Bush re-elected President	2004	Julie and Kevin married
Iraq War	2003	
	2002	Jordan III graduated from college
9/11 Terrorist Attack	2001	
George W. Bush elected president	2000	Julie graduated from college
	1999	
	1998	Jordan graduated from high school
	1997	
	1996	Julie graduated from high school Jordan and Joyce moved to Fremont Hills
	1995	
	1994	
	1993	
	1992	
Persian Gulf War	1991	Jordan and Joyce moved to Nixa
	1990	
	1989	
	1988	
	1987	
	1986	
Internet	1985	Jordan and Joyce moved to Bolivar
	1984	
	1983	
	1982	
	1981	
	1980	Jordan III, son born
	1979	
	1978	Julie, daughter born
	1977	
1st personal computer	1976	
	1975	
	1974	
End Vietnam War	1973	Joyce began teaching career
Watergate	1972	
	1971	
	1970	Jordan and Joyce graduated from high school
1st man on moon	1969	
MLK Jr. assassinated	1968	
Continue with years and events	1967	

From *Teaching Elementary Information Literacy Skills with the Big6™* by **Joyce Needham**. Columbus, OH: Linworth Publishing, Inc. Copyright © 2009.

LESSON PLAN 19.8

LESSON TITLE: PAUL REVERE VIA PRIMARY AND SECONDARY SOURCES

Grade Level: 4th and 5th	**Time Frame:** ■ One 30-minute session
Content Objective: History—Revolutionary War ■ Social Studies Theme: Time, Continuity, and Change	**Information Literacy Objective:** ■ Practice using the steps of the problem solving process ■ Information Seeking Strategies: primary and secondary sources, reliability of sources

Materials and Sources:

■ Copy of poem, "Paul Revere's Ride" by Henry Wadsworth Longfellow
■ Web site: American Revolution.org (<http://www.americanrevolution.org/revere.html>)
■ Web site: American Revolution Spy Letters. April/May 1775—Rachel Revere to Paul Revere (<http://www.si.umich.edu/SPIES/index-people.html>)

PLAN

Problem:

■ Share painting of Paul Revere at American Revolution Web site. Ask: Is this a photograph or portrait? Do you know who this is? What did he do for a living? What historical event he is connected to? *It is a portrait. His name was Paul Revere. He was a silversmith by trade. He also helped in the American Revolution. He was a messenger.*

■ Share Longfellow's poem about Paul Revere. This is a secondary source of information about what happened that night. Longfellow was not there. He used other sources to find out what happened and to write his poem. Is this a reliable source? How could we find out? Would you like to find out?

Task Definition (What):

■ What is our task? *To verify if Longfellow's poem is an accurate source.* In the process we are going to learn more about primary and secondary sources and reliability.

Information Seeking Strategies (What):

■ What source could we use to verify the poem's accuracy? *An encyclopedia or book.* That would work because books and encyclopedias are usually reliable. They are both what we call secondary sources. What if we could actually see Paul Revere's account or retelling of that night? Would his account be primary or secondary? *primary*

■ What is a primary source? *An account by a person who was actually there, such as a letter, diary, journal, photos, original documents.* What is a secondary source? *A source that relies upon primary sources and other secondary sources to provide the information.*

■ With access to the Internet, it is possible to view many primary documents which previously only scholars could access. For instance, we can access Paul's account of the night Longfellow writes about.

Location and Access (Where):

■ Using computer and projector, model for students typing in URL for the American Revolution Web site and skim and scan to locate Paul Revere's account of the night.

Use of Information:

■ Randomly call on students to read parts of Paul Revere's account of that night.

■ Discuss differences in the poem and Paul's account. For instance, was the purpose to notify the country side or to notify Hancock and Adams? Was Paul alone or with others? What happened to Paul that night?

Note: Students may need to use a dictionary (online or print) to understand the meaning of some words not used frequently in today's speaking language.

Synthesis:

■ Which is primary source? Which is secondary source?

■ Using projector and overhead visit another primary source regarding Paul Revere, American Revolution Spy Letters. Share letter written by Paul's wife and given to the doctor who was actually a Loyalist.

Evaluation:

■ Product: Ask students to evaluate, thumbs up/thumbs down: Did we verify the accuracy of Longfellow's account of Revere's ride?

■ Process: What is a primary source? What is a secondary source? Is it important for you to know which you are using in your research? Is one source always better than the other? Why or why not?

Note: Other primary documents available on the Internet which may be of interest to students include Lewis and Clark's journals and journals and letters written by Civil War soldiers and their families.

From *Teaching Elementary Information Literacy Skills with the Big6™* by **Joyce Needham**. Columbus, OH: Linworth Publishing, Inc. Copyright © 2009.

LESSON TITLE: COMPARING FAMOUS AMERICANS

Grade Level: 1st-2nd	**Time Frame:** ■ One session for each person studied ■ One follow-up session ■ Additional sessions for culminating activities
Content Objective: History—Biography ■ Social Studies Theme: People, Places, and Environments	**Information Literacy Objective:** ■ Practice the steps of the problem solving process ■ Use of information: Note taking, Charts/Tables, Venn diagram, if culminating activity is completed

Materials and Sources:
- Paper to create class chart
- One source for each person studied
- Optional (culminating activities): Paper for student to create report on favorite person
- Optional (culminating activities): Blank Venn diagram for comparing

PLAN

Problem:
- There are many famous Americans. People we remember for one reason or another even after they die. Can you think of some famous people?
- Let students help create a list of famous people. Might want to distinguish between famous and popular. For instance, lots of sports players, musicians, actors are popular at the time. This does not always mean they will be famous or whether people will remember them in 50 or 100 years.
- Would you like to know more about some of these people? Maybe learn why we remember them, where they were born, and who they were? What if we created a chart or table with five or six famous people and some facts about each? Would you know more about them?
- I wonder . . . are famous people alike? Or can people be famous and be different? Could we look at our chart and see if these people are alike and or different?

Task Definition (What):
- What is your task? *To learn about famous people by creating a chart comparing them.*
- Would it be easier to read and compare our famous people if we wrote in paragraph style with complete sentences or would it be easier to compare if we used a table or chart and wrote only keywords? *Table or chart with keywords.*
- What information do we want to compare about each person?
- Create a chart with categories to be completed. Categories included could be: age if alive today, sex, race, state in which person was born, and keyword or phrase identifying why they are famous. With class input determine which six of the famous people on brainstormed list will be included on the chart. When selecting it is suggested that a diverse group be chosen, e.g. men and women, African American and Caucasian, etc.

Information Seeking Strategies (What):

- What source can we use to find the needed information? Do you have the information in your brain or prior knowledge? You know the name. You may know their race. Do you know how old they would be today? Do you have all the important information? Would a book about the person be helpful in finding the needed information? What about an encyclopedia? Internet?

- Model using a variety of sources to locate the information, using one source for each person being researched. Using a different source for each person exposes students to a variety of sources and allows students to understand more than one source of information normally exists.

Location and Access (Where):

- Model going to the shelf or the computer and locating the source.

- Model finding the keyword (person's last name) by using guide words or index/menu of the source.

Use of Information:

- After information is located or found for one person, ask students: How are we going to get the information on our chart? Can I just copy all this information?

- Discuss how we must engage by reading, inputting information in the brain, and then extracting, pulling the important information, before we can write our notes.

- Explain to students what use will look like: Since reading might be difficult for you and since there is only one copy of the text, would it work if I read to you? How will you engage and input this information in your brain? *Listen.* What will you need to do as you listen?

- Model and practice letting students extract information as they listen, e.g. listening for keywords, raising hand when keyword is heard.

- Begin reading information. Stop when students raise hands indicating the important information or the keyword has been found. Ask students to listen as you read that section again. Randomly call on students to identify the needed information or the treasure.

Synthesis:

- As students identify the needed information record it on the chart.

- Repeat until the chart contains all the needed information about one person.

- *Note: Some answers will not be found in the text because of the various levels of questions. Students will need to use information from the text and add prior knowledge to find the information needed for the chart. For instance, the age of the person if they were alive today will probably not be found in text. Students will find the birth year of the person in the text. Students, possibly with teacher help, will need to apply prior knowledge of math and compute how old the person would be today. It is desirable to present the information in this way because it allows students to practice combining new and old information and also helps develop a sense of time, of how long ago the person lived.*

- *Note: It is acceptable to use prior knowledge as a source if some facts are known. For instance, students may agree the person is male and Caucasian. At the same time it is important to emphasize the importance of verifying information when doing research.*

Information Seeking Strategies, Location and Access, Use of Information, and Synthesis:

- Repeat until all of the information is found and recorded for all six people.

Synthesis:

- Randomly call on students to use the chart and identify similarities and differences between the people studied. Students may make their own comparisons or teacher may ask questions requiring students to compare. For instance: Which are women? Who was born in the same state? Which are African American? Who lived the longest time ago? Who lived most recently?

Optional Culminating Activities:

- Create a report about favorite person. Each student selects his or her favorite person from the chart. Provide the student with a picture of that person. Each student creates a report, using the picture and information on the chart. The report includes the name of the person, a picture of the person, and one or two sentences written by the student incorporating the facts written on the chart.

- Create a Venn diagram. Select two people from the chart and model creating a Venn diagram. Give each student a blank Venn diagram. Have students choose two people from chart and write comparisons on the diagram. Students may be asked to turn their Venn diagram, which contains phrases, into a two-paragraph paper on the similarities and differences of the two people compared.

- Line Ups. Cut chart into strips with one famous person per strip. Randomly hand the six strips to students. Direct students with strips to use one category of information to line up or group themselves according to similarities. For instance, line up from youngest to oldest, by race, by region of birth.

Evaluation:

- Product: Ask students to write the names of the six famous Americans studied without accessing the chart. Randomly call on students to share one fact about a specific person studied. If culminating activities are used, be sure to evaluate them also.

- Process:
  - Ask students to indicate with thumbs up or thumbs down: Did we follow the steps of Big6? Did these steps make it easy to solve our problem? Can we use these steps if we need to learn about people in the future?
  - Randomly call on students to identify: Which step did you like best? Which step did you like least? How do you engage or use information that is text? *Read.* How do you engage or use information if it is spoken? *Listen.*

From *Teaching Elementary Information Literacy Skills with the Big6™* by **Joyce Needham**. Columbus, OH: Linworth Publishing, Inc. Copyright © 2009.

LESSON PLAN 19.10

LESSON TITLE: FAMOUS AFRICAN AMERICANS
(Any group of people, e.g. inventors, explorers, famous people from your state, Revolutionary War leaders, could be substituted for Famous African Americans)

Option: This lesson could be used as a springboard to in-depth study of one person. Students may use the knowledge gained about individuals in this lesson to successfully choose one person for further in-depth study.

Grade Level: 3rd-5th	**Time Frame:** ■ One 45-minute session

Content Objective: History—Biography ■ Social Studies Theme: Individuals, groups, and institutions. ■ Cultural Awareness	**Information Literacy Objective:** ■ Practice using the steps of the problem solving process. ■ Location and Access: Locate needed information in encyclopedia by scanning and skimming. ■ Synthesis: Identifying keywords ■ Information Seeking Strategies: Compare organization and use of dictionary and encyclopedia. *For students who have no prior experience with encyclopedias.*

Materials and Sources:

■ Blank chart to be completed: needs to be 4 cards wide and long enough to allow all names to be attached in first column
■ One card with name of famous African American written on it
■ One card with picture (no name) of famous African American (Lay these out on table at front of room.)
■ Two blank cards
■ Encyclopedias

PLAN

Problem:

■ Call out names of famous African Americans. Have students respond by raising one hand if they recognize the name and two hands if they know why they are famous. Include both familiar and unfamiliar names.

■ Connect to Black History Month and desire to learn about famous African Americans: If we do a report, we learn about the one person we research. How can we use our limited time to learn about lots of famous African Americans? (Hint: Point to empty table or chart and help students determine that creating a class chart or table is an effective solution.)

Task Definition (What):

- What is our task? *To learn a little about many famous African Americans.*
- What information do we need? What do we want to include in table or chart? Guide students to include:
    - name of person
    - year of birth and death or place of birth (city or state)
    - picture
    - why they are famous
- Discuss: Will we want to write complete sentences or keywords or phrases in our chart? Will we have a lot of room to write on our chart? Which will be quicker to read as we try to learn information? Complete sentences or keywords?
- I already wrote names of famous African Americans on cards. I also have a picture of each person although you will have to identify who they are. I also have two blank cards. What do you suggest we write on each card? *Year of birth and death or birth place on one and why famous on the other.*
- Do we all need to find the information on every person? How could we make this easier? Work smarter not harder? *Work in pairs, each pair research one person.* Good idea, but we have more people than we have pairs. *When we finish researching and entering data on chart for one person, we take another person until we find all people.*

Information Seeking Strategies (What):

- Would the encyclopedia be a good source? Why?

For students who have no previous experience with encyclopedia:

- What source can we use? Would a dictionary be a good source? Why not? Would it be ok if we use an encyclopedia? You have not used it for a project yet and it is a source you need to learn about this year. (For introduction to encyclopedia see Figure 3.3 and Chapter 3.)

Location and Access (Where):

- Guide students before they begin searching:
    - Where are the encyclopedias?
    - What will your keyword be? *Person's last name.*
    - How will you know which volume you need? *First letter of last name of person.*
    - How will you find information in the encyclopedia? *Scan or match guide words.*
    - To find birth date and death date you will scan for what type of information? *Numbers, specifically four digits or a year.*
    - What might you skim for to find why they are famous? *Famous, accomplishments, best known for, etc.*

Use of Information and Synthesis:

Students work in pairs:

- Pick up three cards, one card with name and two blank cards.
- Use the appropriate encyclopedia to record dates of birth and death on one card and keywords telling why famous on another card.
- From table select picture of the famous person.
- Bring all four cards to chart and tape in appropriate columns.
- Repeat process until all names are researched.

Evaluation:

Ask students to respond to evaluation questions with thumbs up or thumbs down or by sharing with partner:

- Product: Did we complete our task? Did we find a lot of information about famous African Americans? We have the information, but do we know it? How can we learn this information? See follow-up activities.

- Process: Was this a good way to solve our problem? Share with your partner something that worked well with the process. Share something that was negative with the process. Randomly call upon students to share positives and negatives.

- *Students who were introduced to the encyclopedia:* Tell your partner one way encyclopedias are like dictionaries and one way they are different.

Follow-Up Activities:

- Create a timeline using the cards from chart.

- Play memory or concentration. Remove cards from chart and lay print side down.

- Students select one person from the chart for in-depth research. Complete a report or project about that one person.

- Create a living museum to share information. Each student becomes an exhibit or the person researched. Scatter students throughout the library or all-purpose room or museum. Using artifacts or dressing like the person under study, the student comes to life and gives a speech as if he were that person when visitors tap his button or sticker placed on back of hand.

From *Teaching Elementary Information Literacy Skills with the Big6™* by **Joyce Needham**. Columbus, OH: Linworth Publishing, Inc. Copyright © 2009.

LESSON PLAN 19.11

LESSON TITLE: TIMELINE OF AMERICAN PRESIDENTS

Grade Level: 2nd-5th	**Time Frame:** ■ Two 30-minute sessions

Content Objective: History—Biography and Geography ■ Social Studies Theme: Time, Continuity, and Change; People, Places, and Environments	**Information Literacy Objective:** ■ Practice using the steps of the problem solving process ■ Information Seeking Strategies: selecting the best source ■ Location and Access: Scanning for dates, scanning guide words ■ Synthesis: creating a product that solves our needs

Materials and Sources:

■ Paper or string to create timeline circling the room (adding machine tape works well)
■ List in alphabetical order of the American presidents
■ Index cards (One for each president, with president's name written in marker. Will be used to record information.)
■ Encyclopedia or Internet

PLAN

Problem:

■ How many presidents has the United States had? *Ending with George W. Bush there have been 43 presidents.* How many can you name? Do you think the president has much impact on what happens in our country while he is president? As American citizens would we have a better understanding of our country if we knew who was president when . . . Lewis and Clark made their trip west? . . . man first landed on the moon? . . . on 9/11? Are you interested in learning who was president when you were born? Which state has produced the most presidents? Has a Missourian ever been president? Would you like to know more about who our presidents have been? . . . their names? . . . when they served? . . . in what state they were born?

Task Definition (What):

■ What is our task? *To identify the presidents, when they served, and in what state they were born.*
■ How can we best share this information? . . . three-page report? . . . chart? . . . timeline? Discuss pros and cons of each format of synthesis.
■ When discussing timeline, suggest it be posted all year. Events may be added, as studied, to the timeline. This will create a picture of what happened in our country during each president's term. Ask: Would this help us better understand our presidents and our history? Thumbs up/thumbs down. Do you like the idea of creating a presidential timeline?
■ If we create a timeline, do you each need to research every president? How could we organize to better use our time? *Each student or pair of students could research one president.* If each student or each pair researches one president, will we have information on all 43 men? What can we do? *When you finish researching one president you could research another until all presidents had been researched.*

Information Seeking Strategies (What):

- Let students brainstorm list of sources. After brainstorming, guide students in determining advantages and disadvantages of each suggested source. For instance, an advantage of using the encyclopedia in this particular assignment is you have less information to scan than in a book. Another advantage is with over 20 volumes in an encyclopedia set, more students can access the source at the same time than one book about presidents.

- Depending upon objectives, e.g. students may need to learn about a specific source, teacher may decide upon a specific source, or allow students to choose an appropriate source from list.

Location and Access (Where):

- If needed, model for students locating the source.

- Remind students to scan, or match one letter at a time, for the keyword. Identify the keyword, which is the president's last name. Encourage students to use text aids, such as guide words or index/menu to find the keywords.

- Guide students to scan for numbers, specifically four digits, when identifying what years the president served. Verbalize for students the first years found after the president's name, usually in parenthesis, will probably be birth and date deaths. May also point out the need to skim headings for keywords such as term of office, elected, etc.

Use of Information:

- Students read and extract needed information. Information should be recorded on card containing the president's name.

- When students have completed the card for one president, they should take a card and research another president. This continues until all presidents are researched.

Synthesis:

After all cards are completed:

- Designate various areas of the room as geographical locations or regions of the U.S., e.g. corner by white board is the East, window area is the West, center of room is Midwest, etc. Each student, using one of the president's cards, goes to the appropriate region in which their president was born. May want to group by state within the region.

- Attach timeline around the perimeter of room. Have students attach their president's card to the appropriate location on the timeline. Discussion of the timeline might include: How many presidents served more than one term? What president served the shortest period of time? The longest? Who was president when you were born?

- Throughout the year, as events are studied, add them to the timeline and note who was president at the time. Discuss the effects of the event on people at the time and upon future events and people.

Evaluation:

Evaluate by having students respond, thumbs up or thumbs down, to teacher questions:

- Product: Did we complete our task? Did we determine in what state each president was born? Did we identify when each president served as president? Did we identify what was happening when each president served? *Students should respond thumbs down, but acknowledge we will need to do this as we continue studies this year.*

- Process: Did our synthesis solve our problem? Did the timeline work to quickly and easily solve our problem? Did we select a good source to use? Did we scan and skim rather than read when locating the information? How did that work for us? What did you learn that will help you the next time you have a problem to solve? What would you do differently?

CHAPTER 20
PARTING THOUGHTS

B ig6 . . .

- rocks because it turns brain busters into no brainers!
- does not give you the answer, but it helps you get the answer.
- makes you think a little bit harder.
- helps me when I am confused.
- has helped me in real life with real problems.
- has made all my homework and my life easier.

Our goal as teachers and library media specialists is to teach students. The perceptions of the above 4th grade students, after being introduced to and using Big6, offer an incentive to include Big6 in that teaching (Mullins 2002). There are other reasons to include problem solving instruction as a part of our curriculum.

Why Teach Problem Solving?

Knowledge and information expand daily. If today you could claim possession of all of the knowledge known to mankind, tomorrow that claim would be false. Living in a constantly changing world, where new information emerges daily, demands that students become lifelong learners. Problem solvers are lifelong learners. They are able to tackle and solve new and unfamiliar problems by utilizing problem solving skills.

Eisenberg's variation of the fish parable helps explain the power of teaching problem solving:

- Give a man a fish and he will eat a meal.
- Teach a man to fish and he will eat for a lifetime.
- Teach a man how to find information on how to fish and he will teach himself to fish and anything else he needs to know (Eisenberg 2003).

Students are being taught to fish when they are taught processes such as reading, writing, and problem solving. When the process being taught is problem solving or information literacy, they are being taught to find information and solve their own problems. Improved problem solving skills and increased learning results when students assume responsibility for their learning by tackling problems. The ability to solve problems, without relying upon the skills of others and without having previously experienced the problem, is the mark of an information literate individual and a lifelong learner.

Why the Big6 and Not Another Problem Solving Process?

Problem solving or information literacy skills are identified as " . . . the ability to access information efficiently and effectively, evaluate information critically and competently, and use information accurately and creatively" (AASL 8). The Big6 problem solving process provides a logical, sequential approach to mastering the skills required to be information literate.

There are other problem solving strategies from which to choose. If you examine the problem solving processes, you will find the steps identified in each process are very similar (Eisenberg & Berkowitz 6). The number of steps varies from four to 10 depending upon how the sequence is broken down. Most follow the same basic sequence. Perhaps the biggest variation exists with identification and location of sources (Big6 #2 and #3). These two steps are often implied, rather than stated, unless the problem solving process is designed as a research process.

Examination of the various problem solving processes reveals another difference in the strategies: terminology. Each process has its own set of vocabulary to describe the steps of the process. Many of the processes, such as scientific inquiry, were designed to solve a specific type of problem and so the vocabulary fits when solving that type of problem. The vocabulary, however, may not fit when attempting to solve other types of problems. Therein lays the power of Big6. The vocabulary of Big6 may be applied to solve a wide variety of problems. For instance, task definition and evaluation are applicable to problems students must solve in reading, writing, math, science, social studies, research problems, and even personal problems. The authentic nature of the Big6 vocabulary helps make the problem solving process visible and concrete for problem solvers. In addition, the Big6 vocabulary is both kid-friendly and adult-friendly.

The versatility of Big6 allows students to learn and use one process and set of vocabulary to solve any problem. The opportunity for repetitive practice and mastery exists when the same process and vocabulary are used to tackle all problems. This familiarity with the Big6 may be utilized to help students more quickly learn new problem solving processes. When introduced to new processes, such as scientific inquiry or math problem solving processes, students are able to make connections between the processes. These connections lead to a deeper understanding of problem solving.

The Big6 process of problem solving supports how we learn (Chapter 3), teaching process (Chapter 4), and using problems to teach (Chapter 6). Finally, it is possible to use the Big6 strategy in conjunction with and to support other effective strategies such as cooperative learning, differentiated learning, Love and Logic (Fay & Funk), reading strategies as suggested in *Reading with Meaning* (Miller) and *Nonfiction Matters* (Harvey), and other suggested research-based strategies (Marzano, Pickering, and Pollock).

Teaching the Big6: Are You Ready to Tackle the Problem?

The introduction to this book identified three parts of learning: **What** you are learning, **why** you need or want to learn it, and **how** you learn it. If this book has met its challenge, at this point you have determined **what** to teach your students: the Big6 problem solving process. You have also identified **why** your students may need or want to learn the Big6 process. The third part, and the most challenging, is **how** to teach Big6. This book contains many tips, strategies, and lessons which may be helpful as you tackle the problem of teaching your students Big6 problem solving. If you are feeling a bit overwhelmed, or not sure where to begin, the Big6 itself may help solve your problem (see Figure 20.1).

Helping Our Students Succeed

As teachers and library media specialists, you are driven by the desire to see your students succeed. Part of this success means mastery of the basics: reading, writing, arithmetic, and **problem solving.** You realize how much simpler life is for students who master the basics. The power of reading, writing, and arithmetic has been recognized for many years. Today the importance of information literacy is also recognized. As effective problem solvers, students will not:

- turn in the wrong problem because they did not **define the task**
- use a dictionary or almanac to write a 10-page report because they did not use **information seeking strategies**
- stand in the library and expect information to come to them or turn page after page in a book to find information because they did not use their **location and access** skills
- sit in class and daydream or sit in front of the television for hours with a textbook in their lap because they did not **engage** and **use information**
- copy word for word from a book because they did not **extract and use information**
- get a zero for failing to turn work in on time because they did not **synthesize**
- turn in assignments with blanks they accidentally skipped because they did not **evaluate**
- view mistakes as failures rather than as opportunities to learn

Creation of a classroom or library where Big6 is a visible, concrete strategy is a viable option for making student success a reality. Students, who master the Big6 process, become problem solvers and information literate individuals. These individuals are empowered to become critical thinkers and lifelong learners who can and do solve their problems. They have the opportunity to be successful in our information-rich world.

Teaching Big6

#6. Evaluate	*What does problem solving currently look like in your classroom?*		
Level 1 Teacher or library media specialist solves problems.	**Level 2** Teacher or library media specialist lets students solve problems		**Level 3** Teacher or library media specialist lets students solve problems and makes them aware of the process being used to solve the problems.
——▶			

1. Task Definition	
1.1 What is the task?	Teachers and students solve problems all day every day. The task is to switch from simply **using** the problem solving process to teaching **students** the process and letting students solve their problems.
1.2 What information is needed?	■ What adjustments are needed in my teaching?* ■ Strategies for teaching problem solving. *Note: In most cases only minor adjustments are needed, not major overhauls. For instance, assume you are in your car and push the button to clean your windshield. Instead of spraying water on your windshield, water sprays on the car parked beside you. There is a definite problem. The solution does not require a major overhaul. What is needed is a minor adjustment, physically bending the spout that emits water. Moving from using Big6 to teaching Big6 only requires minor adjustments.*
2. Information Seeking Strategies What sources may I use?	*Teaching Elementary Information Literacy Skills with the Big6* Prior knowledge
3. Location and Access	Might refer to table of contents or index to locate information or begin by referring to adjustments and strategies suggested below:
4. Use of information	
4.1 Engage or read the information to the right. 4.2 Extract the needed information.	Change your habits. This requires conscious thought and repetition. The following may be helpful: ■ Post the Big6 process in a visible spot in your classroom. ■ Review the process in your mind daily at first and then weekly ■ Use the Big6 vocabulary, e.g. What is your task? What source will you use? Evaluate.
	Level One: ■ Pose problems instead of telling students, e.g. ask what needs to be done rather than giving instructions. ■ Model solving problems for students.
	Level Two: ■ Introduce the six steps by solving a student problem, e.g. signing up for community soccer program or planning your birthday party. ■ Verbalize the steps as you solve problems, making the process visible for students

Figure 20.1 Task: Teaching Big6

	■ Frequently stop students and ask where they are in the problem solving process at this moment? e.g. Are you evaluating, defining the task, or using information? ■ For one week insist all students be able to identify their task at any time. ■ Require students to evaluate every problem solved. Evaluate both the process and the product. Evaluation may be as simple as thumbs up/thumbs down response to an evaluative question such as, How did you do? ■ Integrate Big6 and allow students to use the process in solving a multitude and a variety of problems, i.e. guide students in using Big6 to solve problems in all content areas, classroom management, research, and test taking.
5. Synthesis	Use the strategies extracted above and from the book to help students solve their own problems and become aware of the steps of Big6 as they solve problems.
6. Evaluation	Product: Who is working harder . . . you or students? Who is solving problems . . . you or students? Are students aware of problems and the strategy used to solve them? Process: Can students identify the six steps in the problem solving process? Are the students using the six steps to solve their problems? *Note: Once students have mastered the process, they may solve problems automatically without consciously thinking of each of the six steps unless they are attempting to solve a difficult problem.*

From *Teaching Elementary Information Literacy Skills with the Big6™* by **Joyce Needham**. Columbus, OH: Linworth Publishing, Inc. Copyright © 2009.

Figure 20.1 Task: Teaching Big6 continued

Works Cited

American Association of School Librarians [and] Association for Educational Communications and Technology (AASL). *Information Power, Building Partnerships for Learning.* Chicago, IL: American Library Association, 1998.

Eisenberg, Michael. Pre-AASL National Conference Big6 Workshop. Kansas City, MO: 2003. Eisenberg, Michael and Robert Berkowitz. *Teaching Information & Technology Skills, The Big6 in Secondary Schools.* Worthington, OH: Linworth Publishing, Inc., 2000.

Fay, Jim and David Funk. *Teaching with Love and Logic, Taking Control of the Classroom.* U.S.: The Love and Logic Press, 1995.

Harvey, Stephanie. *Nonfiction Matters; Reading, Writing, and Research in Grades 3-8.* Portland, ME: Stenhouse Publishers, 1998.

Marzano, Robert J., Debra J. Pickering, and Jane E. Pollock. *Classroom Instruction That Works, Research-Based Strategies for Increasing Student Achievement.* Alexandria, VA: Association for Supervision and Curriculum Development, 2001.

Miller, Debbie. *Reading with Meaning, Teaching Comprehension in the Primary Grades.* Portland, Maine: Stenhouse Publishers, 2002.

Mullins Fourth Grade Class. Notes to the author. October 2002.

APPENDIX A

PICTURE BOOKS AND INFORMATION LITERACY SKILLS

Information Literacy Skill	Title	Author
1. Task Definition	Aunt Lucy Went to Buy a Hat	Low, A
1. Task Definition, power of vocabulary	Book Book Book	Bruss, D
	Baloney, Henry P	Scieszka, J
2. Information Seeking Strategies	Souperchicken	Auch, M
	Our Librarian Won't Tell Us Anything	Buzzeo, T
	Henry and the Buccaneer Bunnies	Crimi, C
	Library Dragon	Deedy, C
	Livingstone Mouse	Edwards, P
	Going Someplace Special	McKissack, P
	Earthquack	Palatini, M
	Aunt Chip and the Great...or Triple Creek Dam Affair	Polacco, P
2. Information Seeking Strategies, sense of sight	See the Ocean	Condra, E
2. Information Seeking Strategies, thesaurus	Web Files	Palatini, M
2. Information Seeking Strategies, unabridged dictionary	Frindle	Clements, A
2. Information Seeking Strategies, book safety	Mr. Wiggle	Craig, P
	Stella Louella & the Lost Book	Ernst, L
	Edward and the Pirates	McPhail, D
3. Location and Access, organization	I Spy CD-ROM, Oops Hoops	CD-ROM
4. Use of Information	Wretched Stone	Van Allsburg, C
4. Use of Information, prediction	Charlie Anderson	Abercrombie, B
	The Whingdingdilly	Peet, B
5. Synthesis	Grandpa Toad	Kasza, K
Big6, intro research process	George Washington's Breakfast	Fritz, J
Big6, Steps in the process	Superdog: The Heart of a Hero	Buehner, C
	Goldie Socks & the Three Libearians	Hopins, J
	Baby BeeBee Bird	Massie, D
	The Little Red Hen Makes a Pizza	Sturges, P
	Bertie was a Watch Dog	Walton, R
	Knufflebunny	Wilem, M
	What was I Scared of?	
Need for Change	Sneetches	Seuss
Need for Collaboration	Don't Laugh Joe	Kasza, K

HISTORICAL FICTION PICTURE BOOKS, AMERICAN HISTORY

Information Literacy Skill	Title	Author
Early Explorers	The Encounter	Yolen, J
Colonial Era	Samuel Eaton's Day	Waters, K
	On the Mayflower	Waters, K
Revolutionary War	Redcoats & Petticoats	Kirkpatrick, K & Himler, R
	Katie's Trunk	Turner, A
	Boston Tea Party	Edwards, P
Slavery Period	Nettie's Trip South	Himler, R & Turner, A
	Sweet Clara & the Freedom Quilt	Hopkinson, D
	Drinking Gourd	McKissack, P
	Mr. Lincoln's Whiskers	Winnick, K
	Barefoot, Escape on the Underground Railroad	Edwards, P
Lewis and Clark	Seaman's Journal	Eubank, P
Civil War	Pink & Say	Polacco, P
	A. Lincoln & Me	Borden, L
Westward Movement	Hog Music	Helldorfer, M
	Dandelions (Nebraska territory)	Bunting, E
	Lewis & Papa	Josse, B
Gold Rush	Nine for California	Levinton, S & Smith, C
	Boom Town	Levinton, S & Smith, C
Turn of the Century Life 1990s	Growing Seasons (farm life)	Splear, E
	My Tour of Europe	Roosevelt, T
1914	Mailing May	Tunnell, M & Rand, T
World War I	Casey Over There	Rabin, S
Dust Bowl	Children of the Dust Days	Coombs, K
Migrant Workers	Working Cotton	Williams, S
Immigrants	Streets of Gold	Wells, R
	Grandfather's Journey (Japanese-1920s)	Say, A
	A Day's Work	Bunting, E
	Going Home	Bunting, E
	Peacebound Trains	Balgassi, H
Depression (1930s)	The Gardner	Stewart, S
	The Babe & I	Adler, D
	The Bat Boy and the Violin	Curtis, G
	The Rag Coat	Mills, L
1930s	Amelia and Eleanor Go for a Ride	Ryan, P
1940s	The Sunday Outing	Pinkney, G
World War II	Hilde & Eli	Adler, D
	The Butterfly	Polacco, P
	So Far From the Sea	Bunting, E
	Faithful Elephants	Tsuchiya, Y
	Sadako	Coerr, E
Civil Rights Movement	Smoky Night (1990s)	Bunting, E
	Going Someplace Special	McKissack, P
Vietnam Era	The Wall	Bunting, E

Created by B. Holland, M. Butler, K. Gallion, and J. Needham

APPENDIX C

SCIENCE CONTENT AND PICTURE BOOKS

Science Content	Title of Book	Author
Camouflage	Clara Caterpillar	Edwards, P
Environment	Alejandro's Gift	Albert, R
	I Stink (Garbage Truck)	McMullan, K & McMullan, J
	The Stranger	VanAllsburg, C
Food Chain	Some Smug Slug	Edwards, P
	The Dory Story	Pallotta, J
Inventions	The Button Box	Reid, M
Life Cycles	Farfallina & Marcel	Keller, H
	The Caterpillar & the Pollywog	Kent, J
Measurement	Librarian Who Measured the Earth	Lasky, K

INDEX

6+1 Writing Traits 39, 41-42

A

A Functional Model of Information Processing (Figure 3.1) 18
A Functional Model of Information Processing through the Big6 Lens (Figure 3.2) 20
AASL 3, 298
Accurate Evaluation (Figure 12.1) 132
Addressing Faulty Behavior (Figure 16.4) 198
American Association of School Librarians 3, 298
American Revolution Journal Entry (Figure 19.2) 266
An Australian Rainforest Living Museum (Lesson Plan 18.5)
analogy 25
    child learning to walk/ learning to solve problem 207
    hand and fingers/communication arts 37-38
    lifting heavy object/learning 22
    raindrops/information 114
    recipe/Big6 process 13, 25
    sports practice/learning session 22
Animal Classification Riddle Step Book (Lesson Plan 18.9) 244-246
Answering a Simple Research Question (Lesson Plan 13.1) 150-151
answering questions from text
    application of Big6 to the process 175-177
    implementing effectively 173-174
Answering Questions from Text (Figure 15.1) 175
Association for Educational Communications and Technology 3
Author Study (Lesson Plan 13.2) 152-153

B

Bagwell, Janell 201
behavior expectations 190-191, 239
Berkowitz, Robert 65, 105, 112, 122, 126, 129, 131, 133, 142, 208, 218, 298, 302
bibliography
    information literacy picture book titles 303
    science picture book titles 305
    social studies picture book titles 304
Big6 xv, 4, 6
Big6
    advantages of 4, 298
    answering questions from text 175-177
    as a research strategy 145
    beginning to teach 5
    student success 224, 299
    terminology 4, 208, 221-222, 298
    steps 4, 6-7, 13, 21, 25, 29, 40, 41-42, 146, 147, 178, 180, 222, 223
    versatility 298
    vocabulary 4, 29, 191, 208, 298
Big6 Math Organizer (Figure 17.5) 209
Big6 Math Organizer—How Many More Dogs Than Snakes (Figure 17.2) 203
Big6 Math Organizer—Marbles (Figure 17.3) 204
Big6 Organizer (Figure 4.1) 33
Big6 Organizer for Math Problem (Figure 17.1) 202

Big6 Problem Solving Process with the Little 12 (Figure 1.1) 4
Big6 process
    breaking into small steps 4, 13, 29, 206, 207, 210
Bloom, Benjamin 52, 62, 88, 129, 161
Bloom's Taxonomy 50, 51, 62, 125
Brennan, Marilynn xiii, xvi
Butler, Margaret 304

C

citation 117, 120, 121, 122, 168
citing sources 39, 71, 120
    how to 121, 122, 168
    need for 120-121
    scaffold 71
    why 120-121
Civil War Study (Lesson Plan 13.4) 159-161
Class Animal Book (Lesson Plan 18.4) 232-234
Class Luau (Lesson Plan 19.3) 276-277
Classification of Animals (Lesson Plan 13.3) 154-155
classroom management 185
    advantages of implementing Big6 as strategy 185
    behavior 192
    behavior expectations 190-191
    changing habits 190
    impact of consequences and consistency 186-189
    making the process visible 191
    posing problems 193
    problem solving 185
    providing opportunities for student evaluation 193
    routines and procedures 185
    students accepting responsibility 185, 186
collaboration xiii, 32, 33
communication 29-30, 34, 123, 127
    one-way 127
    two-way 127
Compare Student Research Process with Big6 Process (Figure 13.1) 146
Comparing Famous Americans (Lesson Plan 19.9) 289-291
Comparing the Dictionary and Encyclopedia (Figure 3.3) 24
Comparison of Answering Questions from Text to Answering Questions on Tests (Figure 15.4) 181
Comparison of Book Publication and Internet Publication (Figure 8.1) 86
Comparison of Directing to Questioning (Figure 16.1) 187
Comparison of Faulty Research Process with Big6 Process (Figure 13.2) 147
Comparison of Scientific Inquiry, Technological Design, and Big6 222
concrete behavior expectations 190
Connecting Electronic Testing to Paper and Pencil Testing (Figure 15.3) 179
connections 15, 25
    answering questions from text/test taking 181
    classroom management
    communication arts 37, 38, 39, 43
    new learning to prior knowledge 22, 23, 70
    power of 23, 24

reading 37, 38, 43
science 221, 223
social studies 182, 263, 275
technology 40, 106
test taking/answering questions from text 187
test taking 23, 24
to prior knowledge xiv, 19, 30, 38
writing 37, 38, 41, 43
Connections between Big6 Process and Communication
  Arts (Figure 5.1) 39
consequences 51, 135, 136, 186, 188, 189
consistency 13, 186
content x, 13, 24, 25, 29, 34, 201, 221, 223, 224, 263, 305
cooperative learning 65, 139, 299
Creating a Math Strategy Bank (Figure 17.11) 214
Creating a State Scrapbook (Lesson Plan 19.5) 280-281
Creating our Safety Rules (Lesson Plan 18.7) 240-241
Culham, Ruth 41, 42, 44, 56

D

Denniston, JaDene 47, 52, 187, 200
differentiated learning 299
Differentiating between Scanning and Skimming
  (Figure 9.4) 104
Dinosaur Report (Lesson Plan 18.3) 229-231
drawings 213, 229

E

Eisenberg, Mike xvi, 4, 7, 40, 43, 62, 65, 71, 88, 105, 112,
  118, 122, 126, 129, 131, 133, 142, 208, 210, 218, 288,
  302, 309
engaging 113, 116, 117
  oral sources 91, 165
  print sources 68, 96, 106, 165
Establishing a Classroom Management System Utilizing
  Big6 (Figure 16.3) 197
evaluation 131
  ask specific concrete questions 138, 139
  consequences for 136-137
  effectiveness 137
  efficiency 138
  importance of 133
  instead of lecturing and nagging 135
  learned skill 132, 133
  math word problems 132, 210
  of Internet sources 87, 88
  of likes and dislikes 138
  of returned tests and assignments 137
  other terms to identify 131
  peer evaluation 137, 138
  process 138
  product 137
  strategies 135-142
  student 136
experience
  one year or 25 years 133
Exploring our City (Lesson Plan 19.6) 282-283
extracting
  impact on problem solving
  important information 114, 115
  needed information 114, 115, 118
  phrases 117, 118
  scaffold 117
  treasure 118

F

Famous African Americans (Lesson Plan 19.10) 292-294
Fay, Jim 188, 200, 299, 302
feedback 34, 63, 66, 87, 131, 136, 191, 217
Figure 6.1: Examples of Good Student Problems
Figures (See Table of Figures) viii-ix
fish parable 298
Following One Problem through the Process (Figure 17.8)
  212
Funk, David 188, 200, 299, 302

G

Gallion, Kristie 304
graphic aids 77, 93, 96, 108
Guide Word Champ (Figure 9.3) 100

H

Harvey, Stephanie 299, 302
History Timeline (Lesson Plan 19.7) 284-286
Holland, Barbara 304
How Do We Cite Sources? (Figure 10.2) 121

I

Identifying the Best Source and Locating Information
  (Lesson Plan 9.3) 109-111
important information
  clues in oral presentations 168
  clues in written sources 168
information
  explosion 9, 10, 174
information literacy
  definition 3
information seeking strategies
  brainstorming 40, 233, 265, 296
Integrating Big6 Process with the Writing Process and
  6+1 Traits of Writing (Figure 5.3) 42
integration
  classroom management 190, 191, 200
  math word problems 201
  reading 38
  science 223, 224
  social studies 269
  technology 123
  within elementary school 14, 34, 38
  writing 38
Internet
  accessing information 94
  conducting a search 95
  developing evaluation skills 87
  importance of keywords 96
  locating source of Web site 94
  location and access 94
  menus or indexes 94
  navigating 94
  need for skills 85
  reliability 86, 87
  search engines 86, 93. 94, 95
  teaching skills 106
  URL 94, 121, 248, 288
  variety of sources 86
Internet Index or Menu (Figure 9.1) 94
Internet Scavenger Hunt: Earthquakes and Volcanoes
  (Lesson Plan 18.10) 247-249

Introduction to Sources (Lesson Plan 8.1) 72-75
Introduction to Reference Sources (Lesson Plan 8.3) 79-82
Invention Timeline (Lesson 18.14) 258-260
Inventions and Our Life (Lesson 18.13) 255-257

J

Jansen, Barbara xv, xvi, 114, 118, 119, 122, 168, 172

K

Keyword Organizer (Figure 9.5) 105
keywords 33, 39, 56, 59, 60-62, 65, 66, 68, 87, 89, 91, 93,
    95, 96, 105, 106, 109, 110, 111, 118, 140, 147, 161, 174,
    175, 176, 183, 212, 213

L

Landforms Book and Game (Lesson 19.2) 272-275
learned helplessness 136
learning
        characteristics 17-19, 47
        functional approach to 17, 18
        what 17
        why 49
        how 17, 18, 19
        level of 50-51
        strategies 21-25
Learning About our State (Lesson Plan 19.4) 278-279
learning process 17
lesson plans (See Table of Lesson Plans) x
level of learning 50-51, 124, 125
Life Cycles (Lesson Plan 18.2) 227-228
List of Questions (Figure 7.2) 61
List of Sorted Questions (Figure 7.3) 61
listening 37, 38, 58, 64, 74, 91, 113, 164, 165
Little 12 4, 7, 157
location and access of information
        impact of technology on 90-91
        importance of in today's world 89-90
        importance of keywords 93, 96
        motivation to learn 89-90
        two guiding questions 97
long-term memory 17-19, 20-21, 55, 58, 113
Love and Logic 188, 200, 299, 302

M

Marzano, Robert 34, 36, 116, 122, 164, 172, 211, 218, 299,
    302
Maslow 134, 142
Math Concepts (Figure 17.4) 206
Math Strategy Bank (Figure 17.10) 215
math word problems
        basic math concepts 206
        Big6 organizer 202, 209
        identifying strengths and weaknesses 210-214
        marble problem 202-205
        pet shop 201-203
Miller, Debbie 299, 302
Missouri Department of Elementary and Secondary
    Education 183-184
Mnemonics 149, 210
Mnemonics (Figure 17.6) 210
Mullins, Laura 214, 215, 223, 297, 302

N

National Academy of Sciences 221, 222, 224, 261
National Council for the Social Studies 263, 269
Necessity is the Mother of Invention (Lesson 18.12) 253-
    254
nonfiction text 107, 174
Nonlinguistic Representation of Note Taking (Figure
    14.1) 164
nonlinguistic representations 116, 164
note taking
        access information from print or oral sources 165
        closed book note taking 171
        extracting 165
        extracting important information 165
        giving sources credit 168
        identifying the treasure 168
        modeling note taking 170
        organization 169
        organizers 169
        phrases 169
        purpose of 164-165
        recording the important information 168
        teaching skills 165
        the process 163
        timed reading and writing 170-171
        used for synthesis 165
note taking organizers 117, 126-127
        computer programs 127
        data chart 118, 160, 169
        file folder with envelopes 154, 160
        notebook paper 127
        Venn diagram 30, 117
        webs 169
note taking test 169

O

objectives
        addressing with synthesis 125
        addressing with task 59
        determining level of learning 50-51
Objects in the Sky (Lesson Plan 18.6) 238-239
Opportunities for Choice (Figure 13.3) 157
organization
        Eisenberg's magazine pictures 126

P

Paul Revere via Primary and Secondary Sources (Lesson
    Plan 19.8) 287-288
Payne, Ruby xiii, xvi
Pickering, Debra 34, 36, 122, 172, 218, 299, 302
plagiarism 51, 117, 120, 233
        reasons for 120-122
        strategies to prevent 117, 120
Planets Brochure (Lesson 18.11) 250-252
Planning Form (Figure 4.2) 35
Pollock, Jane 34, 36, 122, 172, 218, 299, 302
practice
        opportunities for 33, 47, 51
        prescriptive xiv, 14, 34, 53
print sources
        importance of keywords 36, 68, 93
prior knowledge 3, 13, 18, 19, 20, 25, 27, 30, 31, 55, 67, 68
problem solvers 4, 5, 9

dependent 12
independent 12
semi-dependent 12
problem solving
why teach 13
motivation 9-12
Problem Solving and Science (Figure 18.1) 222
Problem Solving Continuum (Figure 2.1) 12
problem solving process
visualizing 206, 213, 217
conscious use of 13, 25, 32
problem solving processes 221, 298
problems
authentic 5, 48, 49, 124, 141, 200, 222, 263
creating "good" problems 48-50
creating a purpose for learning 49-50
definition of 4
engaging 48
ownership by students 48, 49, 59
ownership by teachers and library media specialists 51
posing 25, 47, 50, 193, 194, 269
presenting learning goals as 49, 52
student 48-50
as a teaching strategy 47
level of learning 50
process
autopilot 28
teaching 27, 29-34
process evaluation 131, 132, 141, 224
product evaluation 131
Properties of Objects: Comparing, Sorting, and Describing (Lesson Plan 18.1) 225-226

Q

questioning 25, 28, 60, 141-142, 158, 173, 187, 194-196
questions
answering from text 175-181, 183
quotes 117, 118, 119, 120

R

Ratcliff, Jeannie 160
reading 3, 27, 28, 37-43, 180, 182
research
develop questioning skills 158
focus on one step at a time 158
incorporating student choice 157
intermediate students 157-161
levels of learning 158
organizing questions 161
primary students 149-155
sample lessons 150-155, 159-161
topics for primary students 149
retrieval 18, 19, 20, 206
Rotation (Figure 17.7) 211
rubrics 39, 132

S

Sample Diagnostic Practice (Figure 17.13) 219
sample problem
connections to prior learning 44-45
economics social studies test item 182
electronic test vs. paper-and-pencil tests 179
failure to read assignments 188
ink marks in library book 69
Journal entry of citizens during the American Revolutionary War 266
library catalog 48
loss of worksheet 135
low mid-quarter grades 51
luau project 277
Native Americans project 133
overdue books 69, 189
sources needed in Kansas City 68-69
student lack of awareness of process weaknesses 14
synonym and antonym worksheet 135
using study guide vs. using text chapters for test-preparation 115
voting location 69
westward movement social studies test item 177-178
Sample Reading Selection Questions (Figure 15.5) 182
Sample Test Item (Figure 15.6) 182
scaffolding instruction 31
behavior 192
classroom routine 191
developing questioning skills 141
guiding 157, 170, 191
independent practice 171, 191
modeling 157, 170, 191
scanning 91, 92, 96
importance of scanning quickly 99
strategies to increase scanning speed 99-100
teaching 98
schema 68
Schiller, Pam 19, 26, 32, 36
science 221
definition of 221
sample lessons 223-260
Science Content Standards 224
Science Content Standards 224
Science Content Standards (Figure 18.3) 224
scientific inquiry 221, 222, 223, 298
Scientific Inquiry and Big6 Planner Figure 18.2) 223
self-evaluation 134-135
active learning 134-135
importance of 134
non-threatening 134
senses 17, 18, 19, 20, 55, 58, 91, 114, 115
sensory memory 17-21 58
short-term memory 17
Simple Machines and Westward Expansion (Lesson Plan 18.8) 242-243
skimming
teaching 105
social studies 263
creating lesson plans 265
definition 263
integrating Big6 into existing lessons 267
integration of social studies skills 263-265
primary and secondary sources 287-288
sample lessons 270-296
student questions 268
timelines 268
Social Studies Skills and Big6 Skills (Figure 19.1) 264
Social Studies Test Item (Figure 15.2) 177
sources 19, 67
characteristics of good sources 69
connecting new sources to familiar sources 70

criteria for selecting 71
electronic reference sources 85
identifying 67-68
Internet 68
locating information within 91
location of 89
need for 68-69
possible information sources 67
print reference sources 71, 79-82
prior knowledge or schema 68
reference 67, 71
selecting 69-70
the "I Know' pitfall 71
speaking 37-40
strategies
think aloud 70, 97, 98, 106
Strategies to Help Know or Identify Task (Figure 7.4) 64
Strategies to Help Students Understand the Task and
Identify Information Needed (Figure 7.5) 65
student achievement xiii, 23, 24, 36, 57, 85, 132, 134, 138,
152, 173
student choice 157, 251
Student Evaluations (Figure 17.12) 217
Student Selection of Sources for Research (Lesson Plan 8.4)
83-84
students
as problem solvers 51
responsibility for learning 134
Suggested Evaluation Questions (Figure 12.2) 139
synthesis 21, 123
authentic problems 124
communicating 127
forms of 128
impact on level of learning 125
importance of 124
organizational skills 124, 126
providing authentic audiences 125
purpose for communicating solution 124
student choice 128
technology tools 127
Synthesis Forms (Figure 11.1) 128

T

task definition 19, 22, 55
definition 55
effect upon learning efficiency and effectiveness 57
faulty 57
importance of task 56
listening 58
Task: Teaching Big6 (Figure 20.1) 300
Teaching Extracting Skills (Figure 10.1) 118
technological design 221, 222
technology
impact on careers 10
impact on lives 11
Technology Integrated into Big6 (Figure 5.2) 40
Telling vs. Questioning (Figure 16.2) 194
Test Preparation Sources: What source do I use to study for
tests? (Lesson Plan 8.2) 76-78
test taking
Big6 as strategy 180
connections to answering questions from text 181-182
importance of communicating answer 178
importance of evaluation 179

importance of task definition 180
mandated tests 178
preparing for tests 178
reading selection tests 180-181
two parts of 178
text aids 93, 96
Text Aids, Features, or Conventions: The What and Why
(Lesson Plan 9.2) 107-108
text conventions 108
text features 30-31
time
instructional time saved with extracting xiv, 114
instructional time saved with location and access
skills 91
required to integrate Big6 28
Timeline of American Presidents (Lesson Plan 19.11)
295-296
TSE 208

U

Unit Plan for Guide Word Champ: Building Scanning
Ability and Speed (Lesson Plan 9.1) 101-103
use of information
engaging 116, 117
extracting 117, 165
Using Big6 to Solve an Authentic Problem (Figure 1.2) 6
Using Drawing and Visualization (Figure 17.9) 213
Using Picture Books to Teach Social Studies (Lesson
19.1) 270-271

V

Venn diagram 25, 30, 106, 117, 125, 128, 215
vocabulary 191, 208, 264, 298, 300

W

Web of Questions (Figure 7.1) 60
Wilson's Creek Battle (Figure 14.2) 166
Wolfe, Patricia 13, 14, 17, 18, 19, 20, 21, 28, 55, 56, 115
Word Search (Figure 9.2) 99
writing 3, 28, 32, 37, 41, 42
Writing a Fiction Animal Story (Lesson Plan 5.1) 44-45

Z

Zay, Traci 223